The Historical Film

Rutgers Depth of Field Series

Charles Affron, Mirella Jona Affron, Robert Lyons, Series Editors

Edited and with an introduction by
Marcia Landy

The Historical Film

History and Memory in Media

Rutgers
University
Press
New Brunswick,
New Jersey

Library of Congress Cataloging-in-Publication Data

The historical film : history and memory in media / edited and with an introduction by
  Marcia Landy.
       p.   cm. — (Rutgers depth of field series)
  Includes bibliographical references and index.
  ISBN 0-8135-2855-0 (cloth : acid-free paper) — ISBN 0-8135-2856-9 (pbk. : acid-free
paper).
  1. Historical films—History and criticism.   I. Landy, Marcia, 1931–   .   II. Series.

  PN1995.9.H5   H577   2000
  791.43'658—dc21   00-028080

British Cataloging-in-Publication data for this book is available from the British Library

This collection copyright © 2001 by Rutgers, The State University
For copyrights to individual pieces please see first page of each essay.

Manufactured in the United States of America

Contents

Preface

The objective of this book is to identify changing theoretical positions toward conceptions of history in the critical literature. Toward that end, the essays are selected to make available to both the general and the specialized reader representative examples of how media critics and historians write about history as it is portrayed in film and television. The essays address the commanding role that media—including documentaries, films, and television programs—have come to play in altering and complicating our understanding of historical events. In particular, the essays investigate what it means to "read" films historically, and how the methods of historians and media critics work toward that end. I have selected the essays with an eye toward fulfilling the goals of the Depth of Field series: they "appeal to an audience of students or general readers who have an interest in visual culture but who have no great familiarity with current theory or with more specialized academic studies in this area." In order that the reader can view the film texts under discussion by the critics, the essays chosen for inclusion here deal with works readily accessible to the public. The writings in this volume work toward two ends: to find a critical language for addressing the ways in which history is invoked in the cinema, and to establish methods for evaluating the current penchant for memorialization in film and television.

This collection of essays focuses on four aspects of the cinematic uses of the past. It is geared, first of all, to the question "How can we understand and account for the changing perceptions of film scholars and of historians in the project of 'writing' history on film?" Second, the essays explore what is at stake culturally and politically in this enterprise and how it is different from traditional forms of historicizing. Third, the writers of these essays outline issues that film critics and historians have articulated as necessary for the creation of a responsible analytic methodology to treat the character of cinematic and televisual media. And finally, the essays collected here offer examples of different—sometimes conflicting—theoretical and methodological positions on the filmic treatments of history; they are intended to represent different perspectives on what the critics mean when they talk about the uses of the past. Written by both film critics and historians, these critical discussions of films and television productions are designed to represent different styles of filmmaking from different parts of the globe. In most instances, the writers focus on representative films that illuminate the cultural problems posed by the various treatments of history and memory in the work of particular filmmakers.

I want to thank the editors, Mirella Affron, Charles Affron, and Robert Lyons for inviting me to contribute a volume to the series and for their helpful comments on the manuscript. I am extremely grateful to Leslie Mitchner at the

Rutgers Press for her support of this book and to Carol Mysliwiec and Sara K. Morriss for their assistance in preparing the manuscript, collating the essays, and in securing permissions from presses and authors. I acknowledge support from the Richard D. and Mary Jane Edwards Endowed Publication Fund.

The Historical Film

Marcia Landy

Introduction

What can we learn from engaging the question "What Is History?" This book focuses on uses of the past and on the nature and role of history and memory. The essays collected here shed light on the ongoing theoretical and practical problems posed by forms of historical representation through cinema and television; and they present methods of analysis that can overturn the conventional (and often negative) judgments about the historicizing potential of the media.

The first section of the book explores problems that stand in the way of analyzing the nature of popular history on film and offers suggestions for how to understand popular representations of the past. The second section discusses specific works of silent and sound cinema produced in Europe and the United States; here, the many cultural sources and styles drawn on in portraying history on film are identified. The third section focuses explicitly on the cinema of postcoloniality and the different forms it can take in the important enterprise of recollecting, rethinking, or challenging versions of the colonial past. The fourth and final section addresses current debates on postmodernism and their relation to questions of history and memory through television.

In their discussions of history in film and in television, the essays provide insight into methods for understanding the proliferation of works that return to the past. Increasingly, cultural and media critics, filmmakers, television programs, and numerous novels and biographies are engaged in re-creating and interpreting major crises of twentieth century life—two world wars, the Holocaust, and worldwide national liberation movements and the aftermath of their struggles in former colonized nations. As these events become more and more remote, they are reexamined and invested with great importance and intensity by filmmakers, television programmers, novelists, and museum curators. The media's representations of the past are a barometer of the social and cultural life of the last decades of the twentieth century. Memory becomes a bulwark against forgetting or altering the chronicling of events. But whose past and what ends are involved in the fetishizing of memory? And what do critics of the cinema have to contribute to an understanding of film and the uses of history? The essays in this collection seek answers to these questions.

I

There is by no means unanimous agreement about the nature, role, or forms of historicizing, and the essays selected for this volume reflect serious differences and problems concerning the meaning and importance of understanding the past. A brief overview of the controversies surrounding the means and ends of historical representation offers a sense of what is at stake in reexamining the past. For example, at one extreme there are such writers as Francis Fukuyama who have propounded the notion of "an end to history," seeing the new era as one which is self-regulating, and in which there is no need to have recourse to the past to determine the present.[1] But there are other writers—Walter Benjamin, Michel Foucault, Gilles Deleuze, and Felix Guattari—with different and more complex views on the motives of traditional historiography; these critics resist monolithic views and especially the penchant for teleology.[2] They do not forsake history; rather, they urge the abandonment of monolithic, messianic and deterministic views toward the past, suggesting instead that the material of history takes many forms and, moreover, that these forms are not innocent nor purely "objective." These writers are suspicious that too often existing forms of history are disseminated by the victor and therefore deserve to be challenged as well as reexamined so that different conceptions of social and cultural change may be developed.

Historicizing has played a key role in consolidating notions of national, gendered, ethnic and racial identities, presenting deterministic and essentialist conceptions of time and human action. In the words of Etienne Balibar:

> The history of nations . . . is always already presented to us in the form of a narrative that attributes to these entities the continuity of a subject. The formation of the nation thus appears as the fulfillment of a "project" stretching over centuries, in which there are different stages and moments of coming to self-awareness, which the prejudices of historians will portray as more or less decisive.[3]

This quotation is a reminder that national boundaries (geographical and cultural), the nature of the "citizen-subject," the forms of education, and conceptions of rights and duties are all dependent on constructed versions of the past. Versions of history thus play a powerful role in determining how individuals and groups inherit and understand their social and cultural milieu. History and memory have also played a part in destabilizing conceptions of the nation.

In twentieth century debates over representations of history, the work of the philosopher Friedrich Nietzsche has been extremely influential, especially for dissecting forms of historicizing and their relations to knowledge and power. In particular, his essay "On the Uses and Disadvantages of History for Life" is an examination of modes of treating the past. Here, Nietzsche argues for the necessity of remembering the past, but he is critical of what he considers the excesses of attachments to the past. He invites his readers to contemplate that *the unhistorical and historical are necessary in equal measure for the health of an individual, of a people and of a culture.*[4] Nietzsche outlines three dominant forms of historical construction—the monumental, the antiquarian, and the critical—arguing that to a degree each of these is necessary for regarding the past.

Monumental history is "an engagement with the classic and rare of earlier times . . . the greatness that once existed."[5] However, according to Nietzsche, too great an attachment to the monumental past is destructive:

> As long as the past has to be described as worthy of imitation, as imitable and possible for a second time, it of course incurs the danger of becoming somewhat distorted, beautified . . . incapable of distinguishing between a monumentalized past and a mythical fiction.[6]

Monumental history as purveyed in the cinema has certain defining characteristics. In its uses of narrative it relies on a vision of the past during moments of crisis and heroic conflict, and it reveals a penchant for the actions of heroic figures, such as Napoleon, Elizabeth I, Rembrandt, and Louis Pasteur. These figures come to define an age, and their actions are considered as models to be emulated. While unique, they are not isolated from the moral and social climate of their times; to the contrary, they are inseparably integrated into their era. In this view of history, there is often an implied contrast between the greatness of that past and the decadence of the present. However, monumental history may become rigidified and prescriptive, and, in its too-great attachment to, and veneration of, the past, thus block new conceptions.

Antiquarian history takes a different, though related, direction. The positive contributions of this type of history reside in its preservation of and reverence for "ancestral goods." In its portrayal of the past, it focuses on the artifacts of the past in minute detail; it probably has a greater claim to "objectivity" than monumental history. But this form of history can also be insidious for, like monumental history, it "knows only how to *preserve* life, not how to engender it; it always undervalues that which is becoming; . . . it hinders any resolve to attempt something new."[7] Thus, what might be a necessary means for understanding uses of the past is in danger of becoming a destructive enterprise.

Critical history attempts to "break up and dissolve a part of the past,"[8] concerned with what is deemed to be a necessary reexamination of the methods and values that have animated historians; but this form of history can also be excessive. In challenging the past without a regard for what is to be maintained and what is to be forgotten, the historian employing this method can end up disillusioned, completely denying the past, and refusing to understand and accept imperfection and injustice.[9]

From Nietzsche's comments, it is possible to draw several caveats about how history is understood, and how this understanding is acted out in practice; the conception and handling of history inevitably have an impact on how history is represented. First of all, in the cannibalizing of monuments and antiquities, any sense of critical comprehension of the relation between past and present is obliterated. The monumentalization of people and events can "inspire the courageous to foolhardiness, and the inspired to fanaticism."[10] Second, the antiquarian's veneration of historical objects destroys the critical discrimination necessary to enter into any assessment of what deserves remembering. Moreover, these objects take on a life of their own, completely disconnected from past or present. The cynicism that attends critical history lends itself to judgment and litigation rather than critical insight; on the positive side, this form of history can challenge prevailing and restrictive assessments of good and evil; on the negative side, when excessive, it inhibits alternative ways of thinking about the past.

Nietzsche's ideas on history are seminal for an understanding of how history continues to be represented and how critical challenges to traditional investments in the past can be expressed. Given the cataclysmic events of the twentieth century—two world wars, the rise of Fascism, and the Holocaust—and given the role of media in disseminating reductive and non-analytic monumental and antiquarian renditions of these events, philosophers and historians have been compelled to ask questions not only about the presentation of these events, but, even more, to ask, "What *is* history?"

Following Nietzsche, the writings of Michel Foucault have been instrumental in rethinking the relations of forms of historicizing to the creation, legitimization, and exercise of power through western cultural institutions. In exploring the past, Foucault sought to avoid the excesses of history in contemporary culture and politics. In his essay "Uses and Disadvantages of History for the Present Time" in *Logic, Counter-Memory, and Practice*, Foucault rehearses the three major lines of argument outlined in Nietzsche's *Untimely Meditations*; Foucault focuses finally on the importance of counterhistory as "effective history."[11]

According to Foucault, following Marx's *The Eighteenth Brumaire of Louis Bonaparte*, history repeats itself, first as tragedy, then as farce. In Foucault's terms, counterhistory is "farcical." Related to Nietzsche's conception of critical history, farcical history serves to undermine existing views of history as linear, as tending toward a purposive end (teleology), and as progressive. In the Nietzschean vein, counterhistory relinquishes its absolute claims to truth about the meaning and direction of history.[12] Instead, counterhistory offers questions about the role of history as myth contributing to the consolidation of the nation-form, the State, and citizenship.

Foucault's analysis of hisoricizing has occasioned much commentary in the critical literature and in representations of history in literature and film. His work (and, in a different vein, the writings of the Annales historians in France and the New Historians in the United States) has fueled many of the current debates on history. The proliferation of historical monuments and museums has been concomitant with the phenomenal increase of historical texts—academic, literary, biographical, cinematic, and televisual.

The essays in this book dramatize the characteristics and impact of changing theories of history as they are applied to cinema and in its uses of the past. Nietzsche's conceptions of the three modes of drawing on the past are often replicated in the styles of filmmaking as they draw on past modes of thinking about the past to dramatize that past. However, as the essays demonstrate, changing aspects of social and cultural life are revealed in the media's making of history now.

In this respect, the work of Jacques Derrida has been a major critical force in the reevaluation of historical thought. From *Of Grammatology* to *Archive Fever,* Derrida's writings have been influential in challenging received notions of representation and have had important philosophic implications for rethinking questions of language, history, memory, and the impact of electronic media in altering how we think about the past.[13] His deconstructive process, with its complex attention to the indeterminacies of language in speech and writing, is an assault on unitary and totalizing thought that have characterized Western narratives and especially history-writing, obscuring its multiple voices and reducing history to repetition and sameness. In the deconstructive focus on the multiple and ironic play of language, "what Derrida offers as history," writes Paul Bové, "is repetition and trace."[14] Unfortunately, Derrida's writing against history has, in the name of textuality, often been appropriated in such a way as to obscure the "materiality of the very discourses it claims to deconstruct," and thus "fails to understand the realities of power."[15] In the hands of many imitators, the deconstructive process can become another institutionalized academic mode of formal textual analysis shorn of any conceptual grappling with the nature or importance of understanding the political and cultural objectives in confronting the uses and abuses of the past. In this moment of postmodernity and globality, the assault on classic storytelling and "master narratives" instead can also serve opportunism, relativism, and cynicism, fueling the sense that meaning, and hence cultural transformation, is not only impossible but superfluous. However, in another direction, Derrida's work has been productive for French and American feminists and for writers on postcoloniality in their quarrels with received history as they reveal gaps and misunderstandings, but also traces of other submerged, forgotten, and unexamined truths concerning gender, sexuality, and race.

Not only are conceptions of the past being revised, but histories of both film and television have had to be rewritten in the light of reeamined and altered conceptions of social development and change. New forms of media history have challenged reductive notions of historical development, especially the idea that historical change is linear, moving from the simple to the complex, and from the primitive to the technologically advanced. The films themselves—as well as the criticism of them—have played an increasingly important role in reshaping representations of history. Rather than reflecting history through verisimilitude, films reflect our received notions of the past and offer, either reflexively or obliquely, an understanding of how cinematic history is constituted in monumental, antiquarian, and critical fashion as well as in ways that counter the excesses of these modes.

One of the most challenging theoretical discussions of the changing aspects of cinema from its beginnings to the present can be found in Gilles Deleuze's two-volume study, *Cinema 1: The Movement-Image* and *Cinema 2: The Time-Image.* Drawing on Nietzsche's theories of history, Deleuze provides a map for charting how cinema capitalizes on its uses of the past and present. In the first volume, the reader is introduced to the various ways in which pre–World War II cinema was attached to an "organic" form of narration in which the image of time was indirect. In this form of narration, the emphasis is on action and on a narrative whose parts are related to the whole. Examples can be found in the works of Abel Gance, Jean Renoir, Sergei Eisenstein, and Fritz Lang, who relied on sameness, repetition, and self-identity; in their creation of character and milieu, they emphasized affective forms of perception, not thought.

From the standpoint of early commercial cinema, the historical film—a staple of most cinemas—resembles the monumental and antiquarian forms described by Nietzsche.[16] As Deleuze frames it: "The American cinema constantly shoots and reshoots a single fundamental film, which is the birth of a nation-civilisation."[17] The decay of the movement-image is nowhere so blatantly exhibited as in the Nazi cinema where the past has been atrophied, where "the revolutionary courtship of the movement-image and an art of the masses become subject was broken off."[18]

Deleuze gives us a new conception of the uses of the past and present, indicating how the work of filmmakers such as Alfred Hitchcock and neorealists such as Roberto Rossellini opened the way to new conceptions of the image and its relation to the passage of real time and to objects and empty spaces. Instead of indirection, these filmmakers provided a sense of the everyday, of fantasy, or of a dream: the image takes on a sense of indeterminacy where the boundaries between the real and the imaginary blur. Instead of the monumental hero, the protagonists have become falsifiers, counterfeiters, somnambulists, and even children. Instead of the images of "truth," the audience is given images of the "false," in a "crystalline" narration, a surface that reflects many layers and many discrete perspectives.[19] Moreover, instead of the unifying dimensions of action and affect, there is a new kind of narration, one that is discontinuous and fragmenting, rather than connected and unified. Both the characters in the film and the external audience become observers acutely aware of seeing and of recognizing images differently. In his analysis of the later films of Italian director Roberto Rossellini, Deleuze writes:

> Whether it is in Socrates, Christ, Augustine, Louis XIV, Pascal, or Descartes, the speech-act is torn away from the old style, at the same time as space forms a new layer which tends to cover the old: every where a struggle marking the itinerary of the difficult birth of a new world, under the double forceps of words and things.[20]

In short, if one is to follow Deleuze, one learns not only that the cinema is a major source for learning about the various forms that history has taken in the twentieth century, but also that particular cinematic styles signal important cultural changes closely tied to pedagogical conceptions of the nation or its critique.

I find that the contributions of Italian philosopher Antonio Gramsci are particularly helpful in understanding the powerful hold of the past on the present. Although most of the essays contained in this volume do not invoke the particular figure of Gramsci, his work has been central to many British critics in their attempts to understand historical representation. Such writers as Stuart Hall were responsible for a reintroduction in the 1970s of Gramsci's writings to the

English-speaking world. Gramsci's work has been useful (especially for work of the Birmingham Centre for the Study of Contemporary Culture) in delineating new methods for rethinking the nature of popular and mass culture in relation to the uses of the past.[21]

The aspects of Gramsci's thought that appealed most to the Birmingham school stressed the workings of "common sense as folklore" as an instrument for forging consensus.[22] In this view, the past is not inherited in a consistent, logical, and unified fashion. Rather, history is circulated in a form that is often clichéd, based on legalistic forms, oratory, and aphorisms. Gramsci's examination of common sense exposed the various ways in which movement toward consensus is dependent on these contradictory and fragmented forms of knowledge derived from the past. The shards of the past are embedded in these inconsistent, illogical, and disunified forms of common sense. Most important is that the cement for these fragments is affective, for the investment in the past is melodramatic. This component of Gramscian analysis is useful in identifying the persistence of certain models and formulas. Whether or not critics allude specifically to the notion of "common sense as folklore," I contend that they are eager to rethink the ways in which folklore is being understood and even combated by historical films.

II

From earliest embodiments in the cinema, the penchant for documenting the past has been evident. Early cinema focused on novelties, spectacles, funerals, marriages, sports, military exercises, and the activities of the rich and famous. A demand for "veracity" and "facticity" was raised early, especially around staged events on film purported to be "authentic." With the appearance of longer films and with genre differentiation in the teens and twenties, as well as the distinction between "fiction" and "nonfiction," historical and fantasy (or escapist) films became common. Given the scrutiny of any cinematic work according to these standards of factuality and nonfictionality, it is not surprising that the "historical film" was seldom considered to be a conduit for any believable and legitimate sense of history.

The major genres that rely on images of the past are historical films and costume dramas, and the tendency to describe these films as unhistorical, escapist, and unrealistic has been a dominant trend of film and historical criticism until recent decades. Film criticism has begun to rethink the cinematic representations of political events that occurred during the twentieth century. In particular, concomitant with the criticism that has sought to understand the historical preoccupation with nation formation, the academic study of cinema has focused on relations between cinema and nation as attempts have been made to describe and analyze what is meant by a "national cinema."

The sound films of the 1930s and 1940s—the biographical film ("biopic"), the costume spectacle, and the historical film—depicted significant individuals and events associated mainly with traditional and watershed moments of a country's past. Historical films employed major stars and celebrated significant events in the forging of national identity. These films frequently served as a form of collective morality as well as source of morale. They were often produced on a grand scale in the mode of "monumental history," and they have been instrumental in establishing conventions about the commercial cinema's uses of spectacle in its treatment of the past.

The genre of the historical film often reveals the excesses of monumental history and its fascination with both the spectacle and the heroic figure—embodied in stars who assumed the roles of the rich, famous, and powerful. This kind of historical film flourished up to (and to a lesser extent during) the World War II years; examples include *Queen Christina* (1934), *The Scarlet Empress* (1934), *The Grand Illusion* (1937), *Young Mr. Lincoln* (1939), *Ivan the Terrible* (1942–1946), and *Young Mr. Pitt* (1942). Their uses of folklore and legend temporarily waned in the late 1940s and 1950s in the aftermath of World War II and during the Cold War. The cinematic "epic" of ancient Rome and Greece was resurrected beginning in the 1950s, characterized by such films as *Spartacus* (1960) and by Italian spectacles involving Hercules in particular.

The post–World War II years witnessed the rise of neorealism in cinema, expressed in such films as *Rome, Open City* (1945), *Paisan* (1946), and *The Bicycle Thief* (1948). In its wake, filmmakers reacted negatively to genre films, such as costume dramas and historical films, advocating a focus on the present and a rejection of monumental and antiquarian forms of filmmaking. Emphasizing a "new realism," these filmmakers sought to convey a different sense of the social milieu. Not only did notions of acting change (extending even to the use of nonprofessional actors), but there was also a reaction against the conventional melodramatic distinctions between hero and villain. By implication, not only was history on trial, so was the history of the classic cinema.

Significantly, in the occupied and "defeated" countries of Japan and Germany, the occupying governments established limits, if not prohibitions, on the historical film as a "precautionary" measure against films that exalted militarism. In Eastern Europe only in the late 1950s and 1960s was there a reemergence of historical films (such as the films of Andrej Wajda). These films focus specifically on World War II and raise the question of the uses of that historical event in relation to current events in "communist" countries such as Poland and Hungary.

More recently, the historic political convulsions in Europe in 1968 had an impact on how history was to be represented generally and on the cinema in particular. Throughout the sixties and early seventies, films identified as "New Wave" played a key role in the further globalization of cinema. Their impact was felt from Hong Kong to Hollywood and they were instrumental in the styles of both experimental and popular films. New Wave filmmakers, like François Truffaut, Jean-Luc Godard, and Pier Paolo Pasolini, were engaged in forms of criticism and filmmaking that would alter the course of cinema and conceptions of the time-image and, hence, of history. These filmmakers, first of all, took a fresh look at Hollywood cinema; they developed a critical terminology, in journal essays and on film, designed to rescue cinema—and particularly commercial and mass cinema—from its stigma of escapism and unreality. Moreover, in the ways that they employed cinematic language, these filmmakers broke down the classic realist cinema's structures of continuity editing: their narratives were episodic and fragmented. They employed star images and genre forms reflexively, increasingly calling critical attention to how the commercial cinema, identified with Hollywood, had forged its mythology.

Following the precedent of the neorealists, in these films the protagonists are no longer the "heroes" found in earlier cinema, but instead are either flawed or pasteboard figures. The earlier emphasis on action-oriented narratives gave way to a paralysis on the part of the characters, who are seen as observers like their audience. These films are multilayered and intertextual, emphasizing the role of looking and hearing instead of action and transformation of the social milieu. In these ways, the spectator is enlisted to view and to rethink the uses of time and of the past. These New Wave films had a profound impact in several ways: they initiated new forms of narration; they produced new relations to the actor/stars; and they offered a "pedagogy" of spectatorship and of film history in such films as the Antoine Doinel cycle, *Breathless* (1960) and *Alphaville* (1965).

In the 1970s and 1980s, a new generation of German filmmakers (Rainer Werner Fassbinder, Volker Schlondorff, Hans-Jürgen Syberberg, and Helma Sanders-Brahms, to name a few—all influenced especially by Jean-Luc Godard), were eager to challenge their elders' silence about the Nazi past. They experimented with cinematic methods, seeking to develop a language that would be able to communicate their understanding of Germany's suppressed history. At the same time, film and television became a major source for portraits of historical events; examples include the television series *Holocaust* and the film *Heimat*. An important precursor of, and model for, treatments of the Holocaust on film had been Resnais's *Night and Fog* (1955), considered by most critics of historical films to be a "truthful" and unsentimental examination of that event. The Holocaust continues to be a subject of interest to filmmakers. In France, during the 1980s, two documentary films—Claude Lanzmann's *Shoah* (1985) and Marcel Ophuls's *Hotel Terminus* (1988)—examined the history of the Holocaust by means of interviews with both former Nazis and Holocaust survivors. Films employing a fictional format, such as *Au revoir les enfants* (1988), have sought to address the ravages of the Nazi past, using melodrama in ways that can create an affective relation to events, re-animating a sense of a past that is becoming increasingly remote in time. Commercial cinema and television have not been far behind in their productions of Nazism and the Holocaust; both media have triggered debates about the uses of history in film and television. The vehement discussions of the film *Schindler's List* (1993) are a case in point. Most recently, the war between documentation and "fiction" film continues in the assessment of Roberto Benigni's *Life Is Beautiful* (1998). Both of these commercial films are considered, by and large, to falsify events, to attempt to put into pictures what is inherently inexpressible, and thereby to display disrespect for victims of the Holocaust.

The production of history has proved popular and profitable. Since the late 1970s, Britain has experimented with what Andrew Higson has termed the "heritage film." In this form of filmmaking, "the evocation of pastness is accomplished by a look, a style, the loving re-creation of period details," producing "a fascinating but self-enclosed world."[23] The heritage film is exemplified by such diverse texts as *Chariots of Fire* (1981), *Another Country* (1984), *Scandal* (1984), *Dance with a Stranger* (1985), *Maurice* (1987), and *Carrington* (1995). Unlike these heritage films, a number of critical films on Ireland—such as *Four Days in July* (1984), *In the Name of the Father* (1993), *Michael Collins* (1996), and *The Butcher Boy* (1997)—are less preoccupied with a detailed representation of a period in the Irish national past than they are with offering unsettling versions of familiar national conflicts through their revision of history. In the United States, the blockbuster historical film continues into the 1990s with Hollywood films that have been concerned with revisiting the past cinematically; examples include *Malcolm X* (1992), *Forrest Gump* (1994), *Panther* (1995), *Amistad* (1997), and *Titanic* (1998).

The historical film and documentary filmmaking are also experiencing a revival in the cinemas of Asia, Africa, and Latin America. In the wake of postcoloniality and its preoccupation with memory instead of with official history, African cinema has sought to create a counterhistory of colonialism and imperialism; examples may be found in such films as Kwah Ansah's *Heritage Africa* (1988) and Ousmane Sembène's *The Camp at Thiaroye* (1989). In contrast to the action cinema of Hong Kong, the mainland Chinese cinema has contributed to the rethinking of the past in such films as *Raise the Red Lantern* (1991) and *Farewell My Concubine* (1993). Diaspora films, including *Mississippi Masala* (1992) and *The Joy Luck Club* (1993), also play a part in rethinking histories of the nation and conceptions of national identity. The questions raised by these films, and others coming from Asia, Africa, and Latin America, are closely tied to the redefinition of contemporary culture as "postmodern." For many who write on the "postmodern condition," history is regarded as an assemblage of images, as part of the world of information commodities, endlessly recyclable and transformable, repeatable and devoid of meaning.

Television also constitutes a major venue for the dissemination of historical images. As cable stations proliferate, we have growing numbers of channels devoted to biography and history, offering miniseries that replay different moments in history—especially the ones that have captured the national imagination, such as the Civil War. World War II has been a perennial source of new programming and reruns of older programs. Periodically, historically interesting events of shorter duration and narrower scope—such as the "disasters" (as they are termed on television) of John F. Kennedy's assassination and more recently the events surrounding the death, mourning, and funeral of Princess Diana—

enlist the devices of historical memory.[24] What are the effects of this proliferation of history on television?

Umberto Eco offers a disturbing answer to this question: "It doesn't matter what you say via the channels of mass communication. . . . The important thing is the gradual uniform bombardment of information, where the different contents are leveled and lose their difference."[25] Anton Kaes, too, in writing about the proliferation of films and television programs dealing with the Holocaust, has questioned the effects of repetition, whether this "bombardment" dulls the thinking and makes it impossible to see or understand the very events that are purportedly under examination.[26] Has the ability to discriminate been eradicated? In place of discrimination, is the spectator treated to discrete and indigestible bits of "information," an endless procession of substitutable disaster? If so, history becomes tabloid, catastrophe, and scandal; or, at its worst, historical representation appears as "opinion" in a world of conflicting opinions, where there is no way of arriving at unassailable "truth."

In one sense, this complaint about film and television has been around a long time, focusing always on mass and popular culture. These negative views are especially relevant to any attempts to assess the uses of history in media. How is it possible to understand the inevitably changing aspects of history? And what is to be made of the impossibility of irrevocably "fixing" attitudes toward and judgments about the past? Is there a methodology that will help to deliver us from the vicissitudes of relativism? It is obvious that a "belief" in the possibility of reconstructing the past with absolute objectivity "as it was" already founders on one of the Nietzschean caveats about the effects of an excess of history. Moreover, the nature of investments in the past—whose investments and toward what end—can be revealing of another excess: namely, a belief in the possibility of total objectivity, absolute truth, and complete veracity.

From another side, the attack on media history is launched in terms of its sentiment. When a critic seeks to attack popular history, the pejorative term usually directed at the "fiction" is that it is "melodramatic," which implies that this type of representation is unhistorical. In this view, popular history relies on clichés, on wisdom inherited from the past, and on an emotional investment in the past. This folklore inheres in melodrama, which seeks to make sense of the past, but does so in formulaic terms. In recent decades, critics have taken a serious look at melodrama in an effort to understand its language and cultural basis in the context of modernity. Taken seriously, melodrama "becomes the principal mode for uncovering, demonstrating and making operative the essential moral universe in a postsacred era."[27]

I have argued, in a discussion of films on the Italian Resistance and on the Holocaust, that the presence of melodrama is important in the enterprise of understanding popular forms of historicizing.[28] In films employing melodrama, the investment in reliving the past through flashback, somnambulism, or fetishism of certain objects is evident. Forms of religiosity and legality are also central to melodrama; they play key roles in attempts to expose the criminality often at the heart of the historical event. Inherent in the "melodramatic imagination is the imperative of judgment that attends the preoccupation with the past. The quest for assigning responsibility is common to both high and mass culture. Melodrama is thus not ahistorical but central to the folklore that inheres in popular history."[29]

Historically, the study of film is a relative latecomer to cultural analysis. From the 1970s onward, the field of film studies has derived intellectual sustenance from, and sought to accommodate, various philosophical positions. It has sought to establish a critical and political language for cinematic analysis examining the history of the medium, its development within certain national contexts, its relation to the other arts, and, more recently, its relation to other disciplines, such as philosophy and history. The emphasis has begun to shift from the necessary initial accumulation of data about film, from interpretations of individual texts, and from the exclusive attention to individual auteurs, to addressing questions of the cultural impact and reception of film and television. The appearance of a number of books on the topic—such as Rosenstone's *Revisioning History,* Pierre Sorlin's *The Film in History,* Vivian Sobchack's collection of essays, *The Persistence of History,* and my *Cinematic Uses of the Past*—testify to the rethinking the relationship of media to historical representation.

III

The essays in the first section of this book, "Regarding History," address the question of what is at stake in the project of identifying the specific properties of the historical film. The study of cinematic history requires methods other than the purely academic. Robert Rosenstone remarks:

> The academic or Dragnet historian ("Just the facts, ma'am") looking at film has to face difficult questions: what criteria are applicable for judging visual history? How does film contribute to our sense of the past? The easiest answer (and the most irrelevant because it ignores the change in the medium) is to assess how true a work remains to "the facts." But you do not have to see many films to know such an approach is ridiculous.[30]

The insistence on the part of traditional historians and film critics for "accuracy" is a major obstacle inhibiting a proper assessment of the uses of the past in cinema. In reviews of such films as *Schindler's List* and *Michael Collins,* for example, both critics and public figures excoriate the films for not providing an accurate image of the events the films allegedly represent. The media critic cannot merely overlook the elimination of certain data, the distortion of certain characters, and the mingling of fact and fiction; a critic writing about history in film must find a method for describing and analyzing these departures from empirical data.

In place of the standards of judgment about "truth" and "falsehood," the critic—whether specialized film scholar or historian—has to develop new ways of thinking. Instead of maintaining a disciplinary divide, film scholars and historians need to pool their knowledge and work together in the interest of developing new methods for understanding history through images and fictional forms. Toward that end, the scholars represented in this section—Rosenstone, Sorlin, Custen, and Harper—have had to move beyond the formal assessment of a single film text. In fact, they have been compelled to examine what they mean by a "cinematic text." Their work acknowledges that the straightforward paths to "interpreting" events, by means of explaining and judging the fidelity of the events represented in a text according to an "external" reality, do not do justice to the complex ways in which the visual image functions as history.

Therefore, critics have had to educate themselves about the nature of the cinematic image and how to understand the basis of the historicity of a film. Does historicity reside in the document itself, as created at a given moment of history? Does the subject matter itself make the film historical? Is historicity to be found in the complex nature of narrative, sound and images that have their roots in the history of art, of folklore, of popular culture, and even of the avant-garde? For historians, too, the translation of the images into content analysis is unsatisfactory for an understanding of historical representation. The transparent reading of film narratives has to give way to a methodology that allows for an exploration of the properties of the visual medium, and particularly properties of both popular and unpopular history.

In "How to Look at an 'Historical' Film," Pierre Sorlin, one of the pioneers of history and film, provides specific guidelines for identifying, describing, and evaluating the "historical film." In his quest to identify different strata and techniques of films that purport to treat historical subjects, Sorlin develops a method for observing these films and for accounting for the ways in which they might be seen as creating a sense of the past. Sorlin takes as his text Eisenstein's film *Oktober* to demonstrate how one might address the subtleties and formal dimensions that can account for the film's uses of the past; these approaches could be applied to other films.

Rosenstone's essay, "The Historical Film: Looking at the Past in a Postliterate Age," confronts the seemingly unbridgeable gap between professional historians and scholars of popular culture. His questions about history in film are addressed to historians, film critics, and filmmakers. Rosenstone acknowledges that the many existing forms of historicizing on film can be reduced for critical purposes to three main categories: history as drama, history as document, and history as experiment. The author confronts the pieties normally attached to documentation and examines the character of mainstream feature films in an attempt to describe their strategies (for example, their indirect discourse and their closed versions of the past). Rather than denigrating the uses of the image for historical purposes in these films, Rosenstone seeks to find a language to situate the ways they work. His own bias appears to lean toward filmmakers who employ experimental or oppositional forms of historicizing (for example, Eisenstein, Kluge, and Godmilow, among others). In short, his essay is an attempt to forge new methods and a new language that can better account for "visions of the past."

While Sorlin and Rosenstone examine possibilities and limitations for a range of historical films, George Custen's essay, "Making History," addresses the popular biographical film (the "biopic") and traces its generic properties, its relation to audiences, and its connections to noncinematic forms of biography. His essay explores the pedagogical and propagandistic dimensions of the biopic. Through an examination of issues relating to production, he is able to demonstrate the multiple influences on this form of popular history—books, music, and studio publicity (especially the publicizing of the films as "historically accurate" and impeccably researched). The essay discusses the appropriateness of the appearance and acting of the stars to their historical subjects, the choice of directors, and the various thematics that guide different types of biopics and the connections between these films, Hollywood culture, and American culture at large.

Sue Harper's essay, "Historical Pleasures: Gainsborough Costume Melodrama," focuses on a specific moment of the costume drama in British cinema of the 1940s. Her essay examines the relationship between melodrama and history, but a form of history that "grants a freedom to the [largely female] audience to maneuver its own way through narrative codes." Harper's analysis reveals how these costume dramas provide a sense of the past particularly tailored to female audiences in their treatment of class and of gender transgression. The films are not empty escapist texts, but reveal conflicts concerning gendered, sexual, and class relations. Through their opulent visual language and excessiveness in costume, hair-dos, and sexual behavior, the films allow for "the expression of anxieties about the boundaries of political power and moral value." They are tailored to a certain type of British actor of the time and are the result of the particular production practices of the Gainsborough Studios during World War II. By rejecting the charge that these films are ahistorical and by shifting her analysis to the psychosocial through melodrama, Harper expands the notion of popular history. She establishes that the films, in presenting the past as a "site of sensual pleasure," make a particular contribution to conceptions of historical representation.

The second section of this book, "History as Trauma," focuses on specific moments in film history (in both silent and sound films) and specific texts that offer insights into the stylistic qualities and the cultural sources for historical films. The essays range from a discussion of early examples of monumental and antiquarian history to an analysis of more recent treatments of the past, from the spectacular to the everyday, from the national to the international, from nonfiction to fictionalizing, and from folklore to critical historicizing.

From its beginnings, the cinema has been fascinated with history, recording and documenting on film the sights and sounds of contemporary life, the ceremonials of a now-gone aristocracy, the weddings and funerals of the great, the emergence of technology (for example, the train, the airplane, and the automobile), and the nature and movements of the masses. The silent era saw the production in Europe of historical texts such as *Cabiria* (1914), *The Last Days of*

Pompeii (1913), *The Birth of a Nation* (1915), *Intolerance* (1916), *Potemkin* (1925), and *Napoléon vu par Abel Gance* (1927). These "monumental" forms of cinematic history were instrumental in forging a modern identity through the movement-image and through grand narratives of social upheaval and social transformation.

The production of history in silent cinema was not restricted to Europe and Hollywood. In the early years of the Japanese and Indian cinema, the mythology of a pre-modern past was central to the development and financial health of these countries' film industries. Nor are the connections between national identity and cinema restricted to the early cinema, as the following essays reveal; for the contemporary cinema has not abandoned the project of nation formation, although post–World War II films may look with a more critical eye on national history.

Maria Wyke's essay, " Projecting Ancient Rome," focuses on a prominent but rarely examined form of historical film—the "epic film" which is identified with European and Hollywood cinema. In particular, she describes the character and persistence of images of ancient Rome. Films that feature this classical past were popular in the silent cinema and returned to the Hollywood and European cinema during the 1950s and early 1960s. Central to her argument is the thesis that representations of ancient Rome are especially instrumental in the formation of Italian national identity. For example, she explores the concept of "romanità" as indispensable to Italian literature and cinema, to visions of republicanism as well as to Fascism. Her discussion focuses on relationships among representations of gender, sexuality, and politics as they are orchestrated in these images of a classical, but frequently resurrected past.

In "You Remember Diana Dors, Don't You," I explore the many and intertextual layers of popular history. The British film *Dance with a Stranger* (1985), starring Miranda Richardson, is a biopic that returns to the 1950s and dramatizes the life of Ruth Ellis, the last woman to be executed in England. Richardson appears in the film as a blonde, and her image evokes values associated with the "blonde" star, epitomized by Diana Dors—sexual promiscuity, class misalliance, violence, and a style of life associated with the urban milieu and with marginality. In its focus on the female "offender," *Dance with a Stranger* evokes parallels between the world of the 1950s and that of the 1980s. By focusing on these incarnations of the folklore of the blonde in the history of commercial cinema, I explore connections among stardom, femininity, fashion, cinematic representation, sexuality, criminality, and politics as they indicate continuities and discontinuities between past and present in British cinematic culture.

Miriam Hansen's "*Schindler's List* Is Not *Shoah*" makes an eloquent case for reconsidering the means and ends of memorializing so as to avoid simplistic judgment about cinematic uses of the past. The essay offers a nuanced investigation of the problems of comparing nonfiction films to fiction films if only (as many do) in order to relegate the fiction film to a lesser place in representations of history. Concerned with the issue of "public memory," Hansen examines the arguments mounted against the Spielberg film that are, unfortunately, not based on a careful analysis of the text. Instead, critics attack the film for its Hollywood origins, its "commercialization" of the Shoah, its uses of "fiction," and its reliance on a genre form that requires "resolution." These aspects, such critics argue, debase the memory of the Shoah; Spielberg's film, they assert, stands in direct contrast to the Lanzmann film, which is respectful of the past by not indulging in commercial histrionics. Hansen's essay calls attention to the need for textual analysis of films that treat history, to the need to situate the cinematic uses of the past in the present time, and the need to avoid simplistic and binary distinctions between various forms of film (such as between documentary and fiction).

Anton Kaes's "The Presence of the Past" addresses the issues of history and memory in relation to German history as represented in the contemporary German cinema of the last decades of the twentieth century, and particularly in their relation to Nazism. Most conspicuous in the probing of memory is the work of German director Rainer Werner Fassbinder; Kaes discusses the work of memory as exemplified in Fassbinder's *The Marriage of Maria Braun* (1979). Through Fassbinder's use of melodrama the film questions silences about the war and Nazism that characterized his generation. The film exposes "the unresolvable dual status of historical narratives, as document and fiction."

The Marriage of Maria Braun spans from the end of the war to the late 1970s. The film is composed in a cinematic style that uses multiple voices and the creation of images that resemble historical newsreels and photographs. The film, a blending of fiction and documentary, official history and memory, is self-reflexive, both about itself as cinema, and about the efficacy of representations for thinking differently about the past. Kaes's concern is with the effects of this kind of filmmaking: Does the film, despite its work of returning to and exploring the past, join other numerous films that portray images of the Nazi past to become part of a legacy of eradicating history and memory, lost in the proliferation of "postmodern" commodification of information and images?

Sumiko Higashi's "*Walker* and *Mississippi Burning*: Postmodernism Versus Illusionist Narrative" offers another perspective on the question, "Is history dead?" Referring to various commentaries on the end of history—both Fukuyama's wished-for end and Fredric Jameson's very different assessment of the "end of history"—Higashi takes two texts, *Walker* (1987) and *Mississippi Burning* (1988), as examples of the persistence of historical investigation, reinvigorated through the works of such historians as Fernand Braudel. For these historians, film is evidence of both the conventional and the innovative aspects of historical representation.

Walker represents events in chronological and linear fashion but then engages in a selfconscious dialogue about the ways past and present are constructed in relation to each other, and not merely as a linear unfolding of time. Furthermore, the film exploits contradictions about prevailing views of history, frustrating genre conventions and audience expectations. Stylistically, it utilizes image and sound disjunction, montage, and a complex mode of narration. In contrast, *Mississippi Burning* is modeled on "illusionist cinema" and what the public construes as a "legitimate" historical film. The essay thus indicates that history is not dead; it lives on in both traditional and innovative forms, though the more innovative form has less appeal in box office terms.

The third section of this book, "History, Fiction, and Postcolonial Memory," examines postcolonial quarrels with history. The nature and mode of historical representation that characterize non-European contemporary culture, as well as what has been termed "postcoloniality," are discussed as they relate to the work of particular films and filmmakers. The essays in this section are concerned with the distinction between official history and memory; and they explore how some filmmakers from formerly colonized nations have sought to create a cinematic style that addresses this distinction. The essays are also engaged in examining representations of the effects of decolonization, on the colonized as well as on the former colonizers. They reflect the contemporary academic and popular interest in rethinking historical representation in literature and film. The films discussed by the essays are tied to the emergence of increasingly vocal social groups—national, sexual, gendered, and ethnic—which have, since the end of World War II, increasingly asserted their claims to international attention in literature, media, the other arts, and in armed struggles as well.

One of the major concerns in the literature on and by subaltern groups is the need to rewrite the past, to challenge the official histories shaped largely by Eurocentrism. Official history, it is claimed by postcolonial critics, has erased the struggles of marginalized groups, has articulated history from the perspective of the victor, and has posed the history of western culture as the standard of universal justice and reason—in the process rationalizing colonialism, imperialism, racism, and phallogocentrism. The essays address distinctions between traditional historicizing and the workings of myth and memory in the context of postcolonial theories and practices.

A number of currents have contributed to the veneration for and the unsettling of traditional forms of historicizing. In the years before and during World War II, Fascism, Nazism, and Stalinism first challenged and then re-instituted their own versions of official history. These movements commemorated a past based on monuments and media. The effects of that era still reverberate in the memories of those years and in the unresolved questions that have arisen about the origins and modes of these various regimes that have been "documented" in photography and on film. In the aftermath of World War II, the rise of struggles for national liberation in formerly colonized sections of the world had generated different readings of the past, readings at odds with the version presented by the colonizing nations; these revisionary readings were to have a broad impact on the future of historiography.

The Vietnam War, involving France and, later, the United States, altered the social and cultural life of the twentieth century on a worldwide scale. The sheer violence of these struggles and the attempts to halt the violence and genocide have made an impact on film production as well as on the ways in which history in film is written. The conflict surrounding the war contributed to a rethinking of the nature and role of written and visual language, the meaning of textuality, and the meaning of consensus.

Naomi Greene's essay, "Empire as Myth and Memory," explores two films that are reflections on the French colonial past. The films rely on memories of decolonization, and Greene examines how they shed light on the workings of memory. The Algerian war offered a particularly problematic reminder of an unpopular war and a war that evoked memories of Nazi atrocities. Discussing two films—*Le Crabe-tambour* (1977), and *Outremer* (1991)—Greene examines two dimensions of the decolonization experience. In the case of *Outremer*, the film focuses on ritualistic encounters between the French settlers and the indigenous "Other" in a dreamlike style; while *Le Crabe-tambour* is preoccupied with the military and with memories of betrayal and the decline of an empire. In the case of these two films, Greene sees them as exemplary versions of how history and myth are sundered and of how myth becomes a bulwark against incursions from the past.

In a different vein, Ismail Xavier's essay, "*Black God, White Devil*," examines the use of allegory in Glauber Rocha's film of the same name. Through allegory, argues Xavier, the film becomes a "decentered and problematic reflection on history itself." The essay concerns not the fidelity to dates and documents but parable, popular memory and music. In any representation of revolutionary struggle and subsequent social transformation, historical thinking is central as it relates to the text's treatment of history as heterogeneous and different from official history. Drawing on a different conception of popular culture than that of commercial cinema, the film does not romanticize, condescend to, or sentimentalize popular culture. It takes a glance at the peasant world through a form of cinematic language that conveys both the hopes and fears of history in Brazil.

The final essay in this section Mbye Cham's "Official History, Popular Memory: Reconfiguration of the African Past in the Films of Ousmane Sembène," focuses on Senegal and its history. Consistently, Sembène has been engaged in a rethinking of the forms of history that constitute the Senegalese inheritance. Cham traces and examines the various forms of history and memory represented in Sembène's films—the history of negritude, official Eurocentric and dominant versions of Africa and Africans, the political and cultural role of language, neocolonialism, and the role of popular memory in the reconstruction of Euro-Christian and Arab-Islamic history. In Sembène's films, the position of women in popular memory is highlighted as part of Senegal's past. Most centrally, Cham regards Sembène's films as evoking a critical and demystifying examination of myth and official history; that is, his films are not nostalgic for a past that cannot be resurrected and may never have existed; rather, they offer a pedagogy for thinking about the future.

———

The book's final section, "History and Television," explores the problem of historicizing from the vantage point of writings on postmodernism and the fate of history in the last decades of the twentieth century, and as a consequence of the televisualization of the globe. The literature on postmodernity has contributed to an undermining of traditional conceptions of (in E. H. Carr's words) "What Is History." The impetus to rewrite (or even abandon) history is related to the fall of Communism and to the dizzying speed of worldwide capitalization that has contributed to the increasing division between rich and poor, and between people of color and whites. Concomitantly, the global role of televisual media has also contributed to dislodging notions of "universal" truth and faith in essential and commonly shared conceptions of reality.

These issues have been examined in the writings of such thinkers as Jean-François Lyotard, Guy Debord, Jean Baudrillard, and Fredric Jameson; these writers questioned prevailing beliefs in realism and in the role of history as moral arbiter, and they have introduced readers to the notion of the hyperreal, the society of the spectacle. This literature has led to conceptualizations of an "end to history" or at least an end to certain versions of history. What was new about these writings was their examination of the effects of past and present events received through cinematic and televisual images. Here again, the "grand narratives" of history have come under attack. Ien Ang has suggested that perhaps all we have left now are small narratives—but ones that come closer to addressing the differences that have been buried under the rubric of universalistic sameness.[31] As a consequence of the sustained attention now paid to media, televisual analysis has become more imperative and incisive. And in the case of television and video (as well as cinema), one sees a lessening of the tendency to see the media as a reflection of reality together with a greater emphasis on learning to identify the formal properties of media and their impact. These critical positions are fruitful for adopting different methods for examining and rethinking the nature of historical representation and, more generally, of the media in and as history.

History bombards us twenty-four hours a day in the numerous productions that feature "biographies," in the cinema, in the books that proliferate opening up new local and international narratives of the past; and the effects of this bombardment are yet to be analyzed and understood. The replays of history in the media may, on the one hand, have the effect of destroying any belief in the efficacy of historicizing. An alternative position would argue that with the death of European "grand narratives," we are now witnessing the emergence of new, smaller, and different narratives of justice and social transformation. In either case, we are now confronted with the problem of how to evaluate the nature and effects of historical representation on television; the final essays address these issues.

Mary Ann Doane, in her essay "Information, Crisis, Catastrophe," provides a context in which to evaluate how television works in ways that are antithetical to inherited conceptions of the role and importance of the past for understanding the present. She focuses on television's immediacy and the various means by which that information is transmitted. Television lives in the present, particularly in its obsession with disaster and death—we need only look at its treatment of Chernobyl, Bhopal, plane crashes, and earthquakes. In its focus on catastrophe, and in the various ways in which it records and comments on events, the medium thrives on discontinuity. In Doane's words: "What is at stake in television catastrophe is not meaning but reference." Though continuous in the flow of information, its mode of presentation is discontinuous, its techniques disruptive, serving to annihilate memory, explanation, and accountability.

In related fashion, Richard Dienst's essay, "History, the Eternal Rerun," is situated within a larger theoretical consideration of television. Dienst argues that the televisual medium is ubiquitous: it cannibalizes images. It runs twenty-four hours a day—even as we sleep—and it is hungry for all kinds of news. In order to understand its uses of the past, Dienst discusses the television series *Crime Story*. In particular, *Crime Story* flies in the face of traditional conceptions of history, eschewing the familiar markers we associate with monumental, antiquarian, and critical history. Bits of the past erupt into the present, shorn of context but indicative of a world where knowledge is dismembered. Thus, in order to understand the impact of television on our inherited conceptions of the past, one cannot merely focus on discrete programs but must have recourse to the nature and effects of the total medium.

Taylor Downing's essay, "History on Television: The Making of *Cold War*, 1998," offers a different analysis of the uses of history on television. This essay, like the Edgerton essay that follows, regards popular history on television affirmatively. Downing contends that the uses of history in media have increased in frequency and popularity in the last two decades. Contributing to this growth is the proliferation of history programs on BBC 1 and 2 as witnessed by *The Great War* and *The World at War* and the creation of a history channel in the United Kingdom and the United States. While these programs and channels constitute good television, Downing asks: are they "good" history?

The answer to Downing's question is not clear-cut. In making television documentaries, filmmakers as historians have undervalued the "power of the image." In particular, they have not often confronted how the use of oral history presents philosophical and methodological problems. Major difficulties in producing such programs involve the judicious use of archival material and the critical use of interviewees. *Cold War*, Downing argues, is a good illustration of attempts to confront these problems: the series relied on historical advisors; it introduced new archival footage; it offered a more varied selection of subjects to be interviewed; and, in addition to the commentary of government officials, the series drew on personal accounts of surviving individuals who experienced that epoch. In short, Downing seeks to make television history conform to rigorous standards of documentation.

Also concerned with the making of popular history, Gary Edgerton discusses *The Civil War* in "Ken Burns's Rebirth of a Nation: Television, Narrative, and Popular History," contrasting the television program to the film *The Birth of a Nation*. Edgerton regards the television miniseries as responding to the cultural stereotypes of the 1915 film with its nationalistic, stereotypic treatment of race, and its "great man" and monumental approach to the Civil War. Critically acclaimed, *The Civil War*, according to Edgerton, offers a "popular" and "a fresh emphasis on social and cultural history" in its focus on a "bottom-up" treatment of the war. This "bottom-up" perspective focuses on "African-Americans, women, immigrants, workers, farmers, and common soldiers in the conflict." Furthermore, Edgerton regards this program as treating history from the vantage point of consensus rather than conflict, presenting speakers whose interests might clash, but ultimately highlighting agreement and promoting a liberal pluralist perspective.

Shawn Rosenheim, in his essay "Interrotroning History," questions whether there is hope for television's representation of history. Television has been a major purveyor of historical narratives, chronicling such events as the Rodney King beating, the O. J. Simpson trial, and the Civil War. In response to what he perceives as "badly told" reportage, he proposes a documentary series, what he terms "mentalité TV," the kind of presentation that *Errol Morris: Interrotron Stories* would offer. This kind of format, which Rosenheim describes as "interrotroning," depends on a revelation of "what happened" but also an exposure of normative history as myth. Central to this series is an interview that allows viewers to look into the camera directly and view the presentation of a nuanced interaction between the subject and the interviewer. The interaction is based on Morris's treatment of the interview in his films.

The Interrotron refines the uses of the medium; the audience is invited to see the interaction between camera, studio setting, and interviewed subject. Rosenheim compares the interrotron mode to Dziga Vertov's *kinoglaz*. In Vertov's films, the "camera eye" calls attention to the artifactual and constructed nature of the filming. Rosenheim sees this form of television as a composite of documentary images, dramatic re-creation of events based on interviews, direct address with Max Headroom teleprompters. Thus the spectator is bombarded with constant reminders of events as staged. In this way the slipperiness of memory can be highlighted and the viewer is treated to a "thoroughly postmodern" version of history, replete with pastiche, parable, and suspicion about motivation.

In its concerns with the media's uses of the past, and as an index to contemporary anxieties, this book offers the reader an opportunity to identify and differentiate what is at stake in the complex theoretical formulations historical thought. The essays address the commanding role that media have played in shaping our understanding of the world and explore methods to assess and gauge the effects of this explosion of historical subjects. The writings are representative of the debates that characterize critical thinking on the making (and unmaking) of history and, hopefully, they guide the reader to a better understanding of the beleaguered role of history at the end of the twentieth century.

NOTES

1. Francis Fukuyama, *The End of History and the Last Man* (New York: Maxwell Macmillan, 1992).

2. Walter, Benjamin, "Theses on the Philosophy of History." In *Illuminations*, ed. Hannah Arendt, trans. Harry Zohn (New York: Schocken Books, 1976), 253–64.

3. Etienne Balibar, "The Nation Form: History and Ideology." In *Race, Nation, Class: Ambiguous Identities* (London: Verso, 1995), 86.

4. Friedrich Nietzsche, "The Uses and Disadvantages of History for Life." In *Untimely Meditations*, ed. J. O. Stern. and trans. R. J. Hollingdale (Cambridge, Mass.: Cambridge University Press, 1991), 63.

5. Ibid., 69.

6. Ibid., 70.

7. Ibid., 75.

8. Ibid., 73.

9. Ibid., 76.

10. Ibid., 73.

11. Michel Foucault, "Nietzsche, Genealogy, History." In *Logic, Counter-Memory, Practice: Selected Essays and Interviews*, ed. Donald F. Bouchard (Ithaca: Cornell University Press, 1988), 139–165.

12. Ibid., 160–63.

13. Jacques Derrida, *Of Grammatology*, trans and ed. Gayatri Chakravorty Spivak (Baltimore: Johns Hopkins University Press, 1976); *Archive Fever: A Freudian Impression*, trans. Eric Prenowitz (Chicago: University of Chicago Press, 1996).

14. Paul Bové, *Mastering Discourse: The Politics of Intellectual Culture.* (Durham, N.C.: Duke University Press, 1992), 74.

15. Ibid., 75.

16. Gilles Deleuze, *Cinema 1: The Movement-Image*, trans. Hugh Tomlinson and Barbara Habberjam (Minneapolis: University of Minnesota Press, 1986), 150.

17. Ibid., 148.

18. Deleuze, *Cinema 2: The Time-Image*, trans. Hugh Tomlinson and Roberta Galeta (Minneapolis: University of Minnesota Press, 1989), 64.

19. Ibid., 126–31.

20. Ibid., 248.

21. Stuart Hall, *The Hard Road to Renewal: Thatcherism and the Crisis of the Left* (London: Verso, 1984).

22. Antonio Gramsci, *Selections from the Prison Notebooks*, ed. and trans. Quintin Hoare and Geoffrey Nowell Smith (New York: International Publishers, 1978), 323–33, 419–25.

23. Andrew Higson, *Waving the Flag: Constructing a National Cinema in Britain* (Oxford: Clarendon Press, 1995), 113.

24. Wheeler Winston Dixon, *Disaster and Memory* (New York: Columbia University Press, 1999).

25. Umberto Eco, *Travels in Hyperreality: Essays*, trans. William Weaver (San Diego: Harcourt Brace Jovanovich, 1986).

26. Anton Kaes, *From Hitler to Heimat: The Return of History as Film* (Cambridge, Mass.: Harvard University Press, 1989), 198.

27. Peter Brooks, *The Melodramatic Imagination: Balzac, Henry James, Melodrama, and the Mode of Excess* (New York: Columbia University Press, 1985), 15.

28. Marcia Landy, "History on Trial: The Case of *Porzus.*" In *Screening the Past*, Arthur Lindeman and Anthony Guneratne, Latrobe University (April, 1999), www.latrobe.edu: np.

29. Marcia Landy, "Cinematic History, Hollywood, and the Holocaust," in *Humanity at the Limit: The Impact of the Holocaust on Christians and Jews* (Bloomington: Indiana University Press, 2000).

30. Robert Rosenstone, *Revisioning History: Film and the Construction of a New Past* (Princeton: Princeton University Press, 1995), 7.

31. Ien Ang, "Hegemony-in-Trouble: Nostalgia and the Ideology of the Impossible in European Cinema." In *Screening Europe: Image and Identity in Contemporary European Cinema*, ed. *Duncan Petrie* (London: BFI, 1992), 21–32.

Regarding History

Pierre Sorlin

How to Look at an "Historical" Film

I must first ask my readers to be patient. Before studying the films themselves—which are, I admit, the most exciting part of our work—we must first specify the methods to be used and define the subject of our interest, which is, roughly speaking, the study of the cinema considered as a document of social history that, without neglecting the political or economic base, aims primarily at illuminating the way in which individuals and groups of people understand their own time. We will of course return to the ideas I am discussing here, but I would like to warn the reader that I am describing research which is still in progress, a stage in working out a method; I shall give very few final results, I shall ask questions to which there can be no reply and I shall point out problems for which I can find no solution.

The Audiovisual Age

Audiovisual material—by which I mean material that reaches the senses and establishes communication through a combination of moving pictures and sounds, particularly television and the cinema—is a part of our daily life. It is a source of much of our knowledge, information and entertainment. But as historians, we demand very little of it. The cinema is barely ninety years old, although it has drawn considerable crowds since the beginning of the century; there are few places in the world today where television is unknown. And yet, until 1960, audiovisual material was almost completely neglected by historians. At the most, they dealt with it in a few paragraphs on art and culture. For reasons which are worth examining, historians have stressed the artistic aspect of cinema, failing to speculate on its documentary value, its possible influence in moulding opinion, or its interest as an historical source.

In 1960, or thereabouts, the situation began to change: we now have cinema periodicals specially intended for historians, we have established organizations like the Slade,[1] and a number of universities have developed courses on audiovisual studies. I believe that television is at the root of this change. Historical documentaries are an inexpensive and convenient way of filling screen time. As editing and the addition of a commentary are usually all that is needed, a programme built up of old films involves on average one tenth of the cost of a television play. Successful series like *World at War* have exposed the public to an unfamiliar type of history—visual history, designed to strike by its evidence and through immediate contact, instead of convincing through reason and deduction.

The integration of film into the material used by historians is not the result of deliberate choice: filmed documents have been imposed on historians through the use made of them by nonspecialists or by specialists with no training in history. A comparison with written sources might be useful. All over Europe, scholars have collected and corrected texts relating to antiquity and the Middle Ages. Historians were on their own territory: no one disputed their right to work on the manuscripts, and they realized that if they did not complete the task a large proportion of the documents were in danger of disappearing. The effort to construct a positive history, respectful of its sources, is inseparable from the discovery and publication of the texts on which that history is based.

If we turn to audiovisual material, I think we can distinguish three new features which completely alter the situation. First, historians have no monopoly over the material, nor are they alone in studying and disseminating it. For example, television has made most of the interesting material relating to the Second World War widely available. In this respect, the historian's task is no longer to compile otherwise unknown sources and make them available to all: he must learn instead to use material that is already widely available. If the scholars of the past had not accomplished their enormous task, there would be no positive history, no "scientific" history. But if historians today neglect audiovisual material, it will exist in spite of them as a history through pictures. Furthermore, the public will lose all interest in specialists, and the specialists themselves will be in a curiously divided position, conducting their research shut away in libraries, but turning to television when they want information on the present. Historians must take an interest in the audiovisual world, if they are not to become schizophrenics, rejected by society as the representatives of an outmoded erudition.

This introduces the second point, that access to filmed records is very expensive. If we had to pay to consult Roman inscriptions or medieval documents, and pay again if we quoted them, historical publications would be few in number, and historiography would become the privilege of a few public foundations and wealthy individuals. We cannot discuss the cinema without bringing up the central question of money. As there is heavy demand, due mainly to the requirements of television, the film companies charge high prices. We have to make do with one film, when for the purposes of comparison we would prefer to use ten. In the book from which this essay is taken, we are going to discuss a number of films, but if the reader were to see them all it would prove to be an expensive undertaking. I hope that my accounts will suffice.

We can read a text once and then discuss it; we are all used to this kind of exercise. With a film it is more difficult: we are trained to read, rather than to watch. And here we come to the third point. Hitherto, the historian produced a new text after having read existing documents. In both, the medium of expression was the same—language. Cinema, however, although it too uses language, can manage without it. There are many films in which not a single word is spoken. In any case, when language is used in the cinema, it forms part of a whole: the raw material of cinematic expression is an indissoluble combination of picture, movement, and sound. Anyone who is interested in the audio-visual—historian or otherwise—must translate a system with several components into a system with only one—language. Starting from pictures, he must produce a written text. It is an unsatisfactory method, and I accept that in writing this book, I place myself and my readers in a rather absurd position: it is difficult for us to obtain the necessary material, and we do not quite know how to use it. I am convinced that more and more we will use another film medium, video, to express our feelings about cinema film. So why embark on an unsatisfactory study that will be out of date in twenty or thirty years? For the moment, we have no alternative: we must begin somewhere, and we can argue that getting used to pictures no doubt begins with getting used to reading.

We will not be considering the whole of world cinema, of course, and I would like to explain the choices I have made. I have chosen 1960 as a *cut-off point*, when television had become a commonplace in nearly every country in the world and when light, inexpensive recording equipment became more generally available, at least in the West. If we were concerned only with the United States, we would naturally have to go back to 1950, whereas in other countries 1970 might have been a more appropriate date at which to end the study: 1960 is taken as an average boundary. Before then, television was of only slight importance and audiovisual material was limited to the use made of it in the motion picture industry: film equipment was cumbersome and expensive; only a few companies used it for specific purposes, which we will discuss later. Production was restricted to a few, select circles, and an inventory of the audiovisual film output of the pre-1960 period would be a brief one: most of the existing material on the Second World War, for example, has been located.

Since 1960, the television companies have been filming constantly to provide programme material. The availability of small cameras and video means that companies, political groups, and private individuals have recorded on literally miles of film or tape. To take only one example: three years after the *coup d'état* in Chile there were at least three feature films and several short films on the failure of the "Union Popular" and the events of September. We know not only the official truth—elections, parliamentary debates, speeches, processions—but we also have filmed records of dozens of incidents unknown to the press—the occupation of land, the shopkeepers' strike, confrontations between workers and lorry drivers, and arrests made by the army in September and October. Of Hitler's accession to power, the cinema shows us only the official version—Hitler in the Reichstag, the screaming crowd in the streets, the enthusiasm of the victors. There exist only a few photographs of the hunting down of opponents, the prisons, and the first concentration camps, whereas we have several hours of film on the internment camps in Chile. The history of the American involvement in the Vietnam War, the *coup d'état* in Chile, or the Portugese Revolution will be known through audiovisual records as much as through written ones, but an inventory of this material will first have to be drawn up, and this will need lengthy research by international teams. We have not yet reached this stage.

In short, we have a stage of limited development in the evolution of audio-visual material, followed by a stage of ultra-rapid expansion. We will restrict ourselves in this book to the first stage, which is the only one for which we can achieve a fairly clear general view. For this period, the exploratory research and archive work is well advanced. The Slade Film History Register can be consulted by subject (mines, strikes, bombing, etc.) or by period. In addition to newsreels, all British films stored in the National Film Archive are listed in a printed catalogue and the catalogue of the other films is available on demand.

How Films Are Made

At this point, it would perhaps be useful to summarize what a motion picture is, from a material point of view. Everybody knows this as well as I do, but we must agree on the technical terms we are to use. A motion picture is first of all a strip of film on which frames are printed; during filming, as during projection, the number of frames filmed or projected is constant for a given period, generally twenty-four frames per second. The filming begins when the motor is switched on, and the sequence of frames taken continuously, without stopping the motor, is called a shot. When a cameraman comes to the end of a reel he has the raw material of a film; several consecutive shots which may have no connection with one another. The film is constructed when some passages are cut out of certain shots, and shots that the director wishes to bring together, for reasons of completion or contrast, are spliced end to end. This is the editing. Several related shots, for instance showing the arrival of a person who gets off a plane, into a car, and drives away, form a sequence.

It is essential to bear these points in mind if we are to understand what kind of document we are working with. It is very rare to find raw material—a shot as it was filmed by the cameraman: most if the films we see have been edited. It is impossible to reconstruct the originals, because what is not used is nearly always thrown away, for lack of room. But you must not imagine that what has disappeared was of great value: in most cases the cameraman responsible for filming an event, such as the opening of an exhibition by the king, took three times more than was necessary to be sure of having clear pictures, in which the king and the people welcoming him were easily recognizable. The problem for the historian is not that shots have been eliminated, but that what he sees is the result of a subjective choice, where the effect of editing is involved; that is, the influence that the different shots making up a sequence have on one another. On top of this, since 1930 there is the further problem of the sound track. We must remember that before magnetic recording came into general use, sound recording was an extremely delicate operation, requiring complex, cumbersome equipment. Speeches were recorded easily, because the speaker did not move; but in the previous example, an enormous effort would have been needed to follow the king as he walked through the exhibition, speaking to different people. Nobody thought it was worth taking the trouble. In spite of appearances, the cinema before 1960 consists of silent films to which sound has been added. In the sequence of the royal visit, vague crowd noises, voices, applause, and a commentary were added later. When we watch such a film, we are conscious of an atmosphere, and we feel a sense of involvement; but the sound effects, which play a large part in our impression, are artificial and have nothing to do with the scene that was filmed. Let us try to make a comparison: there is a great difference between a telex from a news agency reporting an event and a comment on this event in the *Times* or the *Guardian*. Exactly the same thing is being dealt with, but the article develops, shifts and modifies it. There is an even greater transformation between the filmed shot and the shaping through editing and the addition of sound effects. In most cases we know only the finished version of filmed events.

So I propose to make a first distinction between the filmed document as raw material, and the film which gives an interpretation, a particular point of view. I am stressing this difference because it is generally ignored in studies of the cinema. A classification should be made among films; several studies, in particular the article by Roads on film as historical evidence,[2] have laid down rules for this; and I do not think it is necessary to repeat here what you can easily find elsewhere if you are interested. Suffice to emphasize the difference between information films and feature films.

They can first be contrasted by stressing that the very great majority of feature films are fictional; the few exceptions, like Walt Disney's films on the desert, and documentaries on the sea, and on animals, are not very important. Information films are directly connected with the world of social relations, certain aspects of which they claim to reveal. To borrow a term from semiotics, we will say that they have a referent. For instance, it is decided to film a race that should interest the public. The purpose is the contest; the film of course shows only a few aspects, interpreted by the shooting and the editing, and transformed by sound effects. But the film exists only in relation to its pretext, and if we want to study it we must compare it with the referent. A fictional film is its own event; technicians and actors have been brought together, and for several weeks they have formed a social group, the manifestation of which is a long strip of film. The motion picture is both the cause and the result; it has no referent.

This involves a great difference in the way in which the audience is addressed. An information film seeks the best viewpoint of the event, the clearest picture; it concentrates entirely on the scenes and the people to be shown. A fictional film has less need of clarity and precision, but as it refers to nothing other than itself, it must grip the audience, making them participate actively, guess what is not shown, and feel sympathy or repulsion with what is happening on the screen. Brecht has explained perfectly the justification and function of this phenomenon of identification; he studied it mainly in the theatre, and we shall have to make a closer examination of the mechanisms by means of which the feature film involves the audience.

On the one hand we have the feature film, often unrelated to current events, and in any case conceived as a self-contained work, an enclosed universe; on the other hand, we have the information film which is only a kind of relay, a reflection that is no doubt distorted but that was originally based on direct observation of an event. It would seem that for the historian the information film is the preferred audiovisual document, the one from which he can get most. From sources of this latter type, the British Inter-University History Film Consortium has made five very interesting films on the years between 1936 and 1940 (*The Munich Crisis: The End of Illusions; From Munich to Dunkirk; The Spanish Civil War; The Winter War in its European Context; Neville Chamberlain*);[3] and the Open University has edited the War and Society series.[4] I am nevertheless going to criticise this kind of document. My proposition is that the information film is of undoubted but extremely narrow value, and that for the period we are dealing with, that is, for the years *before 1960*, the most original source is the fictional film.

Moving, Talking Newspapers: The Newsreels

Newsreels were born with the cinema: in 1896 or 1897, Dickson in the United States and Lumière in France were filming scenes of daily life. Until about 1910, cinema shows had no programme; people went without knowing what they would see, just to watch moving pictures. The performances were short and included about ten items, a mixture of newsreels and fictional scenes. Even at that time, the principal market was already the United States. In Europe, cinemas were open only a few hours a day, whereas in the United States the nickelodeons, which started in 1905, were so popular that within five years there were nearly 10,000 of them, open from morning till night; programmes changed daily, which meant that there was a considerable demand for films to renew the shows.[5] For technical reasons, mainly because they owned the patents, the market was dominated by a few companies—Edison, Biograph, and Pathé. In 1908, they came to an agreement and founded the Motion Picture Patents Company which had a monopoly of production and sales in the United States. Pathé dealt particularly with newsreels; this company already had subsidiaries in most European countries, and to supply this vast circuit the company sent cameramen all over the world to make films that could be shown equally well Russia or in England, and in the east or the west of the United States. The dominance of a company which supplied an extremely diverse clientele set a model for newsreels at the beginning of the century. This pattern did not change until 1960 and remains unchanged in countries like Italy, where newsreels are still shown in cinemas.

There are various reasons for this permanence. Let us briefly mention some technical considerations, although these are not the main factor. Those of you who have used a cine-camera know how difficult panning is—swivelling the camera to follow a moving object—if a tripod is not used. The exploits of Buster Keaton in *The Cameraman*, following the stages of a gigantic fight step by step, would be almost impossible with the lightweight equipment available today; it was out of the question with the old cameras, which were far too heavy. In addition, emulsions were slow, and filming was only possible in a good light. For a film to be successful, it was advisable to choose a good position, set up the equipment beforehand, and wait for sufficient light; so the simplest thing was to film events announced in advance, such as exhibitions, sporting contests, and military parades. If there was a violent demonstration or a fight, the still photographers took a few snaps and the cine-cameramen arrived when it was all over.

But we must take into account other phenomena, with which historical research is directly concerned.

The first important question is the organization of the film industry and its position with regard to the public. The habit of going to the cinema spread remarkably quickly in the West, from the first decade of the century. Twentieth-century historians seem to forget that the film was a perfectly common information vector well before the First World War. In his articles, which I recommend you to read,[6] N. Pronay has shown that no English newspaper ever reached a public comparable with that of the newsreels, which were seen every week by more than half the population of Great Britain during the 1930s.[7] The newspapers have their public, whose characteristics they approximately know, and for whom they adapt their style. Newsreel producers[8] do not know whom they are addressing; the same films are shown in a small agricultural town, a working-class suburb, and the West End, depending on the distribution circuit, so they have to try to please everyone.

We know the instructions given to Gaumont-British cameramen—give priority to traditional events, festivities, and sport; when abroad, do not miss either official ceremonies or events in which the English are involved.

People dealing in news items and entertainment in other media often take care not to offend their public; but the fear of shocking the audience never seems as acute as it is in the cinema. Filmmakers have always avoided what might annoy their audience, using a self-imposed censorship to avoid any kind of "excess." Just before the First World War, the British Cinematograph Exhibitors' Association, fearing the loss of a part of its audience, urged the Association of Kinematograph Manufacturers to establish a system of censorship: a British Board of Film Censors was established in January 1913. The filmmakers were not obliged to refer their films to this new private institution, but it became more and more difficult to find cinemas ready to show a film without the certificate delivered by the Board. The cinema had created its own limits.

The big European cinema networks, of which Pathé was the best example, did not survive the First World War. After 1920 they broke up into national companies and the market was taken over by firms in the United States, which were now the most powerful. For their sales abroad, and for their purchases of foreign films, almost all the producers went through the United States. The circuits had changed, but the old rules endured—to reach every social group within any one country, to satisfy audiences in very different countries, and to concentrate on a few well-defined fields of interest which people had become accustomed to since the earliest newsreels.

We must also take into account a conception of news which places the event in the foreground. As historians, we should wonder how, in each period, the public is informed of current events; for reasons that we do not have time to analyse, we should note a tendency, in the late nineteenth and early twentieth centuries, to put the emphasis on exceptional facts, which can be dated precisely and described in a few words or a few pictures. An attempt was made in the cinema to develop magazines dealing with a single subject, but they had little success and filmed news which was almost entirely limited to a series of brief, superficial glimpses of a small number of events.

Excellent studies have already been made of newsreels from Britain and the United States,[9] and I will therefore deal more with German films. The Bundesarchiv collection in Coblenz is far from complete for the period of the 1920s, but the period from 1929 to 1932 is covered more satisfactorily. There, we would expect to find material on the German crisis, unemployment, rioting, the rise of the Nazi organizations, but in fact newsreels made during this time are no different from those of previous years, and remarkably similar to newsreels produced in other European countries in their general conception. Sport is prominent, appearing weekly and frequently taking up more than half of the programme. Regional festivities featuring dancing, costume, and music appear to be the next most popular subject, followed by film of official ceremonies. The crisis is mentioned only indirectly, and coverage of politics is confined to what might be called "recognized" circumstances—elections, inaugurations, and visits of foreign dignitaries.

Documents of this sort are of only limited value, although they are not entirely worthless. They invite an interesting comparison with the concerns of the written media in 1932. The newspapers of the period continually refer to the rise of Hitler: if we took them as our only source, we might deduce that the Germans were interested in nothing but politics. Newsreels counterbalance this impression, reminding us that the economic and political crisis overlay ordinary activities without affecting them. The same Germans who, through political meetings and the newspapers, lived in a state of permanent tension, found their country apparently unchanged when viewing newsreels at the cinema.

Filmed news was never intended to cover developments over a long period; it deals only with particular facts, occurring at a definite point.[10] It is at its best when dealing with diplomatic agitation, military preparedness, or the effects of war.[11] Hardly surprisingly, the five British Inter-University History Film Consortium films all deal with the origins or the early years of the Second World War, three of them focusing entirely on the fighting. The material gives us a good idea of what was at stake (such as the strategic importance of Madrid), the conditions in which fighting took place (winter in Finland), the rival forces, and the principal battles.

Newsreels themselves are questionable as pieces of evidence. What can be gleaned from an analysis of them? John Grenville[12] proposes a distinction between primary and secondary evidence, giving as an example the Gaumont-British special feature on the Munich Conference and Chamberlain's return to Great Britain. The film gives us very little information on the diplomatic discussions themselves: here it provides only secondary evidence. But it gives primary, direct evidence in the sequence showing Chamberlain reading a report on the results of the Conference. Primary evidence of this sort, however, is hardly very useful. Newspapers published the report in full, and in this respect the film made no great contribution to the evidence already available elsewhere. I think we must see the film in a rather different light. The film shows Chamberlain being driven home along a road lined with crowds. The people raise their arms and the soundtrack records long shouts of applause. The evidence here is secondary rather than primary. The filmmakers wanted to show that the British people supported Chamberlain's policy, and that they were prepared to unite in support of their leader. The British filmmakers were in fact imitating their German counterparts. Interestingly enough, the same film footage was re-edited in France for French audiences, with the French Prime Minister Daladier taking the place of Chamberlain. In the English version, Chamberlain's return is featured prominently: in the French film, Daladier's return is dealt with much more briefly. Knowing that newsreels are composed entirely of shots chosen to produce a desired effect, and with a completely fabricated soundtrack, we should not conclude that the British were more satisfied with the results of the Munich Conference than the French were. All we can say is that the filmmakers themselves had two completely different sets of objectives. Films tell us all we need to know about the policies and opinions of their makers, and no more, but as we are aware of the importance of newsreels in influencing opinion, we must also understand what those policies and opinions were.

Newsreels show the world as filmmakers would like to see it, as is obvious in their choice of topics and even more apparent in the style of the various sequences. In spite of its brevity, every part of a weekly newsreel can be edited in various ways.[13] Official ceremonies, for example, are described in suitably solemn manner. The Prince of Wales visits allotments given to poor country people: we see the Prince arriving, speaking, smiling, digging, cutting corn. His exploits are not of intrinsic interest and might even be described as faintly ludicrous, but the filmmakers were interested in making the point that the Prince was prepared to try. Today, we can learn little of value about the Prince of Wales from the film, but we can at least gain some information about rural life in the 1930s by examining the faces of the ordinary people ranged behind him in the film.[14] Another reel[15] covers the street fights between Communists and fascists in London: a few brief shots and a shouted commentary make both demonstrations appear shocking and offensive.

We are obliged to treat newsreels as "distorted" or rather as "directed" images of society. Events that were of little importance at the time are endowed with a greater significance through repetition. Penelope Houston underlines this point: "Look at enough news film and one begins to feel that the most constant image of the 1930s is of a mounted police charge into an unarmed street crowd. But I realise, as I write this, how little real idea I have of the facts. How often was this scene actually enacted, in London, or Paris, or Madrid, or Berlin? How far is it an impression gained from well deployed screen use of a few unfailingly dramatic shots?"[16] Newsreels give us a highly selective view: if we want to use newsreels as evidence, we must expose the concealed rules governing that selectivity.

Newsreels illustrate diplomatic and military history, but they might also be useful in another way if we were prepared to consider them as ethnographical documents.[17] If we look, for example, at film of German crowds leaving a stadium, and if we ignore the clothes, the uniforms and the surroundings and consider only the mannerisms, the way of walking, the priority given to women and children, and the composition of the groups, we are presented with a number of interesting details. We can guess that half a century ago, social life modelled behaviour in very different ways, but we lack the means to prove it. In this respect, films are a potentially useful source of evidence, but perhaps we are still too close to the period and should leave research of this sort to the historians of the twenty-first century.

Imagine that a catastrophe destroyed all newspapers everywhere with the sole exception of *Life* magazine; who would dare to use this sole source as a basis for writing history? What happens with newsreels is rather like that. This is not an imperfection peculiar to the cinema, but a situation connected with the production and distribution of newsreels in the first half of the twentieth century. This fact must be acknowledged, and we must limit the use of news films to the restricted field for which they are suitable, and look elsewhere—in fact to feature films—for an instrument for research.

History and Historiography

Up to now we have discussed the relationship between the cinema and historical research as though the purpose of this research was obvious to everyone. I am not sure that we are in complete agreement on this point, and before considering the use of feature films I think it is essential to make it clear, at least as far as I am concerned, how I see the historian's work.

In the first stage, history is an attempt to clarify—to sort out what is probable from what is false, to establish the chronology of events, to show the relationships between them, and to detect periods of strong social or political tension and define their characteristics. We can call this positive history, the methods of which were devised two centuries ago and have lost none of their value. Today, we must go beyond this stage. We know that history is a society's memory of its past, and that the functioning of this memory depends on the situation in which the society finds itself. Out of the almost infinite mass of incidents and encounters which perpetually occur, a certain number are identified and described, and in this way become fixed as events, particular moments, the memory of which will be passed down and adopted by later generations. Sometimes it is a matter of chance whether a name or date stands out or disappears, but we should not attach too much importance to this. The essential part of what remains was made to be kept; even if we restrict ourselves to material traces, we find what was built to last—the towns, the houses of the powerful, the palaces. Our task is not only to reconstitute the past; we must also understand how, and according to what interest, the bases of our future documentation accumulated. We must realise that our work is largely conditioned by the organization of the period in which we are interested.

Most societies, at any rate Western societies, create their history as they evolve. And in these societies, certain groups, social classes, political parties, and socio-professional communities define their own version of the past. To clarify matters, we will use the word "historiography" to refer to the work of historians (or any other people) based, in principle at least, on all the available documents; and we will call the descriptions proposed by the groups belonging to the same society "historical traditions." I will make this clearer by an example that I would like you to bear in mind, concerning Russian films about the October revolution. In Russia it has always been the rule to refer to history, and particularly to the experience of the revolution; before the opposition was crushed by Stalin, it defined its position against the party leaders in terms of its own version of the events of 1917. The conflicting trends in the Bolshevik Party were marked by revisions of the previously accepted historical traditions. Today, now that the opposition is reappearing, it presents the reassessment of October and the period of Lenin as an essential stage. The Russian example is particularly obvious, but the same phenomenon can be found in many other countries.

The historical tradition defended by each group and class is of course only an instrument for talking about the present; the conflicts that divide a society, and the goals pursued by the opposing forces, are transposed in the semblance of past events. So I think that historiography—the history of history—is the ideal instrument for approaching the study of the problems that are current concerns in a society and for understanding the picture it has of its future.

I now come to what seems to me the second aspect of historical research—an aspect complementary to and inseparable from positive research. With the methods available to us—defining the socioeconomic base, analysing production methods and yields, studying quantitative data—we describe a period or a social sphere from the outside. But our research remains firmly rooted outside its object unless we can go beyond our scientific problematics and try to discover how the society we are dealing with defined itself, how it interpreted its own situation.

Let us return to the example of Soviet Russia. For a decade, the Bolshevik Party was simply not strong enough to administer a country of that size without some additional support, and so the Bolsheviks re-created a precariously privileged class in the form of a vast bureaucracy. Half a century later, we can now see this process as a whole, and we can begin to understand its significance and the various stages in its evolution; we must now discover how those who were involved in the process understood it, and the extent to which their actions were guided by their perceptions. In research of this kind, the greatest obstacle is the dearth of documentary evidence. The leaders of a political struggle have of course left their own accounts of the period, but how can we discover the point of view of those who did not write in newspapers or speak at congresses, but who nevertheless had an important part to play in a period of open struggle? At this point, we must turn to other material, including feature films.

Not all films are of equal interest, however, and we will first of all discount mass-produced imitations of an earlier success, on the grounds that these simply cashed in on a fashionable and popular theme. Mass production would be of interest if we were studying public reaction, but that is not our concern here.

On the other hand, the success of a new film must be taken into account, although I admit that this criterion is a very ambiguous one: bad films can be transformed by good publicity and vice versa, but we have no other method of assessment. We can measure the size of audiences and the length of runs, and this will give us a rough index of the correspondence between the message of a particular film and certain public expectations of that film.

We will also consider the character of a film. Nearly all films refer, if indirectly, to current events, but references of this sort are frequently obscure. For reasons of economy, we will concentrate on overtly political films. In view of what we have said about the importance of historical traditions, I think it would repay our interest to analyse historical films in which we have a chance of finding a view of the present embedded within a picture of the past. Finally, I have chosen films produced during periods of tension, rather than those that were released in a period of relative calm.

To sum up, I would therefore propose four rules for selection: the originality of a film, its relationship to current events, its favourable reception by the public, and the fact of its being produced and distributed during a time of crisis. On this basis, we could analyse several films from the same period (those films made on the tenth anniversary of the Russian Revolution in 1927, for example), but as we are attempting a comprehensive view, rather than an exhaustive one, I think it would be best to select a number of different examples, rather than restrict our choice to films made at a certain time. In 1914–1915, for example, when war broke out in Europe, very few historical films were made, and yet *La Marseillaise, La Grande Illusion* and *Gone with the Wind* were all made at the time of the Spanish Civil War, when the sins of German and Japanese aggression were first apparent and war seemed imminent. Not all historical films were exceptional: many of them were mass-produced. In studying the film I have selected, I will say why I consider it to be original, why it can be classified as an historical film, what kind of reception it had, and—because we are concerned with "history in film" rather than "film in contemporary history"—with the period covered in the film itself, rather than the period at which it was made.

What is an "Historical" Film?

Before beginning the individual analyses, I think it is essential to raise a few general questions about the nature of the historical film and the methods of research already in use.

When we want to characterize a film briefly, we try to isolate the features it has in common with other films, so that it can be classified as a type. Most of the types that we are familiar with—westerns, thrillers, comedies, science fiction, horror—developed within the world of the cinema, despite their literary origins, and they no longer exist except as cinematic types. The peculiarity of historical films is that they are defined according to a discipline that is completely outside the cinema; in fact there is no special term to describe them, and when we speak of them we refer both to the cinema and to history. This is a point that should be of interest to historians: it would seem that audiences recognize the existence of a system of knowledge that is already clearly defined—historical knowledge, from which filmmakers take their material.

A spectator watching an unfamiliar film can type-cast it within minutes. In the case of the historical film, what are the signs by which it can be recognized as such? There must be details, not necessarily many of them, to set the action in a period which the audience unhesitatingly places in the past—not a vague past but a past considered as historical. The cultural heritage of every country and every community includes dates, events, and characters known to all members of that community. This common basis is what we might call the group's "historical capital," and it is enough to select a few details from this for the audience to know that it is watching an historical film and to place it, at least approximately. When the period is less well known, or does not belong to the common heritage, then the film must clearly stress the historical nature of the events.

A well-known American film, *Intolerance,* illustrates both these processes. The film consists of four stories, three of them taking place in the past and one in the present, which are shown alternately rather than in chronological sequence. Two episodes, the life of Christ and the religious wars of the sixteenth century, are easily recognizable: they can be identified by the costumes, the attitudes, famous scenes, and occasionally portraits. But one of the episodes is set in ancient Babylon, a period virtually unknown to audiences, so the film provides abundant detail to establish the period, informing the audience that a certain object was found during excavations, that a particular custom is described in Greek or Babylonian texts. By compensating for the gaps in the audience's knowledge, it emphasizes the historical nature of what is shown.

What I think is important in both cases is the understanding that is formed, with no difficulty, between the filmmakers and the audience: for both, something real and unquestionable exists, something which definitely happened and which is history. The contingent aspect of the historical tradition, with which historians are deeply concerned, is completely ignored by the producers of historical films. It must be said that this type of film is not an historical work: even if it appears to show the truth, it in no way claims to reproduce the past accurately.

So I think that when professional historians wonder about the mistakes made in an historical film, they are worrying about a meaningless question. They would do better to concentrate on other problems.

We have noted some of the methods by which a film identifies itself as historical and allows the audience to find its bearings. In this way every historical film is an indicator of a country's basic historical culture, its historical capital. Which characters do not even have to be introduced, which have at least to be named, and which need to have some details given about them? What scenes, meetings, and events are recognized unhesitatingly? When, and on what points, do explanations have to be given? Behind the common knowledge, we can detect what is much more important: the underlying logic of history. What facts does the film select? How does it develop them? What connections does it show between them? The historical film is a dissertation about history which does not question its subject—here it differs from the work of the historian—but which establishes relationships between facts and offers a more or less superficial view of them. The understanding of historical mechanisms as developed in the cinema is another field for our research.

Historical films are all fictional. By this I mean that even if they are based on records, they have to reconstruct in a purely imaginary way the greater part of what they show. Scenery and costumes similar to those of the period represented can be based on texts and pictures, but the actors alone are responsible for the gestures, expressions and intonations. Most historical films (though not all—this does not apply to *October*) combine actual events and completely fictitious individual episodes. It is very seldom that a film does not pass from the general to the particular, and arouse interest by concentrating on personal cases; this is one of the most direct forms of the appeal to identification, an appeal which is in fact not specific to the cinema. Fiction and history react constantly on one another, and it is impossible to study the second if the first is ignored. The same type of analysis can be applied to an historical film as to any feature film.

Every Film Has Its Own "History"

When we begin the study of a film, the first question that arises is which document to use. Some of my readers may undertake research in this field, and I would draw their attention to this point. A film is analysed from a copy, but a copy is not like a book; it always has a career and sometimes a history. Its career is the use that has been made of it previously; a copy wears out and gets torn, and to repair it the damaged parts are removed. Before a film is shown, its condition should be checked, and any cuts noted, so that the missing passages can be replaced from another copy. But this is a comparatively minor thing. We must also realize that many production companies print copies for the domestic market (domestic prints) and copies suited to foreign audiences (foreign prints). We must always bear in mind the origin of the print used and the audience it was intended for. The essential thing is the history—in other words, the way in which the film has been marked by the political variations of its time. Many films that we are going to study have undergone important alterations. For some of them there are no more than the scissors of the censor to account for and things are quite simple: for a long time, *La Grande Illusion* was shown without the passage in which a German woman and a French soldier live together; the original version was not restored until 1958. With *October* and *The Birth of a Nation* things are far more complicated. I think it useful to give some information on the subject. Erudition is only the first and by no means the most interesting stage in the study of films, but it is absolutely necessary because all too often people discuss a film without knowing they have seen completely different films with the same title.

October was filmed and edited in a few months, at the end of 1927. In many of the authoritative studies of the Soviet cinema, the film is said to have suffered cuts in a number of scenes because they dealt with Trotsky. That is not true; Trotsky played a very small role in the original print: the shots showing him were cut out, but their omission only shortened the film by a few minutes. The cut shots were not burnt, as had been done for those cut in *The Birth of a Nation*; instead, the cut scenes were deposited in the Moscow film archive. The film, in its first version, was shown for several months in Russia after its release. However, audiences found it somewhat disappointing; the general impressions were that it was too difficult to follow and too intellectual. As a result the film was stored away and forgotten. A German company, which had acquired a print, finding it too long and subversive, made a concise version and sold it under a title borrowed from John Reed's book *Ten Days that Shook the World*. In 1966, the Russians took the first version out of storage and sold it to Western companies. As the Western newspapers, even the communist ones, had given the film good reviews, the government decided that the film was a useful propaganda vehicle in Soviet Russia and abroad; but *October* was still said to be too difficult for "average people" and another, shorter, re-edited version was assembled: all the subtitles were modified;[18] and the sequences in which oppositions were used (one photograph followed by the same photograph horizontally reversed; when Kerenski is endlessly climbing the steps of the Winter Palace inversions are extremely important in emphasizing his helplessness) were simplified. As we shall see later, the time scale is broken up: in the second part of the film, night and day constantly overlap one another; the 1967 version tries to "restore" the chronology by editing first the day shots and then the night shots.[19]

Here again things are simple: it is not difficult to ask which of the three different versions is going to be shown. Nobody can tell us where a print of *The Birth of a Nation* comes from. It is well known that the original 13,500-foot version, which showed the negroes in a hostile, racist manner, was strongly criticized; the producers cut out 500 feet which have never been recovered.[20] In the following years, the film was projected all over the United States; depending on the audience, the distributors[21] sometimes shortened the copy, sometimes altered the editing, sometimes added, cut out, and modified subtitles.

The producers themselves made changes,[22] and in 1930, Griffith himself issued a new short sound version.[23] It is impossible today to say which is the original print or how many prints are in distribution.

My conclusion on that point will be extremely clear: you must never study a film without referring to the origin of the print you have seen.

Problems of Interpretation: From Kracauer to the Present

Only what is relatively important politically is censored, and here we find another indication for measuring the popularity of films. When we follow the career of the prints, and reconstitute the original, we are again only doing a job of pure erudition, to which the methods of positive historical research are well suited. The uncertainty begins when we try to read and to interpret the film. Historians seem to experience a particular difficulty in this field. Thirty years ago, two books by Kracauer, *From Caligari to Hitler: A Psychological History of German Film* (1947) and *Nature of Film: The Redemption of Physical Reality* (1961), opened the way to a sociology of the cinema, but they were not followed up. In spite of their inadequacies we are still compelled to quote from them. Kracauer developed two different points of view, which are not contradictory, but for which he proposed no synthesis. In *Nature of Film,* he tried to show that feature films are realistic, in spite of their fictional character: "Film is uniquely equipped to record and reveal physical reality and, hence, gravitates towards it. . . . The only reality we are concerned with is actually existing physical reality—the transitory world we live in."[24] If we ignore the plot and the characters, we discover aspects of life which the camera has recorded all the more accurately because the cameraman did not even notice them. Take a film like *The Servant.* Today we are interested in the story and we think the setting unimportant, but in a hundred years' time, historians will find in it valuable information about dress, homes, public places, and relationships in London in the middle of the twentieth century. This is what I have called the ethnographical aspect of the cinema; Kracauer was right to draw attention to it, to show that it changes according to the period and the director; and he points out that certain social spheres are often shown while others, such as the country and factories, are forgotten. Looked at in this way, films are only a series of documentary illustrations; the frames remain, but the film disappears as a system of expression with a specific character. As it is difficult to work with film, for material reasons, and as there are very good collections of stills in the archives, it is possible to avoid the cinema altogether, if this is all we expect from it.

Kracauer also drew a parallel between the unhealthy atmosphere in the German cinema in the 1920s and the political situation under the Weimar Republic. There is certainly a connection between the two, but the author does not show where it lies; he underlines a few major trends in the cinema—mysticism, a feeling for nature, and an exaltation of the irrational—that he also finds in Nazi propaganda, but this parallel, which is sometimes forced, proves nothing.

Starting from an interesting intuition, Kracauer was content to give brief impressions, never really analysing the material of the cinema and never wondering what links there were between films and the society which produces them. I will return to these questions later.

Since 1960 there have been studies of individual films, but I know of only one attempt at a methodological synthesis—a work written by six Danish historians, *Film Analyses: History in Film*. As the book raises important questions, I will discuss it at some length.[25]

The authors look at films in relation to the historical and social circumstances in which they were produced. They think that while all films reflect a background reality, this reality is not directly reflected, but rather transformed by a series of processes. The book begins with an outline of the sociohistorical position, and then analyses twenty-three films produced in the United States and Western Europe in the fifty years since the end of the First World War, beginning with Lang's *Doctor Mabuse* (1922) and ending with *The Godfather* (1971).

The authors argue that during this period, the rise and crises of capitalism in the United States have forced the entire world into a ceaseless motion called development, which has destroyed the old social order. As capital tended towards an even greater concentration, independent producers were reduced to the status of wage-earners: "The centralizing tendency of capitalism and *proletarianization* of independent producers led to a new world where self-sufficiency has been abolished, a world strange and threatening for those who based their way of life on self-sufficiency."

Most people who work in the film industry are wage-earners, but their situation is such that they are in many ways placed in the same position as independent producers—whether they sell their products, if they are writers, freelance journalists, or musicians—or whether they are allowed enough freedom in their work that they become less conscious of the economic background determining it. "The intellectuals are to a high degree in the same position as the *proletarianized* independent producers but the mainly immaterial characteristics of intellectual work can lead to a concealment of the economic circumstances in which it takes place, so that there is in this work process the basis for a mixture of real insight and mystification." Films are not a direct reflection of reality, but give a distorted image of society, restricting social conflicts to a limited environment, transferring from the social to the individual plane and arbitrarily shaped by the conventions of the genre.

Let us look at John Ford's *Stagecoach* as an example of the most widespread types of distortion. First, some social conflicts are transposed and take place in the framework of a mini-society, a small, closed universe. Secondly, the subject matter of social conflict is transposed to the personal, individual level; the hero's problems with agriculture and the breakup of the family (remember that the film was produced in 1939: its social background is the economic depression of the 1930s) are seen as being caused by personal conflicts between the hero and certain wicked individuals. When these conflicts are resolved, the hero can return to his farm and restore the family idyll. Thirdly, *Stagecoach* is a western; the course of events proceeds within the limits of the conventions of a particular genre which requires a fixed organization of the story material.

The general approach in *Film Analyses* is at least an advance on Kracauer. The latter never separates a film from its "author"; he imagines that a film, like a book or a painting, has a single creator whose biography throws light on his creations. The Danes realize that such a notion cannot really be applied to the cinema: a film is always made by a team. To a large extent a writer or a painter is an independent producer: he does not need to find a publisher or a dealer until he has completed his work. But filmmakers have to find financiers before they can begin, and during shooting they are constantly making compromises with the actors and technicians. The director is a leader and an arbiter, but he has nothing of the author; for reasons of convenience his name may be attached to the title of the film, but the details of his life cannot be used as elements for an explanation. If we want to put films back into their context, which is very important, we must consider the circuit as a whole—the financing, the shooting, and the distribution. Kracauer also has a tendency to tell the story of the film, to concentrate on the scenario, and to comment on the psychology of the characters. The Danes, on the other hand, try to get away from fiction, and, beneath the anecdote, to discover the hidden expression of social conflict.

In spite of this progress, I see two serious objections. The first concerns the connection made between the background and the film. The sociohistorical analysis in *Film Analyses* seems to me a little too simple; even if it were taken further, the technique of defining a model and then trying to find proof of it in films is still not a very satisfactory method. With this procedure, we are sure to find at the end only what was postulated at the outset. The twenty-three studies lead to constantly recurring conclusions: the middle class is more and more threatened with losing its freedom, and independent work is giving way before monopolies. [The book from which this essay is drawn] covers half a century of the cinema in the United States and Europe: if, over fifty years, thousands of films have only repeated the same thing, dealing with the cinema is a waste of time.

In logic, when we are trying to classify terms, it serves no purpose if we have a category into which all the items can be placed, because it allows no distinction to be made. The same applies to an explanatory model which does not show the differences between films. Instead of describing society and then seeing how it is transposed to the cinema, we should move in the opposite direction—start with the films, study their specific characters, group together those which have features in common and separate those which are different, even on secondary points. But such an analysis cannot be made simply by seeing the films; it demands a preparation that many commentators prefer to dispense with.

Filmmaking and Film Analysis

How are films made and produced? News items or events or even a novel, or the biography of an important person, might suggest suitable themes: the filmmaker's first job is to write a short account of the subject and to present it for a producer. This simple, untechnical plan is called a *treatment:* Renoir and his scriptwriter wrote several unused treatments for *La Grande Illusion* and one of them is easy to get hold of:[26] it is quite different from the final film. If a producer and a group of actors are interested in the scheme, the director or the scriptwriter rewrites the text in order to give a full list of shots, described in their order, with stage directions and technical terms clearly marked; this is the scenario. There is a good scenario of *October* written by Eisenstein himself[27] but, once again, it is far removed from the three finished versions of the films we can see today. It is difficult to put into practice what was decided beforehand, and important alterations occur in the course of production. Two examples illustrate the point. One of the most spectacular effects of *October* is the opening of the main bridge of Petrograd; the carcass of a dead white horse, which is slowly raised with the bridge, eventually falls into the water; the scene was not even in the original scenario and was introduced later on: one morning, whilst filming another scene, the director, seeing the opened bridge on the skyline, decided to include its slow and irresistible motion in the film and to dramatize it by adding a carcass.[28] *La Grande Illusion* ends with two French prisoners of war escaping from the camp through snow, mud, and cold. The snow, which produces a very impressive effect, was not in the scenario; it had snowed just before the sequence was shot and the quite accidental effect of snow enhanced the mood of the scene.

Another difficulty may arise from the novel that the film was inspired by. It is tempting to make a study of the transposition of the written text to the screen, to list differences and likenesses, to dwell on the novel and on its relationship with the film, in a word, to take into account the sources. It is well known that the subject of *The Birth of a Nation* was suggested by two novels by the Reverend Thomas Dixon;[29] many apparently unnecessary or secondary details can be easily explained by referring to these books; for instance, the scene where Ben Cameron, injured, is visited by Elsie in hospital, follows the book closely, which explains why it is so long; we are then told that the same character is to be executed "on a false charge" but we do not know what this charge is: the book is more precise; the military surgeon tells Ben's friend that the young man was "sentenced by court-martial as a guerilla. It's a lie, but there's some powerful hand back of it."[30] The novel is less ambiguous than the film, but, as we shall see later, this lack of precision about the causes of events was one of the salient features of the film;[31] the film itself was greatly admired in spite of its vagueness.

If we were interested in the process of filmmaking, it would be important to compare the novels and the scenarios with the film. If we only want to study the films in their final form, however, as they were shown to the public, if we are asking what the films show us about their period, such comparisons are less relevant. Publishers print "the text" of some films; one must bear in mind that there is an enormous gap between a shot-analysis and dialogue: dialogue only gives the cues, the spoken part of the film; the book published with the title *Grande Illusion* is not very useful because it does not include information on centring, motions, stage management, or editing. On the contrary, Theodore Huff did very well when he described the making of *The Birth of a Nation* giving, shot by shot, any necessary information on shooting, staging and editing:[32] although it is rather a good work, I think the writer did not pay enough attention to the changes which were made from one print to another—especially from the silent to the sound version—and I prefer to use a more comprehensive analysis.[33]

A film is not simply a story played out by actors, even if the plot and characters are very important. It is also a series of shots which exert an influence through their content and through their relationship with one another. Again, it is a succession of information through language and, in sound films, a musical accompaniment and sound effects. When we first look at a film, we react to certain particular aspects of the picture. If we try to explain our feelings, we can find that our remarks are misunderstood or that they are not intelligible to others. One reason for this lack of precision is that in discussing our feelings about a film, we fail to provide enough detail to expand and substantiate our comments. Feelings are rarely a particularly useful basis for discussion or argument. If we want to argue about films—and as historians we have to argue about documents—we must begin with a description of what we are arguing about, namely films. Of course, the particular, specifically emotional quality of a film is only in part reducible to words and sentences. A description is no more than a brief discussion document. Semiologists would describe it, barbarically, as a meta-text, by which they mean another text, a byproduct of the first, rewritten in terms which enable historians to understand one another. A meta-text enables us to gauge the importance of data like style, shooting and editing. Many people maintain that a verbal description of this sort merely stifles intuitive creation and comprehension. They may be right but they miss the point completely. Intellectual, theoretical research is an abstraction: if we want to understand a film, we must ignore its presence; if we want to discuss it, we must isolate it and examine it from a distance. Objective consideration of this sort is probably less satisfying than pure, unalloyed "feeling," but at least it can form the basis of further discussion.

A filmed story and its constituent images cause us to react with approval or disapproval. We accept what we have seen or we reject it, and after the performance we all enjoy discussing what we felt. I have often observed that audiences are disturbed by the portrait of negroes in *The Birth of a Nation*, and that they react with very violent criticism. Too many discussions on the cinema consist only of obvious remarks and hasty judgements. It is easy to say that *The Birth of a Nation* is a racist film which condones lynching and violence. This may be true, but it is far too obvious a comment to serve any purpose. If we want to understand the reason for this racism, and its place in American life, we cannot be content with such general remarks. We must get a grip on the film, and to do so we must analyse it more deeply.

Many essays on the cinema try to assess the meaning of a film in terms of the director's purpose. In my opinion, a film *has* no meaning, and we should not be concerned with the purpose of the filmmaker. As both of these statements are highly contentious, I will try to make them more precise.

On the question of meaning, I would say that a film does not *necessarily* demonstrate anything. If it does make a point, it does so in such an obvious way that it is simply not very interesting. *The Birth of a Nation*, for example, suggested that blacks were a threat to the South and that the Ku Klux Klan were right to attack them. This point is made perfectly clear in the film, and we would waste valuable time in discussing it further. A film shows various things and poses many questions. We cannot hope to find and clarify them all. We must choose a middle way between discussing the obvious and losing ourselves in a maze of largely unanswerable questions.

What about following the director's intentions? Griffith certainly had a purpose in filming the American Civil War, and we can study what he wanted to "explain" and why he used particular details in his film. But Griffith is not the film. If we wanted to write his biography, we would have to decide to what extent his life and his experience are involved in his films. But he did not make the film single-handed: many older and younger people from all over the United States worked with him and had an effect on the film. And the thousands of Americans who saw the film and enthused over it did not care about Griffith's "purpose." *The Birth of a Nation* was a milestone in Griffith's life, but to the extent that we regard the film as a document of social history, we are concerned only with analysing the finished work and studying its effects.

History in "Historical" Films

One film mixes together a lot of information. Some of it is shaped by the cultural habits of a period or society: some of it is new and unfamiliar. Put together, old and new make the film; as far as we are concerned, it is important to know how details, notations, and pictures react upon one another. A film is made in more than one way; there are many connections, each of them structuring the whole of a film or a part of it, sometimes only one sequence. A good method for examining a film in detail is to take one or two themes and see how they are treated throughout the film. For us, history provides a convenient starting point. What is shown of it? Are the "historical" scenes long and detailed or short and imprecise? How are they edited?

Most books and reviews on the subject of history in film compare the events shown in film with a written description of those same events, but such an approach is ineffective. What should we compare? The history of the American Civil War as we now know it and a film of the war made in 1914? It would be an absurd comparison. We are in a position to see many things and relations which were unsuspected at the time: after the black revolt of the 1960s and 1970s we do not look at American blacks as people did before the First World War. We must, instead, compare the film with the version of history given at the time, but in 1914 there were many versions of the war, many accounts, none of them with a monopoly on the truth. *The Birth of a Nation* is one such account, no more or less so than any other book or film. If we were studying an historical text written at the same time, we would not compare it with the film version to see if it was true. We would instead try to understand the political logic of the account given in the book, asking why it emphasized this question, that event, rather than others. We should keep the same preoccupation in mind when analysing films.

As my argument is rather theoretical, I will give an example. Take Austin Stoneman, a character in *The Birth of a Nation*. We can try to identify him by looking beyond the film to the House of Representatives, where a parliamentary leader called Thaddeus Stevens had considerable influence during the Civil War and in the period of Reconstruction. During the war, Stevens was an aggressive extremist: in 1864 he spoke of the need to "exterminate" the rebels, and at the end of the war he urged the President to reduce the South to a "territorial condition." In this respect, the character of Stoneman closely resembles Stevens—but I would add that such a conclusion is not particularly interesting. Stoneman or Stevens—what is the difference? Let us go further: if we want to deal with the "context," our comparison should not stop there. In many ways, Stoneman and Stevens are very different. Stevens was elected in 1848, whereas Stoneman was "rising to power" in 1860; Stevens never married, whereas Stoneman had two children; Stevens never visited the South, whereas Stoneman travelled there "to see his policies carried out at first hand." More important, Stevens's close friend, Charles Sumner, supported the same programme and was one of the senators whose hostility towards the South wrecked Johnson's and Lincoln's policies. In *The Birth of a Nation*, Sumner urges a less dangerous policy in advocating extension of power to the newly free negroes.

Stevens or not Stevens? We cannot decide. Why is this so? We will have to accept that it is impossible to list all the characteristics of class, group, and character given in the film. We can enumerate some qualities, but we can never be sure that we have exhausted the possibilities or that we have grasped the relevance of a particular quality. Is it important that Stoneman was married, or that he very often remained seated when speaking to other people? We cannot answer that without putting Stoneman—or any other character—into a system of mutual relations. Most phenomena are only inadequately described if they are analysed piece by piece. The appearance of any element depends on its place and its function in the pattern as a whole. The shots do not simply stand "additively" next to each other, but assume quite different shades of meaning through this juxtaposition. Our vision does not involve mechanically recording the elements, but grasping significant structural patterns.

I know that the word "structure" is anathema for many historians. Structural analysis is not a pure formalism, nor a self-sufficient system: the structures do not exist by themselves, at least when we are working on a limited object like a film; they are conceptual models which help us in describing the organization and mutual relations of a particular complex whole. The structural analysis begins by discovering opposing principles (Stoneman as anti-Lincoln, for example) and goes on to emphasize the process of development of the opposed characters, groups or alliances.[34]

In "reading" a film, we must make a detailed examination, on the screen and more slowly on the viewing table, of all the elements in a film, to assess material and to see how it stands in relation to other material. At this stage we must ask: What is happening? How does it work? What is the film stressing? What fictional mechanisms is the film using, and behind them, what social mechanisms are concealed? It is not a matter of "explaining" the film, nor of finding out what the film "means." Under the unifying veneer of the story, multiple threads run through a film, some of them vanishing immediately, while others are developed at length. Analysis must draw out this multiplicity, showing that several approaches are possible to any one film. . . .

NOTES

1. "In January 1969 the Slade Film History Register started to comb the film collections systematically for material of use in the study of the twentieth century. The main selection criterion was to include every newsreel item ('story') which related to personalities (politicians, statesmen, inventors, artists and 'ordinary people') who made news, events (wars, strikes and elections) and subject themes (aircraft development, welfare services, economics, women and society, fascism, etc.) . . . Selections were based on the issue sheets of the newsreel companies and their accessions registers, together with additional information from any catalogues which existed, shot sheets, and the viewing of some of the material." ("The Slade Film History Register." In Frances Torp, ed., *A Directory of British Film and Television Libraries* (London, 1975). The lack of finance resulted in the closure of the Register at the end of 1975; its files can be consulted at the British Universities Film Council, 72 Dean Street, London.

2. C. H. Roads, "Film as Historical Evidence," *Journal of the Society of Archivists* (1966), 183. See also R. M. Barsam, *Nonfiction Films: A Critical History* (New York: Dutton, 1974), chap. 1; and William Hughes, "The Evaluation of Film as Evidence," in *The Historian and Film*, ed. P. Smith (Cambridge: Cambridge University Press, 1976), chap. 3.

3. Created in 1967, the British Inter-University History Film Consortium comprises the history departments of the Universities of Birmingham, Edinburgh, Leeds, Nottingham, Reading, the London School of Economics and Political Science, Queen Mary College, London. See John Grenville, "The Historian as Film-maker," in *The Historian and Film*, chap. 7; Tony Aldgate, "The Production of the 'Spanish Civil War,'" *University Vision* 11 (1974), 16, and 12 (1975), 42; and Tony Aldgate, *Cinema and History: British Newsreels and the Spanish Civil War*, (London: Scolar Press, 1979).

4. The third-year history course "War and Society," prepared by the Open University, includes thirty-two lectures. Students receive, alternately, one radio programme every fortnight and one TV programme every fortnight. The 16 TV programmes comprise, for instance, "The Social Consequences of World War II," "The Afro-American and World War II," "Guerrilla Warfare in Algeria." See Arthur Marwick, "Film in University Teaching," in *The Historian and Film*, chap. 8; and Milton Keynes, *Archive Film: Compilation Booklet* (London: The Open University, 1973).

5. "Today it would be hard to find a nickelodeon in the country that is not furnishing a change of program every day. In some instances . . . two changes a day are offered." *Views and Film Index* (28 December 1907). In Lewis Jacobs, *The Rise of American Film* (New York: Harcourt Brace, 1939), 53.

6. Nicholas Pronay, "British Newsreels in the 1930s," *History* (1971), 411; and (1972), 63.

7. "By 1934 the circulation figure for the cinema was already 43% of the [British] population [excluding the young people]. . . . In 1938–39 over half the population, excluding the very

young, saw each week what was communicated by means of the screen." Pronay, "British News-reels," (1971), 412–13. See also Aldgate, *Cinema and History*, 54 ff.

8. Gaumont-British, Movietone, Pathé, Paramount, Universal.

9. Raymond Fielding, *The American Newsreel* (Norman: University of Oklahoma Press, 1972).

10. According to N. Pronay, the newsreels were very popular among the working class for their "personification of political issues and their directly personal style; by way of contrast the cult of impersonality adopted by the BBC and by the documentaries appealed to the middle class." Pronay, "British Newsreels," (1972), 69.

11. "The newsreels of the 1930s belonged much more to the world of journalism than to the film world." Ibid., 63. See Aldgate, *Cinema and History*, 34 ff.

12. John A. S. Grenville, *Film as History: The Nature of Film Evidence* (Birmingham: University of Birmingham, 1971).

13. We cannot agree with N. Pronay when he says, "The 44 stories were constructed to move as fast as possible. . . . The professed reason for this technique was to cut before anyone in the audience became bored. It was, however, also another way of saying 'cut' before anyone could have had a chance of going over the story again in his mind. . . . Much the same applied to the sound tracks: the points were made to sink in through speed, loudness and repetition." Pronay, "British Newsreels," (1972), 63.

14. *British Movietone News* (24 April 1933), included in the Open University programme quoted in note 17 below. See "Great Britain 1750–1950: Sources and Historiography," (London: The Open University, 1974), 16.

15. *British Paramount News*, 664 (8 July, 1937), 4. "Blackshirts and Reds clash."

16. Penelope Houston, "The Nature of the Evidence," *Sight and Sound* 36:2 (1967), 91.

17. By selecting some short sequences devoted to precise aspects of social life and editing them the Open University had opened this field; its programmes on "Images of the working class in films of the Thirties" and "Slum clearance" used feature films, newsreels and documentaries. The OU's television programmes have been drastically reduced by lack of money.

18. Alterations often give information on what is supposed to be understandable for an "average citizen" in 1967. For instance the first subtitle, which was originally "February" has been completed by a caption telling the audience that February was the first step in the Revolution!

19. Unfortunately the most common version, distributed by the BFI, is the last.

20. We can imagine what the cut shots were by reading some reviews written after the first screenings. For instance: "We are told both in pictures and in titles that African Slaves were brought to this country by Northern traders who sold them to the South. Puritan divines blessed the traffic, but when slave trading was no longer profitable to the North, the 'traders of the seventeenth century became the abolitionists of the nineteenth century.'" *The Moving Picture World* (13 March 1915). This sequence was suppressed.

21. At that time a distributor acquired all the rights (including changes) for the whole of a State.

22. The second caption tells us: "All pictures made under the personal direction of D. W. Griffith have the name 'Griffith' in the border line. . . . There is *no exception* to this rule." It is easy to distinguish the captions written by the producers from those which were made by the distributors. Very often two or more different captions, having the name "Griffith" in the border line are edited at the same place in different prints.

23. Billy Bitzer, Griffith's cameraman, writes: "Ten years after the first showing, Mr. Aitken [the producer] who still owned *The Birth of a Nation* consulted me and I deemed it best we insert film twins—two identical picture frames coupled where one had been. Thereby we doubled the original twelve reels to feed into the new, more rapid projector." George William Bitzer, *Billy Bitzer, His Story* (New York: Farrar, Straus, and Giroux, 1973), 112.

24. Siegfried Kracauer, *Theory of Film: The Redemption of Physical Reality* (New York: Oxford University Press, 1960), 28.

25. *Filmanalyser. Historien i Filmen* by Michael Bruun Andersen, Torben Grodal, Søren Kjørup, Peter Larsen, Peter Madsen, Jorgen Poulsen (Copenhagen: Røde Hane, 1974). Quotations taken from the introduction, translated by the authors.

26. See André Bazin, *Jean Renoir* (New York: Simon and Schuster, 1973), 172.

27. Sergei Eisenstein, *Three Films* (New York: Harper & Row, 1974).

28. Having given Eisenstein's account we may add that another film devoted to the Russian Revolution, *The End of St. Petersburg,* which was shot during exactly the same period, includes some shots of the same opened bridge, which means either that one of the two directors (which one?) was influenced by the other or, more likely, that this bridge was seen as a symbol of the Romanovs' capital. With regard to the white horse, we must remember all the dead horses in Dostoevsky's novels. Bridge and horse are not mentioned in the original scenario of *October* (see note 27 above). It is interesting to see they were "spontaneously" added to the film during the shooting.

29. In 1915 many people thought that the "author" was Dixon, the writer of the novels which Griffith drew his inspiration from. See *Fighting a Vicious Film* (Boston: Boston Branch of NAACP, 1915), a pamphlet against the picture in which the film is attributed to Dixon.

30. Thomas Dixon, *The Clansman: An Historical Romance of the South* (New York: Doubleday Page and Co., 1905); and Thomas Dixon, *The Leopard's Spots: A Romance of the White Man's Burden* (New York: Doubleday, 1902), whose epigram is very symptomatic: "Can the Ethiopian change his skin or the leopard his spots?"

31. Sorlin, *The Film in History,* 93–94.

32. Theodore Huff, *A Shot Analysis of D. W. Griffith's "The Birth of a Nation"* (New York: Museum of Modern Art, Film Library, 1961), 62.

33. "Special Griffith," *L'Avant-scène du Cinéma* 193/194 (October 1977). All the captions are given in English.

34. In the lecture he delivered to the seventh Conference on History and the Audiovisual Media (München, September 1977), "A structural analysis of the film 'Sisimiut' with reference to an assessment of the applicability of semiotics in historical film research, Karsten Fledelius gave an excellent restatement of the question. The main objection is that the structural analysis is too time-consuming but it enables us to observe some patterns or 'modes' of expression which seem to possess, several of them, some ideological values. Perhaps these were not realized by the filmmaker, at least on the conscious level, but nevertheless they are there and they exert their influence on the message of the film as the potential of meaning is either narrowed or broadened by certain ways of building up the syntax of the film. In this way structural analysis becomes of fundamental value for the 'close reading of the film—the sign analysis'" (p. 40). See also Karsten Fledelius, "Film Analysis; the Structural Approach," in *Politics and the Media,* ed. M. J. Clark (Oxford and New York: Published for the British Universities Film Council by Pergamon Press, 1979), 105–126.

Robert A. Rosenstone

The Historical Film: Looking at the Past in a Postliterate Age

Historians and Film

Let's be blunt and admit it: historical films trouble and disturb professional historians—have troubled and disturbed historians for a long time. Listen to Louis Gottschalk of the University of Chicago, writing in 1935 to the president of Metro-Goldwyn-Mayer: "If the cinema art is going to draw its subjects so generously from history, it owes it to its patrons and its own higher ideals to achieve greater accuracy. No picture of a historical nature ought to be offered to the public until a reputable historian has had a chance to criticize and revise it."[1]

How can we think of this letter today? As touching? Naive? A window onto a simpler age that could actually conceive of Hollywood as having "higher ideals"? All of these? But if the attitude seems dated, the sentiments surely are not. Most historians today would be capable of saying, or thinking, the same thing. Give reputable scholars the chance to criticize and revise scripts, and we will surely have better history on the screen.

Question: Why do historians distrust the historical film? The overt answers: Films are inaccurate. They distort the past. They fictionalize, trivialize, and romanticize people, events, and movements. They falsify history.

The covert answers: Film is out of the control of historians. Film shows we do not own the past. Film creates a historical world with which books cannot compete, at least for popularity. Film is a disturbing symbol of an increasingly postliterate world (in which people can read but won't).

Impolite question: How many professional historians, when it comes to fields outside their areas of expertise, learn about the past from film? How many Americanists know the great Indian leader primarily from *Gandhi*? Or Europeanists the American Civil War from *Glory*, or—horrors!—*Gone with the Wind*? Or Asianists early modern France from *The Return of Martin Guerre*?

Dislike (or fear) of the visual media has not prevented historians from becoming increasingly involved with film in recent years: film has invaded the classroom, though it is difficult to specify if this is due to the "laziness" of teachers, the postliteracy of students, or the realization that film can do something written words cannot. Scores, perhaps hundreds, of historians have become peripherally involved in the process of making films: some as advisers on film projects, dramatic and documentary, sponsored by the National Endowment for the Humanities (which requires that filmmakers create panels of advisers but—to disappoint Gottschalk—makes no provision that the advice actually be taken); others as talking heads in historical documentaries. Sessions on history and film have become a routine part of academic conferences, as well as annual conventions of major professional groups like the Organization of American Historians and the American Historical Association. Reviews of historical films have become features of such academic journals as the *American Historical Review, Journal of American History, Radical History Review, Middle Eastern Studies Association Bulletin,* and *Latin American Research Review.*[2]

All this activity has hardly led to a consensus on how to evaluate the contribution of the "historical" film to "historical understanding." Nobody has yet begun to think systematically about what Hayden White has dubbed *historiophoty*—"the representation of history and our thought about it in visual images and filmic discourse."[3] In essays, books, and reviews, the historical film is dealt with piecemeal. Yet it is fair to say that two major approaches predominate.

The explicit approach takes motion pictures to be reflections of the social and political concerns of the era in which they were made. Typical is the anthology *American History/American Film,* which finds "history" in such works as *Rocky* (problems of blue-collar workers), *Invasion of the Body Snatchers* (conspiracy and conformity in the fifties), *Viva Zapata* (the cold war), and *Drums along the Mohawk* (persistence of American ideals).[4] This strategy insists that any film can be situated "historically." As indeed it can. But it also provides no specific role for the film that wants to talk about historical issues. Nor does it distinguish such a film from any other kind of film. Which leads to this question: Why not treat written works of history in the same way? They, too, reflect the concerns of the era in which they were made, yet we historians take their contents at face value and not simply as a reflection of something else. Why consider history books in terms of contents and historical films in terms of reflections? Is it that the screen itself only reflects images? That the analogy to Plato's cave is too close to allow us to trust what messages the shadows deliver?

The implicit approach essentially sees the motion picture as a book transferred to the screen, subject to the same sorts of judgments about data, verifiability, argument, evidence, and logic that we use for written history. Involved here are two problematic assumptions: first, that the current practice of written history is the only possible way of understanding the relationship of past to present; and, second, that written history mirrors "reality." If the first of these assumptions is arguable, the second is not. Certainly by now we all know that history is never a mirror but a construction, congeries of data pulled together or "constituted" by some larger project or vision or theory that may not be articulated but is nonetheless embedded in the particular way history is practiced.

Let me put it another way: historians tend to use written works of history to critique visual history as if that written history were itself something solid and unproblematic. They have not treated written history as a mode of thought, a process, a particular way of using the traces of the past to make that past meaningful in the present.

The notion of history as constituted and problematic is hardly news to anyone familiar with current debates in criticism, but it needs to be stressed. For to talk about the failures and triumphs, strengths and weaknesses and possibilities of history on film, it is necessary to pull back the camera from a two-shot in which we see history on film and history on the page square off against each other, and to include in our new frame the larger realm of past and present in which both sorts of history are located and to which both refer. Seen this way, the question cannot be, Does the historical film convey facts or make arguments as well as written history? Rather, the appropriate questions are: What sort of historical world does each film construct and how does it construct that world? How can we make judgments about that construction? How and what does that historical construction mean to us? After these three questions are answered, we may wish to ask a fourth: How does the historical world on the screen relate to written history?

Varieties of Historical Film

We cannot talk about the historical "film" in the singular because the term covers a variety of ways of rendering the past on the screen. (Written history, too, comes in different subcategories—narrative, analytic, quantitative—but we have the notion that they all are part of some larger story about the past. Film seems more fragmented, perhaps because there exist no broad film histories of nations, eras, or civilizations that provide a historical framework for specific films.) It is possible to put history on film into a number of categories—history as drama, history as antidrama, history without heroes, history as spectacle, history as essay, personal history, oral history, postmodern history—but for heuristic purposes this essay will collapse all of these into three broad categories: history as drama, history as document, and history as experiment. Most of what follows will focus on history as drama, the most common form of historical film.

If you say "historical film," history as drama is probably what comes to mind. A staple of the screen ever since motion pictures began to tell stories, this form of film has been regularly produced all over the world in the United States, France, Italy, Japan, China, Russia, India—wherever films are made. Some of the most beloved motion pictures have been dramatized history, or at least dramas set in the past. Among them are the kind of works that have given the historical film such a bad reputation—*Gone with the Wind, Cleopatra,* and *The Private Life of*

Henry VIII. It has been suggested by Natalie Davis that history as drama can be divided into two broad categories: films based on documentable persons or events or movements (*The Last Emperor, Gandhi, JFK*) and those whose central plot and characters are fictional, but whose historical setting is intrinsic to the story and meaning of the work (*Dangerous Liaisons, The Molly Maguires, Black Robe*).[5] But this distinction does not in fact have much explanatory power, for the categories quickly break down. A recent film, *Glory*, which I will analyze later in this essay, follows the common strategy of placing fictional characters next to historical characters in settings alternately documentable and wholly invented.

History as document is a more recent form than history as drama. Growing—at least in the United States—out of the social problem documentary of the thirties (*The Plow that Broke the Plains*), it was given a boost by the post–World War II patriotic retrospective (*Victory at Sea*), and an even bigger boost by public money, which has been funneled by the National Endowment for the Humanities into historical films in the past two decades. In the most common form, a narrator (and/or historical witnesses or experts) speaks while we see recent footage of historical sites intercut with older footage, often from newsreels, along with photos, artifacts, paintings, graphics, newspaper and magazine clippings.

Professional historians trust history as document rather more than history as drama because it seems closer in spirit and practice to written history—seems both to deliver "facts" and to make some sort of traditional historical argument, whether as a feature (*The Wobblies, Huey Long, Statue of Liberty*) or as a series (*The Civil War, Eyes on the Prize*). But a major problem for documentary lies precisely in the promise of its most obviously "historical" materials. All those old photographs and all that newsreel footage are saturated with a prepackaged emotion: nostalgia. The claim is that we can see (and, presumably, feel) what people in the past saw and felt. But that is hardly the case. For we can always see and feel much that the people in the photos and newsreels could not see: that their clothing and automobiles were old-fashioned, that their landscape lacked skyscrapers and other contemporary buildings, that their world was black and white (and haunting) and gone.

History as experiment is an awkward term for a variety of filmic forms, both dramatic and documentary and sometimes a combination of the two. Included here are works made by avant-garde and independent filmmakers in the United States and Europe as well as in former communist countries and the Third World. Some of these films have become well known, even beloved (Sergei Eisenstein's *Oktober* and *Battleship Potemkin*, Roberto Rossellini's *The Rise of Louis XIV.* Some have achieved local or regional fame (*Ceddo* by Senegal's Ousmane Sembène, *Quilombo* by Brazil's Carlos Diegues). Others remain intellectual and cinematic cult films, more written about by theorists than seen by audiences (Alexander Kluge's *Die Patriotin*, Trinh T. Minh-ha's *Surname Viet Given Name Nam*, Alex Cox's *Walker*, Jill Godmilow's *Far from Poland*).

What these films have in common (apart from lack of exposure) is that all are made in opposition to the mainstream Hollywood film. Not just to the subject matter of Hollywood but to its way of constructing a world on the screen. All struggle in one or more ways against the codes of representation of the standard film. All refuse to see the screen as a transparent "window" onto a "realistic" world.

Why, you may ask, discuss such films? Why take time for works few people want to or can see? Because, as I have argued elsewhere, such works provide the possibility of what might be called a "serious" historical film, a historical film that parallels—but is very different from—the "serious" or scholarly written history, just as the standard Hollywood film parallels more popular, uncritical forms of written history, the kind history "buffs" like. At its best, history as experiment promises a revisioning of what we mean by the word *history*.

How Mainstream Films Construct a Historical World

The world that the standard or mainstream film constructs is, like the world we live in and the air we breathe, so familiar that we rarely think about how it is put together. That, of course, is the point. Films want to make us think they are reality. Yet the reality we see on the screen is neither inevitable nor somehow natural to the camera, but a vision creatively constructed out of bits and pieces of images taken from the surface of a world. Even if we know this already, we conveniently forget it in order to participate in the experience that cinema provides.

Less obvious is the fact that these bits and pieces are stuck together according to certain codes of representation, conventions of film that have been developed to create what may be called "cinematic realism"—a realism made up of certain kinds of shots in certain kinds of sequences seamlessly edited together and underscored by a sound track to give the viewer a sense that nothing (rather than everything) is being manipulated to create a world on screen in which we can all feel at home.

The reason to point to the codes of cinema (which have a vast literature of their own) is to emphasize the fundamental fiction that underlies the standard historical film—the notion that we can somehow look through the window of the screen directly at a "real" world, present or past. This "fiction" parallels a major convention of written history: its documentary or empirical element, which insists on the "reality" of the world it creates and analyzes. The written work of history, particularly the grand narrative, also attempts to put us into the world of the past, but our presence in a past created by words never seems as immediate as our presence in a past created on the screen.

History as drama and history as document are, in their standard forms, linked by this notion of the screen as a window onto a realistic world. It is true that the documentary—with its mixture of materials in different time zones, with its images of the past and its talking heads speaking in the present—often provides a window into two (or more) worlds. But those worlds share, both with each other and with history as drama, an identical structure and identical notions of document, chronology, cause, effect, and consequence. Which means that in talking about how the mainstream film creates its world, it is possible to make six points that apply equally to the dramatic film and the documentary.

1. The mainstream film tells history as a story, a tale with a beginning, middle, and an end. A tale that leaves you with a moral message and (usually) a feeling of uplift. A tale embedded in a larger view of history that is always progressive, if sometimes Marxist (another form of progress).

To put it bluntly, no matter what the historical film, be the subject matter slavery, the Holocaust, or the Khmer Rouge, the message delivered on the screen is almost always that things are getting better or have gotten better or both. This is true of dramatic films (*Glory, Reds, The Last Emperor*) and true of documentaries (*The Civil War*). It is also true (perhaps especially true) of radical documentaries like *The Wobblies, Seeing Red, The Good Fight,* and other hymns of praise to lost causes.

Often the message is not direct. A film about the horrors of the Holocaust or the failure of certain idealistic or radical movements may in fact seem to be a counterexample. But such works are always structured to leave us feeling: Aren't we lucky we did not live in those benighted times? Isn't it nice that certain people kept the flag of hope alive? Aren't we much better off today? Among those few films that leave a message of doubt about meaningful change or human progress, one might point to *Radio Bikini*, with its lingering questions about the possibility of controlling atomic energy or regaining an innocent faith in government, the military, or the scientific establishment. Or to *JFK*, with its worries about the future of American democracy, though the very fact that a big star like Kevin Costner, playing New Orleans attorney Jim Garrison, expresses these doubts tends to reassure us that the problems of the security state will be exposed.

2. Film insists on history as the story of individuals, either men or women (but usually men) who are already renowned, or men and women who are made to seem important because they have been singled out by the camera and appear before us in such a large image on the screen. Those not already famous are common people who have done heroic or admirable things, or who have suffered unusually bad circumstances of exploitation and oppression. The point: both dramatic features and documentaries put individuals in the forefront of the historical process. Which means that the solution of their personal problems tends to substitute itself for the solution of historical problems. More accurately, the personal becomes a way of avoiding the often difficult or insoluble social problems pointed out by the film. In *The Last Emperor* the happiness of a single "re-educated" man stands for the entire Chinese people. In *Reds*, the final resolution of a stormy love affair between two Americans becomes a way of avoiding the contradictions of the Bolshevik Revolution. In *Radio Bikini*, the fate of a single sailor stands for all of those who were tainted with radiation from the atomic bomb tests of Operation Crossroads.

3. Film offers us history as the story of a closed, completed, and simple past. It provides no alternative possibilities to what we see happening on the screen,

admits of no doubts, and promotes each historical assertion with the same degree of confidence. A subtle film like *The Return of Martin Guerre* may hint at hidden historical alternatives, at data not mentioned and stories untold, but such possibilities are never openly explored on the screen.

This confidence of the screen in its own assertions can trouble even historians who are sympathetic to the visual media. Natalie Davis, the historical consultant on the film, worries about the cost of the "powerful simplicity" of *Martin Guerre:* "Where was there room in this beautiful and compelling cinematographic re-creation of a [sixteenth-century] village for the uncertainties, the 'perhapses,' the 'mayhavebeens' to which the historian has recourse when the evidence is inadequate or perplexing?"[6] Davis followed her work on the film by writing a book (with the same title) in order to restore this important dimension to the story of Martin Guerre. But anyone other than an expert viewing a historical film is confronted with a linear story that is unproblematic and uncontested in its view of what happened and why.

This is equally true of the documentary, despite the fact that it may call on various witnesses and experts who express alternative or opposing points of view. Through editing, these differences are never allowed to get out of hand or call into question the main theme of the work. The effect is much like that of dissenting minor characters in a drama, people whose opposing positions heighten the meaning of whatever tasks the heroes undertake. Ultimately, these alternative viewpoints make no real impact. They only serve to underline the truth and solidity of the main world or argument.

4. Film emotionalizes, personalizes, and dramatizes history. Through actors and historical witnesses, it gives us history as triumph, anguish, joy, despair, adventure, suffering, and heroism. Both dramatized works and documentaries use the special capabilities of the medium—the closeup of the human face, the quick juxtaposition of disparate images, the power of music and sound effect—to heighten and intensify the feelings of the audience about the events depicted on the screen. (Written history is, of course, not devoid of emotion, but usually it points to emotion rather than inviting us to experience it. A historian has to be a very good writer to make us feel emotion while the poorest of filmmakers can easily touch our feelings.) Film thus raises the following issues: To what extent do we wish emotion to become a historical category? Part of historical understanding? Does history gain something by becoming empathic? Does film, in short, add to our understanding of the past by making us feel immediately and deeply about particular historical people, events, and situations?

5. Film so obviously gives us the "look" of the past—of buildings, landscapes, and artifacts—that we may not see what this does to our sense of history. So it is important to stress that more than simply the "look" of things, film provides a sense of how common objects appeared when they were in use. In film, period clothing does not hang limply on a dummy in a glass case, as it does in a museum; rather, it confines, emphasizes, and expresses the moving body. In film, tools, utensils, weapons, and furniture are not items on display or images reproduced on the pages of books, but objects that people use and misuse, objects they depend

upon and cherish, objects that can help to define their livelihoods, identities, lives, and destinies. This capability of film slides into what might be called false historicity. Or the myth of facticity, a mode on which Hollywood has long depended. This is the mistaken notion that mimesis is all, that history is in fact no more than a "period look," that things themselves *are* history rather than *become* history because of what they mean to people of a particular time and place. The baleful Hollywood corollary: as long as you get the look right, you may freely invent characters and incidents and do whatever you want to the past to make it more interesting.

6. Film shows history as process. The world on the screen brings together things that, for analytic or structural purposes, written history often has to split apart. Economics, politics, race, class, and gender all come together in the lives and moments of individuals, groups, and nations. This characteristic of film throws into relief a certain convention—one might call it a "fiction"—of written history: the strategy that fractures the past into distinct chapters, topics, and categories; that treats gender in one chapter, race in another, economy in a third. Daniel Walkowitz points out that written history often compartmentalizes "the study of politics, family life, or social mobility." Film, by contrast, "provides an integrative image. History in film becomes what it most centrally is: a process of changing social relationships where political and social questions—indeed, all aspects of the past, including the language used—are interwoven."[7] A character like Bertrande de Rols in *Martin Guerre* is at once a peasant, a woman, a wife, a property owner, a mother, a Catholic (but possibly a Protestant), a lover, a resident of Languedoc, a subject of Francis I of France.

How Experimental Films Construct a Historical World

The only collective way to characterize history as experiment is as films of opposition: opposition to mainstream practice, to Hollywood codes of "realism" and storytelling, to the kind of film described above. Certainly most experimental films will include some of the six characteristics of the standard film, but each will also attack or violate more than one of the mainstream conventions. Among films defined as history as experiment, it is possible to find the following: works that are analytic, unemotional, distanced, multicausal; historical worlds that are expressionist, surrealist, disjunctive, postmodern; histories that do not just show the past but also talk about how and what it means to the filmmaker (or to us) today.

How does history as experiment contest the characteristics of mainstream film? Here are some examples:

1. History as a story set in the framework of (moral) progress: the director Claude Lanzmann suggests in *Shoah* that the Holocaust was a product not of madness but of modernization, rationality, efficiency—that evil comes from progress. Alex Cox, in *Walker*, highlights the interpenetration of past and present and points to Manifest Destiny (with its assumptions of political and moral

superiority and uplift) not as an impulse confined to pre–Civil War America but as a continuing part of our relationships with Central America.

2. History as a story of individuals: Soviet directors in the twenties, particularly Eisenstein in *Potemkin* and *Oktober,* created "collectivist" histories in which the mass is center stage and individuals emerge only briefly as momentary exemplars of larger trends (much as they do in written history). The same strategy has been pursued more recently by Latin American filmmakers (Jorge Sanjinés in *Power of the People,* Carlos Diegues in *Quilombo*).

3. History as a closed, uncontested story: Jill Godmilow in *Far from Poland* presents a "history" of the Solidarity movement through competing voices and images that refuse to resolve into a single story with a single meaning. Chris Marker in *Sans Soleil* and Trinh T. Minh-ha in *Surname Viet Given Name Nam* both dispense with story in favor of historical incident, pastiche, rumination, essay.

4. History as emotional, personal, dramatic: Roberto Rossellini made a series of sumptuously mounted but wholly dedramatized films, including *The Rise of Louis XIV* and *The Age of the Medici,* in which amateur actors mouth lines rather than act them. The Brazilian Glauber Rocha achieves a similar Brechtian, distanced, unemotional past in such works as *Antonio das Mortes* and *Black God, White Devil.*

5. History with a "period look": Claude Lanzmann in *Shoah* tells a history of the Holocaust without a single historical image from the thirties or forties; everything was shot in the eighties, when the film was made. The same is largely true of Hans Jürgen Syberberg's *Hitler, a Film from Germany,* which re-creates the world of the Third Reich on a soundstage with puppets, parts of sets, props, actors, and random historical objects, all illuminated by back-projected images.

6. History as process: the director Alexander Kluge in *Die Patriotin* creates history as a series of disjunctive images and data, a kind of collage or postmodern pastiche. Juan Downey in *Hard Times and Culture* uses a similar approach in a study of fin de siècle Vienna. Chris Marker in *Sans Soleil* envisions the past as made up of disconnected, synchronous, and erasable events.

———

History as experiment does not make the same claim on us as does the realist film. Rather than opening a window directly onto the past, it opens a window onto a different way of thinking about the past. The aim is not to tell everything, but to point to past events, or to converse about history, or to show why history should be meaningful to people in the present. Experimental films rarely sanitize, nationalize, or reify the past, though they often ideologize it. They tend to make bits and pieces of our historical experience accessible, sometimes in all its confusion. Such films rarely claim to be the only or the last word on their subject; many hope to make us think about the importance of a subject ignored by written history.

Experimental films may help to re-vision what we mean by history. Not tied to "realism," they bypass the demands for veracity, evidence, and argument that are a normal component of written history and go on to explore new and original ways of thinking about the past. Although such films are not popular, and although "reading" them can at first seem difficult for those who expect realism, their breakthroughs often are incorporated into the vocabulary of the mainstream film. The revolutionary montage effects of Eisenstein were long ago swallowed up by Hollywood. More recently, a German film, *The Nasty Girl*, uses a variety of avant-garde techniques (back projection rather than sets, composite shots, overtly absurdist elements) to portray the continuing desire of middle-class Germans to deny local complicity with the horrors of the Third Reich.

Reading and Judging the Historical Film

Our sense of the past is shaped and limited by the possibilities and practices of the medium in which that past is conveyed, be it the printed page, the spoken word, the painting, the photograph, or the moving image. Which means that whatever historical understanding the mainstream film can provide will be shaped and limited by the conventions of the closed story, the notion of progress, the emphasis on individuals, the single interpretation, the heightening of emotional states, and the focus on surfaces.

These conventions mean that history on film will create a past different from the one provided by written history; indeed, they mean that history on film will always violate the norms of written history. To obtain the full benefits of the motion picture—dramatic story, character, look, emotional intensity, process—that is, to use film's power to the fullest, is to ensure alterations in the way we think of the past. The question then becomes: Do we learn anything worth learning by approaching the past through the conventions of the mainstream film (conventions that are, through the global influence of Hollywood, understood virtually everywhere in the world)?

A slight detour: it must always be remembered that history on film is not a discipline in which historians participate (to any great extent). It is a field whose standards historians may police but, with rare exceptions, only as onlookers. When we historians explore the historical film, it is history as practiced by others, which raises the ominous question: By what right do filmmakers speak of the past, by what right do they do history? The answer is liberating or frightening, depending on your point of view. Filmmakers speak of the past because, for whatever reasons—personal, artistic, political, monetary—they choose to speak. They speak the way historians did before the era of professional training in history, before history was a discipline. Today the historian speaks by virtue of this discipline, by virtue of special training and the standards of a profession. Filmmakers have no such standard training, and no common approach to history. Few, if any, devote more than a minor part of their careers to history; it is more likely that they are moved over the years to make one or two historical statements on film. (Though some major directors have devoted major parts of their careers to history, including Roberto Rossellini, Akira Kurosawa, Masahiro Shinoda, Carlos Diegues, Ousmane Sembène, and Oliver Stone.) One result: history on film will always be a more personal and quirky reflection on the meaning of the past than is the work of written history.

The haphazard nature of history on film and the lack of professional control make it all the more necessary that historians who care about public history learn how to "read" and "judge" film, learn how to mediate between the historical world of the filmmaker and that of the historian. This means that historians will have to reconsider the standards for history. Or learn to negotiate between our standards and those of filmmakers. We will have to adapt to film practice in order to criticize, to judge what is good and bad, to specify what can be learned from film about our relationship the past. The film world will not do this, for it has no ongoing stake in history (though some individual filmmakers do). The best we historians can hope for is that individual filmmakers will continue to create meaningful historical films that contribute to our understanding of the past. For only by studying how these films work can we begin to learn how to judge the historical film.

Among the many issues to face in learning how to judge the historical film, none is more important than the issue of invention. Central to understanding history as drama, this is the key issue. The most controversial. The one that sets history on film most apart from written history, which in principle eschews fiction (beyond the basic fiction that people, movements, and nations all live stories that are linear and moral). If we can find a way to accept and judge the inventions involved in any dramatic film, then we can accept lesser alterations— the omissions, the conflations—that make history on film so different from written history.

History as drama is shot through with fiction and invention from the smallest details to largest events. Take something simple, like the furnishings in a room where a historical personage sits—say Robert Gould Shaw, the chief character in *Glory*, a colonel and leader of the Fifty-fourth Massachusetts Regiment of black troops in the American Civil War. Or take some process, such as the training of the black volunteers who served under Shaw, or the reconstruction of the battles they fought. The room and the sequences are approximate rather than literal representations. They say this is more or less the way a room looked in 1862; these are the sorts of artifacts that might have been in such a room. This is more or less the way such soldiers trained, and the battles they fought must have looked something like this. The point: the camera's need to fill out the specifics of a particular historical scene, or to create a coherent (and moving) visual sequence, will always ensure large doses of invention in the historical film.

The same is true of character: all films will include fictional people or invented elements of character. The very use of an actor to "be" someone will always be a kind of fiction. If the person is "historical," the realistic film says what cannot truly be said: that this is how this person looked, moved, and sounded. If the individual has been created to exemplify a group of historical people (a worker during a strike, a shopkeeper during a revolution, a common soldier on a battlefield) a double fiction is involved: this is how this sort of person (whom we have created) looked, moved, and sounded. Both can obviously be no more than approximations of particular historical individuals, approximations that carry out some sense that we already have about how such people acted, moved, sounded, and behaved.

The same is true of incident: here invention is inevitable for a variety of reasons—to keep the story moving, to maintain intensity of feeling, to simplify complexity of events into plausible dramatic structure that will fit within filmic time constraints. Different kinds of fictional moves are involved here, moves we can label *Compression, Condensation, Alteration,* and *Metaphor.*

Consider this example: when Robert Gould Shaw was offered command of the Fifty-fourth, he was in the field in Maryland, and he turned down the offer by letter. A couple of days later, urged by his abolitionist father, he changed his mind and accepted the position. To show the internal conflict expressed in this change within a dramatic context, *Glory* compresses Shaw's hesitation into a single scene at a party in Boston. The actor, Matthew Broderick, uses facial expression and body language to show Shaw's inner conflict. When he is offered the command by the governor of Massachusetts, he says something noncommittal and asks to be excused. There follows a scene with another officer, a kind of alter ego, an officer who voices Shaw's own unspoken doubts about the costs of taking such a command. These doubts register on Broderick's face, and we literally watch Shaw make this difficult decision, see that accepting the commission is a matter of conviction triumphing over fear. All of this scene, including the fellow officer, is invented, yet it is an invention that does no more than alter and compress the spirit of the documentable events into a particular dramatic form. In such a scene, film clearly does not reflect a truth—it creates one.

The difference between fiction and history is this: both tell stories, but the latter is a true story. Question: Need this be a "literal" truth, an exact copy of what took place in the past? Answer: In film, it can never be. And how about the printed page, is literal truth possible there? No. A description of a battle or a strike or a revolution is hardly a literal rendering of that series of events. Some sort of "fiction" or convention is involved here, one that allows a selection of evidence to stand for a larger historical experience, one that allows a small sampling of reports to represent the collective experience of thousands, tens of thousands, even millions who took part in or were affected by documentable events. One may call this convention Condensation too.

But isn't there a difference between *Condensation* and invention? Isn't creating character and incident different from condensing events? Is it not destructive of "history"? Not history on film. On the screen, history must be fictional in order to be true!

Why? Because filmic "literalism" is impossible. Yes, film may show us the world, or the surface of part of the world, but it can never provide a literal rendition of events that took place in the past. Can never be an exact replica of what happened (as if we knew exactly what happened). Of course, historical recounting has to be based on what literally happened, but the recounting itself can never be literal. Not on the screen and not, in fact, in the written word.

The word works differently from the image. The word can provide vast amounts of data in a small space. The word can generalize, talk of great abstractions like revolution, evolution, and progress, and make us believe that these things exist. (They do not, at least not as things, except upon the page.) To talk of such things is not to talk literally, but to talk in a symbolic or general way about the past. Film, with its need for a specific image, cannot make general statements about revolution or progress. Instead, film must summarize, synthesize, generalize, symbolize—in images. The best we can hope for is that historical data on film will be summarized with inventions and images that are apposite. Filmic generalizations will have to come through various techniques of condensation, synthesis, and symbolization. It is the historian's task to learn how to "read" this filmic historical vocabulary.

Clearly, we must read by new standards. What should they be? At the outset, we must accept that film cannot be seen as a window onto the past. What happens on screen can never be more than an approximation of what was said and done in the past; what happens on screen does not depict, but rather points to, the events of the past. This means that it is necessary for us to learn to judge the ways in which, through invention, film summarizes vast amounts of data or symbolizes complexities that otherwise could not be shown. We must recognize that film will always include images that are at once invented and true; true in that they symbolize, condense, or summarize larger amounts of data; true in that they impart an overall meaning of the past that can be verified, documented, or reasonably argued.

And how do we know what can be verified, documented, or reasonably argued? From the ongoing discourse of history; from the existing body of historical texts; from their data and arguments. Which is only to say that any "historical" film, like any work of written, graphic, or oral history, enters a body of preexisting knowledge and debate. To be considered "historical," rather than simply a costume drama that uses the past as an exotic setting for romance and adventure, a film must engage, directly or obliquely, the issues, ideas, data, and arguments of the ongoing discourse of history. Like the book, the historical film cannot exist in a state of historical innocence, cannot indulge in capricious invention, cannot ignore the findings and assertions and arguments of what we already know from other sources. Like any work of history, a film must be judged in terms of the knowledge of the past that we already possess. Like any work of history, it must situate itself within a body of other works, the ongoing (multimedia) debate over the importance of events and the meaning of the past.

False Invention/True Invention

Let me compare two films that invent freely as they depict historical events—*Mississippi Burning*, which uses "false" invention (ignores the discourse of history), and *Glory*, which uses "true" invention (engages the discourse of history).

Mississippi Burning (directed by Alan Parker, 1988) purports to depict the Freedom Summer of 1964, in the aftermath of the killing of three civil rights workers, two white and one black. Taking for its heroes two FBI men, the film marginalizes blacks and insists that though they are victims of racism, they in fact had little to do with their own voting rights drive. The resulting message is that the government protected African-Americans and played a major role in the voter registration drive of Freedom Summer. Yet this is palpably untrue. This story simply excludes too much of what we already know about Mississippi Freedom Summer and the rather belated actions of the FBI to solve the murder of the three civil rights workers.[8] The central message of that summer, as responsible historians have shown, was not simply that blacks were oppressed, but that they worked as a community to alleviate their own oppression. This is the theme that the film chooses to ignore. By focusing on the actions of fictional FBI agents, the film engages in "false" invention and must be judged as bad history. Indeed, by marginalizing African-Americans in the story of their own struggle, the film seems to reinforce the racism it ostensibly combats.

Glory (directed by Edward Zwick, 1989) is as inventive as *Mississippi Burning*, but its inventions engage the historical discourse surrounding the film's subject: the Fifty-fourth Massachusetts Regiment commanded by Robert Gould Shaw, and, by implication, the larger story of African-American volunteers in the American Civil War. Here are examples of how specific strategies of invention work in *Glory*.

Alteration. Most of the soldiers in the Fifty-fourth were not, as the film implies, ex-slaves, but in fact had been freemen before the war. One can justify this alteration by suggesting that it serves to bring the particular experience of this unit into line with the larger experience of African-Americans in the Civil War, to generalize from the Fifty-fourth to what happened elsewhere in the Union to slaves who were freed.

Compression. Rather than creating characters from regimental histories, the film focuses on four main African-American characters, each of whom is a stereotype—the country boy, the wise older man, the angry black nationalist, the Northern intellectual. The filmic reason is obviously dramatic: such diverse individuals create a range of possibilities for tension and conflict that will reveal character and change. The historical reason is that these four men stand for the various possible positions that blacks could take toward the Civil War and the larger issues of racism and black-white relations, topics that are not solely "historical" or that, like all historical topics, involve an interpenetration of past and present.

Invention. Although there is no record of this happening, in the film the quartermaster of the division to which the Fifty-fourth belongs refuses to give boots to the black troops. His ostensible reason is that the regiment will not be used in battle, but the real reason is that he does not like African-Americans or think them capable of fighting. Clearly, this incident is one of many ways the film points to the kinds of Northern racism that black soldiers faced. Another way of showing the racism might have been by cutting to the antiblack draft riots in New York, but such a strategy could vitiate the intensity of the film and the experience of our main characters. This incident is an invention of something that could well have happened; it is the invention of a truth.

Metaphor. Robert Gould Shaw is shown practicing cavalry charges by slicing off the tops of watermelons affixed to poles. Did the historical Shaw practice this way? Does it matter? The meaning of the metaphor is obvious and apropos.

Question: Does using a white officer as a main character violate the historical experience of these African-American volunteers? Answer: No, it provides a different experience, a broader experience. Even if the decision to have a white main character was in part made for box office reasons (as it surely must have been), the film provides another explanation. Throughout *Glory* we see and hear Robert Gould Shaw saying (in voiceover extracts from actual letters) that though he admires them, he cannot comprehend the culture of these men he leads. The clear implication is that we too will never fully understand their life. We viewers, in other words, stand outside the experience we are viewing just as Shaw does. Which suggests that film itself can only approximate that lost historical life. We do not understand the life of the soldiers because we are always distant spectators of the experience of the past, which we may glimpse but never fully understand.

For all its inventions, *Glory* does not violate the discourse of history, what we know about the overall experience of the men of the Fifty-fourth Regiment—their military activities, their attitudes, and those of others toward them.[9] At the same time, the film clearly adds to our understanding of the Fifty-fourth Regiment through a sense of immediacy and intimacy, through empathic feelings and that special quality of shared experience that the film conveys so well. To share the up-close danger of Civil War battles as rendered on the screen, for example, is to appreciate and understand the possibilities of bravery in a new way.[10]

There is no doubt that the film simplifies, generalizes, even stereotypes. But it proposes nothing that clashes with the "truth" of the Fifty-fourth Regiment or the other black military units that fought for the Union—that men volunteered, trained under difficult conditions, and gave their lives in part to achieve a certain sense of manhood for themselves and pride for their people. Only the moral may be suspect: when the bodies of the white officer and one of his black men (the angriest, the one most suspicious of whites, the one who refuses to carry the flag, the one who has been whipped by this same officer) are pitched into a ditch and fall almost into an embrace, the implication seems to be that the Fifty-fourth Massachusetts Regiment and the Civil War solved the problem of race in America. How much more interesting, how much truer, might have been an image that suggested that the problems of race were to continue to be central to the national experience.

A New Kind of History

Of all the elements that make up a historical film, fiction, or invention, has to be the most problematic (for historians). To accept invention is, of course, to change significantly the way we think about history. It is to alter one of written history's basic elements: its documentary or empirical aspect. To take history on film seriously is to accept the notion that the empirical is but one way of thinking about the meaning of the past.

Accepting the changes in history that mainstream film proposes is not to collapse all standards of historical truth, but to accept another way of understanding our relationship to the past, another way of pursuing that conversation about where we came from, where we are going, and who we are. Film neither replaces written history nor supplements it. Film stands adjacent to written history, as it does to other forms of dealing with the past such as memory and the oral tradition.

What, after all, are the alternatives? To try to enforce Gottschalk's dicta? To insist that historians begin to make films that are absolutely accurate, absolutely true (as if this were possible) to the reality of the past? Not only is this impossible for financial reasons, but when historians do make "accurate" films (witness *The Adams Chronicles*), they tend to be dull as both film and history, for they do not make use of the full visual and dramatic power of the medium. A second alternative: history as experiment. But whatever new insights into the past experimental films provide, they tend to give up large audiences. A final alternative: to wish film away, to ignore film as history. But this would be to surrender the larger sense of history to others, many of whom may only wish to profit from the past. Worse yet, it would be to deny ourselves the potential of this powerful medium to express the meaning of the past.

It is time for the historian to accept the mainstream historical film as a new kind of history that, like all history, operates within certain limited boundaries. As a different endeavor from written history, film certainly cannot be judged by the same standards. Film creates a world of history that stands adjacent to written and oral history; the exact location of the understanding and meaning it provides cannot yet be specified.

We must begin to think of history on film as closer to past forms of history, as a way of dealing with the past that is more like oral history, or history told by bards, or *griots* in Africa, or history contained in classic epics. Perhaps film is a postliterate equivalent of the preliterate way of dealing with the past, of those forms of history in which scientific, documentary accuracy was not yet a consideration, forms in which any notion of fact was of less importance than the sound of a voice, the rhythm of a line, the magic of words. One can have similar aesthetic moments in film, when objects or scenes are included simply for their look, the sheer visual pleasure they impart. Such elements may well detract from the documentary aspect, yet they add something as well, even if we do not yet know how to evaluate that "something."

The major difference between the present and the preliterate world, however obvious, must be underscored: literacy has intervened. This means that however poetic or expressive it may be, history on film enters into a world where "scientific" and documentary history have long been pursued and are still undertaken, where accuracy of event and detail has its own lengthy tradition. This tradition, in a sense, raises history on film to a new level, for it provides a check on what can be invented and expressed. To be taken seriously, the historical film must not violate the overall data and meanings of what we already know of the past. All changes and inventions must be apposite to the truths of that discourse, and judgment must emerge from the accumulated knowledge of the world of historical texts into which the film enters.

NOTES

This essay began as a presentation to a conference on the broad theme of "How We Learn History in America," held at the University of North Carolina. While others wrestled with major issues of the profession—the historical canon, Western civilization courses, textbooks, how to teach race and gender—I used the occasion to explore the question of how film creates a world of the past that must be Judged on its own terms. Here for the first time I attempted to specify just what those terms are and how we can use them to distinguish between good and bad works of history on film.

1. Quoted in Peter Novick, *That Noble Dream: The "Objectivity Question" and the American Historical Profession* (Cambridge: Cambridge University Press, 1998), 194.

2. There is no single book that satisfactorily covers the topic of history and film. The broadest discussion takes place in a forum in *American Historical Review* 93 (1988), 1173–1227, which includes the following articles: Robert A. Rosenstone, "History in Images/History in Words: Reflections on the Possibility of Really Putting History onto Film"; David Herlihy, "Am I a Camera? Other Reflections on Film and History"; Hayden White, "Historiography and Historiophoty"; John J. O'Connor, "History in Images/Images in History: Reflections on the Importance of Film and Television Study for an Understanding of the Past"; Robert Brent Toplin, "The Filmmaker as Historian."

3. White, "Historiography and Historiophoty," in ibid., 1193.

4. John E. O'Connor and Martin A. Jackson, eds., *American History/American Film: Interpreting the Hollywood Image* (New York: Ungar, 1979).

5. Natalie Zemon Davis, "'Any Resemblance to Persons Living or Dead': Film and the Challenge of Authenticity," *Yale Review* 76 (1987), 457–82.

6. Natalie Zemon Davis, *The Return of Martin Guerre* (Cambridge, Mass.: Harvard University Press, 1983), viii.

7. Daniel J. Walkowitz, "Visual History: The Craft of the Historian—Filmmaker, " *Public Historian* 7 (Winter 1985), 57.

8. Books on the Mississippi Freedom Summer include Doug McAdam, *Freedom Summer* (New York: Oxford University Press, 1988), and Mary A. Rothschild, *A Case of Black and White: Northern Volunteers and the Southern Freedom Summers, 1964–1965* (Westport, Conn.: Greenwood Press, 1982). For an older account that remains useful, see Len Holt, *The Summer That Didn't End* (New York: Morrow, 1965).

9. For a history of the Fifty-fourth Regiment, see Peter Burchard, *One Gallant Rush: Robert Gould Shaw and His Brave Black Regiment* (New York: St. Martin's Press, 1965).

10. James McPherson, "The *Glory* Story," *New Republic* 202 (January 8, 1990), 22–27.

George F. Custen

Making History

It is personalities, not principles, that move the age.
—Oscar Wilde

In 1944 Leo Lowenthal, a member of the Frankfurt School, published his now famous article "Biographies in Popular Magazines." In it, he proclaimed that twentieth-century capitalism had created a new set of myths—what he called "mass culture." Rather than being indigenously produced by a people, mass culture was instead manufactured for audiences by organizations we now refer to as mass media of communication. These myths—in this particular instance, a set of biographical sketches of famous men and women published in mass circulation magazines—were manufactured like the commodities of other industries that had come to dominate the American landscape; story form and content, like items on any assembly line, were standardized for easy consumption. Readers could thus peruse the pages of *Collier's* or the *Saturday Evening Post* and in the tales of the life of a Henry Ford and Ronald Reagan (when he was only a movie star) receive a kind of pseudo-education, one that reduced history to organized gossip.

In selecting to discern in these magazine biographies patterns over time, Lowenthal noted a shift both in the subjects of biography and in the explanations proffered for why a particular life was meritorious. His content analysis of 1,003 issues of *Collier's* and the *Saturday Evening Post*, covering sixteen sample years, found that while magazines of the first decades of the century had focused their attention on the biographies of what he called "idols of production" (captains of industry, the military, and other members of conventional ruling elites), later magazines, inspired by the new media, radio and the motion picture, chose to highlight what Lowenthal called "idols of consumption." In this change from idols of production to idols of consumption, he detected a shift in American values and a shift in the morality lessons—"lessons of history"—that readers might derive from these magazines. Power through the making of the world had been replaced by power through ownership of its coveted items. Consumerism had replaced community as a way of life. This new power was attained through the appropriation of a proper and glamorous appearance. In this world, Andrew Carnegie was replaced by Hattie Carnegie as a figure to be admired.

Lowenthal shared with other members of the Frankfurt School (notably Theodor Adorno, Walter Benjamin, and Max Horkheimer) a fearful contempt for the products of the mass media which, according to his view, increasingly manipulated audience members into an authoritarian view of history cum popular entertainment. Fearing that the simplifications found in items like biographies in popular magazines, when not downright harmful, were "corrupting the educational conscience by delivering goods which bear an educational trademark but are not the genuine article,"[1] Lowenthal felt that biographies performed another, more powerful function. In particular, biographies, like the earlier "Lives of the Saints," helped prepare average people to accept their place in the social structure by valorizing a common, distant, and elevated set of lives that readers could hope to emulate. More than examples of entertaining education, these biographical sketches were also propaganda that prepared readers for acquiescence in a status quo; in this world of biography, there would always be readers on the outside and those figures inside the covers whose lives were read about, admired, and emulated.

If he feared the impact of magazines (with their relatively modest circulations) as agents of socialization, one wonders what Lowenthal made of the infinitely more glamorous biographies manufactured and released by the Hollywood studios. For just as biographies in popular magazines played some part in socializing readers into a particular vision of America and the lived American life, movies, with their attractive stars, swelling, emotionally manipulative musical scores, and powerful publicity engines, were rival sources of information about the lives of the famous. Movie biographies offered the public the possibility of connecting concretely with a glamorous image of a famous historical person in the guise of a contemporary movie star. One could admire the past life depicted while worshipping the very real current incarnation of this life on the screen, and off the screen, in publicity materials.

Movies created a rhetoric of fame that was essentially different from that of print. In movies, the actor portraying the eminent figure had an actual, corporeal existence outside the narrative frame of a particular biographical life that may or may not have been congruent with the figure depicted; in print, there was no such double life, except to the extent that print biographies, sanitized and censored as their movie equivalents, were as far removed from the real life as any film.[2] Stated another way, movie biographies presented a double level of the articulation of fame. At the first level, one was absorbed by the narrative constructed about selected episodes in the life of the subject. At the second level, one encountered the famous figure in other filmic contexts as well as through repeated exposure to publicity materials. Combined, these two levels of image created the facets of what Richard Dyer perceptively refers to as the polysemic star image. Here, the moviegoer is drawn to resonant aspects of the impersonator as well as the life impersonated. In this light, perhaps one admires Queen Elizabeth I for her statecraft but also because she is Bette Davis.[3]

Marketing Research

Biopics were often sold to the public as accessible versions of history. Credits within the film and publicity for the films made sure to highlight this research angle. For example, a title credit for Fox's *Stanley and Livingstone* (1939) acknowledged the researchers for the film as well as the director, producer, and screenwriters. The intensity of the research effort expended on a project was part of the publicity campaigns for many biopics. Bordwell, Staiger, and Thompson, in *The Classical Hollywood Cinema,* have noted that both the spectacular and novel aspects of a film were commonly used to differentiate one product from the next.[4] Extravagant research efforts became, for the biopic, a way of reassuring consumers that every effort had been expended to bring them true history in the guise of spectacle, as well as suggesting that the research for each film was, for the first time, bringing to the screen a true portrait, or at least a singularly true version or the accurate characterization of a person.

In part, the focus Hollywood accorded biopic research was like Leonardo's aging painting of *The Last Supper:* parts of the fresco were vividly drawn, with the most minute detail given emphasis. In other places, the image lacked clarity. With the full awareness of some of the personnel on a film, the most outrageous misrepresentations sometimes passed as the norm. In part, research for a biopic was shaped by particular expectations regarding what historical errors audience members and critics might catch, and what they were likely to overlook. Such slippage had to be avoided at all costs, for it could suggest that the product had been accorded less than the deluxe treatment.

The studios files are full of letters from fans who wrote gleefully to point out real or imagined mistakes. For example, Corporal Maurice G. Smith, an RAF pilot, wrote Warners Research Department on October 30, 1946, that some of the personnel in a hospital scene in the Cole Porter biopic, *Night and Day,* were wearing inappropriate decorations. Hetta George, of Warners Research, defended the accuracy of the costumes: "Our uniform expert, however, who incidentally is an ex–Royal Navy Officer, assures us that the ribbon worn by the British Medical Officer in our picture was carefully checked by him and is absolutely correct." Similarly, a preview card from MGM's *Parnell* (1937), in May 1937, contained a query from an audience member about the accuracy of the film's narrative. Although praising one of the film's stars ("Anything with Myrna Loy suits me"), the anonymous viewer noted, "Also, I thought Parnell and O'Shea were married after her divorce."[5] From its earliest days, film audiences seemed to demand a loose code of realism in certain cinematic contexts. Kevin Brownlow writes:

> The alibi, "The audience will never notice" was given lie early in *Photoplay*'s "Why Do They Do It?" column which was entirely devoted to blunders made in movies. . . .
>
> Audiences spotted every conceivable error, and specialists in various subjects had a field day when films appeared dealing with their favorite topic.[6]

He suggests that both the demand for accuracy on the part of the audience, and the studios' means of satisfying that demand, were in existence by the 1920s.

Particularly because biopics were films differentiated from other narratives by dint of their historical nature, the studios maintained a watchful eye upon their use of facts. While most critics were willing to accept a certain amount of poetic license in biopics and other historical narratives, a film that wandered too far into biofantasy inevitably drew sarcastic critical comment. Thus, H. T. Jordan, a critic from the *Cincinnati Times-Star,* under a review for Fox's *Cardinal Richelieu* titled "Bad History," lectured:

> In the motion picture *Cardinal Richelieu* featuring George Arliss, there is an incident which is so contrary to truth and so palpably a distortion of historical facts that the entire production, despite its extravagant beauty of setting, is rendered distasteful to any well-informed person.
>
> It is realized that a writer of motion picture plots is permitted some freedom with historical facts, but when one of the greatest characters in history is introduced wantonly and unnecessarily into the plot structure and in a manner derogatory and despicable, the occasion gives rise to protest.

The critic refers to the depiction of King Gustafus Adolphus of Sweden as a kind of drunken lout, a portrayal that drew a protest from the Swedish government. Geoffrey Shurlock, of the MPPDA, took note of the protest, and suggested to Fox that such an error "serves to remind us how very careful we will have to be with regard to these historical pictures."[7] Fox, in an unusual capitulation, eliminated the offensive scenes.

For the biopic of the Brontës, *Devotion* (1946), the anonymous critic for the *New York World Telegram* noted that while "the picture can look forward to the popularity that goes to all slickly produced tear jerkers these days," the creators of the wildly inaccurate narrative of the Brontë family "should have their knuckles rapped for making up such fibs about their elders."[8]

Although some critics and viewers lay in wait to catch the slightest slip, the attitude of most audience members, as well as producers, seemed to be that unless the error was particularly outrageous, or the events were so recent that many patrons would recall the facts, an odd mixture of careful research, of compromised whimsy, and of outright fabrication characterized the sets, the costumes, the characters, manners and mores, and the narratives of most biopics. As Darryl Zanuck, in a memorandum of August 12, 1950, notes of some of the fabrications of the life of Ben Hogan, *Follow the Sun* (1951), "No one, in my opinion, will ever pin us down to dates except the later dates in the past two or three years which are clearly remembered." Zanuck believed if the film were entertaining enough, no one would attend to a minor glitch or two. When Kenneth MacGowan, the associate producer of a Zanuck favorite, *Lloyds of London* (1936), complained that some of the depictions of financial operations of nineteenth-century insurance companies were inaccurate, Zanuck, in a memo dated July 28, 1936, lectured film neophyte MacGowan on what audiences would and would not accept as film history:

Technicalities of this type never cause any trouble. In *Rothschild* I made Rothschild an English Baron and there never was a Rothschild a Baron. I had the King of England give him the honor, and at this time there was no King of England as the king was in the insane asylum and the Regent had the gout and couldn't stand up, but I used Lumsden Hare and the picture in England got the same wonderful reviews it received in America and no one ever mentioned these technical discrepancies.[9]

Research and historical accuracy were woven among the threads of narrative demands, producer's taste, and the marketing strategy in which a film could be exploited for its "spectacular" research.

We see this approach to exploiting research in the road show and souvenir books printed by each studio for the premieres of important films. Typical of these efforts is MGM's booklet for their prestige production of *Marie Antoinette* (1938). The campaign book for the film is filled with numerical data, informing exhibitors that "during the four years in which the picture was in preparation, 59,277 . . . questions were answered. This required compiling a bibliography of 1,538 volumes, gathering 10,615 photographs, paintings and sketches, and mimeographing 5,000 pages of manuscript containing more than 3,000,000 words."[10] It seems that Metro could now boast that they had more researchers, as well as more stars, than in heaven, for no detail was too small to demand attention. According to the *Antoinette* campaign book, sharp-eyed director W. S. Van Dyke spotted one extra, amid a crowd of 250, wearing anachronistic and inappropriate pants; he would not shoot the scene before this minuscule detail was rectified. Selling the film as historically accurate, as an epic of research, was key in differentiating the biopic genre from other studio fare. Thus, MGM's book for the West Coast premiere of *Madame Curie* suggests that

> The research task to achieve authentic realism was one of the most thorough ever attempted for a motion picture. Fortunately, many photographs of the Curies, of their laboratories and of Paris during the turn of the century were available. A treasure of Curie photographs was obtained from Mlle. Curie. They furnished accurate guides for make-up, costuming and sets. . . . Whenever possible, these photographs were brought to life. . . . Miss Garson's make-up as Marie in her later years, of Pidgeon as Pierre, Travers as Dr. Eugene Curie and Dame Whitty as Mme. Curie, were carefully matched to family portraits.

Sometimes, producers attempted to attain the active participation of the surviving family members of the great man or woman. Their imprimaturs were valuable publicity commodities, though only occasionally were their contributions more than symbolic. Producer Sidney Franklin even tried to get Marie Curie's daughter, Eve, whose book, *Madame Curie,* was the source material for the Paul Osborn and Paul Rameau script, to speak the opening narration, noting in a draft of a letter to Eve Curie that, "Since the words are yours, it seems to us it would be most fitting that the voice should be yours, also."[11] Eve Curie demurred, and the poetic opening was spoken in classic dulcet narrator tones by

Cambridge-educated novelist James Hilton who had, earlier, written the screen-play for another Greer Garson/Walter Pidgeon hit, *Mrs. Miniver* (1942).

Similarly, the program for the press preview of MGM's *Edison, The Man*, which took place at Grauman's Chinese Theatre on May 16, 1940, avers how research aided Spencer Tracy in his portrayal.

> Before the picture, Spencer Tracy visited Edison laboratory in Greenfield Village, talked with Henry Ford, who has collected the Edisoniana, and visited Mrs. Mina M. Edison Hughes, widow of the inventor. . . . During production, Mrs. Madeleine Sloane, Edison's daughter, watched many scenes during a trip to Hollywood.

Further, copious newsreel footage of Edison was assembled by the research department, and "Tracy studied them many times to capture the inventor's mannerisms and actions."

Never one to be outdone in the serious business of ballyhoo and promotion, Cecil B. DeMille claimed, in the souvenir book for the West Coast premiere of Paramount's Jean Lafitte biopic, *The Buccaneer* (1938), that he was descended from the governor of Tennessee who financed the War of 1812. DeMille, the master showman, thus connected himself in a deeply personal way with the narrative; it became a tale of his own ancestor, as well as a reconstruction of history. RKO claimed a similar genealogical link for Katharine Hepburn to a character she portrayed, Mary Queen of Scots.

Publicity campaigns, then, asserted that the film seen by the viewer was the end product of copious research efforts on sets and costumes. in verification of historical chronology, and in accuracy of mannerisms. These prodigious efforts to bring the authentic life to the screen were overseen by surviving relatives or experts whose presence, in addition to providing valued publicity, also served as a guarantee of authenticity.

This issue of authenticity, stressed in every road show publicity book for every biopic, could be reframed as the question, "To what extent did studios consciously attempt to cultivate a sense of accurate history in film biographies?" Here, I am interested in the kinds of research that went into narratives about the famous, and in a general way, the kind of history Hollywood producers felt they were creating for viewers. Was Warners' effort on *Juarez* (1939) typical of Hollywood's approach to understanding biography? For this film, the vice consul of Mexico acted as a technical advisor while the producer, star, and director toured and studied their way through a six-week trip to Mexico to acclimate themselves to Juarez's milieu. The final product of this jaunt seemed to be neutralized by other Hollywood conventions, notably the demand for heterosexual love; the film canted the frame of history more toward the romance of Maximillian and Carlotta than toward the struggle of Benito Juarez. The luxury of a six-week tour of Mexico was not a common agenda item for the Warners research department. However, every biopic, and many nonbiographical films, made extensive use of the studio's own in-house research departments at every stage of film production.

Research came into play before a script was written, during actual shooting, and for publicity purposes prior to release. The kinds of questions asked of the research departments as well as the use to which such findings were put in film production are important signposts on the road to Hollywood history.

Star Actors

While there may be large, overarching structures formed by the corpus of biographical films, individual factors, like the personality of the star, are also significant features of the biopic. To an extent, every famous figure, from Henry Fonda's Lincoln to Barbara Stanwyck's Annie Oakley, is filtered through the persona of the star image in two ways: inside the frame by the tradition of the actor's performance, and outside the film by publicity and public relations materials. Because events outside the film (the life depicted) interact with our responses to the actor inside the film, the meaning of this body of films is both multivalent and interactive.

The very real strengths and limitations of the actors under contract to any particular studio at a given time influence the life selected for depiction and its manner of enactment. While Paramount had Betty Hutton under contract, they cast her in films that presumably used the attributes that made her enormously popular. Thus a Betty Hutton film featured the singing, dancing, and above all the vibrant, at times abrasive, energy that made her a top box office draw of the 1940s. After she scored a major hit in Preston Sturges's *The Miracle of Morgan's Creek* (1944), she appeared in three biopics in the 1940s, culminating in 1950 with a starring role, as a replacement for an ailing Judy Garland, in MGM's *Annie Get Your Gun*. Hutton could only play tough, heart-of-gold types and the lowest of physical comedy. Producers, realizing this, cast her exclusively within this type. Thus, her Pearl White, in *The Perils of Pauline* (1947), is constantly played off against the high-art manners of Shakespearean actor Michael Farrington (John Lund) and the good-natured grand dame gestures of her companion, Miss Julia Gibbs (Constance Collier). When audiences heard Pearl White referred to, in the film, as too kinetic for Shakespeare but just perfect for the silent movies, they knew the line referred as much to the so-called Blonde Bombshell's performance style as to the historically created character of silent movie queen White. This illustrates what Dyer has suggested as one dichotomy of the star: star-as-star/star-as-actor.[12] Betty Hutton, actress, seems incapable of acting like anything but the star Betty Hutton. The Pearl White biopic trades on our realization of this: when Pearl is allowed to "be herself" she succeeds; forced by her high-toned love interest to be some other personality, she fails.

On the other hand, there is some difference between the performance characteristics of stars and their personal history outside the frame. For the part of the dissolute John Barrymore in *Too Much, Too Soon* (1958), the producers cast Errol Flynn, whose own fading career (he made but two more films) and declining health (he died, at fifty, less than a year after completing the film) were used as palpable hooks for the viewer. As they watched the story of John Barrymore, they knew they were also watching Flynn perform in his own cautionary tale. Here we have what Dyer refers to as a dichotomy in which star-as-self/star-as-role interact. These individual factors, and their patterned deployment, are part of the code of the biopic. They are as significant a determinant of the film biography as any sense of ideological history producers or other film personnel may have had.

Studios as Sites of Production

In addition to looking at a body of films as constituting a code of biography, and the star as a set of lenses through which the life is rendered meaningful, biopics can also be studied as in-house reflections of the community of producers, in the way, say, that Muriel Cantor, in *The Hollywood TV Producer* (1971), studied the culture of production of American popular television. George Jessel's production of six biographies for Zanuck at Fox—*The Dolly Sisters* (1945), *I Wonder Who's Kissing Her Now, Oh, You Beautiful Doll* (1949), *Golden Girl* (1951), *The I Don't Care Girl, Tonight We Sing* (1953), and for Paramount *Beau James* (1957)—all placed vaudeville at the center of the universe. These films might be seen less as an example of house style than as reflections of Fox's available talent pool of Betty Grable, Mitzi Gaynor, and company, including Jessel's own, highly limited skills. Producer Jessel, in preserving this crepuscular form, created a mythology: that vaudeville was the only legitimate form of entertainment, and that the era of vaudeville was a privileged, halcyon time. This perspective of biopics as a product of a culture of producers suggests that, in addition to the studio's own house-style ideologies asserted by these films, each studio was also shaping biography based on the talent pool available under contract, both above and below the line.

House style might include not just the studio personnel and their repeated, conventional deployment, but also an ideology of biography. It seems that in a general way, studios had different class attitudes toward their biographical materials. Studios selected careers they opted to use as film materials, with certain studios showcasing common people who performed feats uncommonly well. Even given common material (say, entertainer biopics), studios manifested significantly different attitudes toward a life. Fox tended to showcase vaudeville stars and stars of the stage, luminaries from popular entertainment, while MGM opted for headliners from high culture, with films of Enrico Caruso (Mario Lanza), Jenny Lind (diva Grace Moore), Clara Schumann (Katharine Hepburn), and the like.

In fact, the differences between conventional formulations of high and popular culture are themes of the performer and entertainer biopics. This distinction is at the heart of the movies picturing themselves. One of the stranger biopics in the sample—it is the only starring vehicle for that mainstay character actor S. Z. "Cuddles" Sakall—*Oh, You Beautiful Doll* clearly illustrates this tension. Sakall plays Fred Fisher, composer of hugely popular songs "Chicago," "Peg o' My Heart," and the title number. Alfred Breitenbach, though trained as a classical composer, shamefacedly moonlights under the name of Fisher to support his family (daughter June Haver and "Mama" Charlotte Greenwood). Unable to support himself or his family as a serious artist, though hugely successful as a popular balladeer, he flees his home after denouncing his family as being Fishers (popular artists) interested only in money rather than Breitenbachs (serious artists) whose only interest is art. Fisher/Breitenbach tells his family, "Money, what is money, but the vulgar implement to tempt man's soul." By making him ridiculous—his character is a portly figure whose malapropisms and spoonerisms are the stuff of good-natured humor—the film suggests that his artist's point of view is also, like the befuddled Fisher/Sakall, silly, if somewhat endearing.

A key scene in the film illustrates this high art/popular art formulation, and articulates Hollywood's own attitude toward movies as a cultural form torn between pretensions of high art and the lure of popular acceptance. Fisher has gone to his (popular) music publisher, Ted Harris, an amiably tone-deaf capitalist, to get out of his contract. They argue, and Fisher asks how he, the publisher, who admits to knowing nothing of music, can predict when a song will be a hit, when Fisher himself, a trained classical musician, is unable to predict such a thing. The publisher replies, "Because it's my business to make it a hit. Tin Pan Alley is just a huge company to make people listen. Get them so used to it, they like it. Then, they buy it. Good or bad, it's our job to make it a hit, anyway." This justification of selling music as a commodity rings with the tone of self-justification. Earlier, even Fisher's future son-in-law, a resourceful song plugger, compares the peddling of Fisher's operas turned into ragtime to selling groceries, or to serving leftover meat reheated with the horseradish of syncopation. In the end, it is the popular Fisher, and not the classical composer of serious classical works like *Der Finstervald*, who triumphs as a composer, as Mama and others have secretly schemed to have his music played at a concert at Mayolian (sic) Hall. And, while the name announced in the program is Breitenbach, the orchestra, arrangements, and the conductor are classical, the music is popular, like the Boston Pops's dreadful, bloated renditions of Beatles songs. Breitenbach is resolved to being Fisher, as Mama, always the voice of common sense, tells him, "You see, Papa, good music is good music. Some people like it played slower, some people like it played faster." Fisher has lived out Adorno's nightmare of how popular music impoverishes the classical. In the movie view of the world, Breitenbach embraces Fisher with enthusiasm, or *con brio.*

These attitudes reflect, in part, the attitudes of the production heads toward what constitutes culture, including what kind of culture Hollywood itself constitutes. Zanuck at Fox repeatedly voiced his democratic leanings, his feeling that film should be in accord with audience tastes and desires. Mayer, at MGM, had a somewhat variant view of movies as morally uplifting; it was his duty, in selected films, to bring culture and taste, in the form of enlightenment, to the masses. These differences suggest that each studio signed up the talents they deemed fit to carry the studio colors at the box office. If you signed up photogenic and lively soprano Grace Moore, and if she made a biopic, it would have to be one that showcased her talent, singing. It is difficult to imagine Betty Hutton, say, as

Jenny Lind or Marie Curie; her robust personality was better suited to brash nightclub hostess Texas Guinan or physically active Pearl White.

Thus, if the 1950s saw a dominance of biographies about performing artists (28 percent of all biopics made in this time) this curious fact could be seen as the swan song of producers' ideas of "good entertainment" in a world where vaudeville and the live stage was being usurped by Elvis, the LP record, and television. One could also see these films as products utilizing an available—and predictable—pool of talent at each studio in a highly conventionalized way, a way that controlled for the unpredictability of different content with the ritualistic and repeated use of certain stars and producers in successful star/genre formulations. That is, in this loose application of principles derived from the sociology of work, singers under contract make biopics about singers, George Arliss portrays great statesmen of a certain age, and James Stewart, once he passed the age deemed suitable for romantic leads, and once, as a freelance artist, he could select his own roles, can portray anything from aviators (Charles Lindbergh) to wounded athletes (Monty Stratton). The universe of figures on film we have come to accept as great or important are venerated equally for the morality of their deeds and the convenience and availability of their talent.

Formal Elements

Given all the possible variables—star casting and available personnel, censorship, the power of some producer's point of view, legal considerations—that can influence the shape of a life on film, how do these films situate themselves as historical narratives? Unlike most films, almost every biopic opens with title cards that place the piece in context or with a voiceover narration that historically "sets up" the film. For example, *The Stratton Story* (1949), the biopic of Monty Stratton, who overcame a crippling shotgun wound to continue pitching in baseball, opens with the title "This is the TRUE story of a young American—Monty Stratton—and it starts one fall afternoon near Wagner, Texas." The title here serves the function of avowing that the film that follows is true. This convention of the biopic, the introductory assertion of the truth, serves as a reminder of a fact so obvious that we might overlook it: that most films made in Hollywood are not supposed to be taken as true. This use of the title sets up one of the genre's distinctive qualities, a claim to truth.[13]

The title also sets up the moment of a life when we can witness the birth of a particular talent—seldom the character's literal birth. *The Stratton Story* opens, *in medias res,* at the jumping-off point of Stratton's fame, on the eve of his being discovered by a scout. Similarly *The Pride of the Yankees* opens with young Lou Gehrig demonstrating his ability, as a juvenile, to hit the long ball for which he would become famous as a New York Yankee. Many film lives selectively highlight a part of a life so well known that a portion of it bears closer scrutiny (*Young Mr. Lincoln, Young Tom Edison* (1940), *Young Daniel Boone* (1950), *Young Bess* (1952), and *Young Jesse James* (1960). The formulation "young" in a film's title performs several functions. It seemingly permits the viewer to be present at the creation, witnessing the birth or the first display of the traits that will make the older version of the biographee famous. Second, it also suggests that fame is often largely a genetic predisposition, present from a very early age. Thus, "young" Mr. Lincoln, although only a moderately successful lawyer in Springfield, Illinois (at least in John Ford's version of history), nevertheless possesses the keen judgment, the ability to "balance" two sides of an issue, which will become his hallmarks as a senatorial candidate and, later, president. "Young" Tom Edison displays the persistence needed to struggle through many false starts as well as the ingenuity that are the core of cinematic inventor's trial and error.[14]

Some films eschew the opening written word for the spoken word. Director William Wellman's *Buffalo Bill* (1944) opens with a rather long narration by an omniscient, anonymous narrator who informs us that

> In 1877, a young man rode out of the West and overnight his name became a household word. He was not a great general, or great statesman, or a great scientist. Yet, even now more than sixty years later, the legends which surround him are as vivid as they were then. His name was William Frederick Cody. But to the young and old, rich and poor, king and commoner, he's known as *Buffalo Bill*. This is the story of his life.

From the outset the film is set up in contrast to one of Lowenthal's biographies, with a kind of selfconsciousness that its subject is not one of the conventional great men about whom movies might be made. Throughout the film that follows, Bill Cody will be presented as a link to the common audience member, as the champion of the authentic, of the West versus the East, of the rights of Indians to live on their own terms and not the Indian Bureau's, and as a proponent of entertainment as education. In Wellman's vision, Cody's "Wild West Show" is created to give the American people a true image of the West. Wellman's version of Cody's life may well be a displacement, in which Cody is Wellman himself and the Wild West Show is Hollywood. If Cody could make the truth a popular hit, so can Wellman.

Even in the very rare cases in which the biopic starts without an assertion of truth, some signifier of the "facticity" of the film is present. For example, *The Actress* (1953) opens with a family photo album, suggesting that the drama will be an intimate domestic tale based on a photographic re-creation of a life. Similarly, *Madame Du Barry* (1934) opens with a series of oil portraits of the historical figures in the film. Cleverly, these portraits, created by the art department of Warners, made certain that Louis XV looked like his filmic impersonator Reginald Owen, and that other royal figures were painted as the actors who portray them. The opening shot of *Roughly Speaking* (1945) tracks into an engraved funeral invitation for the leading figure's father, setting the stage for the life of Louise Randall Pierson, a woman who was able to make her way, from the title on, independent of male dominance. *The Left-Handed Gun* (1958), Arthur Penn's revisionist history of Billy the Kid, opens, selfconsciously, with a ballad that intones a series of questions about Billy's motivations in his short life. The film is thus located as a piece of (pseudo) folklore, attempting to narrate a life of one of America's folk bandits in the appropriate musical genre. It is the rare film, for example, *My Wild Irish Rose* (1947) or *Shine On, Harvest Moon* (1944), that dispenses with an opening claim of veracity, and moves directly into the story. Presented thus with an assertion of truth, viewers are given the limited option— which they may or may not take—of believing that what they see is, in fact, true.

The introductory titles of biopics thus help to prepare at the outset the conditions under which the film will operate. Rather than being a mere formula, the phatic "Once upon a time . . ." that assures us that the storytelling machine is in order and operating, titles can give us a key to what will follow. Much the same way Orson Welles's voiceover opening ode signals his somewhat ironic nostalgia for the vanished magnificence of the age of the Ambersons, the adjectives used to describe time and place in the first biopic titles set the tone for and assert the value of their subjects.

Warners' *Pride of the Marines* (1945) illustrates this setting of the ideological stage with the correct props through writer Albert Maltz's judicious title. The film is the story of a marine, Al Schmidt, who loses his sight during a battle. The film focuses on his coping with this disability, and his subsequent readjustment to his new life, aided by a sympathetic fiancée. John Garfield, as Schmidt, speaks the introduction.

> This is Philadelphia, 1941. Everybody's got a home town. My name is Schmidt, Al Schmidt. Maybe you've heard of me, maybe not. Anyhow, one way or another, what I've got to tell you started here in Philly. I grew up here. . . . But it could have begun anywhere. It could have begun in your hometown, maybe. And what happened to me might have happened to you.

Although we see the sights of Philadelphia—Independence Hall, the Betsy Ross House—the stage, as the voiceover suggests, could be anytown. Philadelphia is really Schmidt's hometown, but it is also rife with symbols connecting the current struggle of World War II to past struggles, specifically the founding of the American republic. Schmidt is a rare famous person in Hollywood in that he was unknown before a misfortune singled him out. Thus, the goal of the film seems to be to connect "regular guy" Schmidt to every member of the audience. Unlike other ordinary men—Audie Murphy, Alvin York—who perform heroic feats during the war, the focus in this film is on the social readjustment Schmidt must accomplish if he is to be reintegrated into postwar society. Made in 1945, as the war was winding down, the film situates itself as an instructional text for family and friends of the wounded serviceman.

It is interesting to note the strength of the title convention in the biopic, for it is definitely not a convention of most other sound-era films. Bordwell, Staiger, and Thompson note that title credits were a staple of silent film, and were used to "announce the salient feature of the narration. In the sound era, other film techniques take on this role of foregrounding the narration."[15] Titles or introductory voiceovers were also conventions of documentaries of the period and it is likely they were appropriated by biopics as a recognizable signal that the film was true. Luis Buñuel, in *Land Without Bread* (1932) and, later, Woody Allen in *Zelig* (1983) would, in different ways, acknowledge the ironical function such verbal framing devices can perform in fiction films purporting to be true. But films that purport to be true seldom use this device ironically.

Avowals of the truth of the film can take other forms. John Sturges's *The Magnificent Yankee* (1950), the biography of jurist Oliver Wendell Holmes, opens with an aural narration by an actor playing the writer Owen Wister (author of the popular, much-filmed novel *The Virginian*) who informs us, "You might have read one of my books, *The Virginian*. It was fiction, but this story is true." We have in *Yankee* a clever bit of disingenuous conjuring; one mediated form (the novel) is used, in its ficticity, to create the fiction of truth for another mediated form, a film. "Wister's" preface serves as a kind of pseudo-celebrity endorsement of the veracity of the film's content. Nevertheless, this endorsement is rendered ironic because it is an actor whose voice informs us that he knew about the events that were about to unfold, and not the actual writer who witnessed them.

Occasionally, if they are still living, the filmed subjects themselves lend ultimate credibility to a film. In several films in the purposive sample, the signed endorsements of the actual figures appear, attesting to the truth value of the film. *Somebody Up There Likes Me* (1956), directed by Robert Wise for MGM, opens with a title card that assures us, "This is the way I remember it, definitely" and this characteristic assertion, which we will hear repeatedly in the film that follows, is signed by Rocky Graziano, the former middleweight boxing champion.[16]

Another example of the function of the opening credit with its verbal or written avowal of truth is Delbert Mann's *I'll Cry Tomorrow* (1955). It opens with the poignant but enigmatic inscription that makes sense only after the film is over. The inscription, "My life was never my own. It was charted before I was born," is more of a teaser for the viewer than a helpful piece of information. Signed by singer Lillian Roth, whose battles with her possessive stage mother and (her own) subsequent alcoholism the film chronicles, it serves neither as validation of truth nor as temporal marker. Instead, it functions as a kind of leitmotif in an overture, one whose variations will be specifically spelled out in the work to follow. A later film, Robert Wise's *I Want to Live!*, for which Susan Hayward won her only Oscar, is signed at both the beginning and end by the journalist whose stories inspired the film treatment. The appearance of his signature, without any sound on the soundtrack (a pseudo-documentary marker in a film using an otherwise obtrusive cool jazz score that reminds us of the seedy, nighttime world Barbara inhabits), as well as a magnificent gray scale and a plethora of newspaper headlines all signal the film as factual.

In-Person Avowals of Truth

Rarer still is the biographee who plays him- or herself. In the complete sample, only seven films—RKO's *The Flying Irishman* (1939), the story of Douglas

"Wrong Way" Corrigan; *Harmon of Michigan* (1941) with the gridiron star imper-sonating himself for Columbia, Columbia's 1943 *Is Everybody Happy?*, the biopic of entertainer Ted Lewis, in which Jolson impersonator Larry Parks, antic-ipating his stardom in *The Jolson Story* (1946), plays a role; United Artists' *The Fabulous Dorseys* (1947); *The Jackie Robinson Story* (1950); Allied Artists' *The Bob Mathias Story* (1954); and Universal's *To Hell and Back* (1955), the story of war hero Audie Murphy—meet this criterion.

Of the seven films, only Murphy's and Corrigan's efforts stands out as truly extraordinary. Lewis and the Dorseys are professional entertainers, and Har-mon, Robinson, and Mathias are athletes, all used to performing in public. In the case of athletes, it may have been felt that only the athletes could realistically duplicate—or simulate—the feats for which they were well known. This solution of having professional athletes portray themselves in movies may have been inspired by the case of Gary Cooper who, playing Lou Gehrig in *The Pride of the Yankees*, had to be taught how to play baseball. Cooper, already forty-one when filming began, had never played America's national pastime. Although he learned enough of the fundamentals to approximate a baseball player, he was not able to master Gehrig's left-handed batting stance. Since it was unthinkable that audi-ences would not notice this—Gehrig, who had died only one year earlier, had been one of the most famous ballplayers of that era—producer Sam Goldwyn had a major difficulty to resolve. A. Scott Berg, in his 1989 biography of Goldwyn, says that the editor of the film, Danny Mandell, came up with an ingenious solution to the problem: Cooper batted right-handed, with a specially designed uniform that reversed the New York Yankee letters and numbers, and ran toward third base. The negative was flopped in the printing, and Cooper appeared to be bat-ting left-handed and running in the right direction. Thus, through a trick of the film laboratory, the guise of authenticity was created.[17]

Often, in the stories of athletes in which they do not play themselves, long shots of action key the film as "real," even though the knowledgeable spectator realizes that an overage William Bendix did not remotely resemble Babe Ruth, or that Errol Flynn only passably imitated James J. Corbett's boxing style. The dis-location viewers might feel when confronted with a fictive portrayer simulating real physical feats is compensated for by having actual athletes populate the film in cameo parts, playing themselves.

Nor is this strategy limited to athletes. *The Perils of Pauline* convinces us that it is an accurate picture of the early days of silent films (even though it is not) by having an enormous cast of old-timers appear as themselves alongside Pearl White/Betty Hutton, and *The Great Caruso* (1951), although showcasing the talents of quasi-operatic tenor Mario Lanza as the great Caruso, provides him with genuine opera stars Dorothy Kirsten, Blanche Thebom, and Jarmila Novotna as partners in various ensembles. At the far end of some spectrum of performance verisimilitude are the biopics of pianists—like *A Song to Remem-ber* (1945)—in which inserts of the hands of real pianists (there, José Iturbi) fill in for the star, who is most often filmed from in front of the piano, with the full view of his or her hands blocked.

Short of having famous persons play themselves, the mixture of actors and actual professionals provides an odd bricolage of truth for biopics. But Murphy and Corrigan were not actors, and since neither war hero nor misdirected flyer were performers like musicians and athletes are, it must have caused a sense of dislocation to be playing oneself against actors standing in for family members, friends, and the like. Perhaps the very awkwardness of such performances is meant to be read as sincerity, an attempt to convince us that such people are only playing themselves, and not acting.

Often, participation of the subject of the biography is limited to and credited as "technical advice," as in the Joe Howard biopic *I Wonder Who's Kissing Her Now?* and *The Jolson Story* and its sequel. The case of Jolson is unusual, for although Columbia's publicity for the film suggested Jolson himself trained Parks in performing his routines, this was not the case.[18] Jolson had desperately wanted to play himself in his own life story. But at sixty, he was deemed, even by Harry Cohn, his most worshipful admirer, as too old to pull off this stunt. In actuality Jolson's input into his life story took, for this figure most in need of public approval, an uncharacteristic form; in addition to recording the musical vocal track for the film (a false vocal Jolson would be unimaginable) he appeared in the film, unbilled, and unknown to the movie audience, in long shot, doing his inimitable dance on a theater runway. Like "Jolson" in the film, Jolson couldn't keep away from an audience or duck out on an opportunity to entertain. Only, in *The Jolson Story,* he appears, for once, unbilled and anonymous.

If starring impersonations by the actual subjects of the biography are, for reasons of unavailability or advanced age, rare, as I suggested earlier, cameo appearances by celebrities are fairly common. Sophie Tucker, with an enormous leap of faith into a time warp, plays her 1930s self in the 1957 *The Joker Is Wild*, and Babe Ruth, Sam Snead, and other athletes play themselves in cameos in a number of films. Athletes, in particular, are often used in bit parts in sports films, adding authentic physical business to proceedings the viewer knows are otherwise largely staged. Similarly show business folk often appear in cameos, frequently in comic moments where, breaking the narrative frame created by a film, they are recognized as themselves or in brief performance in benefit revues that increase the entertainment value of a package by adding famous names to the marquee. We see this variation on reality casting when Fanny Brice, later to be impersonated by Barbra Streisand in her own story, *Funny Girl* (1968) and *Funny Lady* (1975), playing "Fanny Brice," does a couple of songs in MGM's *The Great Ziegfeld* (1936), performing alongside fictional portrayers of her actual costars, like Anna Held (Luise Rainer).

A last level of use of stars playing themselves in biopics is the use of a star associated with a historical personality in one film to play that life as a bit part in someone else's life story. Since much of the biopic strategy is based on inter-textuality, such self-referential casting asserts the validity of past film triumphs. Thus, James Cagney, whose memorable 1942 interpretation of the then-living George M. Cohan in *Yankee Doodle Dandy* drew favorable comparisons with the real thing, plays Cohan, some thirteen years later, as a cameo to the leading character of Bob Hope's Eddie Foy in *The Seven Little Foys* (1955). Eddie Foy, Jr., himself a performer in vaudeville and on Broadway, made a minor movie career out of portraying his own father (as in *Yankee Doodle Dandy*) complete with his trademark lisp. Wallace Beery earlier portrayed P. T. Barnum as a supporting part in *A Lady's Morals* (1930), the Jenny Lind biopic, before assaying the great impresario as a leading figure in *The Mighty Barnum*. Charles Laughton played the lead as Henry VIII in the 1933 British *Private Life of Henry VIII* and reprised this character, as a supporting player, twenty years later in *Young Bess*. Raymond Massey, who played Lincoln on stage, transferred the Robert Sherwood *Abe Lincoln in Illinois* (1940) to film, and then played a cameo of Lincoln in the 1963 *How the West Was Won*. He also impersonated a figure linked to Lincoln's history, the abolitionist John Brown, two times: first in *Santa Fe Trail* (1940), and again in *Seven Angry Men* (1955). Bette Davis is unique in her biopic roles, as in so many other aspects of her career, for she is the only female film actor to portray the same leading character (some sixteen years apart), playing the aging Elizabeth I of England in *The Private Lives of Elizabeth and Essex* and later playing the yet older Elizabeth in *The Virgin Queen* (1955). In both cases, the later interpretations of Davis and Laughton seemed mannered, over-madeup versions of earlier performances of great originality, as if merely reappearing as the figure would rouse the collective cinematic memory of the moviegoer without the benefit of a strong script or a well-thought-out performance.

Last, film can establish the realism of its casting by other forms of self-reference. In *Somebody Up There Likes Me*, Rocky Graziano's crusty manager, Cohen (Everett Sloane), tells a young fighter, "Either you wanna be a fighter, or you wanna have fun like Errol Flynn," a reference to Flynn's performance as boxer James J. Corbett in *Gentleman Jim*, and a veiled suggestion that while the 1942 Raoul Walsh film is pure "Hollywood," Wise's film is authentic.

The use of either the actual biographee to play himself, or the repeated use of an actor to play the same historical figure, are both strategies film studios used to anchor the factual fiction of biopics in an undeniable authenticity of casting.

Biography as Differentiation

If the truth value is a distinctive feature of the biopic as a film genre, such a characteristic does more than taxonomize bodies of film. One might argue that in addition to functioning as a framing device that sets up audience and producer expectations for biopics, this feature (the assertion of truth) is yet another strategy used to differentiate a product, be it film genre or star, in a highly competitive consumer market. Warner Brothers seemed aware of this, and as Thomas Elsaesser notes, "Distinctive about the publicity for Warner's biopics was the emphasis on historical accuracy, on the quality of the research materials, the extensive inspection of original locations and the quality of the professional consultancy."[19] One attribute all studios, not just Warners, often foregrounded in publicity for biopics was the historicity of the film. The extravagant effort put into research becomes another example or manifestation of spectacle the studios used to frame their films as marketable commodities.

If we view this truth as a significant selling point of these films, we might see the distinction certain actors associated with the genre attained in another, peculiar light. For example, George Arliss was already sixty-one when he made his first sound film, *Disraeli* (1929). He attained stardom in films by transferring his stage successes to the screen, perhaps lending the new sound medium a patina of Broadway and West End theatrical respectability (as well as providing an example of the great man who speaks with a Mayfair accent)—Seeing Arliss as the definitive biopic actor (*Disraeli, Voltaire* [1933], *Alexander Hamilton* [1931], *House of Rothschild* [1934], *Cardinal Richelieu*, and, in England, *The Iron Duke* [1934]) misses the point; the use of Arliss to play film biographies by both Warners and later Fox is, I think, more significant than the contribution made by his portrayals, for it suggested that film biography was serious, making a contribution to public culture comparable to theater or books.

Producer Darryl Zanuck worked with Arliss at Warners (*Disraeli, Alexander Hamilton, Voltaire*) and later shanghaied the actor to his own studio Twentieth Century-Fox (*House of Rothschild* and *Cardinal Richelieu*). Zanuck was well aware of the public's expectation of how Arliss should be cast. In fact, after the initial strong impression he made in *Disraeli*, which, after all, he had played both on the stage and in silent film, Arliss's great men became, except for a new wig here, and a change of scenery there, remarkably interchangeable. Index finger pointing aloft in justified rage, fists clenched in anger, a benign smile creasing his homely face, the Arliss great man was a kind of crafty favorite uncle, always ready to help young lovers and uphold the honor of the country in which he happens to live. So firmly established was the Arliss biopic persona after his triumph in *Disraeli* that Zanuck permitted the actor to attend story conferences, actually listening to his suggestions on how best to manage the Arliss character. The best judge of the Arliss great man persona was its keeper, Arliss himself.

Zanuck, too, was aware of how entrenched was the Arliss persona, and what kind of narrative could best show it off. In a story conference of January 7, 1935. for *Cardinal Richelieu*, Zanuck urges the writers to come up with a scene like an earlier episode in *Disraeli*, where Disraeli, to show support for young love and to outsmart the French, sends a character on a daring mission. Arliss, present at the conference, concurred and even made suggestions for lines of dialogue.[20] Thus Zanuck had a definite idea how Arliss should be used as a great man; this idea was based on what audiences had come to expect through previous, successful use of Arliss.

Biography presented a category in which actors who did not fit other acting types could be utilized. This might be said of Paul Muni—*The Story of Louis Pasteur, The Life of Emile Zola* (1937), *Juarez, I Am a Fugitive from a Chain Gang* (1932), and as mentor to Cornell Wilde's Chopin in *A Song to Remember*. After Arliss, he is a candidate for the representative biopic actor. Muni was a star of the Yiddish theater whose triumphant film appearances were largely in serious dramatic parts. Biopics gave him an opportunity to display his trademark conscientious preparation in accents, dress, and the re-creation of historical figures. As Thomas Elsaesser has noted, Muni's prestige as an actor could be used to create publicity for the film, just as MGM would invoke Spencer Tracy's two Academy Awards when exploiting *Edison, The Man*. A trailer for Warners' *Juarez* links the film to other serious artistic portrayals by Muni, and attempts to convince viewers that they are participating in an educational, even uplifting endeavor. Biopics gave actors with certain, perhaps difficult qualities a niche in which to excel and offered an attractive strategy for marketing film and actor as culturally valuable commodities.

Of course, having succeeded with Muni and Arliss, studios would try the biopic strategy with other performers after they had attained fame in a biopic role. This was the case with Don Ameche, who made *Swanee River* (1939) (Stephen Foster) and *So Goes My Love* (1946) (inventor Hiram Maxin) after his success in *The Story of Alexander Graham Bell*. Paramount would try this formula, too, with Betty Hutton, placing her in three biopics about vaudevillians and other entertainers after she established her credentials with a portrayal of Texas Guinan in *Incendiary Blonde* (1945). But product differentiation as a strategy to market films and actors was like other Hollywood strategies; it worked some of the time and not at others.

Interestingly, female stars are not usually associated with a series of biopics, though Susan Hayward (*I Want to Live!*, *With a Song in My Heart* [1952], *I'll Cry Tomorrow*, and *The President's Lady* [1953], and, in a supporting role, *Jack London* [1943]) and Doris Day (*Young Man with a Horn* [1950], *I'll See You in My Dreams* [1951], *The Winning Team* [1952], *Calamity Jane* [1953], and *Love Me or Leave Me* [1955]) each made five. Betty Hutton (*Incendiary Blonde*, *The Perils of Pauline*, *Annie Get Your Gun*, and as vaudevillian Blossom Seeley in *Somebody Loves Me* [1952]) made four, and Bette Davis performed in four (the two Elizabeth biopics, *Juarez*, and the 1940 *All This and Heaven Too*), doing a fifth role, a cameo of Catherine the Great, in *John Paul Jones* (1959). This relative absence is in contrast to a number of male stars who were prolific performers in biopics: Jimmy Stewart (4) (*The Stratton Story*, *Carbine Williams* [1952], *The Glenn Miller Story* [1954], *The Spirit of St. Louis* [1957]); Gary Cooper (5) (*The Adventures of Marco Polo* [1938], *Sergeant York* [1941], *The Pride of the Yankees*, *The Story of Dr. Wassell* [1944], and *The Court-Martial of Billy Mitchell* [1955]); James Cagney (4) (*Yankee Doodle Dandy*, *Love Me or Leave Me*, *Man of a Thousand Faces* [1957], and *The Gallant Hours* [1960]); Spencer Tracy (4) (*Boys Town* [1938], *Stanley and Livingstone*, *Edison, The Man*, *The Actress*); and Henry Fonda (5) with two leads (*Young Mr. Lincoln* and *The Return of Frank James* [1940]) and three supporting roles (*The Story of Alexander Graham Bell*, *Jesse James* [1939], and *Lillian Russell* [1940]).

Such an unequal distribution has to do, I think, with the overall configuration of biography by gender. There are almost two and a half times as many male biographies as female biographies. Moreover, the bulk of female biographies are of entertainers and paramours. There is thus a strong chance that the cinematically famous woman depicted must be able to sing, and further must be conventionally beautiful in the paramour mode. Hayward fit these qualifications, or rather historical figures who presumably had these qualities fit Hayward's talent. All of Hayward's impersonations were headstrong, colorful women, marked in some way by tragedy. And, as this was one of Hayward's characteristics as a star—she suffered with sublime intensity—the biopic was a niche into which her talents could be fitted. In general, the distribution of power in society is mirrored by the distribution and limitation of the lives women are allowed to depict. The male shape to biography is further a reflection of the talent Hollywood validated. If stardom is a sign of elevation within the society at large, stars playing great men or women are metaphors that signal the domination of both Hollywood and the larger world by men.

Although biopics were used as a way of differentiating both genres and their stars. only one director has been closely associated with the life on film. William Dieterle was Warners' leading biopic director. Born in Germany in 1893, he studied with theater director Max Reinhardt. Initially his career in Germany was that of an actor, but in 1923 he started to direct. Dieterle came to Hollywood in 1930 at the urging of producer Henry Blanke, who felt he might be able to make German-language films for its lucrative European markets. He was successful in a variety of genres before scoring an enormous triumph, in 1936, with *The Story of Louis Pasteur*. He became one of the few directors in 1930s Hollywood to exercise complete control on a film. Publicity for his pictures inevitably stressed his link to the stories of principle he guided. An article in the January 1940 issue of *Coast* magazine stressed his devotion to ideals and principles ("above all he is the one director in Hollywood who has repeatedly risked his reputation on what are roughly, very roughly, termed 'artistic pictures'"). Dieterle, a man who directed wearing white gloves, was held up as the standard-bearer of Warners' culture and idealism. The films he made at Warners bear a remarkable structural affinity to one another, with a great man (or woman) scorned by an establishment only to be vindicated in a scene of public acceptance.

Dieterle himself appears to have taken his own public image seriously, rarely granting interviews, and, when speaking at all, offering weighty opinions like "I believe that a picture's basic idea is more important than the story that is told. A story can be trivial."[21] He guided six great man or woman films at Warners (*The Story of Louis Pasteur, The White Angel* [1936], *The Life of Emile Zola, Juarez, Dr. Ehrlich's Magic Bullet* [1940], and *A Dispatch from Reuters*), and was signed by that hoarder of prestige, Louis B. Mayer, to direct *Tennessee Johnson* for MGM. He later followed former Warners production head turned independent producer Hal Wallis to Paramount, ending his American career on a low note in 1957 with *Omar Khayyam*. While many major directors worked at least once in the biopic genre (George Cukor, John Ford, Vincente Minnelli, Raoul Walsh, Billy Wilder, William Wyler), few established their reputations largely with film biography. Dieterle stands out as the lone exception to the dictum of director as product differentiation, and Warners used public recognition of his association with the genre as a way of generating publicity.[22]

Narrative Components: Elements of the Life

Just as the patterned use of one kind of formal element—title cards—characterizes the biopic as a unique film genre, the way the narrative of a life is constructed
is also characteristic. For example, the point in the life when the film starts
shapes differing discourses about the role of family in the life of the valorized
figure. Many films commence just at the point of the narrative where protagonists display the talent or behavior that will make them famous. Other films,
however, like *The Great Caruso*, start literally at the character's birth, to show
that the gift that would bring the hero fame was present in some embryonic form
at life's debut. These questions—at what point does a biography commence, and
how does the film account for unusual gifts—are central to understanding the
construction of biography. Fame is presented quite differently if it is seen as a biological predisposition (a gift) or if it is, after a series of trials, earned through
hard work and apprenticeship. Either explanatory schemata is often used as an
argument supporting genetic or environmental theories of character. The implications of presenting either a biologically based or a socially constituted theory
of fame lie at the heart of a culture's ideas concerning social stratification; a road
to fame based on the "accident" of heredity provides marginalized members of a
society a different path to travel upon than one based on the gospel of hard work.
Those films that seem to support the nature route can be seen, in part, to support a theory of society that argues for stability in the form of a caste system.

Family

What part does family play in the hero's life? Are they supportive of a career?
Are they divided in their support? In *Interrupted Melody* (1955), soprano
Marjorie Lawrence's family is shown viewing her singing voice as a proverbial
gift from God; they support the divine mandate, if not the career. While her
father leads the family in a prayer accepting Marjorie-as-God's-tool (after she
has won a singing contest), brother Cyril (a young Roger Moore) is much more
excited; he will become Marjorie's manager and, leaving Australia, travel the
world with her, profiting from her talent. His support is differently motivated
from the rest of the family and, not having a pure interest in his sister's welfare, only in the state of her voice, his support waivers when Marjorie is struck
down by polio.

In *The Jolson Story*, Asa's parents, particularly his father, are initially shown
opposing his entry into show business. Later, his father (played as a generic
Hollywood version of an Eastern European by Austrian Ludwig Donath), more
than reconciled to having a jazz singer in the family, will closely follow his
career, reading Asa's notices in *Variety* to the befuddled, but proud, Mama
Yoelson. A similar formulation of parental support is seen in *The Pride of the
Yankees*. Mama Gehrig wants Lou to be an engineer, like her adored brother
Otto, whose portrait on the wall is a constant reminder of Papa Gehrig's lowly
status (he is a janitor) as well as Mama's strong urge for upward mobility. Resis-

tant at first to Lou's career (and his marriage), once Lou is established as a well-paid hero, the Gehrig parents become experts at baseball, attending games regularly, and, comfortably using baseball slang, knowledgeably analyze the game. Uncle Otto, his portrait turned to the wall by a triumphant Papa Gehrig, is forgotten.

Chopin's family in *A Song to Remember* support his musical career, but they dream only of his obtaining a post at the local conservatory. As Norman Maine might say, their dream is not wrong; it's simply not big enough. More cosmopolitan dreams—a future triumph in Paris—are the province of someone outside the family, Frédéric's teacher, Professor Elsner. Paul Muni plays this fictional creation, Frédéric's artistic and social conscience, and his presence allows the Polish liberation theme to be showcased at a time when Poland was under Nazi oppression, and contemporary classical musicians from war-torn countries (like Italy's Arturo Toscanini and Poland's Artur Rubinstein) were mixing music and Allied propaganda in their public performances.

In Lowenthal's work, the family is a key explanatory frame that provides the appropriate environment for fostering the growth of the future famous person. Here, we will consider the family as the source of support or opposition. We will also see if family members change their minds, as, overwhelmed by their relative's gift, they are forced to become just another member of the public and to admire the prodigal. In *Somebody Up There Likes Me*, Rocky Graziano's father only acknowledges his son's gifts at the end of the film; his hatred and jealousy of his own son have, to an extent, been presented as the motivating force behind Rocky's rage to fight. In *Somebody*, we have fame framed with a Freudian explanation. Compare this to a similar film made three decades later, Martin Scorsese's *Raging Bull* (1980), where little in the way of family environment is specifically offered as an explanation for Jake LaMotta's rage; it exists, pure and unmotivated, in a state of its own.

If You're Ever Down a Well . . . : Close Friends and Guides

Does the hero have a close friend who supports him or her in the quest for fame? Often, the famous figure shown in a negative light is one who has lost touch with the neighborhood and old friends. Old friends are often touchstones, reminding heroes, living in some stratosphere, that they generally came from a less exalted sphere.[23]

The presence of an older figure, the bearer of conventional (sometimes limited) wisdom is a staple of many cinematic biographies. Frank Morgan's old baseball player who discovers the young protégé, Monty Stratton, who will one day outshine him; Jolson's fictional companion Steve Martin (William Demarest), a cellist whose small talent has left him "at liberty" until Jolson puts him on the payroll as a permanent friend in attendance: and Alfredo Brazzi (Ludwig Donath in one of his last performances before being blacklisted), Enrico Caruso's washed-up tenor friend who becomes a kind of combination secretary/conscience are all examples of this figure. In Caruso's case, his faded tenor companion serves also as a reminder of the fleeting nature of fame. Alfredo Brazzi's ruined career and lost voice are cinematic *memento mori*, reminders—like an expug reminds the champion boxer at the top—that one's gifts can vanish in a flash, and that a life lived badly now can later destroy any talent.

Occasionally a peer of the hero aids him or her in attaining fame. In *A Song to Remember* we see Franz Liszt (later the focus of a 1960 biopic *Song Without End*), the reigning piano virtuoso of his day, champion the cause of the unknown Chopin after Pleyel, the leading impresario of the day, refuses even to hear the unknown artist. Although his province is art, his métier is business; Pleyel is still a bureaucrat tied to conventional notions of beauty and novelty in art as well as a conservative sense of social decorum in recognizing who can and cannot play in his salon. Liszt, an accepted star, can; Chopin, an unknown, cannot. Liszt and Chopin, while sharing the same salon with Pleyel, inhabit different spheres from their impresario. With their dramatic long hair and tempestuous natures, they display this movie's as well as the overall cinematic artist's code of (rather tame) contempt for bourgeois notions of propriety. Artists, they speak another language than that spoken unctuously by Pleyel.

The two pianists meet in the salon, and Liszt's curiosity over the unusual sheet music he sees on the piano (Chopin's) prompts a career-saving introduction for the young Chopin. They are introduced while playing a four-handed arrangement of the "Grande Polonaise" (Liszt sight-reads the notoriously difficult piece), exchanging handshakes and names in an orchestrated contrapuntal greeting that both introduces the artists to one another and presents Chopin's music in a favorable light to tastemaker Pleyel. Liszt is presented as secure enough in his talent to recognize fellow genius, and we have here a classical illustration of three motifs that will play a role in performer biopics: resistance by the establishment of the field, advice from an older colleague and a dramatic breakthrough, a lucky break—often in the nick of time—for the novice.[24]

Liszt is also shown playing this benefactor role to Robert Schumann in *Song of Love* (1947). His motives, there, are less pure. Smitten with the married Clara Schumann (Katharine Hepburn), he champions her husband's music to gain favor with her. He is rebuffed in the brusque Hepburn manner.

The examples above are older figures who were involved in the same field as the famous person. However, older advisors can at times be a civilian. Living thus outside the odd world of celebrity, they can offer solicited and unsolicited down-to-earth advice. Thelma Ritter often specialized in parts such as these, and can be seen doing this turn in *With a Song in My Heart*. As Clancy, the Brooklyn-born nurse with a sharp tongue and inevitable heart of gold, she dispenses gutsy common sense along with medicine to the beleaguered Jane Froman (Susan Hayward), injured in a plane crash at the height of her singing career. Because they are not part of the world of the celebrated person, figures such as Clancy have little to gain in the way of professional advancement, and are freer to give advice the hero does not want to hear, but must be told. Their very outspokenness, in a world populated by toadies, is their value to the star.

If the biographee is too old to receive advice from one yet older, then the biopic will show the great person as a kind of master advice-giver, one wise to the world after repeated encounters with treachery, avarice, and the like. George Arliss plays this part—the crafty older statesman—in *Disraeli, Cardinal Richelieu, House of Rothschild,* and *Voltaire.* Because Arliss was already rather old (sixty-one) when he made his first biopic, another actor would have to portray him as a young (and even middle-aged) man. And, unless his youthful incarnation was part of the narrative, the potential situations for receiving advice were rather limited. Besides, this was the point: Arliss, with his monocle and long career, had earned wisdom.

Public Reception of Talent

Often the celebrity is shown attempting the undoable, performing the unconventional, and presuming the impossible. Performing artists (like Lon Chaney, George M. Cohan, Al Jolson, and Marjorie Lawrence) are constantly being told their performance technique is too radical, but it is this violation of performance norms that establishes their unique greatness. In science and medicine, it is a commonplace occurrence in the world of biopics to have all members of a scientific community (save our hero), march to the tune of an outmoded and outdated drum. *The Story of Louis Pasteur, Dr. Ehrlich's Magic Bullet, Madame Curie,* and *Sister Kenny* (1946) all show central characters who must buck both a vituperative scientific establishment as well as impediments to knowledge before they discover the procedures for which they are famous. Such a struggle is not limited to medicine, science, or the performing arts. Henry Stanley (*Stanley and Livingstone*) must overcome prejudice against his professional affiliation and his adopted nationality (American, though born British) before he can convince the Society of British Geographers (led by a bloodthirsty and xenophobic Charles Coburn as British newspaper magnate Tyce) that the maps he presented to them were actually drawn by the "lost" Dr. Livingstone.

A central conflict of the biopic, then, is the hero's antagonistic relations with members of a given community. One might even go so far as to postulate that in this conflict, the hero is attempting to reformulate the boundaries of a given community, to create a Kuhnian paradigm in an already constituted field. As Brecht noted, "The element of conflict in these bourgeois biographies derives from the opposition between the hero and the dominant opinion, which is to say the opinion of those who dominate."[25] It is often in such reactionary poses that tradition is represented. We are told in countless films that Hollywood, as a branch of show business, venerates tradition. Entire songs ("There's No Business Like Show Business" and "Be a Clown," to name two) celebrate this inheritance of the performing artists. Yet, film biography perhaps venerates the star who creates a dramatic new tradition far more than it respects the old. It is both the continuation of a lineage ("the tradition") as well as its reformulation ("uniqueness") that forms the Hollywood code of biography.

For example, Babe Ruth, in *The Babe Ruth Story* (1948), first revolutionizes the game by adding the drama of sudden shifts in the score with his prodigious home runs. In his hitting skills and in his public persona, he is an original. As such, he has run-ins with his tradition-bound manager, Miller Huggins, who presents a contrast to the image of Ruth in both his lifestyle and physique. However, as Ruth's career wanes, the one-time innovator becomes the upholder of a tradition he helped to shape and which in turn shaped the more desirable aspects of his personality His skills fading, Ruth is shown retiring with extraordinary grace, giving his place on the ballfield to the very rookie who had, earlier, scorned him.

BABE: Run for me, kid. Play for me, too. You've got a steady job.

ROOKIE: Babe, I'm sorry for everything. If I can . . .

BABE: Forget it. Be good to the game, kid. Give it everything you've got. Baseball'll be good to you. Come on, get goin'."

Similarly, in *Gentleman Jim* (1942), the soundly defeated heavyweight champion, John L. Sullivan, comes to the victory celebration of the man who vanquished him. James J. Corbett, to acknowledge that a new style of boxing, and a new more refined style of life, is acceding with Corbett's victory.

We see this transition, from one performance style to another, in *The Great Caruso* and *My Wild Irish Rose*, where Jean de Rezske and Billy Scanlon, respectively, acknowledge the arrival of new kings Enrico Caruso and Chauncey Olcott in their domains of singing. Frequently, a physical token completes the ritual of passing the torch, as where Sullivan gives Corbett his championship belt, and Olcott receives a watch given to Scanlon by the Prince of Wales. These graceful transitions—from one era to another—mask the fierce competitiveness that is part of many professions. Any sour grapes over the arrival of newcomers are dealt with by giving the most hostile lines to second-rate talents, whose bitterness is explained by their obvious envy of the newcomers. Thus, the feud between Babe Ruth and Lou Gehrig is glossed over in both the Ruth and the Gehrig biopics, and Cohan's hostile relations with many of his peers[26] is relegated to mere high spirits rather than Cohan's fierce competitive drive or his opposition, as a producer, to any form of theatrical unionization. Sentimentalizing the competition of many professions—suggesting they consist of sororities or fraternities of good will—is a way of eliding the real work, the struggle that might show the world as a place where not all men and women are created equal, and where Injustice and influence often go unchecked. From the point of view of Hollywood as a producer of upbeat images of the world, it is often better, or more economical, to show such struggle through the attenuated means of montage, where reversals of fate can be dealt with in a newspaper headline or two. The romanticization of most professions also throws heroic light on the professions that comprise the motion picture business, sanitizing a Darwinian view of the world by presenting it as a Disneyland. Work is transformed into play, and those who perform these transformations are rendered heroic.

Innovation

What part does innovation play in the construction of fame? Innovation may be the most vaunted quality sold through biopics, whether it is in vaudeville or microbiology. The veneration of innovation is at odds with Hollywood's own marked conservatism in modes of production; where, as Bordwell, Staiger, and Thompson note, innovation is typically slow and occurs within controlled contours.[27] The symbolic function served by innovations in the biopic will be discussed as a kind of homeostatic device to insure not greatness but ordinariness. The public is meant to take innovation-as-deviation as the price of greatness, a price too high for the average spectator to accept and still be a member of the community. One way of dealing with innovation in work is to make the famous person relentlessly normal in other spheres.

The Price of Being Different: Retribution

Does the famous person achieve a sense of vindication over those who opposed their innovations? In *A Song to Remember*, the pompous critic who first denigrated Chopin's talent is later shown as a desperate toady who, once the establishment figure Liszt has given his imprimatur to the young Chopin, will stop at nothing to praise the newcomer.

The degree to which the figure is vindicated suggests a public acceptance of his or her gift; its absence is often tied to tragedy, and tragedy is framed as the lack of fame, as in *The Magic Box* (1951) where the British inventor of the cinema camera, William Friese-Greene, having failed to attain public recognition for his work, dies alone and, except for the existence of the testimonial film, unacknowledged.

Most intriguingly, if the subject of the film is living at the time of its release, vindication can come in the form of the production of the film itself. Thus a celebrity who has passed the time of public visibility, or a figure whose deeds have faded from memory can see, through the public reception of a film, a career revived or witness in the poignant limelight of the projected image the reestablishment of a reputation. Upon the release of *The Jolson Story*, Al Jolson, unhappy in a bitter semi-retirement, experienced one last burst of fame as a result of renewed public interest in his performance: his record sales increased, his radio show received high ratings, and he headlined one last time, entertaining American troops in Korea before his death, from a heart attack, in 1950.

Fortune and Misfortune

To what extent are success and misfortune correlated in biopics? Is such correlation linked to gender, nationality, or other variables? What part does misfortune play in molding the life or in shaping the gift?

Part of any mythology of fame consists of the biographee coping with the misfortune that can level any elevation. Is the hero the agent of his or her own suffering, or merely the recipient of blows from Olympus? The way fame is linked to misfortune and, in turn, happiness, is one of the most powerful instructive lessons biopics display. This is readily apparent in the gender coding of suffering, where women who seek fame are dogged by foiled romance and the specter of life alone in a way their male counterparts—when there are any—are not.

The lesson one learns from biopic vicissitudes, at least on the surface, is quite simple: with an unusual gift comes unusual suffering. As Lowenthal and Adorno suggested of other popular forms of narrative, the audience member viewing a misfortune in a popular film is reassured that a normal, obscure life is perhaps preferable to the proverbial price of fame, life as it is, not life as the movies show it, should be cherished.[28] However, this is far too simple an understanding to take away from a complex body of films. While suffering is often the lot of the famous, it is not distributed evenly throughout the biopic populations.

Thus, more than a rhetoric of suffering, I will try to create a taxonomy of suffering as shown through the biopic. In most cases, no matter how one suffers, salvation is just around the comer in the form of the very institutions that the famous share with most members of the audience: family, community, and home. It is in these tensions—between home and public, between opposing communities, and between definitions of family—that the lessons of fame are created. As Lillian Russell, the already arrived star, tells Chauncey Olcott, the ambitious hopeful, in *My Wild Irish Rose,* "We of the theater live apart from the outside world. We never open our mouths to speak, or our lips to kiss but to further our careers." But, she tells Olcott, who has a "nice girl" waiting for him at home until he gives up the foolishness of the theater, "I'd give the theater away a lot of times if I could do that [have a normal home life]." Although the solution is at hand, and the famous person often articulates his or her desire for the normal life, at times the price of fame is the renouncement of these institutions, though not the values they represent.

In *The Five Pennies* (1959), jazz musician Red Nichols is too obsessed with his career to devote any time to his adoring daughter. When she is stricken with polio, he tosses his cornet from a bridge, only taking up music after a decade of silence when his daughter, now adjusted to walking with a brace, gives him the same pep talk he had earlier given her. It seems that Nichols's success caused his daughter's illness; left alone at a boarding school by a father too busy touring to visit her, she stays out in the rain for hours, contracting the illness shortly after. Several films in my sample question the possibility that the entertainer, seized by the muse, can carry on any relations other than professional ones. This abandonment of family is a harsh price to pay in a culture that venerates family and parenthood.

Historical Era Depicted

There is a tendency in Hollywood to limit the presentation of history to a few periods. While there is no shortage of films set on the American frontier, there are very few films concerning the American Revolution and its heroes. George

Arliss's impersonation of Alexander Hamilton in a film of the same title is the lone exception, though figures from the post-Revolutionary era like Dolley Madison appear in historical romances like *Magnificent Doll* (1946), and the Jean Lafitte biopic, *The Buccaneer*. An analysis of the historical eras depicted will give us an image of Hollywood history. The distribution also suggests that certain eras were more important than others in the formation of the American character. For example, one of the great absences in biopics is the late nineteenth and early twentieth century entrepreneur. Such symbolic annihilation of Henry Ford, Andrew Carnegie, and Henry Frick is all the more significant because written materials of this same period—magazines and newspapers—sang the praises of these men with great frequency. Substituted for the portrayal of capitalists as shrewd and crafty predators was Hollywood's biopic image of the capitalist as a colorful figure who, thwarted in love, has only the domain of finance in which to exercise his energy. Edward Arnold twice portrayed this image of the capitalist as frustrated lover in *Diamond Jim* (1935) as Diamond Jim Brady, and in 1937 in *The Toast of New York* as Jubilee Jim Fisk. Similarly, Hetty Green, the famous pathologically stingy millionaire, was depicted as possessing abundant gold, but little personal emotional wealth in *You Can't Buy Everything* (1934). Other businessmen and women are reframed with nonbusiness references, or else figure prominently in fictive contexts where the figure of the capitalist can either be painted in benign strokes, as in Charles Coburn's depiction in *The Devil and Miss Jones* (1941), or else can be constructed as a threat to all that is decent, as in Edward Arnold's impersonation in *Meet John Doe* (1941). Edison and Bell are framed as inventors, donors of fabulous inventions to the public welfare, and thus are sanitized as capitalists. These absences, as much as what is present, constitute a state of symbolic annihilation (to borrow a term from George Gerbner), in which a sanitized view of history is constructed eliminating problematic areas from public perusal. One needs neither a Ferdinand Saussure nor a Jacques Lacan to tell us that the patterns formed by both presences and absences help cultivate assumptions about history, preserving certain versions of history rather than others.

Character Demographics and Ethnicity

The map of world history via Hollywood is even more inequitable than the Mercator projection. In my analysis, biopics are broken down by key demographic variables to see how the great of the world have been allocated. The degree to which white, North American, or European males of the twentieth century have dominated this canon is staggering.

Since it is a truism that Hollywood is the land of the beautiful and bland, the treatment of ethnicity in biography is problematic; quite often, ethnicity in a film is only dimly alluded to, or else ignored. Presumably, one of the reasons for ignoring ethnicity is that it represents alternative traditions to the mainstream realities represented by all Hollywood films. Ethnicity, in short, could be a threat. One way of dealing with this was to limit ethnic representation to certain stereotypes, even in animated films. Another strategy was to eliminate any reference to ethnic origins and traditions, as if all Americans sprang fully socialized from a small town in the Midwest. Lastly, films sometimes showcased ethnicity, proudly pointing to certain traits and achievements (for example, patriotism for the Irish Americans in *Yankee Doodle Dandy*) that helped, isomorphically, define groups in the melting pot.

Ethnicity is an issue larger than its mere representation in a script. As Ella Shohat notes, "ethnicity is culturally ubiquitous and textually submerged, thus challenging the widespread approach to ethnicity as limited to 'content' analysis."[29] Where a character's ethnicity was alluded to, or indeterminate, the actor portraying the character often had few options but to submit to a kind of ethnic dry-cleaning. A. Scott Berg describes this process with Brooklyn-born Jewish actor Danny Kaye: "Some people suggested he looked too 'sinister,' a euphemism for Jewish. The uninhibited Harry Cohn said he had not signed Danny Kaye because 'he looked like a mountains comic.'"[30] Goldwyn, who signed Kaye to a contract, came up with the solution of dying the former David Kaminski's hair blond, thus altering the purported ethnic way he photographed. Ethnicity, then, is a key component of biography.

Social Class

From what social class does the famous person come? Are talent and genius qualities that are class coded, or are such traits evenly distributed throughout a culture? One of the tensions of modern American life, resolved in part by the lessons taught by the media, is the contradiction between drives that emphasize individualism (stardom, fame, etc.) versus drives that encourage community, and lack of individualism. Different social classes emphasize one trait rather than another, either encouraging individualism or fostering community. Thus, in Warners' *My Wild Irish Rose*, Chauncey Olcott, with his "Irish charm," singing voice, and strong ambition, wishes to be more than the tugboat worker he is presumably, by class restrictions, destined to be. His class-bound friend Joe Brennan, taking note of Chauncey's desire to associate with the powerful and famous (Lillian Russell) tells the upwardly mobile Chauncey (who sits in the balcony dressed as a movie capitalist is, with top hat, cape, and cane), "Let's go home. We don't belong here, Chauncey. We're tugboat people and you've got to get on to yourself." But of course, the famous person, or soon-to-be famous person, will not be held back by conventions, class or otherwise. The class origin of the famous, as well as their families' attitudes toward pursuing a career that will remove their son or daughter from his or her rank, are indicators of Hollywood's attitude toward class, mobility, and innate versus developmental aspects of fame. In Olcott's case, his wise mother (Sara Allgood) resolves the individual/community dichotomy by suggesting Chauncey's voice is heaven-sent, and that "I guess it becomes his duty to share it with the whole world." A mandate, higher than ethnic boundaries or social class, thus frees Chauncey to abandon his community, pursuing his destiny.

The contours of biographical fame will flesh out Hayden White's notion that the construction of history depends not merely on which events are covered. Biography is also shaped by rhetoric. As Leo Braudy argues, fame is not so much a person, but a *story* about a person.[31] Different modes of depiction of the same life constitute different tales. Several of the figures in the sample have had multiple films made about their lives (Billy the Kid, Catherine the Great, Madame Du Barry, Disraeli, Thomas Edison, Elizabeth I, Jesse James, Lincoln, Annie Oakley, Queen Victoria, and François Villon to name a few). The stories they tell, while sharing certain elements in common, are also notable for their differences. These differences suggest that the texts that present fame can also illuminate the processes used in constructing difference. As Hayden White has noted of narrative's role in fabricating history, a filmmaker (similarly) selects plots and orders lives with "choice of the plot structure that he considers most appropriate for ordering events into a comprehensible story."[32] Although the creation of fame is heavily reliant upon a text that helps to establish the famous person, fame is not solely a textual activity. But an analysis of fame's texts will yield much that is significant about public attitudes toward the famous.

NOTES

1. Leo Lowenthal, "Biographies in Popular Magazines." In Paul Lazarsfeld and Frank Stanton, eds., *Radio Research, 1942–1943* (New York: Duell Sloan and Pierce, 1944).

2. This possibility—of a life valorized in print or on the radio being as artificial as a scripted film—was raised by George Cukor in his *Keeper of the Flame* (1942). Filmed during World War II, the movie was almost a Frankfurt primer on the average citizen's duty to keep a watchful eye on both the media and the great figures created by it. Of course, the mask of artificiality, of the "double life" is a truism of theatrical life (for example, *A Double Life* [1947]), and, as Goffman described it, everyday life as well. Today, the concept of theatricality of interpersonal performance is more part of the cultural repertoire than it was fifty years ago when Lowenthal's article appeared.

3. Viewers could later compare Davis's two portrayals in film to those of Flora Robson or Florence Eldridge, or, later, to Glenda Jackson's television portrait, and see which one "fits" more comfortably with one's desired image of the queen.

4. David Bordwell, Janet Staiger, and Kristin Thompson, *The Classical Hollywood Cinema: Film Style and Mode of Production to 1960* (New York: Columbia University Press, 1985).

5. The first letter is in the Warners Collection, University of Southern California. The preview card containing the audience query is at the University of Southern California, John Stahl Collection.

6. Kevin Brownlow, *The Parade's Gone By* (New York: Knopf, 1968), 276.

7. Academy of Motion Pictures Arts and Sciences, MPPDA Collection, *Cardinal Richlieu* file.

8. AMPAS, MPPDA Collection, *Devotion* file.

9. University of California at Los Angeles, MacGowan Collection.

10. University of Southern California, *Marie Antoinette* Campaign Book.

11. University of Southern California, Lewin Collection.

12. Richard Dyer, *Stars* (London: BFI Publishers, 1979).

13. While many of the films in the sample try to finesse this issue of their "truth value" by the use of subtle gradations of opening avowals of veracity, other films are more basic. Thus, Fox's *The Sullivans* (1944), the story of five brothers killed in the service of their country, opens

with the avowal, "This is a true story." The opposite case can be illustrated by MGM's *The Gorgeous Hussy* (1936), which opens with this convoluted disclaimer: "This story of Peggy Eaton and her times is not presented as a precise account of either—rather, as fiction founded upon historical fact. Except for historically prominent personages, the characters are fictional."

14. These "young" versions are, in essence, homunculi of the later figures. They also enabled a studio to showcase young talent in tandem with older players. Thus, Mickey Rooney, MGM's resident teen, and soon to be a major star, impersonates the youthful Edison (*Young Tom Edison*) until the more mature Spencer Tracy can perform his duties as "the wizard of Menlo Park" in another MGM vehicle, *Edison, The Man*.

15. Bordwell et. al., *The Classical Hollywood Cinema*, 26.

16. One of the more unusual examples of the participation of the film biographee is seen in Warners' *Mission to Moscow* (1943). Here, the actual subject of the film, the American ambassador to Moscow Joseph Davies, introduces the film in a lengthy documentary-style, one-camera setup. This introduction both signals the veracity of the subsequent performance by Walter Huston and frames the film as the legitimate and official version of history. Few films have this powerful an imprimatur.

17. A. Scott Berg, *Goldwyn: A Biography* (New York: Knopf, 1989).

18. For more detail on the shooting of either of the two Jolson biopics, see Herbert Goldman's *Jolson: The Legend Comes to Life* (New York: Oxford University Press, 1988) or Doug McClelland's *From Blackface to Blacklist: Al Jolson, Larry Parks, and "The Jolson Story"* (Metuchen, N.J.: Scarecrow Press, 1987).

19. Thomas Elsaesser, "Film History as Social History: The Dieterle/Warner Brothers Bio-Pic," *Wide Angle* 8:2 (1986), 23.

20. University of Southern California, Fox Collection.

21. Robert Joseph, "William Dieterle Gets Hollywood's New Ideas," *Coast Magazine* 3:1 (January, 1940), 8.

22. The less-than-exalted Alfred E. Green—who directed Bette Davis's Oscar-winning performance in *Dangerous* (1935)—piloted four biopics, including the enormously successful *Jolson Story*. He also directed *The Fabulous Dorseys*, *The Jackie Robinson Story*, and *The Eddie Cantor Story* (1953), before ending his career directing for television.

23. Occasionally fame can result in downward, not upward mobility. In *Moulin Rouge* (1952) Henri de Toulouse-Lautrec (José Ferrer), a member of the French nobility, "turns his back" on his noble heritage and pursues a career as an artist. This rejection of his presumed "duties" as a member of a privileged family in favor of a struggling artistic life is the cause of conflict with his reactionary father (José Ferrer again in a dual role). Typically, however, conflict arises when people from the previous (lower) social sphere no longer fit into the higher sphere that comes with fame. At times, the famous people themselves do not fit into the sphere their fame has entitled them to inhabit, and the consequences can be either comic (as the Jolson parents demonstrate with their befuddled perceptions of show business) or tragic (the sad case of Diana Barrymore in *Too Much, Too Soon*).

24. Lowenthal felt that fame as a result of a lucky break, or as the windfall of sudden fortune, alienated the individual from a sense of community, and made irrationality, and not hard work, the explanatory factor in life.

25. Elsaesser, "Film History as Social History," 24.

26. As suggested in Gerald Mast, *Can't Help Singing: The American Musical on Stage and Screen* (New York: Overlook Press, 1987), 34.

27. Bordwell et. al., *The Classical Hollywood Cinema*.

28. Adorno and Horkheimer, in their analyses of cartoons, put the issue quite succinctly, noting, "Donald Duck . . . and the unfortunate in real life get their thrashing so that the audience can learn to take their own punishment" (Theodor Adorno and Max Horkheimer, *Dialectic of Enlightenment* [New York: Seabury, 1944], 362). Perhaps the less cartoonish biopics create a more masked form of the "take your medicine" philosophy. At any rate, the members of the Frankfurt School were exceptionally gloomy about the prospects of the mass audience under popular culture.

29. Ella Shohat, "Ethnicities-in-Relation: Towards a Multi-Cultural Reading of American Cinema." In *Ethnicity in American Cinema,* ed. Lester Friedman (Urbana: University of Illinois Press, 1990), 225.

30. Berg, *Goldwyn: A Biography,* 382.

31. Leo Braudy, *The Frenzy of Renown: Fame and Its History* (New York: Oxford University Press, 1986).

32. Hayden White, *Tropics of Discourse* (Baltimore: Johns Hopkins University Press, 1978), 84.

Sue Harper

Historical Pleasures: Gainsborough Costume Melodrama

Melodrama, like all genres, is historically specific. Stylistic flamboyance and emotional "excess" may be its recurring features, but these will be structured in relation to the class of the target audience, production conditions, and the precise historical period. Melodrama will thus exhibit a variety of relationships between narrative codes, and a range of "permitted" gratifications will be distributed throughout a text in different ways.

I hope to show that a highly popular series of "costume" melodramas produced in England at Gainsborough Studios during and just after World War II achieved that popularity partially because J. Arthur Rank then operated his monopoly in a relatively permissive way, thus allowing a space to be opened up at that studio where ideas about history and sexuality could be expressed which were impossible in existing, more "respectable" signifying systems.

This costume cycle was made with the same production, star, and technical teams.[1] The weekend premier dates for these films are *The Man in Grey* (July 1943), *Fanny by Gaslight* (May 1944), *Madonna of the Seven Moons* (December 1944), *The Wicked Lady* (December 1945), *Caravan* (April 1946), and *Jassy* (August 1947). The films have a rich visual texture and evince a preoccupation with the sexual mores and lifestyle of the upper reaches of the landed classes; they all contain female protagonists (usually visually or diegetically coloured by "gypsyness") who actively seek sexual pleasure and whom the plot ritually excises by the end. There are contradictions between the verbal level of plot and scripts, and the nonverbal discourses of décor and costume; the massive popularity of these films attests that the audience *could* decode their complex and sometimes inconsistent messages. The costume genre at this period thus required a high degree of audience creativity. Gainsborough provided a site for the development of a carefully costed "expressionism," whose practitioners had been manoeuvred out of the theatre or other studios by the dominance of a realist orthodoxy; it was

From *Home Is Where the Heart Is: Studies in Melodrama and the Woman's Film*. Copyright © 1987. Reprinted with permission of the British Film Institute.

precisely in this expressionism that the audience's fears or desires could be pleasurably rehearsed. As I shall indicate, this audience was specifically female, and the films received unparalleled critical opprobrium since they did not conform to the criterion of "good taste." Predictably, their lack of quality is related by critics to their low-status audience:

> A carefully compounded bromide, the lines aiming no higher than *Mabel's Weekly*.[2]

> If Lady E. F. Smith's novel found a large public, this will certainly find a larger. It will certainly make lots of money.[3]

> To enjoy it, you need to have a mind that throbs to every sob of the novelette and a heart that throbs to every exposure of Stewart Granger's torso.[4]

This, and related attempts to cleanse popular forms of their supposed prurience was successful insofar as such films became "invisible" in cinema history until relatively recently. However, they are crucial in any mapping of the field of popular taste in the 1940s and should be given major currency in any debates about the cultural resources or the construction of "femininity" in that period.

The Production Context

J. Arthur Rank's acquisition of Gainsborough in 1941 at first left the existing team unhampered. His philistinism—"Who is Thomas Hardy?"[5]—permitted literati such as producer R. J. Minney to gain intellectual control at the studio until mid-1946, and enabled entrepreneurs such as Ted Black (an associate producer) to exploit their instinct for popular taste. Although financial control rested with Rank, the range and complexity of whose empire rendered him all but invincible, the Ostrer brothers (executive producers) were permitted to run the studio in as tight a way as they wished. It is clear that the Ostrers and Minney parted company, intellectually speaking, with Rank over the question of the latter's definition of culture as basically educational. Minney suggested that a Shakespeare film which could only appeal to a minority audience should only cost £70,000: "the commodity must be what the public wants, and what the public is at present educated enough to like."[6] Rank was increasingly drawn into "quality" films such as *Caesar and Cleopatra*, which as projects had critical kudos but which were financial disasters and necessitated a consolidation of his disparate interests.

All our films except *Jassy* were made under studio conditions dominated by Black, the Ostrers and Minney; the appointment of Sydney Box as producer in August 1946 led to a huge percentage increase in the cost of sets and locations, and probably to the demise of the studio at Shepherd's Bush in March 1949.[7] Management philosophy expressed itself in the area of careful pre-shooting costs and tight commodity control. Very stringent analysis of the shooting diary was in evidence on *The Wicked Lady*: "It had to be kept up to the minute . . . everything had to be kept absolutely . . . we had to be able to explain what the delay was and whose fault it was. Inquests all the time."[8]

Gainsborough producers attempted considerable control over the stars' behaviour, but did not interfere with artistic matters unless the budget was exceeded.[9] There was very little location work, and the rigorous six-week schedule necessitated building sets at night.[10] Such conditions were deemed necessary by studio producers in order to ensure a certain excess profit. Ostrer noted: "I want the whole amount budgeted for the film to appear on the screen in the production, and not to have a large percentage frittered away behind the scenes in extravagant and needless waste."[11]

Black even forbade personal phone calls and kept writing paper at a premium.[12] Also emphasised was the need for careful assessment of market size, advance breakdown of costs, and predictability of the product's visual style and profit.[13] The profitability of the costume cycle was considerably greater than the Gainsborough films in modern dress, since, besides being more popular, the former were cheaper to make due to tighter control. The producers explicitly placed no credence in bad reviews by critics, since high costs could only be justified by mass appeal.[14] Hence the studio's "lowbrow" orientation. Star appearances, elaborate advertising and negotiation of longer bookings, were the means of capturing a large audience.[15]

Further economies were exacted in the area of equipment. The only modern machinery at Gainsborough was the meteorological equipment designed to predict weather conditions, to avoid needless expenditure of time.[16] Wind machines and back-projection equipment were obsolete, there was no illuminated footage in sound-mixing, and the Sound Department were unwillingly obliged to use British Acoustic equipment because it was an Ostrer subsidiary company.[17]

The workforce of the studio displayed a classic "Taylorism" in its structure; all the sections had separate union meetings, and studio union consciousness was difficult to establish. Interestingly, the union structure was precisely analogous to the management's. None of the units were kept informed of the others' filming activities: "It all came from high up, and we were the last in the line."[18]

Everyone I interviewed on the technical side attested to the separateness of management and labour:

They were all so far removed from us;[19]

You'd get the occasional morning visit from Black or Ostrer, but then they'd disappear;[20]

All the heads stuck together. They used to eat together at lunchtime.[21]

The scriptwriters, however, were separated from the rest of the workforce and were in a privileged relationship with the studio management. As I hope to show, they were engaged in making a bid for intellectual power, and their interests were allied with the management's. Only they, the director, and the heads of departments saw the rushes with the producers; comments and criticism were filtered down privately to the technical workers.[22] The intellectual chain of command meant that new script pages were constantly replacing old ones at very short notice.[23] This made an intellectual or critical engagement by the technical workforce impossible, and it deprived them of a sense of corporate responsibility.

That was "carried" by the scriptwriters. They attempted to circumvent production control by defining themselves as "special" intellectual workers. One expression of their struggle was the alteration in class orientation of the popular novels on which the films were based.

Gainsborough's management philosophy produced the conditions for a strong generic cycle. Tight economic control, a strongly hierarchised organisation, a privileged intellectual elite, an insistence that production values appear in visual terms—all these were combined with an uncompromising slanting of the films towards a female audience. Although many audience researchers in the 1940s had problems in defining melodrama,[24] Gainsborough publicists were assailed by no such difficulties. They recognised melodrama's gender bias and suggested that *Madonna* be marketed so as to redefine schizophrenia as a specifically female ailment, with the headline "Split-mind Disorder Gives Idea for Year's Finest Romance!" Cinema managers were advised to appeal "to that great feminine characteristic, curiosity. Trade on this!"[25] Female fascination with dominant males is stressed as a selling point, and H. Ostrer defined the films as the female equivalent to horse racing, the dogs, or boxing—low status anodynes which defused aggression.[26] The poster for *Caravan* displayed Granger, earringed, curled and lipsticked, and bearing a startling likeness to Valentino. While the selling power of his befrilled torso was castigated by such papers as *Sunday Graphic*,[27] the Gainsborough publicists confidently implied that the films would usher the female audience in to an "unspeakable" realm of sexual pleasure. R. J. Minney was largely instrumental in choosing those historical novels for dramatisation which were low-status,[28] since they were by and for women. He defined melodrama as popular fiction *par excellence*, "with blood and thunder," and believed that such films and novels should exemplify a structurally conservative *Ur-text*, "a full-blooded story such as may be found in the pages of the Bible."[29] Against all advice he selected on his own instinct the novel of *Madonna of the Seven Moons:* "The experts all said there wasn't a film in it. The subject had been rejected so often that it was regarded as voodoo. Minney went quietly to work, wrote his own script, planned the production, costed it."[30]

Minney insisted that documentary realism would not fulfil the emotional needs of a mass audience,[31] and ensured instead that the Gainsborough costume cycle was deeply and profitably embedded in popular forms which other studios like Ealing and Cineguild were unable to emulate.[32]

Verbal Languages

I have described in more detail elsewhere the cycle of "new" costume from which the films were made.[33] If we turn to some Mass-Observation material, it is evident that the audience which these profitable "costume" novels attracted was predominantly female. Male readers were uniformly hostile to this type of fiction, demanding realism without sentiment. In a range of replies to an October 1943 directive about reading habits, men asserted that historical romances:

Fairly turn me up;

I hate the mud, blood and midden school;

Real history is more interesting than fiction about it;

A novel dealing with the aristocracy bores me.[34]

A predilection for Hemingway and detective fiction (a genre whose plot structure is more labyrinthine than the historical romance) is clearly, from Mass-Observation material, a male one. Women preferred historical novels as a genre, but many, usually the more educated ones, appeared shamefaced about deriving pleasure from such low-status books. Women make the following comments about historical romance:

> I am sometimes rather snobbishly ashamed of being seen with my current bromide, and would prefer to be reading Meredith.

> I take it as I do cigarettes—nothing so potent as a drug, merely a harmless bromide.

> When a novel has an historical interest, or deals with an economic or social problem, there is a reason for its existence, apart from its literary value.

> They help you to be patient; I found them particularly helpful earlier on in the war, when we were still adjusting our ideas to it.

> It's nice to be able to read about that sort of love and better class people, because you don't notice things as much then.[35]

A sense of proportion, escapism, access to a historically vivid past—these are the alibis most frequently provided by women for historical novels. It was the most heavily subscribed type of light reading among those classified as "serious" readers (that is, the middle class)[36] and high praises for it as a genre came from female students and the occasional female lecturer. Even after the war, middle-class women *in jobs* were those with the most avid interest in historical stories of this type.[37]

These texts present history as unfamiliar, and they also emphasise strongly such nonverbal elements as costume and movement. The novels share a complex series of "framing" devices. *Caravan* and *Fanny* are told through intermediary newspaper reporters; *The Life and Death of the Wicked Lady Skelton* has three initial flashbacks, and *Jassy* is fragmented into four different personas' interpretation of the heroine. This distanciation puts the reader at one remove from history, and the effect is not neutralised by the extreme opulence of the language, which is dense, metaphorical, and "writerly," without exception. Unlike subsequent "bodice-rippers," these novels do not evince a nostalgia for the past. Rather, they express a material change in the composition and style of the aristocracy, and a sense of historical inevitability. The novels select ambiguous groups "on the boundary"—the upper reaches of the aristocracy, gypsies, and sexually aggressive women—and examine them for signs of social pollution. Such groups exhibit exotic energy when poised thus ambiguously, and the audience is encouraged to take *initial* pleasure in their excesses in costume, sexual behaviour, or class power. The novels impel the reader ultimately to judge such excess and to cooperate, so to speak, in its excision. Creativity and complicity are thus inextricably mixed in the readership response demanded by the texts.

All the novels carefully stress the source of aristocratic wealth as rent—a different category from capital and labour—and those who evade the responsibility of office are cast beyond the pale. Hester, in *The Man in Grey*, marrying into the gentry class, abuses the luxuries that the rents produce: "I never knew that such unobtrusive comfort could exist. I never knew flowers could bloom so sweetly in winter, or fires burn so recklessly for people who never came in at all."[38] For a wartime audience, this preoccupation with aristocratic "surplus" would be translated into more immediate concerns about the equitable allocation of limited resources. It is the female protagonist who consumes uncontrollably. Aristocratic energy is linked with that produced by gypsies, who symbolise exotic, eccentric, predominantly sexual energy of a group notoriously de-classed. Gypsy blood in the novels can be inclined to "danger" and sexual excess, but these may be counterbalanced by second sight and "special" knowledge. A third component of this ambiguous "boundary" group in the novels is the sexually aggressive female. If female sexuality is "indissolubly linked with aristocratic excess" it is always categorised as "danger"; otherwise it may be recuperated by marriage and "true love." Oriana's behaviour in the following passage from *Caravan* is later exonerated by her fidelity and death:

> Without a word, he got into bed beside her. And they made love with a fury, a violence, that left him exhausted. . . . He knew her then, at last, for what she was, a sensual woman, who had always wanted him. And as he embraced her, he remembered the sailors' talk of witch-women, of *sorcières* from whom no man could escape . . . he lay there, indulging her wanton ways.[39]

Rosal in the same novel is removed after a series of bold sexual initiatives on her part, and Barbara in *The Life and Death of the Wicked Lady Skelton* sallies forth in search of love and profit by donning male clothes:

> How she had smiled at her own unfamiliar reflection as she dressed herself behind locked doors for the night's adventure, telling herself that she made a very pretty young man . . . beneath the large, flat-brimmed beaver hat her face was provocatively feminine. But a mask would soon remedy that. The high, spurred boots, the leather belt and pistol holder—what a piquant change from muffs, lace cap and painted fans! She drew the loaded pistol from the holster and examined it carefully.[40]

This results in her death at her lover's hands; she is shot as a male highwayman. The novels implicitly correct such *hubris*; the females who survive are domesticated, prolific, and free from desire. "Femininity" (always an ideologically-determined construct) is not equally weighted in these novels with the "gentry" and "gypsy" strands, but none the less the readership is offered the spectacle of a female sexuality poised between self-gratification and predatoriness.

The novels on which the Gainsborough cycle is based suggest via their structure that there is no one secret to unravel, and no single cathartic release. Instead, pleasures are scattered throughout, by a series of intense sensual moments which constitute "the past." It is the historical dimension which is responsible for the novels' popularity; treatment of the aristocracy with a *modern* setting did not capture a mass market in the same way, nor did they permit the fruitful elision of different "strange," marginal groups.[41]

The women novelists insisted on their own similarity to the gypsies, who were outsiders to polite society. Lady E. F. Smith insisted on her own supposed gypsy blood,[42] and Norah Lofts suggested: "If we revert to barbarism, I hope to be allowed to carry my mat from place to place and tell stories for copper coins ... one would thus always be one step ahead of the critics."[43]

Their novels produce pleasure by the ambiguous placing of such groups on the purity/danger axis; the complex negotiations they required of their readers in terms of moral value and "literariness" indicate that they provided a particularly compelling version of history, sexuality, and reading practices. History becomes a country where female refugees from common sense may temporarily reside, but it is a place of banishment none the less; and there, gypsy, gentry and female excess are safely placed. These novels by implication put the readership in a position to envisage (and perhaps regret) a postwar world in which such extravagance would be absent.

The "structures of feeling" contained within the scripts prepared by Gainsborough scriptwriters differ from the novels in important ways. As I have already suggested, the scriptwriters at Gainsborough had a privileged role in the studio. They were a highly specialised group, who had sufficient initiative to found, in March 1937, the Screenwriters Association (SWA).[44] Kennedy, Pertwee, Gilliatt, Minney, Launder, and Arliss were founding members, and continuity existed through until the mid-1940s, with Minney taking a major role.[45] They had a highly developed degree of awareness of their own institutional, material and industrial constraints; I hope to show how they fought to place themselves in a different market relationship from the popular novelists.

The only extant authorship theory advanced by a Gainsborough scriptwriter, Margaret Kennedy, shows a marked advance on earlier professional definitions such as Ursula Bloom's 1938 *ABC of Authorship*. The latter is obsessed with the necessity of reducing artistic discourses to the lowest common denominator, whereas Kennedy, in her *The Mechanical Muse* (1942) expresses as her ideal project a film of "The Eve of St. Agnes."[46] Her whole aesthetic is coloured by contempt for the film audience—"a community which never reads"—and she discourages the novelist from adapting his own text, as he will "break his heart" on realising "how anomalous his position is, and how small the chance that any fragment of ideas will find its way to the screen."[47]

The "illiteracy" of the screen audience produces only three alternatives; to "adapt a second-rate book towards which one has no conscience," to become an "author-cutter" with "directional power," or to develop the "vacant and pensive" writing mood of the director.[48]

It is a familiar argument; that mass culture has lamentably replaced a high one of literary value, and that the employed artist either totally concedes, hack-like, or fights for total control. Either way the original novelist is excluded from the act of mediation. It is of interest that Kennedy's strictures were followed by the studio. There is only one mention of a novelist being on set, as recounted in the publicity material for *Caravan*; otherwise the scriptwriters attempted to augment their power by becoming directors. Minney explicitly suggested this, and it was upheld by the director Crabtree,[49] and more crucially by Arliss who both scripted and directed two of the films.[50] Rank is reported to have been sympathetic to such claims.[51] Although Maurice Ostrer had demanded a "cast-iron script" before shooting,[52] studio practice was to implement last-minute alterations according to screenwriters' interpretations of the rushes. Gainsborough screenwriters had remarkably advantageous notice arrangements.[53] The studio staff were in agreement with the notion of scriptwriter-as-author, and deliberately avoided reading the novels: "We thought that it didn't do to get too involved like that, because you put all sorts of emotions into it, and the script would change a relationship, or chop things, and then you'd be upset."[54]

The exclusion of the novelists meant that the scripts were more directly tailored for a different class of consumption. The scriptwriters separated themselves off as a kind of "aristocracy of labour" from the rest of the workforce, and the Screenwriters Association, which they helped to found and in which they were very active, fought for higher basic payments, for the creation of a jointly-owned "story fund,"[55] for the freedom of radio film-critics,[56] and for the free collective bargaining for a loose affiliation of individuals. Two events suggest that its institutional definitions had become widely acceptable; its being contracted as a "voluntary" workforce for the Ministry of Information (MOI),[57] and the acceptance by the Inland Revenue of its terms of reference: "From what Mr. Williams and Mr. Minney have said, I understand that nearly all screenwriters can be said to exercise a profession, and if they take contracts from time to time, they do so incidentally in the cause of that profession, and not in the intention of obtaining a post and staying in it."[58]

Two disputes further clarify the SWA's definition of authorship as non-industrial and "free." As early as 1943 the Association of Cinematograph Technicians (ACT) had claimed to be the negotiating body;[59] the SWA membership firmly rejected its claims, and Launder noted, "screenwriters are neither reactionary conservatives nor reactionary unionists, but just simple, progressive, benevolent anarchists."[60] By 1947 the SWA felt empowered to act as a trade union, and Cripps reprimanded the ACT for its intransigence.[61] G.D.H. Cole added his support to the SWA's claims for autonomy: "I think the screenwriters must act with authors and other creative artists and must not let themselves be swallowed up."[62]

So notions of writerly creativity and craftsmanship were indubitably linked to a loose guild structure and the institutional power of the SWA was able to defeat the powerful, Rank-backed "Scenario Institute Limited" of del Giudice. Del Giudice suggested that Minney underestimated the audience,[63] and attempted to establish a rival institution more concerned with "culture" and "quality":

his and Rank's Institute would be a quasi-university, with "an intellectual and artistic atmosphere"[64] to raise cultural standards. The SWA took particular offence at the notion that the Institute was "a private commercial venture although not really a speculative one"; del Giudice's proposal to buy up film rights from books before publication[65] was rejected on the grounds of the power this would place in the hands of monopoly capital. The campaign launched by the SWA routed the Institute; even Balcon saw it would produce a "corner" of story wealth.[66] Thus the SWA rejected monopolism and "trade" arrangements; it wished screen authors to be "free" to negotiate a percentage rate for resale of their own work.[67]

The Gainsborough scriptwriters, three of whom were women, produced scripts which endorsed their own class position, clarified lines of class power, and imposed "normative" morality upon deviant females. The novels had spoken to a middle-class audience, conceived as the equals of their authors; the scripts, addressing a working-class and largely female audience, shifted and reinterpreted the "marginal" groups from the novels, profoundly affecting the texts' ideological function.

The novels had all used an extremely complex series of "framing" devices; but the scripts all begin without narrators *in medias res*. Although the film of *The Man in Grey* is structured as a meditation on a portrait, the flashback effect is concealed, *Caravan*'s script begins with a reprise, but from halfway through the narrative. The first *Wicked Lady* script has two modern tramps interrupting Barbara's ghost, but this is removed from the final version of the film;[68] all that remains of "ghostliness" is the camera movement and changed sound quality of her death. Gainsborough screenwriters plunge the audience, with few delayed gratifications, into "unmediated" history; they implicitly suggest that access to it is unproblematical by employing verbal language stripped of literary or historical resonance. They accord more utterance to lower-class characters. Belinda in the novel *Jassy* is a mute, to whom the film grants speech, and the Toby role in *The Man in Grey* is similarly transformed. The audience is encouraged by the scripts to identify with, rather than distance themselves from, historical characters, but this is done by reducing the amount of dialogue in the novels. Information instead is carried by music, a language with easier access to the emotions. Attention to the last fifteen minutes of *Madonna* will show five minutes of dialogue to ten of highly atmospheric music.

The foregrounding of class has a different emphasis in the scripts. Sir Ralph is accused by his fellows of "betraying his own class," and the hero of *Fanny* suggests that "a hundred years from now such class distinctions won't exist." The novels balance the aristocracy against an undefined residuum, whereas the films compare aristocratic excess with "professional" middleclass restraint, to the latter's advantage. Sir Francis in the novel is an amiable invalid—his wife, Oriana, says: "I never had any particular reason for hating him. . ."[69]; whereas the script converts him into a libertine of whom even whores remark: ". . . he's a beast—he's the worst of the lot!" The film Oriana remarks that "He changed the moment we became married—he became evil."

Sir Francis's comeuppance is signalled by the swamp to which he suc-
cumbs, and which the bourgeois hero successfully negotiates, after appropri-
ating his whip. Much more positive roles are accorded to the middle-class male
by the scripts; the architect in *The Wicked Lady*, the librarian in *The Man in
Grey*, the dispossessed farmer in *Jassy*, do not appear as such in the novels.
The aristocratic class is by contrast consistently denigrated: Lord Rohan in
The Man in Grey is converted from an honourable man declaring emotional
severance from Hester[70] into a Byronic figure—"I've yet to meet a woman I
don't despise." He beats Hester to death—"you'll die for it—in my own time and
in my way." The script notes that the brutality of a dog fight "appeals to his
sadistic sense." The aristocratic quartet in the film of *The Wicked Lady* propose
a double divorce and "swap," but the script does not permit them to flout convention in the end.

On the whole, then, the scripts explicitly add to the novels such remarks as
Rokesby's: "I wonder what they [the gentry] ever did to deserve all this." The
scripts present the aristocracy as an unambiguous site of fascination, fear, and
"unspeakable" dark sexuality. Gypsies no longer present, as in the novels, an
exotic eccentric wisdom, but a social threat. The *Caravan* script has them murder and rifle the body, whereas the book insists on their cultural purity; Pertwee
converts the gypsy energy in *Madonna* into dirt and violence[71] and has the virgin heroine raped by a gypsy instead of her husband.[72] Excessive female sexuality is similarly moved from the ambiguous margins into the "danger" category
by the scripts. They foreground the problems of female friendship, and bitchy
vituperation: "You two have shared so much," "I'd rather look worn than dull";
"Wear *that*? I wouldn't be buried in it." Thus the scripts structurally endorse
Mason's gallows recommendation, "Never trust a woman." Hester is ritually
excised because, as the script suggests, "in her black dress . . . she *does* look very
like a witch." The cinematic Barbara wants "a house—children—all the things
I never thought would matter," as a restitution for wanting "a hundred mouths"
to kiss with. The most significant alteration Arliss makes to *The Wicked Lady* is
the revenge, by rape, of the returned Jackson. He is first glimpsed, mouthless, in
a mirror and the sadomasochistic nature of his and Barbara's exchanges is absent
from the book: the film contains the exchanges: "I hate you"; "But I am thrilled
by you," and "I like to drive a hard bargain"; "So do I." All the scripts suggest
that females are an unfathomable, almost pathological, puzzle: "the woman [in
Madonna] is a mystery; she always was," and "I can't think what can have happened to her [the *Wicked Lady* herself]; she used to be so sweet."

Gainsborough scriptwriters, then, strove to place themselves in a different
market relationship from the popular novelists. The latter had arrived, either
by private research or individual instinct, at market dominance; Gainsborough
screenwriters desired instead a loosely strung, quasi-guild authorship. Petty-
bourgeois in origin and outlook, they paid more explicit attention to questions
of mass audience and artistic control than the novelists did. Because of their
rejection of the mass-culture manufactory within which they worked, Gainsborough screenwriters were unable to reproduce the structures of social feeling

of the novels. In the latter, ramshackle though they were in cultural mediation, women, gypsies, the aristocracy are dynamically poised in a sophisticated
balance, and offer a pleasingly "ambiguous" choice to the audience, whose class
anxieties they may then defuse. In the scripts, on the other hand, these groups
are impelled headlong into a dark chasm where only fear and excess reside.
The audience is granted little creativity by the scripts, which is impelled, on the
verbal level of the text, towards perceiving females as greedy and strange, and
the working class as culturally inferior. The institutional struggles faced by the
scriptwriters were clearly instrumental in causing them to draw the boundaries of class and gender more sharply in their texts. The novelists had had an
identity of interest with their readers, since they also were middle-class and
female; whereas the scriptwriters, forced to define their market position with
some rigour, finally took refuge in a rhetoric of dismissal and disdain towards
their working-class female audience.

Visual Languages

The lines of morality, and class and gender power, are very strictly drawn by the
scripts. However, different concepts of knowledge, history and pleasure are contained within the language of the décor and costumes. The art direction of these
films viewed history as a source of sensual pleasures, as the original novels had
done. The department worked under conditions of extreme pressure and difficulty, but managed to gather together a small number of expert "period" artists;
strict control of overspending and overbuilding was tempered by laxity in the
area of historical interpretation. Maurice Carter told me that "provided you could
perform money-wise, and get the sets there on time, they were reasonably happy.
[Executive producers] didn't have much to say on the artistic side."[73]

The art director of "costume" melodrama has to indicate a past which is
both familiar and stimulating; the audience of a successful film must recognise
familiar signs and confidently fill in the "gaps" in the discourse. The "costume"
genre as a whole tends to underplay historical authenticity as such, and the
Gainsborough films of this period avoid "documentation." If it does appear, it is
intensely personalised by a voiceover (as in Clarissa's diary pages in *The Man in
Grey*) or it is so brief as to make only a ripple in the narrative flow (as in the
newspaper cutting in *The Wicked Lady*). The affective, spectacular aspects of
mise-en-scène are foregrounded, to produce a vision of "history" as a country
where only feelings reside, not sociopolitical conflicts. The potency of this for a
wartime audience requires little elaboration.

We should make distinctions at the outset between the various art directors
who constituted the Gainsborough period team, since their origins affect their
respective styles. Maurice Carter, with architectural and furnishing experience,
was a supervising art director, and personally art-directed *Jassy*, *The Bad Lord
Byron*, and half of *The Man in Grey*. He and Vetchinsky, who was an architect
by training, were permanent staff with long-term contracts. Andrew Mazzel,

formerly a commercial artist, did *Madonna,* and John Bryan, with a theatrical background, did *The Wicked Lady, Fanny by Gaslight,* and *Caravan.* The sets of the latter are far more stylised and less concerned with detail than those of the others.

Gainsborough provided a space for those art directors who came from a commercial or applied arts background, and gave the opportunity for those who were opposed to the décor realism of other art directors like Morahan, Relph, and Sutherland, to practise in a non-realist way. The latter-day careers of Carter and Bryan show a clear continuity with the style they developed at Gainsborough; Carter's *Anne of a Thousand Days,* or Bryan's *Blanche Fury,* or *The Spanish Gardener* on which they collaborated, all display an avoidance of naturalist technique.

The influence of continental art directors such as Andre Andrejev, Ferdie Bellan, Vincent Korda and Alfred Junge can be seen far more clearly at Gainsborough than elsewhere. They, along with a number of other art directors from Berlin, had emigrated to Britain, where Junge initially went to Lime Grove and Korda to Shepperton; they had a formative influence on the early attitudes of Bryan and Carter. The art directors from Germany are widely recognised as anti-realist.[74] Their expressionism was filtered through to Gainsborough art directors and tempered their concern with craftsmanship.

If we analyse some of John Bryan's work, we see an interesting selectivity. In *The Wicked Lady,* for example, the interiors are highly eclectic in their construction. Each object is reproduced in an historically accurate way, but it relates to the other objects in an unpredictable way spatially. Generally, the surfaces on which they are placed—bland, unmarked, and plain—throw them into heightened relief. The avoidance of tapestry, carpets, and serried paintings is not historically accurate and cannot be accounted for by wartime shortages or lack of expertise, and it must therefore be "read" as a deliberate aesthetic strategy. A Jacobean door, a Baroque candle-holder, an Elizabethan canopied bed, a Puritan bible, a medieval fire-basket are combined to form an unpredictable and dense visual texture. The past is signified not as a casual, linear structure, but as a chaotic amalgam—an opened cache of objects with uncertain meaning but available "beauty." The undoubted scholarship available at Gainsborough—through period advisers and so on—is always discreetly used so as not to alienate an uninformed audience. *Semper Fidelis* is the only Latin to appear in the film, and it appears inscribed on a plaque which is centrally placed between Roc and Griffiths as they finally affirm their love. The three-cornered gallows in the execution scene had its accuracy carefully proved by Minney,[75] but the first shot of the scene shows miniaturised toy versions of it on display, and this "lightens" any heaviness of tone which the accurate but unfamiliar object might produce. Bryan's décor shows great wit; when Lockwood lowers her eyes on her wedding night, a short dissolve proceeds to compare her expression and posture ironically with the Botticelli madonna on her petit-point tapestry in the next scene.

It is important to note that the only visually explicit sexual scene in *The Wicked Lady* is totally stripped of any historicising mise-en-scène. When

Lockwood and Mason make love by the river, only mist, water and trees are seen; no houses, horses, or accoutrements. Bryan conceals history here; sexuality is presented as "naturally" without codes, practices or historical determinants. Carter remarks that "your instinctive reaction was to make the thing as rich as possible, because that sort of thing was already set by the script."[76] Precisely; the script permits an (idiosyncratic) historicised décor, but not an historicised sexuality. Contemporary analogies are clearly being drawn in the area of sexual pleasure, and "richness" of décor is, by implication, supernumerary when compared with the "richness" of desire.

The complex sets which Bryan designed for *Caravan* were erected and struck with remarkable speed, although they were extremely labour-intensive, especially for the property department.[77] An instructive comparison may be drawn with the representation of the historical past in *The Wicked Lady*. *Caravan's* "Spanish" scenery is an uncivilised wilderness, while the sets indicate a more cultivated disorder. The interiors are crammed with random exotica, spasmodically concealed by darkness. The film presents to its audience a visual cornucopia in which images of Victorian aristocratic décor, Spanish landscape gardening, and gypsy caves are of equal weight. The audience is put in the position of being able to perceive these components as of equal cultural *value*; it is put at the same distance from all these selected, "privileged" locales.

The other art directors in this cycle display a similar avoidance of historical "value," whether expressed tonally, compositionally, or via focus. For example, the ruined Gothic garden and the Florentine "gypsy" interiors in *Madonna* share the same compositional techniques and a picturesque wildness; Mazzel's work as art director here is clearly influenced by his collaboration with Crabtree, whose early training as a cameraman and interest in lighting technique are important signifying features.

Visual style at Gainsborough until the advent of Box in late 1946, then, presented the historical past as a site of sensual pleasure; it was neither regular and linear, nor "closed." Under the different set of managerial constraints instituted by Box, such expressionist (and cheap) set work and design ceased. Extensive and expensive location work was undertaken for *The Bad Lord Byron*, and Box insisted on extreme verisimilitude in using the poet's own furniture.[78] The location work abroad for *Christopher Columbus* was so costly as to nullify any profitability. As the forties progressed, location work came to have a strong "prestige" aroma; Ealing's *Saraband for Dead Lovers* had even been made at Blenheim.[79] Box attempted to follow the practice of the "quality" film by increasing the set allocations for *Jassy* to an unprecedented degree.[80] With the advent of Technicolor, quite different skills came to be demanded of the art department. In many ways, *Jassy* marked a turning point; made at Denham, unlike all the others, and with a different set of technicians, it also displays a markedly different aesthetic and management philosophy.

A set of managerial circumstances permitted a group of likeminded art directors to produce a *visual* aesthetic which at the same time undercut the class positions inscribed in the scripts. Their visual strategies produced contradictions between the verbal level of the scripts and the nonverbal discourses of décor and costume; a carefully costed visual expressionism permitted and encouraged fantasies which combined history and sexuality, in a way which is (paradoxically) not unlike the mode of procedure of the original novels.

If we turn now to the area of costume design in the Gainsborough cycle, we can examine the ways in which different historical determinants affect the "narrative" of dress. Research indicates that the audience preferring costume melodrama was predominantly female and working-class,[81] whilst records of contemporary responses to these films suggest that the style of costume was a very important factor in audience enjoyment.[82] The cycle's costumes foreground sexual difference. For example, breasts are unambiguously displayed as a site of female erotic power—they are not teasingly evoked. The swaying skirts in *Caravan, The Wicked Lady, Jassy,* and *Madonna of the Seven Moons,* and the tinkling earrings of the latter, signal the heroines' combination of pleasure and control through the broad range of movement permitted by these clothes. Jean Kent's dance in *Caravan* is no authentic flamenco; her extreme postural shifts are there to cause the bells on the bodice to ring and the skirts to rustle, and these sounds signify her desire towards Granger. The immobile aristocratic wife in *Madonna* alters her kinesic behaviour once she glimpses the flowing hair and clothes of her "libidinal" gypsy self in the mirror. It is only after she dons exotic costume that she protests "I belong to no one but myself." At her death the supine, desexualised mother again "belongs" in her civilised nightgown, to society. Such "expressionist" costume practice is markedly imprecise historically. *The Man in Grey,* for example, is inaccurate on the hairstyles and the sartorial tastes of the "Young Corinthians," and it is thirty years out in its presentation of a dominant, "mesmeric" relationship.[83]

Turning to the costume narrative which is embedded in *The Wicked Lady* and which contradicts the verbal level of the rather moralistic script, we can examine the possibility that the audience was competent to decode complex visual messages. The phenomenal success of the film, and the marked preference by the female audience for its "costume" aspect, indicate that the audience could read the narrative inscribed into the nonverbal, "unconscious" parts of the discourse.

The costumes of *The Wicked Lady* present Lockwood in an unambiguously positive way while we are prepared for the initial failure of the Patricia Roc/Griffith Jones relationship by their early lack of sartorial "match." He has scrolls and curlicues, flamboyant lace and full cuffs; Roc has military frogging, no cuffs and a straight-cut jacket which makes her appear narrow-hipped. Lockwood's first appearance in the film—androgynously with leather gloves and fur muff—links her with the gorgeous voluptuousness of the Griffith Jones aristocratic male. Her velvet fur-trimmed coat is pulled back to reveal its silken interior and swept round to form giant peplums which emphasise an hourglass figure. Of even greater importance is the back view which we are afforded of this ensemble immediately after her arrival. The satin interior is held in place by a concealed fastening, and from this centre issues a plethora of folds and pleats.

This "secret" view is hidden from the male—he is seen approaching from the other side—but it is displayed to Roc and to the audience. This "female" pattern is echoed in Lockwood's hairstyles here and elsewhere, which radiate, either in plaits or curls, from a hidden centre or vortex. Three of the four hairstyles she sports in the film are like this, the remaining ringlet style is seen only from the front. Such stylised back views of Lockwood's hair and dress ensemble are repeatedly displayed; indeed they might tentatively be called "vulval plaits" and "labial pleats." The genital symbolism of her hair and clothes is not lost upon Mason—"so it's a skirt we have in the saddle." Hence the extended play with the idea of the private room with its "secret passage" to the freedom of the park, and the lost key to that passage which is held by the Puritan servant. The film signals two sorts of female sexuality by carefully differentiating between the two wedding veils. Roc's has cuddlesome, kittenish "ears," whereas Lockwood's is a mantilla, redolent of passion. When Roc's sexual fortunes improve, she changes from austere stripes to frills, curlicues, pearls, and a "vortex" hairstyle, which the newly besotted Griffiths kisses from behind ("I couldn't help it").

Lockwood is presented throughout as a figure likely to give pleasure to a female viewer. She is identified with the mother—rather than the father—principle; her mother's brooch is cradled in her hands in a remarkably long insert, whereas Roc's hands, in a shot near the end of the film, *display* the jewel in quite a different gesture on the flat of her palm. Lockwood combines this with the active pursuit of sexual pleasure, which is facilitated by the donning of male attire; her riverside lovemaking with Mason is conducted in a shoulder-padded, tailored blouse, redolent of maleness *and* of severe 1940s female fashion. Clearly, Elizabeth Haffenden, the designer of the costumes in this and all others in the cycle, uses them to challenge and redefine sexual stereotypes and often to cut across the narrative of the script.

We should turn here to the theatrical origins and aesthetic of Haffenden's early work. None of her early designs in theatrical costume or décor were naturalistic. She worked extensively with masks, notably in Dean's 1939 production of *Johnson over Jordan,* in which Carrick's décor displayed clear continuities with the spectacular, expressionist tradition of mise-en-scène originated by his father Gordon Craig, and by Reinhardt and Appia. Much critical hostility was directed in the late thirties towards these theatrical styles. "Expressionist" was equated with "pro-German," and Haffenden's designs were dismissed as "travesties of well-known types" in an article which insisted that "the alien methods, rather loosely called expressionist, are not interesting or impressive."[84] Comparable defences of a national "addiction to realism" occur throughout the hostile reviews in the late 1930s of Haffenden's theatrical work; the *Bystander* critic notes that the costume and mise-en-scène of one of her plays is "nothing more interesting than our old friend Expressionism repeating its well-worn tricks"[85] and *The Sphere* satirised the "Reinhardian methods of mingling actors and audience" in a play using Haffenden's costumes and Goffin's décor.[86] Clearly, "Englishness" and "realism" had become interchangeable and compelling critical terms in the theatre by mid-1939, and debates about costume drama were confined to moralising or superficialities. In a review of a Haffenden-designed play, the *Telegraph* critic suggests that "we may do worse than look up our histories and reread some of the great novels of the past, particularly those that have played a part in our social developments."[87]

Haffenden's interest in "expressionist" costume could not, therefore, be accommodated within wartime theatre. After staging the 1939 costume pageants for de Gaulle's London visit, she worked almost exclusively from 1942 to 1949 on period films at Gainsborough.[88] Her theatre work in 1945, 1946, and 1949 indicates a continuing concern with costume as a symbolic index, but now the critics praised her "heraldic magnificence."[89] All her postwar theatre designs were period work—either set in, written in, or dressed in, the past—and were nonnaturalistic.[90]

From 1942, then, Gainsborough constituted a space for expressionist costume work, and a site from which to develop. Minney encouraged such stylisation—"one must not copy, one must adapt and evolve"[91]—and he wanted historical models to be creatively and suggestively altered. Such flexibility was banished by Box, who insisted on cumbersome historical "reality" and sent original nineteenth-century fashion plates to Haffenden for faithful "copying."[92] Hitherto, her designs had always been cost-effective, but when Box insisted on verisimilitude of embroidery for the clothes in *The Bad Lord Byron*, the costume department could not complete on schedule; the studio had to compete with Ministry of Labour embroiderers, and as the latter were working on Princess Elizabeth's wedding dress, the struggle was an unequal one.[93] Box even spent time studying the design of Byron's *real shoes*, to ensure that Dennis Price got the limp right.

Management style, therefore, minimised Haffenden's expressionism after *Caravan*; *Jassy* was also the first Technicolor film that she had done, and it affected the design range, necessitating the learning of a different colour "language."

Hedda Hopper, in "Clothes and the British Film Industry,"[94] suggested that the box-office appeal of clothes should be increased by fostering a more intimate relationship between the cinema and fashion industries; but there were important differences between the studios. Male couturiers such as Hartnell, Strebel, Wessel and Molyneux were used by other British studios such as Ealing and British Lion to lend status.[95] Maurice Carter recalled that such designer clothes would be kept by the stars, and their clothing coupon difficulties could thus be circumvented. However, no such arrangements existed at Gainsborough. "Period" clothes could not be appropriated for everyday wear; moreover, period dresses designed by *women* (Haffenden and Joan Ellacott) lacked the trendsetting prestige of Beaton's period work.[96] The modern-dress films at Gainsborough, designed by Yvonne Caffin and Julie Harris, had no stylish couturier pretensions. Our films' relationship to contemporary fashion, then, was not a straightforward one. Even Len England of Mass-Observation worried away at the lack of direct correlation between costume fiction and the dress of its consumers: "Is there a trend in fashion towards bustles and brimmed hats?

And yet surely such books as *Fanny by Gaslight* have been very popular this season."[97]

Although Gainsborough carefully supervised Margaret Lockwood's wardrobe on her promotion tours,[98] it never encouraged direct audience imitation. Mark Ostrer insisted that costume's role was to provide a visual "feast," "pageantry" and "romantic gaiety" for civilians,[99] and the publicity material and press releases stressed the "substitution" aspect of costume. The tie-ups suggested for *Caravan* were restricted to Spanish-style window-dressing and usherettes in gypsy uniform.[100] The *Madonna* material suggested that cinema managers "stir up the feminine interest in the significance of the sign" (*seven moons*) by persuading a hat shop to exhibit a gypsyish hat (hats were coupon-free). *Madonna*'s "wide fashion appeal" was to be taken up through a "dress designing competition" which reproduced its markedly medieval dresses while asking for modern sketches by members of the audience. These, called "elastic" imitations, were to be judged by Haffenden. The only direct area of "fit" suggested was in hairstyles; the film's coiffeurs are pictured and instructions given "which any girl can do herself." The only encouragement to audience imitation of specifically period film dress was in *The Wicked Lady* material especially tailored for American audience and release; the management suggested giving free handkerchieves to the critics: "Have some woman embroider 'The Wicked Lady' on each. The embroidery need not be of the best."[101] The publicity material for *Blanche Fury* campaigned for a new lipstick "Fury Red," and for specially-made blouses—"yesterday's creation is today's fashion"; but this was not a Gainsborough film.

The *Madonna* publicity, rather, suggested that the costume's function is not to inculcate audience imitation, but to signal "passion in the grand manner." This, in the "five terrific love scenes" in the gypsy part, was "located in the hey-day of Valentino and Navarro." Romance, silent film, and exotic dress were synonymous because "modern screen love is anaemic." Respectable underpinning for the whole project was offered by references to the practicality of Haffenden's economies—glamour "with the minimum amount of coupons."[102] Her accurate prediction of the New Look is mentioned in 1946: she "is recognized in the fashion world as an excellent prophet of women's fashions, and in 1944 she forecast in an article the swing over to glamour and to what men would call outrageous fashion. That she was correct is seen in the recent fashion displays of export garments of the big export houses."[103]

The appeal of the garments in the costume melodramas is predicated upon what was not available under contemporary clothing conditions. Clothes rationing had been introduced in 1941 primarily to release 450,000 workers from the clothing industry into munitions.[104] It forced a redefinition and restriction of the female wardrobe, the disappearance of pretty underwear and, post-1942, the banning of the manufacture of heels over two inches high.[105] "Utility" clothes were by law unembroidered, narrow-skirted and single-breasted, and fashion houses restricted the quality of fabrics and the variety of range.[106] Spurning the enthusiasm of the fashion writers for simplicity and economy of means, the female population clearly felt unhappy about its sartorial conditions. A 1941 Mass-Observation survey showed that more than half of women were buying fewer clothes, and that they much regretted the decline in "dressy" evening wear and the equally marked increase in practical trousers.[107] Consolatory hairdressing visits boomed, and the heavy use of cosmetics increased in spite of chronic market fluctuations.[108]

The popularity of the Gainsborough costumes—"tasteless," flared, exotic, excessive—should be seen in the context of the Paris shows of Spring 1946 with their tight bodices, huge layers of material, heavy embroidery and diamanté studs. Dior's "New Look," launched in February 1947, also emphasised the waist, breasts and a swirling largesse of skirt. This quickly became *de rigueur* in England, and not just among the moneyed classes. Clearly the mass aficionados of the Gainsborough costume films shared a definition of "femininity" with those who welcomed the New Look. Both "read" the female body as a flowing mystery—a mobile flower lacking male muscular strength. Such a view would he compelling to a female workforce resenting its dungarees, and in such circumstances frills might have a talismanic significance. Such a notion of femininity might have been a reflection of anxieties about the postwar roles of women, and might have made a retreat into fertility a more attractive prospect.[109]

We may conclude, then, that one reason for the cycle's popularity was its representation, through "costume narrative," of a female sexuality denied expression through conventional signifying systems. The aesthetics and the preoccupations of its designer and studio management techniques combined to form a costume practice which may be termed *anti-fashion*.[110] Like haute couture, this is a rule-based activity with a syntax and semantics;[111] In antifashion, however, the components of the costume ensemble are less strictly related to each other. Pieces from separate garment systems are frequently combined, producing an overall effect which is often inconsistent. Moreover, when garments from different historical periods are worn together, any sense of authenticity is much reduced.

After 1946, a more direct relationship between Gainsborough costume practice and the fashion world became feasible; but by then such clothes may, as I suggested above, have symbolised not female pleasure but a pleasure in retreat.

The Female Audience

The "packaging" of Lockwood was clearly extremely successful. There is evidence to suggest that female adolescents sympathised with her to such an extent as to affect their memory of a film's characters.[112] Black's view that "Lockwood had something with which every girl in the suburbs could identify herself"[113] was extremely astute. However, the female audience was *selective* about the aspects of the Gainsborough films it took on board. Lockwood's energy and self-will produced pleasure for the audience; their accounts of the films suggest that it is the visual, not plot, elements which structure that pleasure.

If we turn to female cinematic taste in the period, we can see that while there was little gender difference in humour,[114] there was an appreciable one in the area of war films[115] and "costume" melodramas. One of the Mass-Observation directives for November 1943 was "what films have you liked best during the past year? Please list in order of liking." The question was not a "priority" one, and it was the last of six, and this must be taken into account. The sample is 104 men, and, unaccountably, 18 women.[116]

The Life and Death of Colonel Blimp figured very largely in the mens' favourites, and *The Man in Grey* was only mentioned by four men. A clerk, 33, liked it because "the restraint and good taste of English films are superior to most of the Americans"; another likes it as "a piece of history," and a technical researcher, 20, praises it thus: "It is 'escapist,' and we forget the present in order to dwell on the past when young ladies were taught what to say to men who asked for their hand in marriage, even though the latter were scoundrels."

"Good taste," "real history," nostalgia for sexual inequality; such are the male alibis for enjoying the films. In Mayer's survey, the males desexualise their response (loving Calvert for her *diction*)[117] or they berate the films' salaciousness.[118] Granger is defensively rejected by a student because "I sincerely dislike *showing off* in films."[119] Even schoolboys noted the bawdiness of *The Wicked Lady*, while ignoring the costumes and settings which so preoccupied the girls.[120]

Female film response differs interestingly. In the 1943 directives, *Random Harvest* is comparable to the men's *Blimp*, and *The Man in Grey* is a favourite of four of the eighteen respondents; two like it for its "good acting," its dramatic qualities impressed another, and a teacher likes its escapism, particularly noting the costumes, setting, and "Becky Sharpe" theme.[121] The film in this survey is favoured by six times as many women as men, and for reasons of star identification and visual pleasure. Mayer's extracts here are useful. A hairdresser, 16½, reconstructs herself after viewing as "the lovely heroine in a beautiful blue crinoline with a feather in her hair."[122] Respondents are quite selective when it comes to *making* the dresses for themselves.[123] Female masochism clearly found ample material in these films: a typist, 17, notes Mason's similarity to Rhett Butler, remarking: "I simply revel in seeing bold bad men."[124] The female audience frequently attests to the films' emotional "sincerity": this gives a respectability to their own cathartic release.[125] This extends into a demand for "realism" by two schoolgirls, but it is clearly a realism of a different *type,* to do with emotional expressivity.[126] The costumes are a major source of pleasure, as are the sets, especially of *Madonna*.[127]

Of paramount importance is the "dream" section in Mayer's 1946 book. The women select as dream-material resonant images from the films which are potent cultural symbols: the mirror and the whip. A typist draws the *seven moons* sign on the mirror *without knowing what it means,* but "nothing further from the narrative";[128] a clerk saw "the terrifying look on James Mason's face as he beat Hester to death."[129] Their dream-work selects out symbols of self-identification and male dominance. What is seen in the mirror is not understood. What is unlike the self is predatory. Clearly the films aid a kind of ritual expression and excision of deep-seated female fears.

It is predictable, therefore, that schoolgirls modelled their body language on such films,[130] and were "speechless with longing."[131] Ideological pressures inevitably directed their taste towards drama and "human relationships."[132]

Of course, caution needs to be exercised with audience findings for the period. Bernstein and the 1943 *Kinematograph Weekly* survey on taste do not distinguish between classes, and Box has a naive belief in the reality of statistics *as such*.[133] Fear of the mass effects of film motivates many academic studies,[134] and Mayer held élitist views on popular culture, evoking Petronius in his distaste for the "decadence" of *The Wicked Lady* and *Madonna*.[135] Mass-Observation work on film favours middle-class respondents, and often shows a peevishness in the face of historical contingency.[136] Nevertheless, it appears clear that the female audience of the period, subjected to the most extreme pressures and anxieties about the future, chose to "read" these texts as an index of pleasure and optimism.

The "gentry" theme in popular texts is a vital and enduring strand in British culture, and the mass audience clearly responded favourably to the Gainsborough style of aristocratic "disguise." Costume melodrama of this sort, I suggest, permits the expression of anxieties about the boundaries of political power and moral value. The function of such films is to articulate the audience's fears on issues of class and gender and (possibly) ritually to excise them. Ideology—that set of relations preferred by a hegemonic class—may be straightforwardly represented, or complicated, or *disguised* by art. The latter is clearly the case with the Gainsborough films. The ideological constitution of culture is such that a confident class will permit (indeed, will *require*) artistic representations of the classes over which it holds sway.

In conclusion, it would appear that the standard and generalised definitions of melodrama do not apply to this case. These melodramas do not foreground the family as an issue, and the mise-en-scène functions quite differently from American forties' historical films of the genre, such as *Forever Amber* or *Frenchman's Creek*. Moreover, what is often referred to as the cardinal sin of male scopophilia does not obtain here. The female stars, as I have shown, function as the source of the *female* gaze both on screen and in the audience; and males, gorgeously arrayed, are the unabashed objects of female desire. Class is an indisputable part of the films' structure of feeling, and is in no way representational of "real events."

It is instructive to compare Ealing historical films of this period. These display the usual realist consonance between different codes: dress, music, script, décor all *reinforce* each other with a quality "gloss" and attention to historical verisimilitude. But the films are monolithic; they do not contain creative spaces or interstices for the audiences, and do not present the past as a place where answers to present predicaments might be found. Rather, the past only contains disappointment and sexual repression, and female attractiveness is predicated on extreme youth and chastity, a combination unlikely to please or comfort all its audience. We may conclude that, in our period, British costume melodrama (as opposed to historical film) manifests a positive interpretation of the past, and grants a freedom to the audience to manoeuvre its own way through narrative codes.

NOTES

1. See *Kinematograph Weekly*, 20 December 1945, 19 December 1946, and *Daily Film Renter*, 29 April 1946 and 9 May 1946, for accounts of the cycle's profitability.

2. *News Chronicle*, 19 November 1945.

3. *Tribune*, 12 April 1946.

4. *Sunday Graphic*, 14 April 1946.

5. Alan Wood, *Mr. Rank* (London: Hodder and Stoughton, 1952), 123.

6. R. J. Minney, *Talking of Films* (London: Home and Van Thai, 1947), 19.

7. The *Times*, 3 March 1949. See *Kinematograph Weekly*, 19 April 1945, for a cost breakdown of *The Man in Grey*, which should be compared with that of Box's *The Bad Lord Byron*, in the *Daily Herald*, 2 March 1948.

8. Interviews conducted by me with Mrs. Paddy Porter, continuity girl at Gainsborough, in unpublished M.A. thesis in Film Studies for the Polytechnic of Central London, 1982.

9. Interview conducted by me with Maurice Carter, Art Director at Gainsborough, in Sue Aspinall and Robert Murphy, eds., *Gainsborough Melodrama* (London: British Film Institute, 1983), 58.

10. Ibid., 56.

11. *Today's Cinema*, 4 January 1945. See also *Kinematograph Weekly*, 21 March 1945. Minney, *Talking of Films*, 77, concurs with Ostrer's ideas about costing.

12. Wood, *Mr. Rank*, 147.

13. *Kinematograph Weekly*, 19 April 1945.

14. Ibid.: "rapturous notices from the critics will be the delight of the highbrows." See Minney, *Talking of Films*, 16.

15. *Kinematograph Weekly*, 20 December 1945.

16. B. Woodhouse, *From Script to Screen* (London: Winchester Publications, 1947), 63–64.

17. Interviews conducted by me with Mr. Bill Salter and Mr. Dennis Mason, sound recordists, in Aspinall and Murphy, *Gainsborough Melodrama*. Lengthier versions of these are in my unpublished M.A. thesis, 1982.

18. Interview with Mrs. Porter, in M.A. thesis, 1982, ix.

19. Ibid. viii.

20. Interview with Maurice Carter in *Gainsborough Melodrama*, 58.

21. Ibid.

22. My interview with Mr. Salter in *Gainsborough Melodrama*, 53.

23. Interview with Mr. Mason, ibid., 55.

24. For example, W. D. Wall and E. M. Smith, "The Film Choices of Adolescents," *British Journal of Educational Psychology*, June 1949, 135–36.

25. *Madonna of the Seven Moons* press-book in BFI library.

26, *Today's Cinema*, 5 January 1944.

27. *Sunday Graphic*, 14 April 1946.

28. Magdalen King-Hall, *The Life and Death of the Wicked Lady Skelton* (London: Peter Davies, 1944); Margery Lawrence, *Madonna of the Seven Moons* (London: Hurst and Blackett, 1931; reprinted 1945); Lady E. F. Smith, *Caravan* and *The Man in Grey* (London: Hutchinson, 1943 and 1941 respectively); Norah Lofts, *Jassy* (London: Michael Joseph, 1944). The only exception to female authorship here is Michael Sadleir, *Fanny by Gaslight* (London: Constable, 1940).

29. Minney, *Talking of Films*, 4; see also p. 35.

30. Norman Lee, *Log of a Film Director* (London: Quality Press, 1949), 34–35.

31. Minney, *Talking of Films*, 43.

32. See E. Britton, *Blanche Fury: The Book of the Film* (London: World Film Publications. 1948) and Vera Caspary, *Bedelia*, ed. William R. T. Rodger (London: Eyre and Spottiswoode/John Corfield Productions, 1946).

33. In "History with Frills: the 'Costume' Novel in World War II," *Red Letters* 14, 1983.

34. These are male replies to the October 1943 directive in the Mass-Observation Archive at Sussex University, from a commissionaire (aged 19), a schoolboy, a commercial traveller (35), and Education Inspector (36), in that order.

35. The first reply is from a female press agent (34) in the Mass-Observation October directive. The second is from Mass-Observation File 2018, p. 85, "C" class female aged 35. The third is ibid., p. 92, housewife (28). The fourth, ibid., p. 93, clerk (35). The last is in Mass-Observation file 2537, p. 34 (unascribed, but female).

36. Mass-Observation file 2018, ix.

37. Reading in Tottenham, Mass-Observation file 2537, 37.

38. Smith, *The Man in Grey*, 139.

39. Smith, *Caravan*, 97.

40. King-Hall, *The Life and Death of the Wicked Lady Skelton*, 97.

41. See my account of John Drummond's 1942 novel, *The Bride Wore Black,* in *Red Letters* 14.

42. See her *Life's a Circus* (London: Longmans, 1939).

43. S. Kunitz and H. Haycroft, *20th Century Authors* (New York: H. W. Wilson, 1942), 842.

44. *Log of a Film Director*, 133.

45. The Executive Committee of July 1944 of the Screenwriters Association contained Launder, Gilliatt, Minney and Arliss, and Minney went on the Association's behalf to conferences in Paris and Madrid. Material on the SWA was formerly in the archives of the Society of Authors, and is now the property of the British Library.

46. Margaret Kennedy, *The Mechanical Muse* (London: Allen and Unwin, 1942,), 39.

47. Ibid., 29.

48. Ibid., 53.

49. Crabtree directed both *Caravan* and *Madonna;* in the BFI press book of the former, he suggests that "it is imperative for a director to be vitally interested in the story."

50. Memo from Launder in SOA files, 15 May 1944. Arliss was co-opted to the Executive Committee to discuss credits in 1946, and he and Kennedy were on council of the SWA until 1954.

51. Lee, *Log of a Film Director*, 133.

52. *Kinematograph Weekly*, 19 April 1945.

53. Letter from Launder to Society of Authors, 11 November 1946, in SOA files. A very highly paid screenwriter could be hired by the week.

54. Interview with Mr. Salter in *Gainsborough Melodrama*, 53.

55. Draft constitution of SWA, 11 March 1937, in SOA files. Resolution 14 is to "provide facilities to encourage the register of stories and scenarios which members might consider to their advantage."

56. Report of the Annual General Meeting of the SWA, 18 July 1944.

57. Letter in SOA files from Launder to the Secretary of SOA, 5 January 1942: "It is our business to suggest or consider stories and ideas with the object of recommending to the Ministry suitable subjects for propaganda films. We believe the majority of writers will not look upon payment." Note that they produce ideas, not actual treatments.

58. Letter from Inland Revenue to Launder, 12 October 1943.

59. See Letter from Launder to the Secretary of SOA, 20 May 1943, and account of a mass SWA meeting, 25 September 1946, in SOA files.

60. Letter from Launder to Screenwriters Guild, June 1947.

61. Letter from Morgan to the Secretary of SOA, 12 October 1947: "I hear that the ACT have been rapped over the knuckles by Cripps, and told to interest themselves a little more in production, and a little less in power politics."

62. Letter from G.D.H. Cole to Morgan, 8 November 1947.

63. *Kinematograph Weekly*, 1 January 1943. See also Wood, *Mr. Rank*, 134–37.

64. Letter from del Giudice to the Secretary of SOA, 10 December 1942.

65. Letter from del Giudice to the Secretary of SOA, 14 December 1942.

66. Rough notes for the private information of Kilham Roberts in SOA files, in what looks very like Balcon's handwriting and bearing his initials. These are undated, but clearly relate to the Scenario Institute.

67. Letter from Launder to Kilham Roberts, 15 April 1943.

68. The end of the script in the BFI library has "thundering hooves" as her spirit makes its exit. These are absent from the actual film.

69. Smith, *Caravan*, 202.

70. Smith, *The Man in Grey*, 245.

71. Lawrence, *Madonna of the Seven Moons*, 14, 155.

72. Ibid., 131: "at last his long-held patience gave way, and he took by force what should only be given in love."

73. Interview with Maurice Carter in *Gainsborough Melodrama*, 58.

74. See Edward Carrick, ed., *Art and Design in the British Film* (London: Dennis Dobson, 1948), 16, 64, 92; and L. Barsacq, *Le Décor du Film* (Paris: Seghers, 1970), 77.

75. R. J. Minney, *The Film-Maker and His World: a Young Person's Guide* (London: Gollancz, 1964), 86.

76. Interview with Maurice Carter in *Gainsborough Melodrama*, 59.

77. *Kinematograph Weekly*, 16 August 1945. See also *The Cinetechnician*, November/December 1948, for an interesting account of the replica work on *Christopher Columbus*.

78. Sydney Box and Vivian Cox, *The Bad Lord Byron* (London: Convoy Publications, 1949).

79. See the press book for *Saraband* in the BFI library.

80. Maurice Carter commented to me that it was "the biggest budget I'd ever had for sets. It was all-out; it was meant to be another *Wicked Lady*."

81. See Jacob Peter Mayer, *British Cinemas and their Audiences* (London: Dennis Dobson, 1948), 144, 252, 257. See also Barbara Kesterton, "The Social and Emotional Effects of the Recreational Film on Adolescents of 13 and 14 years of age in the West Bromwich Area," University of Birmingham Ph.D. thesis, 1948; and W. D. Wall and E. M. Smith, "The Film Choices of Adolescents."

82. See Mayer, *British Cinemas*, 22, 81, 184; and Jacob Peter Mayer, *Sociology of Film* (London: Faber and Faber, 1946), 183, 216.

83. See John Cowie Reid, *Bucks and Bruisers: Pierce Egan and Regency England* (London: Routledge & Kegan Paul, 1971), and Fred Kaplan, *Dickens and Mesmerism* (Princeton: Princeton University Press, 1975).

84. *Illustrated London News*, 11 March 1939.

85. *The Bystander*, 8 March 1939.

86. *The Sphere*, 9 April 1938.

87. *Daily Telegraph*. See also *The Sphere*, 17 September 1938.

88. Information available in the publicity file for *Madonna* in the BFI library. For full credit lists, see Elizabeth Leese, *Costume Design in the Movies* (Isle of Wight: BCW Publishing, 1977), 47.

89. See *The Tatler*, 26 June 1946, and *Picture Post*, 26 March 1945.

90. A complete theatrical list from 1939 is: March 1945, *Three Waltzes*; May 1946, *The Kingmakers*; July 1946, *Marriage à la Mode*; May 1949, *The Beaux Stratagem*; February 1951, *Man and Superman*; June 1951, *Dido and Aeneas*; September 1951, *The Tempest*; November 1953, *Pygmalion*.

91. Minney, *The Film-Maker and His World*, 91, 116.

92. Box and Cox, *The Bad Lord Byron*, 88–89.

93. Ibid., 93–94.

94. *Kinematograph Weekly*, 27 June 1946.

95. See Leese, *Costume Design*, 17.

96. Credit lists in Leese, *Costume Design*, 47; see also Charles Spencer, *Cecil Beaton, Stage and Film Design* (London: Academy Editions, 1975), 81.

97. In Mass-Observation file no. 485 (7 November 1940).

98. Margaret Lockwood, *Lucky Star* (London: Odhams Press, 1955), 112, 135.

99. *Kinematograph Weekly*, 11 January 1945.

100. *Caravan* publicity in BFI library.

101. American publicity material for *The Wicked Lady* in BFI library. *Blanche Fury* material is in BFI library. See also an article by Orrom on tie-ups in general in *Screen and Audience*, 1947, and B. Woodhouse, *From Script to Screen*, 142–47.

102. In the *Madonna* publicity material in BFI library.

103. In *Caravan* material in BFI library.

104. Nicholas Longmate, *How We Lived Then: History of Everyday Life During the Second World War* (London: Arrow Books, 1973), 246.

105. Ibid., 250, 252. See also Julian Robinson, *Fashion in the Forties* (London: Academy Editions, 1976), p. 25 of 1980 edition.

106. Robinson, *Fashion in the Forties*, 16, 25.

107. Mass-Observation file no. 728, *Changes in Clothing Habits* (9 June 1941).

108. Longmate, *How We Lived Then*, 273, 276.

109. Of particular interest here is Mass-Observation report 2059 (8 March 1944), *Will the Factory Girls Want to Stay Put or Go Home?* The Report blandly concludes that "both men and women agree . . . that men should be the breadwinners," but this is not borne out at all by the general restlessness expressed by the younger women. Only those older women who had been at home as housewives before the war unambiguously wished to return there.

110. See Ted Polhemus and Linda Procter, *Fashion and Anti-Fashion: Anthropology of Clothing and Adornment* (London: Thames and Hudson, 1978), 16.

111. As described by Roland Barthes in *Elements of Semiology* (London: Jonathan Cape, 1967), 27, and in his *Systeme de la mode* (Paris: Du Seuil, 1967).

112. Wall and Smith, "Film Choices of Adolescents," 130. Here they note from a retelling of *The Wicked Lady*, adolescent girls called the heroines "Margaret" and "Patricia."

113. Wood, *Mr. Rank*, 146.

114. As indicated by the Mass-Observation survey on *Let George Do It*.

115. Mass-Observation report on Film Themes (17 March 1940), Appendix I. This was a reply to a 1939 question, "do you like a different sort of picture now to what you did before the war?" Mass-Observation concluded that women over 30 were the main objectors to war films.

116. The present Mass-Observation archivists are unable to account for this imbalance.

117. Mayer, *British Cinemas and their Audiences*, 41.

118. Ibid., 49.

119. Ibid., 129.

120. See Barbara Kesterton, Ph.D. thesis, 72: "*The Wicked Lady* was classified as a film whose main appeal is to sex-instinct. Yet it has a lively quick-moving story, and picturesque gowns. It is probably these qualities that give the film considerable appeal for the girls. They, unlike the few boys who mentioned this production, concentrated on the costumes and the settings, rather than the bawdy parts of the plot."

121. A holiday-home manageress (26) likes its "unusual plot and good acting." Two servicewomen praise the female acting style. (It is against Mass-Observation's policy to publish the names of respondents, many of whom must still be alive.)

122. Mayer, *British Cinemas and their Audiences*, 22.

123. Ibid., 81, where chemist's assistant (female, 21) talks about clothes. See also Mayer, *Sociology of Film*, 215, where a female clerk (17) realises that you have to "select"; she proposes to copy a coat from the "civilized" part of *Madonna*, not from the "gypsy" part.

124. Mayer, *British Cinemas and their Audiences*, 73.

125. Ibid., 92, female clerk (20): "it is very seldom that we find faked scenes."

126. Ibid., 161. See also schoolgirl (15), p. 166; female clerk (16), p. 169; female student.(17), p. 179; female clerk (16), p. 174.

127. Ibid., textile worker (18), p. 184. See also Mayer, *Sociology of Film*, p. 183. Female clerk (16): "I also wish we could go back a few centuries and the ladies wear beautiful crinolines." See also Mayer, *British Cinemas and their Audiences*, female typist (191), p. 189. *Madonna* and *The Man in Grey* feature most strongly. On the latter, see ibid., p. 227, female telephonist (25), and p. 234, female housekeeper (46) and female typist (24), p. 214. See also Mayer, *Sociology of Film*, p. 92 (female, 14½) on *The Man in Grey*.

128. Mayer, *Sociology of Film*, 201–202. Respondents were asked to describe any dreams influenced by films.

129. Ibid., 213. See also p. 217, firewoman's dream.

130. See also W. D. Wall and W. A. Simpson, "The Effects of Cinema Attendance on the Behaviour of Adolescents as seen by their Contemporaries," *British Journal of Educational Psychology*, February 1949.

131. Kesterton, Ph.D. thesis, 99.

132. Ibid., 84: 34% of girls like love stories, and only 9% of the boys; p. 79 suggests that 54% of girls and 18% of boys attach importance to "sentiment and pathos." See also pp. 257–58 where 67% of the girls admitted imitating star's make-up (especially Lockwood). This 67% was largely composed of "lower" educational sector.

133. See Kathleen L. Box, *The Cinema and the Public* (London: Central Office of Information, 1946) in Mass-Observation 2429; and L. Moss and K. Box, *Wartime Survey: The Cinema Audience* (London: Ministry of Information, 1943) in Mass-Observation 1871.

134. Such as Kesterton, Ph.D. thesis; or Wall and Smith, "Film Choices of Adolescents."

135. Mayer, *British Cinemas and their Audiences*, 8.

136. Hapless Mass-Observation film-observers were unable to categorise such données as "I can't talk to you now, ducks, I've got no teeth look!" (in Mass-Observation box 15, with loose papers). The Bernstein film questionnaire is unable to decode working-class respondents' jokes and irony.

History as Trauma

Maria Wyke

Projecting Ancient Rome

Invented Traditions

If historical films set in ancient Rome have now become a legitimate object of study for both classicists and historians, then what work needs to be done to write a history of such films? According to the terms recently set for cinema's own strategies for screening history, these films form part of—an integrated regime of—historical representation that constitutes the historical capital of twentieth-century cultures, and the reference period selected for projection ceases to be arbitrary and instead generates historical meaning through its relationship with other, extra-cinematic discourses about the past. Knowledge of those intertexts facilitates the exploration of how historical films function within a culture.[1] The reminiscences of cinema-going in the 1930s offered by Gore Vidal and Federico Fellini, their respective recollections of the neoclassical public architecture of Washington or the various Fascist celebrations of ancient Rome, suggest one important set of intertexts for the production and consumption of films about Roman history—namely the deployment of ancient Rome in the formation of the national identities of the United States and Italy.

The two nations which have been most prolific in their manufacture of cinematic histories of ancient Rome also assiduously created a whole array of "invented traditions" to connect themselves with the Roman past. I use "invented traditions" (a term taken from the historian Eric Hobsbawm) to refer to those discursive practices that, from the mid-eighteenth century, attempted to establish for a modern community a continuity with a suitable historical past. The purpose of these traditions was to cement group cohesion and legitimate action through the use of history, and the communities whose institutions, policies, and social relations were being established, symbolized, or legitimated historically were more often than not the newly formed nation-states. The awareness of an historical continuity, the creation of a cultural patrimony, served to enhance a sense of communal identity, legitimating the new nation and bolstering its sovereignty in the eyes of its own and other peoples. By tracing its origins back into the past, a nation could validate its claims to power, property, and international prestige. And, if rooted in the remotest antiquity, a nation could make claims to the earliest precedent and the greatest dignity.[2]

The United States had constant recourse to an invented tradition of *romanitas* in the early years of the nation's foundation. American national identity had to be forged out of a mass of heterogeneous immigrants who were encouraged to accept and participate in a whole host of rituals and historical discourses which commemorated the history of the new nation and rooted it in a more remote past. Classical antiquity readily supplied America with a usable past—instant, communal history and cultural legitimacy in the eyes of Europe. America was thus created according to the model of an ideally conceived Roman republic. Roman republican ideals of liberty, civic virtue, and mixed government were densely evoked as precedent for and validation of the new republic during the struggle for independence and the subsequent constitutional debates of 1787–1788. In August 1777, for example, when replying to the peace offer made by the British general John Burgoyne, George Washington claimed: "The associated armies in America act from the noblest motives, liberty. The same principles actuated the arms of Rome in the days of her glory; and the same object was the reward of Roman valour." In the early, national period, George Washington in particular became a focal point of efforts to Romanize American history. In pictures and statues and victory arches, he was to be seen draped in a Roman toga or attired in military costume. In the literature of the period, the "father of his country" was hailed as another heroic symbol of the republican virtues of patriotism, self-sacrifice, frugality, and military acumen along the lines of the Roman leaders Cincinnatus, Cato, or Fabius.[3]

America's rhetoric of *romanitas* became more complex and ambiguous as its expansion southward and westward appeared to endanger its republican institutions and its Christian ethics. The international expositions and fairs held throughout the United States from the late nineteenth century until the end of the First World War celebrated the success of America's recent quest for empire through their use of pseudo-Roman imperial architecture, as did similarly designed state capitols, court houses, museums, universities, libraries, and railroad stations. Imperial Rome, however, had supplied the Founding Fathers with a striking anti-model for the social organization and government of the new nation. During the Revolutionary period, British politicians had been regularly clothed in the vices and villainy of the Roman emperors, and British colonial policy had been compared to the tyranny which Rome had supposedly exercised over her provinces. As America's own empire grew from the mid-nineteenth century, so such earlier critiques of imperialism were turned against America itself. By the beginning of the twentieth century, critics were warning apocalyptically that, having forsaken Christianity and fallen into decadence, the nation was heading toward Armageddon. According to Henry Adams, the great-grandson of the Founding Father John Adams, when he looked out of his hotel window at New York in 1905 he "felt himself in Rome, under Diocletian, witnessing the anarchy, with no Constantine the Great in sight."[4]

Scholars, politicians, and intellectuals, ever since, have looked to the decline of the Roman empire to provide support for their dire predictions of America's coming fall. Perpetuated in the public architecture of the United States, allusions to Rome could thus assume a contradictory quality. Nonetheless, parallels between ancient Rome and modern America continued to surface and circulated widely in the popular representational forms of the nineteenth and twentieth centuries, in classical-subject paintings and pyrodramas, toga plays and historical novels.[5] Most notably, General Lew Wallace's religious novel *Ben-Hur: A Tale of the Christ* constructs a stirring narrative in which the fictive Judaean's resistance to Roman rule and his conversion to Christianity effectively cast America as a new Holy Land capable of driving out its imperial rulers and establishing peace through the embrace of Christ. The novel was first published in 1880 and stayed on the bestseller lists for some fifty years. It was spectacularly staged from 1899, was adapted for the screen in 1907, 1925, and again in 1959, and even gave its hero's name to a town in Texas.[6]

American formulations of relationship to ancient Rome, however, have always been less intimate and ultimately less pressing than the Italian conception of *romanità*. A certain confusion reigned over the relevance of both republican and imperial Rome to America because America's place within history, unlike that of European nations, was not clearly demarcated. Material remains of the classical past did not litter America's landscape as they did Italy's.[7] The surviving monuments and iconography of ancient Rome were frequently deployed in Italy during the course of the nineteenth century as political symbols in a struggle for power between the Papacy and the *risorgimento* revolutionaries. The Colosseum was pitted against the Roman forum, the Christian cross against the republican *fasces*. While the Church exploited archaeology as proof of the ultimate triumph of the Christian martyrs over the cruel persecutions of imperial Rome, the emerging nationalist movement sought out and paraded a precedent for a unified, secular Italy that was rooted in an earlier republican tradition of civic rather than religious virtue, of triumvirs and consuls, not tyrants. Thus when Giuseppe Garibaldi was elected to the Constituent Assembly of 1849, he declared (if somewhat prematurely): "I believe profoundly that, now the papal system of government is at an end, what we need in Rome is a republic. . . . Can it be that the descendants of the ancient Romans are not fit to constitute a Republic. As some people in this body evidently take offence at this word, I reiterate 'Long live the republic!'"[8]

After the unification of Italy in 1861, the problem of assimilating its disparate peoples into a single nation was summarized by Massimo d'Azeglio thus: "We have made Italy: now we must make Italians."[9] Needing to justify itself historically, and in the face of continued opposition from the Vatican, the new secular body politic was able to find a major, and apparently self-evident, justification in the ancient civic virtues and military glories of the Roman republic and empire. The invented tradition of *romanità* gave to the heterogeneous Italians a piece of common national history, and, in an epidemic of literary production from unification into the first decade of the twentieth century, historical fictions such as Pietro Cossa's Roman tragedies or Rafaello Giovagnoli's Roman novels attempted to supply a unifying popular culture in which the grand figures of Roman history "get off their pedestals of togaed rhetoric" and speak simply and with a quotidian *verismo* of sacrifices for or betrayals of their country.[10]

Until the 1910s, however, narratives of imperial Rome were often vulnerable to appropriation by religious opponents of Italy's liberal government as gruesome analogies for the state repression of Catholic organizations and as ominous warnings of the Church's certain victory in the continuing struggle to reclaim her temporal power. But by the time the fiftieth year of Italian unity was grandly celebrated in 1911, both state and Church were finding common cause in imperial Rome as historical legitimation for Italy's colonial aspirations in the Mediterranean. In a speech to open an archaeological exhibition held at the Baths of Diocletian during the Great Exhibition of 1911, the Christian archaeologist Rodolfo Lanciani expressed clearly the pressing imperial agenda that now lay behind such Italian displays of its Roman past. According to Lanciani, the *mostra archeologica* ought to form the basis of a future museum of the Roman empire "where Italian youth may seek inspiration for all those virtues which rendered Rome, morally as well as materially, the mistress of the world." On the eve of Italy's war against Turkey to wrest the colonies Tripolitania and Cyrenaica from the Ottoman empire, and despite the reservations of some critics, imperial Rome was everywhere invoked as the model of and reason for a new Italian empire. And, after victory in Africa, the discourse of historical continuity between ancient and modern imperialism continued to circulate widely, as a postcard reproduced in the English magazine *The Sphere* towards the end of 1911 testifies. An Italian sailor triumphantly grasps the sword of empire from the skeleton of a Roman soldier partially buried in the African sands. The caption beneath declares "Italy brandishes the sword of ancient Rome."[11]

Historians of silent Italian cinema, such as Gian Piero Brunetta, have long argued that the war in Africa gave a decisive push toward the meeting of Italian cinematic production and the imperial ambitions of the nation-state. The many grand historical films set in ancient Rome which were produced in the period leading up to the First World War (and which obtained enormous critical acclaim and box-office success both in Italy and abroad) held a crucial role in the formation, interrogation, and dissemination of the rhetoric of *romanità*. Such films were both *about* ancient Rome and *for* modern Italy.[12]

The recently established institutions of cinema changed the relationship between historical narration and its audiences. The practice of cinema-going brought huge numbers of Italian spectators out of their homes into a shared public space and thus rendered their experience of historical reconstruction a more collective event than the private reading of a novel. The technologies of cinema spectacle could also accommodate on screen huge masses of people before whom, or even for whom, the protagonists of the narrative acted. Through these crowds of extras, mass audiences were able to visualize on screen their own collectivity and gain a stake in historical action. Historical films, therefore, became ideal vehicles for addressing the nation's sense of its own identity.[13] In the years preceding the First World War, there was a substantial increase of capital invest-ment in the production of Italian feature-length historical films. Bound to the dic-tates of high finance and to the bourgeois values of its financial backers, Italian historical films began to prosper as an instrument of cultural hegemony. In the logic of their producers, they came to be regarded as a new form of popular uni-versity, capable of shaping the historical consciousness of their mass, largely illiterate audience and transmitting to them the symbols of Italy's recently constituted national identity. Historical films set in ancient Rome became a privileged means for the production and consumption of an imperial *romanità*. The projection on screen of the imperial eagles and the *fasces,* Roman military rituals and parades supplied a concentrated repertoire of glorious precedents for present combative action.[14] Thus, soon after victory in Africa, the celebratory film *Cabiria* (1914) represented a unified Roman community under the leader-ship of the morally upright general Scipio triumphing over a decadent and dis-organized Carthage.[15]

Similarly, despite the relative political independence of the Italian film industry during the early years of the Fascist regime, at the time of the African campaigns of 1935–1936 the Fascist government helped procure considerable capital investment for the production of the spectacular historical film *Scipione l'Africano* (1937), in which the hero is seen to lead a unified, rural, and warlike Rome to victory in Africa. The cinematic construction of the Roman general's character rehearsed a model for the perfect Fascist citizen, and his designed analogy with Mussolini was both exploited by the *duce* himself and recognized by the film's contemporary audience. Even before the March on Rome in Octo-ber 1922, Mussolini had begun to appropriate the militant rhetoric of *roman-ità* to establish historical legitimacy and popular support for Fascism. In a speech reproduced in his newspaper *Il popolo d'Italia* for 21 April 1922, he declared:

> We dream of a Roman Italy, that is to say wise, strong, disciplined, and imperial. Much of that which was the immortal spirit of Rome is reborn in Fascism: the Fasces are Roman; our organization of combat is Roman, our pride and our courage are Roman: *civis romanus sum.* Now, it is necessary that the history of tomorrow, the history we fervently wish to create, not represent a contrast or a parody of the history of Yesterday. . . . Italy has been Roman for the first time in fifteen centuries in the War and in the Victory: now Italy must be Roman in peace-time: and this renewed and revived *romanità* bears these names: Discipline and Work.[16]

In the 1930s, Roman iconography, architecture and sculpture, political rhetoric, and military ritual were systematically exploited to justify historically the Fas-cist aspiration to a colonial empire in the Mediterranean.[17] And, under the impetus of events in Africa, with the conquest of Ethiopia and the ensuing procla-mation of Empire on 9 May 1936, the production of the historical film *Scipione l'Africano* became a work of the regime, on which the Ministries of Popular Cul-ture, Finance, Home Affairs, and War collaborated (the last supplying infantry and cavalry troops as extras for the battle sequences).[18]

Soon after shooting the film, the cinematographer Luigi Freddi (who had been appointed four years previously to run a new film directorate within the Ministry of Popular Culture) avowed that the cinematic representation of Scipio's conquest of Africa had been expressly undertaken to service Italy's renewed imperial project. Writing in *Il popolo d'Italia* for 6 April 1937, he announced that

> *Scipione* was conceived on the eve of the African undertaking and was begun soon after the victory. It was desired because no theme for translation into spectacle seemed more suited than this to symbolize the intimate union between the past grandeur of Rome and the bold accomplishment of our epoch. And it seemed also that no filmic representation was capable of showing and framing, in the august tradition of the race. before ourselves and the world, the African undertaking of today as a logical corollary of a glorious past and an ardent present's indisputable reason for living. Perhaps never, in the history of cinema, has a film initiative been so full of deep spiritual significance derived from active consideration of history.[19]

The film was presented at the Venice Film Festival of November 1937, where it won the Mussolini Cup. Its subsequent distribution was supported by an extensive publicity campaign in the Italian press and by admiring reviews. Its political effectiveness then appeared to be confirmed by interviews with school-children, whose essays on their viewing of the film were printed in a special edition of the cinema journal *Bianco e Nero* for August 1939. According to the introduction furnished by Giuseppe Bottai, the Minister for National Education: "For the children, Scipio is not the Roman hero, it is Mussolini. Through a subconscious power of transposition, the actions of Scipio become the actions of Mussolini. The analogy becomes identity."[20]

The evident meeting between liberal Italy's geopolitical ambitions and the narrative structures of *Cabiria* (1914), the seemingly perfect propagandist match between the Fascist regime's combative discourse of *romanità* and the production, distribution, and consumption of *Scipione l'Africano* (1937), may suggest that films concerning Roman history can be read as effective instruments of ideological control which, through spectacular and engaging historical reconstructions, manipulate their audiences to assent to a celebratory model of national identity. Yet the independently produced *Cabiria* was a huge commercial success in Italy, the (uniquely) state-supported *Scipione* a failure. Furthermore, many successful Italian films of the 1910s and 1920s resurrected ancient Rome's imperial cruelties and Christian martyrdoms rather than its republican triumphs, while Hollywood histories of Rome have appropriated Fascist constructions of *romanità* to turn them back against the regime which produced them, and have constantly exploited the ambiguities and contradictions inherent in the American national discourse of *romanitas* to address iniquities within the United States itself. Screening ancient Rome could supply equivocal history lessons for both Italians and Americans.

In the *New York Times* of 22 November 1959, the film critic Bosley Crowther heaped the highest praise on MGM's latest adaptation of the famous novel *Ben-Hur* for the film's perceived pertinence and timeliness:

Obviously, this story, with its personal conflicts based on religious and political differences, is more concrete to present generations, which have seen tyrants and persecutors at work than it could have been to most of the people who read it in the nineteenth century. And it is this paramount realization of the old story's present significance that properly has been foremost in the reasonings of Mr. Wyler and the man (or men) who prepared the script. It is indeed this realization that has "justified a remake at this time."

Now, in the hero's conversations with Messala, one can hear echoes of the horrible clash of interests in Nazi Germany. In the burgeoning of hatred in Ben-Hur one can sense the fierce passion for revenge that must have moved countless people in Poland and Hungary. And in the humble example of Jesus, most tastefully enacted in this film, one can feel genuine spiritual movement toward the ideal of the brotherhood of man.

As Michael Wood has observed in *America in the Movies* (1975), Hollywood epics of the Cold War era frequently cast British theater actors as villainous Egyptian pharaohs or Roman patricians, and American film stars as their virtuous Jewish or Christian opponents. Thus films like *Ben-Hur* replay in an ancient setting the glorious struggle of "the colonies against the mean mother country."[21] In New Testament epics, the United States takes on the sanctity of the Holy Land and receives the endorsement of God for all its past and present fights for freedom against tyrannical regimes (imperial Britain, Fascist Italy, Nazi Germany, or the Communist Soviet Union). In such narratives, a hyperbolically tyrannical Rome stands for the decadent European Other forever destined to be defeated by the vigorous Christian principles of democratic America.[22] Critics have also argued, however, that such film narratives sometimes exhibit an additional and contradictory analogy between the repressions of the Roman empire and those exercised *within* the United States. When in *The Robe* (1953), for example, the emperor Caligula demands that a Roman soldier infiltrate Christian subversives and name names, Bruce Babington and Peter Evans hear clear echoes of the directives of the House Un-American Activities Committee, which required those called before it to disclose the names of colleagues with Communist Party connections. *The Robe*, momentarily, offers a political critique of the surveillance, investigation, and police-state manoeuvres at work during the course of America's "Red Scare."[23]

If film scholarship has problematized the function of historical film as a national discourse, it often seems to utilize a form of discursive slippage between film and society which requires interrogation. Ever since the psychoanalytic readings of German cinema offered by Siegfried Kracauer in his seminal book *From Caligari to Hitler: A Psychological History of German Film* (1947), where Kracauer posited a relationship between Weimar films and Fascism, many film critics have justified reading the films of a particular nation as a manifestation of that nation's psycho-social disposition as an expression of that society's subconscious fears and desires. Against the trends of auteur theory, films are regarded as the outcome not of an individual creativity, but of a team or social group. Since film needs a public, it addresses itself and appeals to a heteroge-neous mass audience whose desires it must satisfy. If filmmakers and their finan-cial backers then seek to correspond to the beliefs and values of their audiences, films can be considered as reflections of the mentality of a nation. By means of this convenient critical shift from film to society, the historical film in particu-lar can be viewed as a central component of the historical text that a society writes about itself, as a modern form of historiography that, if properly investi-gated, can disclose how a society conceives and exploits its past to construct its own present and future identities. The inadequacies of Kracauer's approach, however, are well documented. Such accounts of the relation between film and society tend to place most emphasis on the social and ideological contexts of film production and to overlook the specificities of the institution of cinema. But only a partial examination of the relation between film and society (or cin-ema and history) can be achieved if any sociological or psychoanalytic exami-nation of film texts is separated from the study of the technical and economic conditions of their production, the formation and development of their repre-sentational conventions, and the process of constructing and consuming their aesthetic pleasures.[24]

The Pleasures of the Look

The cinematic reconstructions of Roman history produced by the Italian and Hollywood film industries have always exceeded in function any imperative to make proprietarial claim on classical virtues and victories (or to question those claims). In the 1910s, for example, they were also utilized to legitimate cinema as a new art form and win international cultural prestige for their country of origin, in the 1930s to showcase commodities, and in the 1950s to combat tele-vision's assault on film industry profits. In all these respects and more, the pro-jection of ancient Rome on screen has often worked to place its spectators on the side of decadence and tyranny.

In the first decades of the twentieth century, a new generation of Italian entrepreneurs began to invest heavily in the production of films (as they had in the manufacture of automobiles and aeroplanes) in order to raise Italy to the ranks of the great industrial powers and to affirm for it a position of commercial prestige on foreign markets. As a result of capital investment, industrial com-petition, and the economic and aesthetic need to increase the artistic status and range of motion pictures, Italian films rapidly increased in length; developed their own formal strategies of editing and camera movement, staging, set design and special effects; dealt with more ambitious themes; and often filled the screen with huge numbers of extras and expensively produced spectacles to rival and outdo theatrical shows and the narrative scale of the novel. Feature-length film narratives set in antiquity, such as *Quo Vadis?* (1913) and *Cabiria* (1914), formed part of a strategy to win over the bourgeoisie to the new cinematic art-form by bestowing on the modern medium a grandiose register and an educative justification. Such films borrowed from the whole spectrum of nineteenth-century modes of historical representation (literary, dramatic, and pictorial) in pursuit of authenticity and authority for cinema as a mode of high culture, and to guarantee mass, international audiences through the reconstruction in moving images of familiar and accessible events of Roman history.[25]

In their search for intertexts that would be familiar to bourgeois spectators, however, Italian filmmakers did not confine themselves to the domestic narratives of ancient Rome available in the novels of Rafaello Giovagnoli or the tragedies of Pietro Cossa, but repeatedly adapted to screen the historical fictions of religious persecution which had permeated the popular literary imagination of nineteenth-century Europe, such as Lord Bulwer-Lytton's *The Last Days of Pompeii* (1834), Cardinal Wiseman's *Fabiola* (1854), or Henryk Sienkiewicz's *Quo Vadis?* (1895), although such fictions were now at odds with the secular *romanità* being promulgated by the liberal government. The commercial and critical success of such film adaptations, therefore, cannot be explained wholly in terms of nationalistic drives. Films like *Quo Vadis?* principally won domestic and international acclaim because they were capable of demonstrating the imaginative power of the cinematic mechanism at a time of virulent attack on the new medium. Putting into the present an exhibitionist spectacle of pomp and magnificence, of grand crowds and monumental architecture, of orgies, seductions, and sadistic martyrdoms, these extraordinarily costly historical reconstructions excited the voyeuristic look of their spectators and provoked the pleasure of gazing on the vividly realized vices and exoticisms of Rome's imperial villains.[26] Even the magnificently depicted scenes in *Cabiria* of child sacrifice in the gigantic Carthaginian temple of Moloch have been described as a double conquest— over the watching Romans within the film's narrative and over the film's external spectators. According to film critic Paolo Cherchi Usai:

> Heroes and enemies— . . . they may hesitate between the duty to defend their country and the temptation to yield to the impulses of luxury—but they are slaves to what they see: the power of the eye, in *Cabiria*, aspires to finality.
>
> The crucial theme of the film is, in this respect, the tragedy of the senses. The most fleeting of all, the look, makes palpable what cinema cannot offer to the touch: the perception of the dimensions of the royal palace's architecture, the movement of the armies beneath the gaze of the cinecamera Moloch, the sway of the figures knelt before the altar of the eternal fire. Demoniacal music accompanies the bloody scenes, the aroma of incense carries onto the film the odours of the temple. . . . For the first time cinema pretends to a total, definitive, conquest of the sensible world.[27]

Early Italian cinematic histories of Rome such as *Quo Vadis?* and *Cabiria* had been released in the United States to critical acclaim, obtained substantial box-office success, and achieved a significant influence over American film production in the years preceding the First World War. After the war, however, Hollywood studios began to standardize both the production and the consumption of their feature-length films according to the formalized codes of a new cinematic representational system now known customarily as "the classical Hollywood style," while nonetheless differentiating their products in accompanying publicity as both original and unique. The classical Hollywood style for representing history departed substantially from the mechanisms for the visualization of the collective that had driven the historical narratives of Italian cinema in the 1910s. Whereas in the earlier aesthetics of Italian silent cinema its protagonists had merged visually in space with the community and its heroes had acted in a socially structured landscape, the protagonists of the classical Hollywood narrative were more frequently isolated from the collective through the use of medium, close, and point-of-view shots and through their positioning in the center of the film frame. Emphasis was now placed on individuals whose psychological motivations were seen to cause historical action. Detached from their surroundings, associated with the personae of the stars who played them, no longer located in a strongly specified historical moment or a socially structured community, they were transformed into characters endowed with traits and in search of private fulfillment. The development, in the late 1920s, of the technologies of synchronized sound also led to a preference for presentist or contemporary film narratives. The protagonists of American sound films in the late 1920s and early 1930s, whether they were housewives, gangsters, newspaper tycoons, Roman emperors, or Ptolemaic queens, spoke in a dialogue that was grounded in the idioms of contemporary America.[28]

Hollywood's classical film style, the development of film technology, and the economic imperatives of the American film industry, all contributed to the privileging of both the individual and the present in the film narratives of the 1920s and 1930s. In a consumer-oriented economy, Hollywood films became showcases for the display of commodities; and the film studios, on the release of their products, encouraged the organization of merchandising tie-ins with other consumer industries. Through their displays of fashions, furnishings, accessories, and cosmetics, the interconnected institutions of cinema and the department store could train the view and orient the material aspirations of their consuming subjects.[29] Pressure was accordingly brought to bear on the studios by their marketing and sales management to produce films with contemporary themes, such as the popular social comedies directed by Cecil B. DeMille in the 1920s. Even films of Roman history, such as DeMille's *Cleopatra* (1934), were subjected to such marketing strategies and commodified—for the Egyptian queen was sold to female spectators in the form of "Cleopatra" gowns, perfumes, hairstyles, soaps, and cigarettes.[30]

The commodification of the past and the solicitation of a consumer gaze frequently generated a conflict between the diegesis and the visual style of films set in antiquity. Thus *Roman Scandals* (1933), the musical comedy which Gore Vidal was forbidden to see, troped imperial Rome in two distinct and antithetical ways. The film's narrative drive abandons any satisfying equation between American society and the civic virtues of republican Rome to present instead an hyperbolic articulation of the Depression's socio-economic problems, where bankers become emperors and the poor dispossessed slaves. In a pointed, populist message, imperial Rome stands in for the corruption and injustice of 1930s America.[31] Yet embedded in this narrative of social protest is a musical sequence that is quite at odds with it. Directed by Busby Berkeley, the elaborate production number is set in the women's baths of the imperial court at Rome, where the hero Eddie (in order to keep up his disguise) is compelled to sing advice to the female slaves on how to "Keep Young and Beautiful." Through the similarity of the women's appearance, and through Berkeley's repetitive choreography and rigid editing, the dancing girls are dismembered into body parts—thighs, nails, lips, hair, and eyes—all of which require attentive cosmetic care, according to the song's lyrics, "if you want to be loved." For the consuming female spectators at this point, imperial Rome no longer stands for corruption and tyranny but for luxury, eroticism, and a glamour available for purchase at their local department store.[32]

Even the godly historical epics produced in the Cold War era, such as *Quo Vadis* (1951), *The Robe* (1953), *Demetrius and the Gladiators* (1954), and *Ben-Hur* (1959), commodified their religious narratives. A substantial part of the enormous profit made by the MGM studio out of their second screen adaptation of General Lew Wallace's nineteenth-century novel, for example, came from the sale of associated "Ben-Hur" merchandise such as toy swords, helmets and armor, model chariots, wallpaper, jewelry, sandals, and even raincoats and umbrellas.[33] Part of the motivation for the production of such historical epics and their deliberate link with the pleasures of shopping lay in Hollywood's economic need to recoup the severe loss of earnings it had experienced in the early 1950s as a result of the competition of television for cinema's audiences. Hollywood's fight against television was conducted as "a duel of screens," in terms of the size of the budget and the size of the image. [34] The industry invested heavily in the technological novelties of Technicolor, widescreen, and stereophonic sound, which it considered necessary to recapture the market, and privileged for big-budget production genres such as the musical, the adventure film, the Western, and the historical epic as, those whose narratives were most capable of accommodating and naturalizing the new emphasis on stylization and ostentatious spectacle.[35]

Grand enough to fill the screen, lavish historical films about the rise of Christianity played a decisive role in Hollywood's battle to reconquer a mass audience during the 1950s. Such epics, as the film theorist Stephen Neale has observed in his discussion of genre, readily supplied many opportunities for cinematic exhibitionism and spectatorial scopophilia.[36] Exotic locations, extravagant sets, colorful decor and costumes, spectacular action (chariot races, gladiatorial combats, Christian martyrdoms, military parades and battles), overwhelming visual effects, and conspicuous costs were all available to the astonished gaze of both the films' internal and external spectators.[37] The films' narratives were also thought capable of matching their spectacle in scale and appeal, offering subjects that were prestigious yet familiar, seemly uncontroversial, educational, spiritually uplifting, and of immense relevance to conservative America's self-portrayal during the Cold War era as the defender of the Faith against the godlessness of Communism.[38] Thus *The Robe* (1953), the first film to be launched in a widescreen format, was based on a vastly popular religious novel published in 1942 by the Congregational minister Lloyd C. Douglas. His account of the conversion of a Roman soldier to Christianity (after witnessing the Crucifixion and coming into contact with Christ's discarded robe) had been immediately bought up by the film producer Frank Ross for its strong market potential. According to an article in *The Tidings* of 27 January 1950, Ross had anticipated that a wartime adaptation to screen of a conflict between Roman decadence and Christian purity would present a parallel with the persecutions currently being instigated by Hitler and Mussolini. Still unmade as a film in 1950, the critic of *The Tidings* suggested an even more pressing parallel now available to the novel's supposedly reluctant adaptors:

> It is easy to appreciate that Mr. Ross and his collaborators were brought to a complete stop when the lights later changed to red and one whom they had regarded as an ally of Democracy became the greatest modern despot of them all.
>
> If, however, there was anything to the idea of extending the Douglas novel into modern parallels. it would seem that the Hollywood dramatists now had more. to go on than ever before. For at last the great struggle between Christ and anti-Christ had been joined, not merely upon political levels but upon the fundamental level of religion also.

When, however, the widescreen version of *The Robe* was finally released by 20th Century-Fox in 1953, in its production, distribution, and reception as much (if not more) attention was paid to its technical virtuosity as to its political parallels with the present. The intense spectacle of CinemaScope threatened to eclipse the film's pious religious narrative in celebration of Hollywood's newly enlarged film frame. In particular, the opening sequence of *The Robe* has been described by Bruce Babington and Peter Evans in *Biblical Epics: Sacred Narrative in the Hollywood Cinema* (1993) as an ultra-dramatic rendering of this moment of technological history in which dark red curtains open in a slow movement to reveal an ever-increasing panoramic spectacle of ancient Rome to the astonished viewer.[39] The self-reflexive invitation of *The Robe* to enter into a newly extended screen space was met with extraordinary enthusiasm at the time of the film's release. A review in *Time* magazine for 28 September 1953, for example, stated admiringly that

> *The Robe* would have been a good movie in two-dimensional black and white. In CinemaScope, which uses a wide-angle lens to throw its picture on a curved screen nearly three times the normal width, it all but overpowers the eye with spectacular movie murals of slave markets, imperial cities, grandiose palaces and panoramic landscapes that arc neither distorted nor require the use of polarized glasses. In CinemaScope closeups, the actors are so big that an average adult could stand erect in Victor Mature's car, and its four-directional sound track often rises to a crescendo loud enough to make moviegoers feel as though they were locked in a bell tower during the Angelus. Obviously, Hollywood has finally found something louder, more colorful and breathtakingly bigger than anything likely to be seen on a home TV screen for years to come.

The Roman historical epics of the 1950s provided a site for the display of the new technologies developed by the Hollywood film industry to rival and outdo television in the pleasure of the look, but what excited that look and drew spectators back into cinemas was as much the widescreen wickedness of the Romans as the piety of their Christian victims. As Michael Wood has argued, despite casting Christians as the diegetic heroes, such Cold War films visually celebrated their Roman oppressors:

> All these stories invite our sympathy for the oppressed, of course—all the more so because we know that by generously backing these losers we shall find we have backed winners in the end. But then the movies, themselves, as costly studio productions, plainly take the other side. They root for George III against the founding fathers, they are all for tyranny and Rome, more imperialist than the emperor. The great scenes in these films, the reasons for our being in the cinema at all—the orgies, the triumphs, the gladiatorial games—all belong to the oppressors. The palaces, the costumes, the pomp . . . are all theirs. It is the Romans who provide the circuses, who give us a Rome to be gaudily burned. It is Nero and the Pharaohs who throw the parties with all the dancing girls.[40]

The pleasures of looking were accentuated by CinemaScope, while the money and labor invested in the manufacture of those pleasures were self-consciously paraded within the widescreen epics and in the extra-cinematic discourses generated around the films' production and exhibition. Unprecedented press, radio, and television coverage, for example, constantly attended the making of *The Robe* and its extravagant worldwide premieres. Its initial screening at the Roxy in New York, on 16 September 1953, was held in a carnival atmosphere, while king-sized searchlights played over the arrival of huge numbers of invited guests and the vast crowds assembled to catch a glimpse of them.[41] Both on and off screen, Hollywood celebrated its capacities to duplicate the splendors of the past. Thus, again in the words of Michael Wood, Hollywood's histories of Rome became "a huge, many-faceted metaphor for Hollywood itself."[42] The reconstruction on screen and exhibition of ancient Rome came to stand for Hollywood's own fantastic excess—its technological and aesthetic innovations, its grandeur and glamour, its ostentation, and the lavishness of its expenditure and consumption. And spectators of Hollywood's widescreen epics were invited to position themselves not only as pure Christians but also as Romans luxuriating in a surrender to the splendors of film spectacle itself.[43]

Case Studies

The projection of ancient Rome on screen has functioned not only as a mechanism for the display or interrogation of national identities but also, and often in contradiction, as a mechanism for the display of cinema itself—its technical capacities and its cultural value. One way, therefore, to interrogate films about ancient Rome is to examine their intersection with the national, political, economic, and cultural identities of the communities in which they are produced while, at the same time, exploring the ways such films reformulate those identities in specifically cinematic terms, building up their own historiographic conventions of style, address, and aesthetic pleasure.[44]

. . . .

According to the historian David Lowenthal:

> The past remains integral to us all, individually and collectively. We must concede the ancients their place . . . . But their place is not simply back there, in a separate and foreign country; it is assimilated in ourselves, and resurrected into an ever-changing present.[45]

The aim of [my book *Projecting the Past*] is to explore, through the consideration of some notable cinematic representations of ancient Rome, the place of antiquity in twentieth-century mass culture. Within the institutions of cinema, ancient Rome performs its own specific operations and that those operations are not uniform. The Roman films so frequently manufactured in the United States and Italy demonstrate a considerable variety and discontinuity in their narrations of Roman history, in the rapport they establish between the Roman past and the present moment of its cinematic reconstruction, in the cultural competences on which the films draw, and in the aesthetic pleasures of historical reconstruction which they offer their disparate audiences. Ancient Rome has been constantly reinvented to suit new technologies for its cinematic narration and new historical contexts for the interpretation of the Roman past in the present. *Projecting the Past* thus aims to disclose the rich variety of functions Roman historical films have had in twentieth-century culture and the diversity of readings of ancient Rome they have offered their millions of spectators.

NOTES

1. Cf. Roberta A. Pearson and William Uricchio, "How Many Times Shall Caesar Bleed in Sport: Shakespeare and the Cultural Debate About Moving Pictures," *Screen* 31:3 (1990), 243–44.

2. Eric Hobsbawm and Terence Ranger, *The Invention of Tradition* (Cambridge: Cambridge University Press, 1983). They locate the proliferation of such "invented traditions" specifically in the period between 1870 and 1914. Cf. David Lowenthal, *The Past is a Foreign Country* (Cambridge: Cambridge University Press, 1985), 35–73.

3. Hobsbawm and Ranger, *The Invention of Tradition*, 279–80; Meyer Reinhold, *Classica Americana: The Greek and Roman Heritage in the United States* (Detroit: Wayne University Press, 1984); Peter Bondanella, *The Eternal City: Roman Images in the Modern World* (Chapel Hill and London: University of North Carolina Press, 1987), 115–50; William L. Vance, *America's Rome. Volume 1: Classical Rome* (New Haven: Yale University Press, 1989), esp. 1–42; Carl J. Richard, *The Founders and the Classics: Greece, Rome, and the American Enlightenment* (Cambridge, Mass.: Harvard University Press, 1994), 12–84.

4. Kennedy postscript in Reinhold, *Classica Americana*; William L. Vance, "The Colosseum: American Uses of an Imperial Image." In *Roman Images. Selected Papers from the English Institute n.s.8*, ed. Annabel Patterson (Baltimore: Johns Hopkins University Press, 1984); Bondanella, *The Eternal City*, 152–71; Karl Galinsky, *Classical and Modern Interactions: Post-*

modern Architecture, Multiculturalism, Decline and Other Issues (Austin: University of Texas Press, 1992), esp. 53–73; Richard, *The Founders and the Classics*, 85–122.

5. Vance, *America's Rome*, esp. 30–67; Theodore Ziolkowski, *Virgil and the Moderns* (Princeton: Princeton University Press, 1993), 146–93; David Mayer, *Playing Out the Empire: "Ben-Hur" and Other Toga Plays and Films, 1883–1908. A Critical Anthology* (Oxford: Clarendon Press, 1994), 1–20.

6. See Mayer, *Playing Out the Empire*, 189–290, which includes a script of the play. Cf. Jon Solomon, *The Ancient World and the Cinema* (South Brunswick, N.J.: A. S. Barnes, 1978), 126–34; Foster Hirsch, *The Hollywood Epic* (South Brunswick, N.J.: A. S. Barnes, 1978), 105–12; Derek Elley, *The Epic Film: Myth and History* (London: Routledge, 1984), 130–35; Gary A. Smith, *Epic Films: Casts, Credits and Commentary over 250 Historical Spectacle Movies* (Jefferson: McFarland and Co., 1991), 22–27; Bruce Babington and Peter William Evans, *Biblical Epics: Sacred Narrative in the Hollywood Cinema* (Manchester: Manchester University Press, 1993), esp. 177–205.

7. Lowenthal, *The Past is a Foreign Country*, 112–16.

8. Clara M. Lovett, *The Democratic Movement in Italy 1830–1876* (Cambridge, Mass.: Harvard University Press, 1982), 20; Carolyn Springer, *The Marble Wilderness: Ruins and Representation in Italian Romanticism, 1775–1850* (Cambridge: Cambridge University Press, 1987), esp. 65–74 and 136–57; Bondanella, *The Eternal City*, 158–65.

9. Quoted in Ranger, *The Invention of Tradition*, 267.

10. As Furio Lopez-Celly, *Il romanzo storico in Italia: dai prescottiani alle odierne vite romanzate* (Bologna: Licinio Cappelli-Editore, 1939), 212–16. Cf. Benedetto Croce, *La letteratura della nuova Italia. Volume 2* (Bari: Laterzi, 1914), 152–57; Giovanni Calendoli, *Materiali per una storia del cinema italiano* (Parma: Edizioni Maccari, 1967), 70–4; Piero de Tommaso, *Nievo e altri studi sul romanzo storico* (Padua: Liviana Editrice, 1975), 110; Giuseppe Ghigi, "Come si spiegano le fortune del 'pepla' su cui sembra che torni a puntare," *Cineforum* 17:2 (1977), 733; Giorgio de Vincenti, "Il kolossal storico-romano nell'immaginario del primo Novecento," *Bianco e Nero* 49:1 (1988), 12–14; Gian Piero Brunetta, *Storia del cinema italiano: il ciinema muto 1895–1929. Volume 1* (Rome: Editori Riuniti, 1993; first edition published in 1979), 151–57; Stefania Parigi, "La rievocazione dell'antico." In *Gli ultimi giorni di Pompei*, ed. Riccardo Redi (Naples: La Macchina dei Sogni A. C. and Electa Napoli, 1994), 67–69.

11. Bondanella, *The Eternal City*, 165–66, discusses the significance of the postcard. See, more generally, on pre-Fascist *romanità*, Anthony Cubberley, ed. *Rodolfo Lanciani: Notes from Rome* (Rome: British School at Rome, 1988), xii; Mariella Cagnetta, *Antichisti e impero fascista* (Bari: Dedalo Libri, 1979), 15–34; Luciano Canfora, *Ideologie del classicismo* (Turin: Piccola Biblioteca Einaudi, 1980), 39–40; Romke Visser, "Fascist Doctrine and the Cult of the Romanità," *Journal of Contemporary History* 27 (1992), 7–8; Claude Moatti, *In Search of Ancient Rome*, trans. Anthony Zielonka (London: Thames and Hudson, 1993; first published 1989), 128; Maria Wyke, "Make Like Nero! The Appeal of a Cinematic Empoeror." In *Reflections of Nero: Culture, History and Representation*, ed. Jas Elsner and Jamie Masters (London: Duckworth, 1994), 16.

12. See, for example, Gian Piero Brunetta, "L'évocation du passé. Les années d'or du film historique." In *Le cinéma italien de La Prise de Rome (1905) à Rome ville ouverte (1945)*, ed. Aldo Bernardini and Jean L. Gili (Paris: Centre Georges Pompidou, 1986), 57; Gian Piero Brunetta, "No Place Like Rome: The Early Years of Italian Cinema," *Artforum* Summer (1990), 123; Gian Piero Brunetta, *Cent'anni di cinema italiano* (Rome: Editori Laterza, 1991), 64–65; Brunetta, *Storia del cinema italiano*, 143–46.

13. James Hay, *Popular Film Culture in Fascist Italy: The Passing of the Rex* (Bloomington: Indiana University Press, 1987), 12–13 and 151–52. Cf. more generally on the social function of early American cinema, John Belton, *Widescreen Cinema* (Cambridge, Mass.: Harvard University Press, 1992), 31–32; Pearson and Uricchio, "How Many Times Shall Caesar Bleed," 260–61; Sumiko Higashi, *Cecil B. DeMille and American Culture: The Silent Era* (Berkeley: University of California Press, 1994), 28.

14. Brunetta, *Cent'anni di cinema italiano*, 64–65, and Gian Piero Brunetta, "Filogensi artistica e letteraria del primo cinema italiano." In *Sperudo nel buio: il cinema muto italiano e il suo tempo (1905–1930)*, ed. Renzo Renzi (Bologna: Cappelli Editore, 1991), 13–16; Aldo Bernardini, *Ciniema muto italiano. Volume 3: Arte, divismo e mercato 1910–1914* (Rome-Bari: Editori Laterza, 1982), 34, and (1986), 34–40; Massimo Cardillo, *Tra le quinte del cinematografo: cinema, cultura e società in Italia 1900–1937* (Bari: Edizioni Dedalo, 1987), 25–37; Monica dall'Asta, *Un cinéma musclé: le surhomme dans le cinéma muet italien (1913–1926)*, trans. from Italian by Franco Arnò and Charles Tatum, Jr. (Belgium: Éditions Yellow Now-Banlieues, 1992), 19–20. Cf. Maria Wyke, "Cinema and the City of the Dead: Reel Histories of Pompeii." In *New Scholarship from BFI Research*, ed. Colin MacCabe and Duncan Petrie (London: British Film Institute, 1996), 143 and Maria Wyke, "Herculean Muscle! The Classicizing Rhetoric of Bodybuilding," *Arion* 4:3 (1997).

15. Roberto Paolella, *Storia del cinema muto* (Naples: Giannini, 1956), 166–70; Calendoli, *Materiali per una storia del cinema italiano;* John Cary, *Spectacular! The Story of Epic Films* (London: Hamlyn, 1974), 7–9; Derek Elley, *The Epic Film*, 81–84; Paolo Cherchi Usai, *Giovanni Pastrone. Il castoro cinema 119* (Florence: La Nuova Italia, 1985); Bondanella, *The Eternal City*, 207–208; Pierre Leprohon, *The Italian Cinema*, trans. Roger Greaves and Oliver Stallybrass (London: Secker and Warburg, 1972), 30; dall'Asta, *Un cinéma musclé*, 20–32; Angela Dalle Vacche, *The Body in the Mirror: Shapes of History in Italian Cinema* (Princeton: Princeton University Press, 1992), 27–52; Mayer, *Playing Out the Empire*, 312–14. Contrast Parigi, "La rievocazione dell'antico," 69, who argues that *Cabiria* is not designed to express a colonialist nationalism.

16. Quoted and translated in Bondanella, *The Eternal City*, 176.

17. Cagnetta, *Antichisti e impero fascista;* Canfora, *Ideologie del classicismo*, 76–146; Bondanella, *The Eternal City*, 181–206; Emily Braun, "Political Rhetoric and Poetic Irony: The Uses of Classicism in the Art of Fascist Italy." In *On Classical Ground: Picasso, Léger, de Chirico and the New Classicism 1910–1930*, ed. Elizabeth Cowling and Jennifer Mundy (London: Tate Gallery Publications, 1990), 345–348; Visser, "Fascist Doctrine and the Cult of the Romanità"; Ziolkowski, *Virgil and the Moderns*, 15–17; Moatti, *In Search of Ancient Rome*, 130–40; Benton (1995); Simonetta Fraquelli, "All Roads Lead to Rome." In *Art and Power: Europe Under the Dictators 1930–1945. Hayward Gallery Exhibition Catalogue*, ed. Dawn Ades, Tim Benton, David Elliott, and Iain Boyd Whyte (Manchester: Cornerhouse Publications, 1995), 130–136.

18. Cardillo, *Tra le quinte del cinematografo*, 158–62; Bondanella, *The Eternal City*, 210–3; Gianfranco Miro Gori, *Patria diva: la storia d'Italia nei film del ventennio* (Florence: La Casa Usher, 1988), 16–25; Jean A. Gili, "I film dell'Impero fascista." In Gian Piero Brunetta and Jean A. Gili, *L'ora d'Africa del cinema italiano 1911–1989* (Trent: LaGrafica-Mori, 1990), 39–112; Dalle Vacche, *The Body in the Mirror*, 27–52, Louisa Quartermaine, "'Slouching Towards Rome': Mussolini's Imperial Vision." In *Urban Society in Roman Italy*, ed. T. J. Cornell and Kathryn Lomas (London: University College Press, 1995), 203–215; Lutz Becker, "Black Shirts and White Telephones." In Ades, et. al., eds., *Art and Power* (1995), 137–139.

19. See Gili, *L'ora d'Africa del cinema italiano*, 4–7, and Quartermaine, "'Slouching Towards Rome,'" 205–206.

20. Cardillo, *Tra le quinte del cinematografo*, 153; Gili, *L'ora d'Africa del cinema italiano*, 99; Quartermaine, "'Slouching Towards Rome,'" 206–207.

21. Michael Wood, *America in the Movies: Or "Santa Maria, It Had Slipped My Mind"* (London: Secker and Warburg, 1975), 184.

22. Cf. Higashi, *Cecil B. DeMille and American Culture*, 202–203, and Alan Nadel, "God's Law and the Wide Screen: *The Ten Commandments* as Cold War 'Epic,'" *Publications of the Modern Languages Association of America* 108:3 (1993), 415–30 on Cecil B. DeMille's *The Ten Commandments* (1956). On the parallels with the present at work in *Ben-Hur* (1959), especially regarding the foundation of Israel, see Babington and Evans *Biblical Epics*, 201–202.

23. Babington and Evans *Biblical Epics*, 210–13.

24. For discussion of Kracauer's work, see Andrew Bergman, *We're in the Money: Depression America and Its Films* (New York: New York University Press, 1971), xiii–xvi; Denys

Arcand, "The Historical Film: Acutal and Virtual," *Cultures* 2:1 (1974), 22; Pierre Sorlin, *The Film in History: Restaging the Past* (Oxford: Blackwell, 1980), 25–26; Thomas Elsaesser, "Film History and Visual Pleasure." In *Cinema Histories, Cinema Practices*, ed. Patricia Mellencamp and Philip Rosen (University Publications of America, *American Film Institute Monograph Series* 4, 1984), 47–84; Robert C. Allen and Douglas Gomery, *Film History: Theory and Practice* (New York: McGraw Hill, 1985), 159–67; Terry Christensen, *Reel Politics: American Political Movies from Birth of a Nation to Platoon* (Oxford: Blackwell, 1987), 6–7; Peppino Ortoleva, *Cinema e storia: scene dal passato* (Turin: Loescher Editore, 1991), 43–53, and Peppino Ortoleva, "Testimone infallibile, macchina dei sogni: il film e il programma televisivo come fonte storica." In *La storia al cinema: ricostruzione del passato, interpretazione del presente*, ed. Gianfranco Miro Gori (Rome: Bulzoni Editore, 1994), 319–28.

25. Ernest Lindgren, "1908–1914: The Years of the Industrial Revolution," *Bianco e Nero* 1–2 (1963), 14–17, Calendoli, *Materiali per una storia del cinema italiano*, 70–74; Solomon, *The Ancient World and the Cinema*, 15–16; Aldo Bernardini, "Le cinéma muet italien, étapes et tendances." In Aldo and Gili, eds., *Le cinéma italien de La Prise de Rome*, 35–40, de Vincenti, "Il kolossal storico-romano nell'immaginario del primo Novecento," 8–10, Brunetta, "Filogensi artistica e letteraria del primo cinema italiano," 14–15; dall'Asta, *Un cinéma musclé*, 19–20. On the comparative development of American feature-length films see, for example, Alan Gevinson, "The Birth of the American Feature Film." In *Sulla via di Hollywood 1911–1920*, ed. Paolo Cherchi Usai and Lorenzo Codelli (Pordenone: Edizioni Biblioteca dell'Immagine, 1988), 146–50; Pearson and Uricchio, "How Many Times Shall Caesar Bleed"; Higashi, *Cecil B. DeMille and American Culture*, 1–33.

26. dall'Asta, *Un cinéma musclé*, 31–32; Parigi, "La rievocazione dell'antico," 67–69.

27. Usai, *Giovanni Pastrone*, 54–55.

28. On the classical Hollywood style see, for example, David Bordwell, Janet Staiger, and Kristin Thompson, *The Classical Hollywood Style: Film Style and Mode of Production to 1960* (London: Routledge, 1985), esp. 1–308; Janet Staiger, "Mass-produced Photoplays: Economic and Signifying Practices in the First Years of Hollywood." In *The Hollywood Film Industry*, ed. Paul Kerr (London: Routledge and Kegan Paul, 1986), 97–99; John Izod, *Hollywood and the Box Office 1895–1986* (Hampshire: Macmillan Press, 1988), 53–57 and 86–87; Barry Salt, "Il cinema italiano dalla nascita alla Grande Guerra: un'analisi stilistica." In Renzo Renzi, ed., *Sperudo nel buio*, 49–54; Leger Grindon, *Shadows of the Past: Studies in the Historical Fiction Film* (Philadelphia: Temple University Press, 1994), 16–22.

29. Charles Eckert, "The Carole Lombard in Macy's Window," *Quarterly Review of Film Studies* 3:1 (1978), 1–21; Jeanne Allen, "The Film Viewer as Consumer," *Quarterly Review of Film Studies* 5:4 (1980), 481–99. Mary Ann Doane, "The Economy of Desire: The Commodity Form In/of the Cinema," *Quarterly Review of Film and Video* 11 (1989), 22–33; Jane Gaines, "The Queen Christina Tie-ups: Convergence of Show Window and Screen," *Quarterly Review of Film and Video* 11 (1989), 35–60; Jane Gaines and Charlotte Herzog, eds., *Fabrications: Costume and the Female Body* (New York: Routledge, 1990); Jackie Stacey, *Star Gazing: Hollywood Cinema and Female Spectatorship* (London: Routledge, 1994), 176–223.

30. Lary May, *Screening Out the Past: The Birth of Mass Culture and the Motion Picture Industry* (Chicago: Unviersity of Chicago Press, 1980), 200–236; Izod, *Hollywood and the Box Office 1895–1986*, 64–67 and 101–104; Mary Hamer, *Signs of Cleopatra: Histories, Politics, Representation* (London: Routledge, 1993), 118 and 121–22; Higashi, *Cecil B. DeMille and American Culture*, esp. 142–78.

31. Richard J. Thompson and William D. Routt, "'Keep Young and Beautiful': Surplus and Subversion in Roman Scandals." In *History on/and/in Film. Selected Papers from the Third Australian History and Film Conference*, ed. Tom O'Regan and Brian Shoesmith (Preth: History and film Association of Australia, 1987), 35–36.

32. Thompson and Routt "'Keep Young and Beautiful,'" 36–43.

33. Solomon, *The Ancient World and the Cinema*, 134. Sample advertisements for such "Ben-Hur" products are to be found in MGM's campaign books which were sent to theater managers to supply ideas for selling the film.

34. Christopher Wood, *Olympian Dreamers: Victorian Classical Painters 1860–1914* (London: Constable, 1971), 169.

35. Stephen Neale, *Genre* (London: British Film Institute, 1983), 34–36; Bordwell, Staiger, and Thompson *The Classical Hollywood Style*, 353–64; Belton, *Widescreen Cinema*, esp. 183–210.

36. Neale, *Genre*, 35. Cf. dall'Asta, *Un cinéma musclé*, 31–32.

37. Penelope Houston and John Gillett, "The Theory and Practice of Blockbusting," *Sight and Sound* 32 (1963), 68–74; Wood, *America in the Movies*, 165–80; Robert Sklar, *Movie Made America: A Cultural History of American Movies* (New York: Vintage, 1975), 294–96; Hirsch, *The Hollywood Epic*, 29, Gianni Rondolino, *Vittorio Cottafavi: cinema e televisione* (Bologna: Cappelli Editore, 1980), 65, Neale, *Genre*, 34–36; Belton, *Widescreen Cinema*; Babington and Evans *Biblical Epics*, 6–8.

38. Cf. on the Cold War rhetoric of Cecil B. DeMille's *The Ten Commandments* (1956), Stephen J. Whitfield, *The Culture of the Cold War* (Baltimore: Johns Hopkins University Press, 1991), 218–19; Nadel, "God's Law and the Wide Screen"; Higashi, *Cecil B. DeMille and American Culture*, 202–203.

39. Babington and Evans *Biblical Epics*, 207. Cf. Belton, *Widescreen Cinema*, 190–91.

40. Wood, *America in the Movies*, 184–85. Cf. Belton, *Widescreen Cinema*, 194–95; dall'Asta, *Un cinéma musclé*, 31–32.

41. See, for example, *Variety* and the *Los Angeles Times* for 17 September 1953.

42. Wood, *America in the Movies*, 173.

43. Houston and Gillett, "The Theory and Practice of Blockbusting"; Wood, *America in the Movies*, 168–73; Neale, *Genre*, 34–36; dall'Asta, *Un cinéma musclé*, 31–32; Belton, *Widescreen Cinema*, 210.

44. Cf. Andrew Higson, "The Concept of National Cinema," *Screen* 30:4 (1989), 42–43, on strategies for the analysis of "national" cinema, and Pearson and Uricchio, "How Many Times Shall Caesar Bleed," 243–44, on strategies for the analysis of Shakespeare on screen.

45. Lowenthal, *The Past is a Foreign Country*, 412.

Marcia Landy

"You Remember Diana Dors, Don't You?" History, Femininity, and the Law in 1950s and 1980s British Cinema

In describing her "love" for the film *Berserk* (1967), Candy Darling (who was sometimes referred to by friends in Greenwich Village as "Diana Doorways") comments: "Diana Dors was in it and she was sawed in half. You remember Diana Dors, don't you? She was England's answer to Jayne Mansfield. Oh you remember a real cheap looking tomatoe [sic] with a tremendous bust, platinumized hair, big lips on a hard trashy face."[1] Allowing for Candy's reconstruction and interpretation of this image, what is significant about this description is its singling out of the star's physical measurements and especially her platinum blonde hair, features rarely associated with British cinema, conjuring up other star images: Jayne Mansfield, Marilyn Monroe, Mamie Van Doren, and before them Jean Harlow and Mae West. One way of disturbing official history and of capturing elusive conceptions of popular memory is by rethinking the historicality of such images and how they resonate and circulate throughout the culture. Candy's comments also invoke the phenomenon of stardom as embedded in a dynamic appropriation of popular history. The interfaces between stardom and value production are located in the heterogeneous, seemingly dissimilar ways in which images as products circulate throughout the culture at many levels and at great speed, revealing the protean, mobile, affective, and effective nature of capital through the forms of its cultural commodities.

Gayatri Spivak has lamented the persistent binary opposition between the economic and the cultural, an opposition

> so deeply entrenched that the full implications of the question of value posed in terms of the "materialist" predication of the subject are difficult to conceptualize. . . . The best that one can envision is the persistent undoing of the opposition, taking into account that fact that, first, the complicity between cultural and economic value-systems is acted out in almost every decision we make; and, secondly,

that economic reductionism is, indeed, a very real danger. It is a paradox that capitalist humanism does indeed tacitly make its plans by the "materialist" predication of Value, even as its official ideology disavows the discourse of humanism as such.[2]

In tracing this complicity between economic and cultural phenomena, questions of subjectivity and affect shed light on the creation, perpetuation, and transformation of value that cannot be measured solely in terms of a cash nexus. Cultural discourses are saturated with affect, circulating seemingly independent of the marketplace. Affective representation is closely tied to social representations that circulate knowledge involving sexuality, gender, and national identity.

The star is a major current in the circuitry of the creation, assignment, and perpetuation of value. The income produced by stars, producers, theater owners, distributors, and exhibitors is the most visible manifestation of the cultural value of economic production. Accounting for the complex character of cultural artifacts as commodities has always been elusive, for as Marx reminds us: "At first glance, a commodity seems a commonplace sort of thing, one easily understood. Analysis shows, however, that it is a very queer thing indeed, full of metaphysical subtleties and theological whimsies."[3] "Subtleties" and "theological whimsies" inhere in the ways value is assigned to the commodity, since "value does not wear an explanatory label. Far from it, value changes all labour products into social hieroglyphs. Subsequently, people try to decipher these hieroglyphs to solve the riddle of their own social product—for the specification of a useful object as a value is just as much a social product as language is."[4] Thus the commodity form functions to occlude the nature of social relations, focusing attention on the concreteness of the commodity itself and concealing the conceptual quality of the creation and perpetuation of value. The "magic of money" is the general measure of value, but the money form of commodities "is distinct from their palpable or real bodily form. It is . . . only an ideal or imaginary form."[5] Marx's concept of fetishism is crucial for an unraveling of the mystery attached to commodity relations. The relation to the commodity is a form of enchantment whereby objects are divorced from social relations and from history, appearing to be part of the natural order of things, sundering mental from physical labor and underestimating and misrepresenting the affective work involved in the construction and maintenance of the value. Marx's concept of fetishism thus provides clues to the indirect and subjective, not merely quantitative and objective, ways in which value functions historically.

Following Marx, Gramsci asks, "How, in the system of social relations, will one be able to distinguish the element 'technique,' 'work,' 'class,' etc., understood in an historical and not in a metaphysical sense?"[6] Gramsci is at pains to locate the affective investment in social and political phenomena, and in so doing he offers clues about the character of affect in his discussion of common sense, art, and intellectuals. In revising historical materialism, Gramsci valorizes "a certain level of culture, by which we mean a complex of intellectual acts and as a product and consequence of these, a certain complex of overriding passion and feelings, overriding in the sense that they have the power to lead men on to action 'at any price.'"[7] Gramsci's uniting of intellect and feeling suggests that he is aware that affect plays a role not as an excrescence but as a fundamental factor in commodity production. His conception of common sense as folklore signals the intricate ways that affect can be regarded as a commodity that circulates and as a basis for ensuring the "fetishistic character of commodity production."

The affective (and historical) dimensions of sexuality and femininity in relation to the family, gender, property, and the law are inextricable from more complex considerations of legality and the state than the traditional notions of relations between base and superstructure, quantified labor and surplus value. The importance of historicizing remains fundamental to this process insofar as an understanding of the dynamics of change helps to track the various ways in which the production of value is constantly on the move but everywhere discernible.

The dependence of melodrama on binarism—femininity versus masculinity, victimization versus domination—and on a scenario of anticipated justice, with its confidence in the law and its obsession with the reproduction of the family, is inextricable from the question of feminine sexuality, and feminine sexuality is inextricable from the personifications of the forces involved in the struggle to sentimentalize "ethics . . . in the working out of poetic justice."[8] Working through the medium of melodrama, the star/diva personality is an embodiment of economic forces and of social forces and the carrier of an all-important affect that serves to guarantee the materiality, legitimacy, and credibility of the represented conflicts. In situating discussions of stardom within the context of melodrama's role in cultural commodification and value construction, it becomes clear that the univalent statement that stardom is the top-down creation of demonic and unscrupulous industry executives is inadequate to account for its popularity. Stardom is a complex mode of production and reception. Like production generally, the creation of this commodity entails manufacture, distribution, consumption, reproduction, and recycling, all of which are dependent on a close affiliation with prevailing hegemonic discourses, especially in relation to affective value's role in the process not as excrescence or superstructure but as the heart of cultural creations. The importance of affect in the determination of value construction lies in its revealing the interested and constitutive, rather than innocent and essential, character of subjectivity. As a person in drag, Candy Darling offers an incisive insight into the multivalent aspects of economics, gender, and sexuality, into their asymmetrical relations to each other, and into the forms of historicizing in the interpolation of subjectivity. Darling writes: "I am not a genuine woman but I am not interested in genuineness. I'm interested in the product of being a woman and how qualified I am. The product of the system is important. If the product fails, then the system is no good. . . . The main thing is will I benefit from it."[9] This passage could have been written by a "genuine" woman but its importance lies in exposing genuineness, in linking sexuality and gender to production, and in highlighting the complex nature of the value associated with this production.

This chapter examines the case of Ruth Ellis, the last woman to be executed in England, who was put to death in 1955 for the murder of her lover, David Blakely. This case—the subject of several books, numerous newspaper articles, and a 1985 film, *Dance with a Stranger*, orchestrates questions relating to the power and the circulation and appropriation of star images to questions of femininity, sexuality, and social class. The particular problem raised in this type of investigation involves a reading of popular history that integrates rather than disjoins the workings of history and modes of popular representation, especially in relation to femininity. The star is not the reflection of externalized social forces, nor is subjectivity the determinant of representations. Representations are the subject and object of history.

In tracing the forms of melodrama, their expression through particular stars, and their specific connection to the case of Ruth Ellis, I concentrate on the star persona of Diana Dors. A British film and television star, Diana Dors was the incarnation of a familiar and popular version of what has been variously called the "blonde sexpot," "blonde Venus," and "blonde sinner." The role she played in the social problem film *Yield to the Night* (1956), which was identified both with Ruth Ellis's plight and with Dors's narrative of her own rise to stardom, sheds light on the direct and indirect bonds between stars and their audiences. I discuss the brief "stardom" of Ruth Ellis, her reincarnation in the press and in the cinema, its connections to the Dors persona, its representation in *Yield to the Night*, and its re-creation in *Dance with a Stranger*. I also examine the social problem film as a conduit through which melodramatic affect flows, generating value in cultural and economic terms in the post–World War II era. Further, I examine the social problem film as a new medium for melodrama and stardom and the relation of both to emerging social discourses that address criminal transgression and juridical discourses central to an understanding of the circulation of affective value through femininity.

Remembering Diana Dors

Photos of Ruth Ellis reveal an image very like the one of Diana Dors described by Candy Darling:

> The star of the show, Ruth Ellis, was brought from the cells. All eyes turned to the wooden dock as she entered. Many of the public were surprised at what they saw. Instead of a dejected young woman, tired-looking, sombre, and about to stand trial for her life, she looked like she was attending a West End show. She was dressed in a two-piece suit with an astrakhan collar, and a white blouse. Her hair was immaculate and dazzling blonde. . . . That her hair looked brassy in its platinum sheen certainly was a mistake as far as the defence was concerned. Jean Harlow and other film stars had equated ultra-blonde hair with a leaning toward "tartiness." . . . So now all eyes were on this woman. This blonde cart, as somebody in the public gallery whispered too loudly, focused around the "theatre." This was to be her stage, and nobody was going to take that away from her.[10]

Allowing for the authors' assumptions about the intentions of Harlow and other film stars, what is striking about their description and about the course of the Ruth Ellis story is the importance of hair color, fashion, versions of Americanness, sexuality, legality, and popular memory. At the time in the 1950s when Ruth Ellis was consolidating her position as a dance hall hostess, Diana Dors (born Diana Fluck) was at the height of her popularity. A brief examination of Dors's recollections of her life and career reveal convergences with Ellis's story. In her autobiography, *Dors by Diana,* Dors describes her family class affiliations as a "climb from working class to *upper* middle class."[11] Reflecting on her aspirations as a child, she says: "I wrote in an essay entitled 'What I would like to be when "grown-up"' that 'I was going to be a film star with a cream telephone and a swimming pool.'"[12] She was wearing makeup at the age of twelve, wore nylons, adored dancing, had elocution lessons, went to dances with American GIs, and won beauty contests ("looking as much like Betty Grable as possible").[13] Of her hair, she comments that it "was now long and fairly honey-coloured—with the help of some lightener."[14] And of blondeness, she adds: "My best friend, Christine . . . sported natural platinum-blonde hair, whereas mine was merely mousy. Somewhere, in the recesses of the mind . . . was born the dream of becoming a blonde, alluring film star, a woman who enchanted men and lived a life of glamour and fame."[15] In a comment that will bear directly on Ruth Ellis's obsession with a glamorous appearance, Dors says that "spectacles were the bane of my life, although I only wore them for reading and at the cinema. My vanity, encouraged by my mother, was prevalent even then and I was terrified of anyone, particularly a boy, seeing me wearing the wretched things."[16] The identification of glasses with an undesirable appearance is a commonplace of feminine representation. For example, in *Now, Voyager* (1942), Bette Davis's "undesirable appearance" is marked by the fact that she wears glasses.[17]

At the age of sixteen, Dors won a scholarship to study at the London Academy of Art, the springboard to her work in first theater and then film. In early films such as *Holiday Camp* (1947), *Here Come the Huggetts* (1948), *Good Time Girl* (1950), *The Weak and the Wicked* (1953), and *A Kid for Two Farthings* (1955), she was primarily cast as a precocious and socially threatening sex symbol. Overall she made sixty-five films, some of them in Hollywood. She also appeared on television in the United States and Britain. Of her major film, *Yield to the Night* (distributed in the United States as *Blonde Sinner*), which she and the critics considered her finest piece of acting, she writes: "At the time everyone thought the film moguls were cashing in on the unfortunate story of the tragic murderess, Ruth Ellis, the last woman to be hanged in England, but strangely enough the story had been written two years earlier by authoress Joan Henry with *me* in mind for the leading role."[18]

Dors was married three times, to men with whom she had violent and financially exploitative relations, all of which were frequently and luridly recounted in the scandal sheets. She became known for her encounters with the law, revenue officers, and morally upright clergy. Of her later career, she writes: "The years went by and my career went steadily down and down, until by the middle sixties, I was forced to leave my children in Hollywood where we had all been living, and come home to England in order to make money by trading on a screen name that had once been big."[19] Her brush with the law, she claims, "did not damage my career. On the contrary it helped to make me a household name, and the public were extremely sympathetic."[20] What is crucial about the shape of her career and relevant in particular for the reconstruction of the Ruth Ellis case is the equation that she, her admirers, and her detractors make between blondeness, tartiness, and self-destructive behavior. The blonde sinner is also associated with the "dumb blonde" as characterized by Marilyn Monroe, Jayne Mansfield, and Judy Holiday; however, this seeming obtuseness turns out in the final analysis to be a form of shrewdness.

Christine Gerahty identifies Dors's star image as a contradictory icon of "vulnerability and knowingness."[21] The qualities with which Dors (along with Brigitte Bardot and Marilyn Monroe) is associated are bodies on display, an "emphasis on experience and sensuality," and a reputation for selecting and being surrounded by incompetent and inadequate men.[22] Gerahty also cites the stormy "often destructive life of the sex symbol . . . as a sign of excessive female sexuality, bankruptcy, [and] decline."[23] Nonetheless, Dors is a survivor and Gerahty attributes this survival to the fact that Dors's image was popular among all social classes. In the construction of Dors's persona, both in her social life and in her films, her identification with working-class experience was an important source of her appeal. This identification was to continue during the period when she became a television personality. David Lusted, who has written about Dors's effect on television audiences, says: "Established initially as a sex symbol . . . [as] she aged, she pushed at the connotations of a variant type known as 'the good time girl,' retaining its characteristic self-regulating search for pleasure, but denying its characterisation as sin."[24] Dors's image makes "connections with women of all ages in a comparable variety of social roles," as well as with "men troubled by conventional models of male-regulated heterosexual relationships."[25]

An examination of Dors's persona reveals how the star is tied to a range of cultural and social positions identified by Richard Dyer: artifice and authenticity, the everyday and the exceptional, the individual and the collective, the private and the public, the accessible and the remote. Most conspicuous in the configuration of the blonde bombshell is the slippery relationship between transgressiveness and conventionality, success and anticipated failure. The narrative that best exemplifies a convergence between Dors's physical appearance, personality, and her reception as a sex symbol is *Yield to the Night*.

Stars, Star Texts, and Cultural Discourses: The Case of *Yield to the Night*

The common sense of melodrama, which provides a sense of naturalness and legitimacy if not rationality, relies on familiar images, sounds, clichés, and popular wisdom, functioning as a collage by bringing together bits and pieces of past and present that create the aura of credibility. In this sense, the social problem films of the late 1940s and 1950s are commonsensical texts. The form of the social problem film is a collage, absorbing elements from pre–World War II melodrama in its various genre guises: women's films, action pictures, film noir, historical films, and biopics. Sensitive to changes in the culture and in the industry, the social problem film is also a distant relative of neorealism and of docudrama. Its amalgam of crime detection, police drama, and melodrama has connections to television as well as to the emergent tabloid culture.

The social problem film emerged in Great Britain during a time of working-class pacification, Keynesianism, growing affluence, consumerism, a rising youth culture, an increasingly overt racism, and concerns over sexual permissiveness (expressed in the Wolfenden Commission, which addressed the status of the family, prostitution, and homosexuality), as well as concerns in the film industry for its health and viability.[26] These issues are tied to the increased international role of U.S. economic and cultural interests in the immediate post–World War II era in Great Britain.[27]

The social problem film was particularly sensitive to the "news of the day" and to immediate social issues that were identified with journalism, social science research, and legislative-political developments. Particularly associated with social problem films were directors and writers such as Basil Dearden, Jack Lee Thompson, Michael Relph, and the Boulting brothers. The scripts were often based on contemporary novels biographies, or exposés as exemplified by the writings of Joan Henry. The narratives focused on threats to the family, criminality, prostitution, same-sex sexuality, juvenile delinquency, and to a much lesser extent racial tensions. Such films as *Sapphire* (1959) dramatized the social problem of race, while *Victim* (1960) addressed the social problem of homosexuality. The hybrid, generic nature of the films, the new faces associated with them, their emphasis on youth, their timeliness, and their greater investment in sexuality addressed several audiences simultaneously: the liberal audience that saw itself as sympathetic to the plight of disenfranchised social groups, another audience that saw itself as sympathetic to the containment of rapidly spreading noxious social practices, a youthful audience that was no longer interested in the traditional offerings of British cinema, and yet another audience that might connect to the more audacious aspects of the subject matter without any ostensible or articulated investment in its politics.

The actors in these films enhanced the sense that there was a changing climate of representation in Britain, and this was certainly true if one contrasts them to earlier British stars. As with Diana Dors and Dirk Bogarde, their physical appearance revealed strong links to Hollywood iconography. The newer actors who played key roles included, among many others, Diana Dors, Yvonne Mitchell, Glynis Johns, Jack Warner, and Dirk Bogarde, though older actors such as John Mills, Laurence Olivier, and even Michael Redgrave made appearances. According to Richard Dyer, the function of bit players differed from its function in conventional genre roles: they now appeared to lend "a certain form of 'realism'" to the role.[28] If there is evidence for the noncomplacent, contradictory nature of class, gender, and sexual antagonisms in the post–World War II era, such antagonisms can certainly be read in the British social problem films of the 1950s as well as in the dramatic works and polemics of the "Angry Young Men." Pieces of an affective collage involving class and gender (and to a much lesser extent race) are embedded in Dirk Bogarde's portrait of a lawyer in *Victim* and in James Mason's portrayal of a schoolteacher in Hollywood's *Bigger Than Life* (1956). Both films portray threats to a respectable middle-class lifestyle arising from over- or underadherence to prevailing notions of masculinity. But the problematic nature of femininity is writ large in the social problem film. In accounting for its importance, however, Dyer errs in adhering to a basic opposition that "places man inside history and women as ahistoric and eternal."[29] Though I agree that women play a prominent role in the films as characters and as actresses, I challenge this binary distinction between active and passive, inside and outside, historical and ahistorical as reductive. The pastiche quality of the social problem film disturbs a monolithic sense of history, a reductive sense of power, and a binary sense of victim and aggressor in relation to gender. As an analysis of Diana Dors demonstrates, the image that emerges of her star persona is far more complex than that of a passive, ahistorical, and excluded victim. Her own narratives, the roles she played, and audience reception of her persona run counter to the notions of center and margin embedded in Dyer's statement. Dyer's taxonomy of social problem films, which situates them between those that address youth and those that address deviance, seems to be too narrative-driven to identify the contradictions posed by these works, especially the complex ways in which they all address issues pertaining to juridical discourses and the state, and their relation to questions of gender, race, and forms of sexuality.

The representation of the blonde sinner as conveyed by Diana Dors in *Yield to the Night* has multiple connections to complex and unexamined, though widely enacted, notions of feminine sexuality circulating in the culture, notions that are inseparable from questions of legality. The film participates in the discursive dimensions of the blonde bombshell through a set of affects relating to physical wantonness, criminality, and anticipated punishment, especially the attribution of being a "bad lot" or the prophecy of "coming to a bad end." Dors herself describes being "probably written off as a thoroughly bad lot from childhood."[30] Later she was denounced from the pulpit "as a wanton hussy." But, she adds, "this was of course before Christine Keeler overthrew the Conservative government."[31] That Dors's "story" and her screen roles parallel those of other young women of the 1950s and particularly that of Ruth Ellis, a convicted murderess, is material worthy in itself of historical inquiry. Dors's comment that Joan Henry's book (on which the script of *Yield to the Night* is based and which accounts for Henry's own brushes with the law) was written before Ellis's execution emphasizes the fact that the problems raised by the life and death of Ellis are endemic to the culture and to its common sense of itself. The narrative confirms that to understand what happened to Ellis one must go beyond the individual facts of her case and situate those events within a specific cultural milieu.

Yield to the Night was identified with the movement to eradicate capital punishment. In summarizing the film, Leslie Halliwell describes it as a "gloomy prison melodrama vaguely based on the Ruth Ellis case and making an emotional plea against capital punishment."[32] Halliwell's designation of the film as a prison melodrama is another reminder of how the social problem film absorbs earlier (Hollywood) antecedents, helping to account for the style of the film and for its use of certain types of character and situation. Though *Yield to the Night* makes claims to realism in its apparently liberal humanistic orientation and in its timeliness in relation to immediate social questions, the film form is more revealing for the contradictions it exposes concerning gender, sex, and class. Like other social problem films, *Yield to the Night* uses location settings and draws from a familiar pool of social problem actors (for example, Dors, Michael Craig, Yvonne Mitchell, Liam Redmond, and Athene Seyler). The focus on legality and on state intervention are integral to the melodramatic treatment of the central character.

The protagonist is a victim, to use a designation that might apply to the protagonists of social problem films generally, but she is also an aggressor, a murderess who expresses little remorse for her actions. That *Yield to the Night*, like many social problem films, has a woman as its protagonist is a testimony to the complex discursive links between femininity and law. Significantly, the other "victim" in this film is also a female, a rival for the affections of the male protagonist, as we learn through a series of flashbacks. Mary Hilton (Dors), married and working as a clerk in a department store, meets and falls in love with a middle-class man, Jim Lancaster (Michael Craig), who is in love with another woman of his own class. For a while he carries on a relationship with Mary, but his own career failures and his rebuff by the other woman, Lucy, drive him to commit suicide. Distraught over his death, Mary seeks vengeance on Lucy, kills her, and is condemned to death. The highly stylized opening of the film builds shot by shot from body parts (legs, hands, and torso, with no facial shot) of an as-yet unidentified woman who shoots another woman; these shots are intercut with shots of a city street. The full form of the first woman, the murderer, is only shown after the murder has been committed. In this fashion, we are made aware of the enigmatic connection between the feminine body and transgression. The images of the second woman, the murdered woman, are also fragmented, revealing her legs and her lifeless braceleted hand as if amputated. This emphasis on female body parts is retained throughout the film.

The film hinges on a number of contrasts. Mary's stripped appearance in prison, without makeup, wearing drab clothing, and subject to the harsh uncovered light bulb in her cell, is contrasted to her appearance in the flashbacks, heavily made-up, wearing clothes—tight dresses, close-fitting two-piece suits, and low cut sheaths—that accentuate her voluptuous body. Mary's face, in the full-face image after the murder, is not heavily made-up, which contrasts with her appearance in the flashbacks that reconstruct the events leading to the murder.

The claustrophobia of her prison cell is contrasted to the sights and sounds of life associated with the nightclub. The contrasts between past and present highlight the differences between her expectations of a better life and the failure of her hopes as she contemplates death. The film also underscores the difference between her own passion for pleasure and the cynical, bureaucratic, or pious attitudes toward sexuality exemplified by the representatives of the law—prison guards, governor, chaplain, and social philanthropists. Her overly feminine image is juxtaposed to that of her masculinized guards. The middle-class portrait of her lover differs from that of her working-class family just as her own appearance differs from that of Jim and from what is shown of the woman she murders.

Significantly, the images of her past in relation to her family, to Jim, and to her work fuse with the images of the prison cell. In spatial and temporal terms, the use of flashback creates a confusion between inside and outside, between society and prison, and in which came first, the crime or the punishment. Similarly, the initial fragmented shots of her body anticipate the later shots in the cell in the ways that the camera and editing focus on shots of her feet, legs, torso, hands, and eyes as if dismembering Mary before the actual execution, reiterating a familiar animus against femininity. In reconstructing Mary in the flashbacks, the text configures her as a familiar 1950s figure of femininity, inextricably associated with social disapprobation, condemnation, and punishment. Despite her identification with biological femaleness and her appearance of superfemininity, Mary as the blonde sinner transgresses by making herself the stalker rather than the stalked and by identifying herself with action rather than reaction, with activity rather than passivity, with recalcitrance rather than submission. As Mary Hilton, Dors is hardly devious and simpering; rather, she is direct (if vulnerable). Like Diana Dors, the character of Mary Hilton is associated with dancing, jazz, popular music, and an interest in fashion.

That notions of femininity are at stake is evident not only in Mary's highly eroticized persona but in the severe, sexually neuter, even masculinized women who are her jailers. The difference between Mary and the most sympathetic of the prison guards, Mac (Yvonne Mitchell), is most striking, highlighting the disjunction between Mary's blatant femininity (even without makeup and in prison uniform) and Mac's plain appearance and restrained behavior. The appearance of the prison governor (Marie Ney) is severe: She is completely covered up, tightly encased in her suits, and rigid in movement. The portrait of the prison guards and the governor connects, perhaps unwittingly, to another aspect of cultural lore relating to women, making the unattractive equation between women in authority and masculinity and raising the specter of lesbianism. In the film's trajectory of feminine types, a contrast is evident between Mary and Lucy, the murder victim. Mary's striking blondeness and buxom nature are set off against the brief glimpse that we have of Lucy as a dark-haired woman dressed stylishly and expensively but conservatively. The differences between Mary and her mother are marked too, the mother belonging to a familiar representation of older British working-class women (the Huggett mother of *Holiday Camp* and *Here Come the Huggetts*, among others): dumpy, indifferent to style, thoughtless, and speaking in a style of speech identified with "lower classes." Mary's speech is indicative of a movement toward "cleansed" pronunciation, and her sensibilities, particularly in relation to familial issues, are clearly superior to the older woman's. Finally, Miss Bligh (Athene Seyler), the prison reformer who seeks to alleviate the pain of Mary's last moments, is a familiar figure to British moviegoers, one largely identified with comic portraits often played by Margaret Rutherford: a de-eroticized, upperclass image that, like the portraits of the prison guards, captures the neutralized and androgynous sense of aging femininity.

The film's representation of masculinity in the figure of Jim Lancaster seems to be particularly at home in the 1950s social problem film. His troubled masculinity is endemic to the genre. He is another instance of transgression against predictable forms of masculinity in ways that are intimately tied to conventional notions of femininity. First of all he is not a sportsman but a pianist. He reads poetry. He had wanted to be a professional pianist but presumably was not successful. His stance is introspective, depressive, morose, pensive, and passive. He is from a middle-class background, and his use of language reveals that he is well educated. Mary describes him in her recollection as "moody." His physical appearance too is 180 degrees removed from that of British actors of the period, such as Jack Hawkins, Stewart Granger, and Jack Warner, who are associated with physicality and virility. His national origins—his mother is Irish and his father, Canadian—also distinguish him from the other masculine characters. His vulnerable masculinity is further underscored by his inability to successfully negotiate a relationship with a woman of his own class. Even his suicide over unrequited love unsettles conventional notions of masculinity. His obsession with Lucy provokes Mary's knowing remark "What's the good of that kind of love?" Moreover he is unwilling to establish a relationship with Mary, attempting to pawn her off on others. His differences from Mary combined with his social failures are suggestive of his inability to come to terms with social (especially sexual and class) expectations.

An important aspect of the portrait of the blonde sinner resides in her inevitable mismatch with the men in her life. The social problem film follows the melodramatic paradigm of denied gratification that Fassbinder once described in relation to Lauren Bacall's role in Douglas Sirk's *Written on the Wind* (1956): "She picks the one with whom things can't possibly work out in the long run."[33] Mary loves Jim who loves Lucy who loves someone else, and this formula for frustrated desire generates obsessional behavior and its attendant aggression. Similarly, one is reminded of the other ungratifying, exploitative, and violent relations that are part of Dors's own narrative. This scenario suggests a malaise with heterosexual cultural expectations packaged in the form of class and gender expectations and often expressed in aggression. The film plants psychological clues, stemming mainly from Mary's lack of accommodation to her own class affiliations, her unsatisfactory marriage to her husband Fred, and her vain attachment to Jim. In fact, her relationship with Jim is developed not so much through an erotic attachment to him as through her fascination for the way he speaks, for his books of poetry, and for his contrast to the working-class image of masculinity offered by her husband and the other men of her own class that she meets. Rather than being exceptional, the ultimately lethal nature of her attachment to him, which culminates in her murder of Lucy, seems to be intrinsic to the scenario of the "blonde sinner," the fulfillment of the often stated prophecy that she will "come to a bad end."

Much like Dors's description in her autobiographies of her youth, Mary's desire to escape the confines of her family life, her desire to be exceptional, and her attention to her physical appearance suggest that Mary identifies such aspirations with a life different from the constrained life of her family and social class. While not a "nightclub queen" (her words) like Dors or for that matter Ruth Ellis, Mary is portrayed as desperately in search of alternatives to the constraints of her life. Of her murder of Lucy she says that she was "sick with hate" and that she planned to kill Lucy in cold blood. This assertion hardly accounts for her act of violence. The film provides no further motive. The flashbacks that take place while Mary is on her bed or walking in the prison yard take on the quality of a dream that offers for analysis only fragments of the relationship between the feminine body, feminine desire, and the pre-scripted scenario of coming to a "bad end."

This bad end is a punishment reserved for those who violate class, gender, sexual, and national expectations. The notion of punishment beyond the ultimate end of hanging by the state is visualized in terms of bodily images and spatial images of constraint. As the flashbacks cease and the execution draws closer, space begins to close in on Mary until she is confined to her bed. The film blurs the temporal sequences, so that it appears that the punishment precedes the crime or rather, that the punishment is not so much for the act of murder as the fulfillment of a prophecy for flaunting and acting on her femininity, revealing Mary as transgressing even before she legally transgresses. When the guard tells her, "If you accept your punishment, not fight it, you will find it easier to bear," the comment carries a dual significance: Though it applies to Mary's facing her execution with equanimity, it applies even more to "punishment" for being feminine.

The absence of a courtroom scene in *Yield to the Night*—replete with expert witnesses, cross-examination of the protagonist, a recounting of the events leading to the murder, and suspense over the verdict of guilt or innocence—has a bearing on the text's investment in the question of punishment: Who is being punished, and for what? The exclusive focus on the prison drama, on the last moments of the protagonist's life, and on whether a reprieve will come at the last moment underscores the film's investment in the question of the ethics of capital punishment. But in the text's visual and narrative obsession with the protagonist's physical appearance, her relations to the men in her life and to her family, culminating in the act of murder, suggest that the punishment precedes and exceeds the crime as a life and death sentence for the sin of femininity and its effects on society. Furthermore, this punishment serves as a reminder that femininity is inseparable from considerations of the family and of the family's ties to other civil, state, medical, juridical, and educational institutions. Elaborating on representations of familial relations within melodrama, Jackie Byars has found that underpinning conflict is a gap left by the family, "a structuring absence expressed through a loss of family." The "function of the female character in these social problem films is to maintain the integrity of the family."[34] Conversely, one might expect that the absence of a character who serves as a guarantor of familial integrity would signify trouble in the text. Mary Hilton's crime incorporates her transgression against the integrity of the family and not merely her criminal act of murder. Through Mary's flashbacks and the scenes of the family visits to the prison, *Yield to the Night* provides a portrait of a disintegrating working-class family. Mary's transgression dooms two families: her parental family and her conjugal family. Her "sin" arises from the conflict between her pursuit of pleasure and the familial obligations that she disregards. The film's dramatization of a disintegrating marital environment includes the prison guard Mac's mentally ill mother who dies shortly before Mary's execution is to take place. The "mixed" marriage—Irish and Canadian—with which Jim is identified is perhaps another indicator of problematic familial relations. One of the last acts of reconciliation that the narrative seeks to effect is familial, between Mary and her mother. Mary repeatedly refuses to see her mother, berating her among other things for bringing her younger brother to see her in prison. Ultimately, with the encouragement of the chaplain, Mac, and others, Mary agrees to make peace with her mother and to allow her to visit.

Prior to any act of criminal transgression that engages public attention through the law, the profoundly disruptive character of the blonde sinner has already blurred the boundaries between home and the world. Her public spectacle is familiar: peroxide blonde hair, usually long and loose, large breasts, a swinging-hips walk, tight-fitting clothing with low backs and necklines that call attention to the body, an availability for play and pleasure, a love of dancing, and a disregard for the opinions of others. Along with such qualities, the blonde sinner is identified with love attachments that are fatal, leading to the demise of herself, of the love attachment, or of both. All this marks her as fundamentally out of step with bourgeois values yet makes her absolutely essential to their representation and maintenance. This figure, so much a part of the cultural landscape of the movies, popular novels, and music, reveals itself not as marginal or exceptional (though it is regarded as unique). Like discourses of sexuality generally, this representation of femininity embodies threatened and thwarted feminine sexuality. In her blatant presentation, the blonde sinner calls attention to the unsuccessful containment of sexuality within the heterosexual family. This publicized form of femininity, because it generates so much interest, is never disjoined from its economically productive dimensions nor can its productive dimensions be concealed: Its affect proclaims its presence. In its obvious exposure of its produced (and disruptive) nature, the blonde sinner threatens to expose the constructed, unnatural dimensions of social cum sexual expectations. It is not surprising that Sir Oswald Mosley compared Dors to "only one other woman of any importance at all, namely, Margaret Thatcher."[35] In the context of reconfiguring the cultural uses of femininity, Mosley's comments are instructive.

Mary's character emerges as more than a passive victim of the social order. She is also an "iron lady," a figure of power and threat. From both sides of the law, femininity comes to take on a more complex appearance. *Yield to the Night* and the much-praised acting of Diana Dors—like Dors's own escapades—seem to touch a number of raw nerves of 1950s culture involving social antagonisms that foreground gender, class, and sexuality and reveal their inextricability from considerations of the role of the state and its juridical apparatuses. Furthermore, Mosley's conjunction of Dors and Margaret Thatcher provides clues to the resurrection of Ellis's story in the 1980s and its relation to contemporary antagonisms involving the history of gendered and sexual representation.

Re-Membering Ruth Ellis

The execution of Ruth Ellis in 1955 was an event that was slow in taking hold of the public imagination but that has now become an important fixture in British popular memory. The effects of that event reverberate and, as these effects show up in movies like *Yield to the Night,* continue to express the continuing and perhaps even increased profitability of woman-centered scandal, especially scandal involved with sexual transgression and class conflict. Peroxide blonde Ruth Ellis, like Marilyn Monroe and Diana Dors, lived in the fast lane. From her teen years, she was keen on dancing, meeting men (especially American servicemen with money to burn), having fun, and escaping the conflicts and dreariness of her family environment, especially the oppressive presence of a father who tyrannized her mother and was dependent on the women in the house. During World War II, she was involved with who promised marriage to her. Unaware that he had a wife at home and pregnant with his child, Ruth learned, too late for an abortion, that he had betrayed her. She delivered the child, Andy, and received support from the father, who had been sent back to Canada, but the support dried up after a year and she no longer heard from him.

A popular figure with men, she moved to London, where she became acquainted with an underworld figure, Morris Conley, who owned clubs where men, mainly professional and upper-class men, would go to get drinks, entertainment, and sex. The women, like Ruth, thought of themselves not as engaging in prostitution but as granting social favors: Sex was part of the job of entertaining the clientele. Ruth's reputation spread, she was much sought after by men at the club as a woman who was great at sex, and she rose to be manager of the Little Club, owned by Conley. It was there she met George Ellis, a dentist who was an alcoholic and could not hold down a job. She married him, left the club, and had a child, Georgina. George tried to stay on the wagon for a while but could not resist the lure of drink, and eventually he not only lost his work but became brutal and abusive toward her. Because of his heavy drinking and his abusiveness, she left him and returned to her work at the club.

It was also at the Little Club that she met David Blakely, also a man of a higher social class (she boasted of the pedigrees of the men who came to the club) and the man whom she would ultimately murder. Blakely, like George Ellis, was another of those men unable to hold down a job, but he was passionately interested in car racing and was supported in this activity by his stepfather. Blakely would come to the club, drink prodigiously, and spend the night with her in the upstairs apartment that she shared with her son, Andy.

At first the relationship was affectionate, but it became physically and verbally abusive. He was engaged to a woman of his own class but assured Ruth that he had broken off the relationship. He invited her to racing events, where she came in contact with his friends the Findlaters and with Desmond Cussen, another man who was to play an important role in her life and death. Blakely was more interested in his racing than in her, and their interactions became characterized by Blakely's indifference to her needs coupled with his unwillingness to let her go.

Public displays of violence between them became familiar to the people who saw them at the club. Ruth was later to claim that the Findlaters were a major cause of the trouble between her and David. They found Ruth, not of their social class, too loud and vulgar. At the same time Ruth was also seeing Cussen. Also of a higher social class, Cussen was described by some of Ruth's acquaintances as sullen and withdrawn. He was in the tobacco business and was generous to her and to her son. After too many violent scenes in which Blakely destroyed property at the club and with the attendant decline in business, Ruth was fired by Conley and forced to leave her upstairs apartment at the Little Club. Cussen, who was paying her son's fees at school, took her to stay at his lodgings, where Andy would also stay during holidays. She continued her relationship with Blakely, a relationship that was becoming even more physically abusive. He and she both carried physical scars from their violent and aggressive interactions. Cussen would tend her wounds after such squabbles. Blakely was also strapped for funds, since he had undertaken the enormous expense of building his own racing car with the aid of his friend, Ant Findlater.

At this time Ellis became pregnant. It is not clear whether she had an abortion or whether, in another of their physically aggressive encounters, Blakely was responsible for the loss of the baby. He had promised to marry her, but he reneged on the promise. She took to chasing him at his various haunts—his apartment, the Findlater's home, and the garage where he and Findlater were working on the racing car. Cussen would chauffeur her as she desperately sought to make contact with Blakely, who had taken to avoiding her. She telephoned incessantly. As a consequence the phone at his apartment and at the Findlaters' was kept off the hook. At one point Ruth broke the windows in his car, and when the police came she claimed that the car was partially financed by her money. She was not arrested, nor was any effort made to restrain her activities. Finally, after Blakely had promised to take Andy out one afternoon but then did not show up, Ellis, filled with liquor and tranquilizers, took a gun that Cussen owned and had taught her to use. On the fatal day, she waited outside Blakely's house until he came out to go to the pub and shot him several times.

Her trial took place during a newspaper strike. It was a brief trial without much attendant notoriety for what gave all the appearances of an open-and-shut case. She did nothing to save herself, and the defense was not aggressive in her behalf. She claimed that she wanted to die. The jury was only out twenty-three minutes, an outstandingly short time considering that a woman's life hung in the balance. According to Laurence Marks and Tony Van Den Bergh, who interviewed one of the jury members many years after Ellis's death: "A member of the jury explained to the authors what went on during the twenty-three minutes they were out. . . . 'The thing that sticks out in my mind was that the others were going backwards and forwards to the toilet. I reckon that of the twenty-three minutes we were out only about thirteen were actually spent discussing the case.'"[36] Public responses, however, were more engaged. Marks and Van Den Bergh describe the case as polarizing the public: "To many people . . . she was . . . a foul-mouthed club hostess who whored on the side. . . . To others, David Blakely was the villain of the tragedy. . . . A third group . . . believed that Desmond Cussen was really responsible for the murder. . . . What sort of man was this who, even though inflamed by jealousy, could provoke a drunken, half-crazed woman whilst he stood watching safely on the sidelines?"[37]

The details of this affair are hardly tucked away in the archives. Rather, it is very much in the public eye almost four decades later, as attested to by the various books, newspaper articles, and scholarly articles that continue to appear and by the 1985 film *Dance with a Stranger*.[38] This brief synopsis of the events leading to the death of David Blakely and the trial and execution of Ruth Ellis reveals a full-blown melodramatic scenario with all the ingredients of a film comparable to *The Weak and the Wicked* (1953), *Yield to the Night*, and of course Hollywood's 1958 prison melodrama about a woman sentenced to be executed, *I Want to Live!*, starring Susan Hayward in her Academy Award-winning performance. The ingredients of the Ellis case are familiar by now: a promiscuous blonde, a mother of questionable fitness, the manipulation of the "sinner" at the hands of her lovers, associations with the underworld, scorn and stigmatization for her working-class credentials, indifference on the part of "respectable" institutional representatives until the major crime occurs, the climactic brush with law.

The urban milieu is major actor in this drama of the underside of respectability—club life, cabarets, gambling, and extortion, along with the selling of sexual favors. While the women's prison dramas usually include a spectrum of female social outcasts—young, first-time offenders as well as recidivist women offenders, women of all ages, classes, and occupations representative of various antisocial acts—in films that focus on a woman facing capital punishment, the narratives tend to isolate the woman, focusing on her struggle to survive and on the psychological effects of her confronting her death, as in *I Want to Live!* and *Yield to the Night*. The fascination with the woman's punishment and the step-by-step involvement in her approach to death seems to parallel the interest in the representation of other forms of violence enacted on women, whether by serial killers or lovers.

Re-Constructing Ellis: *Dance with a Stranger*

Dance with a Stranger returns to the 1950s and to the familiar details of the Ellis case. The names are the same, as is the sequence of events. What is different. is the deliberate absence of either a trial scene or a scene of the women in prison. Like *Yield to the Night* and the later *Scandal, Dance with a Stranger* is not a glossy, expensive film. A product of Goldcrest Films, a company that is identified with such expensive films as *Chariots of Fire,* this film was budgeted at far less money, and the principals involved in its production were not big money makers. *Dance with a Stranger* was the first feature film for Randall-Cutler, the film's producer. The director, Mike Newell, had limited film experience, though he had television work to his credit.[39] Shelagh Delaney, known for her role in writing *A Taste of Honey* and *Charlie Bubbles* for the New Cinema of the 1960s, had not done a script since then and was reluctant to undertake the project. According to James Park, she declared that "she didn't want to write about real people," but Roger Randall-Cutler, the producer, "pleaded that the film would be a fictional account of a love affair with the facts of the case functioning as a springboard for imaginative interpretation."[40] The agreement on the parts of the producer, writer, and director was that this was not to be a "political" film but a "tale of people caught in the dead-end of extreme emotion."[41] In short, it was to be a melodrama. The filmmakers did not acknowledge this but it was also to be a biopic (although hardly a heroic one). The film, in fact, constitutes a transgressive use of the biopic model, which is usually associated with a hagiographic treatment of its subject, as characterized, for example, by Richard Attenborough's *Gandhi.*

Another important dimension of the Ellis story was to be "its hold on the public consciousness." Commenting on the "press write-ups from the period [which] revealed that the Ruth Ellis saga had opened a window into British society that many wanted to keep shut,"[42] the filmmakers sought to provide a set of visual images, through the clothing and makeup—tweed suits, evening dresses, peroxide hair—that could serve as aids to popular recollection. While the film was not considered to be political, the filmmakers were concerned with the public drama and in particular with the "speed with which Ellis had passed through the judicial system [which] suggested that society had been taking its revenge on her for living a fast lifestyle." In its social problem zeal, *Yield to the Night* had also "opened a window onto British society" by addressing antagonisms among social class, gender, sexuality, and national identity through its adoption of the prison drama format. and its tentative explorations of the implications of this "fast lifestyle" and its consequences.

Neither the 1956 film nor the 1985 film *directly* addresses the ways in which the responses to a woman's execution "indicated that the law was out of touch with the public mood in attempting to dam up transformations in social mores that could no longer be held back."[43] Both films, in different ways, are concerned with exposing the profound social disjunctions that are best conveyed through the women's melodrama. In ways that exceed authorial intentionality,

Dance with a Stranger resurrects that mid-1950s world through a 1980s invest-ment in sexual "scandal" and in the centrality of gender and sexuality as a politi-cal phenomenon. Re-creating the club life of the period and the ambiance of a world in which people do not conform to the traditional expectations of public service and familial ideals, focusing on a protagonist who enacts the worst fears of working-class promiscuity and violence, and linking the events of her life to images of film and television through her appearance and through the self-reflexive uses of media throughout, the film links the 1950s to the 1980s and to the conflicts generated by Thatcherite social and economic policies. Thus, contrary to official history, this film offers a multivalent reading that, beyond familiar narrative plotting, is able to mingle the assorted elements of past and present (star images, fashion, music, dance, dialogue, automobiles, and home appliances), focusing on the historic significance of Ruth Ellis as the carrier of otherness. Rather than isolating a specific problem—juvenile delinquency, pros-titution, same-sex relations, racial tensions—the film, through its pastiche of elements of 1950s life, appears to offer itself to audiences as an object of reflec-tion and retrospection. There is no guarantee of a unified reading; rather, it offers a number of contradictory readings. The hybrid way in which *Dance with a Stranger*, like the social problem film, draws on other genres but reconfigures and recycles its borrowings is a further index to the ways in which affect as value production must circulate: remaining the same yet containing difference through combining perennially and erotically charged images with new and threatening dimensions of legal transgression. Gone are the 1950s social agents who are incarnations of the law, the state, and the discourses of social respon-sibility against social chaos: the social workers, psychiatrists, clergy, and reform-ers. Still present are the transgressive and disruptive figures of sexual excess who inhabit the melodramatic landscape, particularly the femme fatale of film noir. The problematic urban world remains, no longer under or outside the world of respectability but at its center.

Like film noir, with its disturbed and violent milieu, its sense of fatality and disaffection, and its ambiguous representation of the law, *Dance with a Stranger* evokes the darkly lit streets, "lonely places," claustrophobic environ-ments, and sense of toughness of the urban, American-like environment, where its inhabitants are mired in cruel, sadistic, and vain struggles to achieve personal and social objectives. This resurgence of film noir in *Dance with a Stranger* sup-ports Mike Davis's claim to the creation of "an elaborate counter-history."[44] From Barbara Stanwyck in *Double Indemnity* (1949), Gloria Grahame in *In a Lonely Place* (1950),[45] Marilyn Monroe in *The Asphalt Jungle* (1950), Susan Hayward in *I Want To Live!*, and Dors in *Passport to Shame* (1958) to Miranda Richardson in *The Crying Game* (1992) and in *Dance with a Stranger*, we are con-fronted with figures of femininity who are victimized but that are also capable of victimizing. Knowing but vulnerable disaffected housewives, prostitutes, movie stars, and political activists inhabit this world where relations with the same sex and with the opposite sex are never transparent or predictable. Others are drawn to this figure in fear, loathing, violence, and inexplicable dependency and fascination. Moreover many of these feminine figures in quest of romance are either destroyed or left destitute. The melodramatic elements follow the course, described by David Rodowick, of the 1950s melodramas: They force the "equation of sexuality and violence," a violence that involves feminine sexuality that is "in excess of the social system that seeks to contain it."[46] (This paradigm also applies to instances in which femininity is not identified with biological women, as represented in such films as *Prick Up Your Ears* [1987].)

Dance with a Stranger is tied to its protagonist; all of the other characters are satellites, and all scenes involve her. Significantly, critics did not know what to make of her role (or, for that matter, of the other characters, especially Blakely). For example, Vincent Canby, working on the model of "new" and "positive" images of women, describes the characterization of Ellis (among other 1980s women's roles) as "active forces in the environments that contain them. They aren't passive little creatures who accept their fate without question. They play roles more often associated with men. They do things." However, he then complains that "they do these things at a certain cost to dramatic coherence. In not one of these films does the woman protagonist have a relationship of any importance with a man who comes up to her collar bone."[47] His qualifying comments reduce gender and sexuality to the naturalized binarism of activity and passivity, to biological conceptions of man and woman, which characterize essentialist address of representation. Moreover old/new/progressive/regressive formulations do not address the complexity of the social antagonisms that Critical Theory has been trying to explore, particularly at the moment when the critique of subject construction has addressed the pitfalls of historicism, especially its linearity, teleology, and reductionism. The heterosexist assumptions about the need for appropriately matched men and women flies in the face of the darker and slipperier aspects in the representation of gendered and sexual relationships that critical investigation has begun to name and describe. The politics of the films, particularly the British films, of the 1980s concentrate "on the everyday lives and memories of 'ordinary people,' and in many cases push female characters to the fore, offering a different range of narrative pleasures and identifications."[48]

One other, perhaps parallel, critical comment about *Dance with a Stranger* deserves attention. A critic from *Variety*, while sympathetic to the film, singles out Rupert Everett as Blakely and complains of the actor's "inability to convey more about David Blakely than that he's set to fail consistently in work and life." This complaint is matched by praise for Ian Holm for his success as "the well-meaning Desmond Cussen whose human decency cannot satisfy Ruth's deeper longings."[49] This reading of the character reproduces the usual strategy of asking for "realist" acting and its corresponding "pop psych" exploration of motivation. For example, the reading of Cussen's character as "well-meaning" does not in any way correspond to the ambiguity of his representation. This characterization seems to spring from the pervasive realist assumption that characters must still be "well-rounded" and transparent. The willful misreading of cultural signs resurrects conventional notions of gender and sexuality. The comments reveal the implicit assumption that masculine figures need to come up to (if

perhaps not compete with) their feminine protagonists by equal time in the narrative. Such comments neglect the ways in which contemporary British films
are engaged in historicizing "in a manner that maintains a complex, bifurcated
perspective shifting between past and present."[50]

An examination of Miranda Richardson's re-creation of the blonde sinner
reveals its imbrication in a number of historically specific events. Her appearance
and her gestures are a calculated simulacrum of Ellis, as can be seen if one looks
at the photographs of Ellis and reads descriptions about her makeup, clothing,
and mode of speaking. This emphasis on her appearance—on its calculated
nature—throws the spectator into the cultural terrain of the 1950s, where the
film's questions about history are generated. The spectacle of Ellis further evokes
the visual memories of 1950s Hollywood stars that are associated with Marilyn
Monroe (whom Ellis seems to resemble most, to judge by photographs). Ellis's
image evokes Diana Dors; as an icon of the period, and it evokes connections to
the consumer culture of femininity. Much of *Dance with a Stranger* presents
images of Ellis before a mirror, primping her peroxide blonde hair, adjusting her
false eyelashes, and fixing her maquillage. In one scene with Cussen, the dialogue
explicitly addresses her appearance. He asks her, "Why don't you let your hair go
back to its natural color?" And she answers, "I'm a blonde now." Unrelenting, he
then says, "I didn't know you wore false eyelashes," and she quips, "I'll wear
anything that improves on nature." She offers to put false eyelashes on him and
to shave his mustache, thus calling attention not only to her construction of
femininity but to the tenuousness of "natural" masculinity as well.

From the first moments of the film, the camera clings to her face and
body, reminiscent of the shots of Dors in *Yield to the Night*. Her dresses are a
reproduction of 1950s feminine attire and especially of 1950s movie attire:
tight-fitting, low-cut, sometimes flared from the waist, rustling, and off the
shoulder-like the gown she wears to the ball with Cussen. Her attire offers a
striking contrast to that of Carole Findlater (Jane Bertish), Ellis's upper-class
detractor, who wears the requisite 1950s middle-class uniform, which is sporty,
even dowdy. Similarly the upper-class women at the dance with Ruth are more
conservatively clad than she is.

Close-ups of the Ellis character reveal the masklike spectacle of her face,
framed by the platinum hair. Rather than conveying great expressivity, this face
seems frozen in its makeup as if we are forbidden to see what, if anything, is
being covered up. Though she wears glasses (and this becomes an important element in the unfolding of the drama), she only wears them at the cinema, when
she is called upon to read a business document, and in the final murder scene.
In the first scene at the car races, she is told in hostile fashion by Carole Findlater
that she could see the event better if she would only put on her glasses, and predictably she responds in the commonsensical vein: "Men never make passes at
girls who wear glasses." The question of looking and of being looked at assumes
a central place in the film through the emphasis on glasses, on mirror shots, and
on chiaroscuro noir scenes as a metaphor for perception and misperception by
Ellis, by others in the film who look at her, and also by the external audience.

Of her peroxide hair, Marks and Van Den Bergh comment that as Ellis got older, her hair got darker, "and she resorted to the peroxide bottle to remedy this. For the rest of her life she was to be inordinately fond of her peroxide blonde hair. She believed the popular saying that 'Gentlemen prefer blondes.' It would not be an exaggeration to say that her fixation to remain blonde was a contributing factor to the poor impression she made when giving evidence at her trial."[51] Putting aside the ways in which Marks and Van Den Bergh presume to "explain" her character and events—though from a sympathetic perspective—what remains from their discussion is the consonance between their descriptions of Ellis, the image of Dors as Mary Hilton in *Yield to the Night,* the linage Dors constructs of herself in her autobiography, and Miranda Richardson's enactment of the character of Ellis.

In this context, another conjunctural aspect raised by the film has to do with the way in which Richardson as Ellis adopts upper-class speech patterns and intonations, managing at the same time to make them seem stilted and affected. Her dialogue is a compendium of clichés, but she is also capable of witty one-liners. In response to one of Blakely's manipulative and insincere pleas for her to marry him, she snaps, "Why? Are you pregnant?" At work in the Little Club, she liberally bestows the appellation "darling" on the various men. Her risqué comments are evident when she is with Cussen, who seems to be more of a prude than the other men in her life. Dangling a banana and taunting Cussen, she says, "Terrible things, aren't they?" She laughs loudly at a pissing dog in Cussen's presence. Marks and Van Den Bergh comment that Ellis was reputed to have been fond of four-letter epithets and used them to shock her auditors (which the film tones down somewhat). In one scene, Ellis rages at David, "I don't give a fuck for your social standing."

As hostess in the club, Richardson plays Ellis as businesslike and competent, ever on the lookout to improve the standing of the club. She manages her boss as well as the other workers to get what she wants. Things only begin to deteriorate when her relationship with Blakely begins to unravel. (The film does not develop her relationship to George Ellis.) She dances gaily with the men and occasionally entertains them with ballads from the time (in fact, she sings the title song, *"Dance with a Stranger,"* in 1950s ballad style). Of the use of music in the film, Richard Combs has said that the "subject—the theme which seems to come through the refrain of the songs—is the social conditioning which shapes this romance."[52] More than a "theme" and "social conditioning" come across through the ballads and dance music. The milieu in which the songs are sung and the lyrics themselves are carriers of the film's invocations on past history.

The image that Richardson/Ellis projects in her speech, dress, and behavior is reminiscent of Gerahty's description of Dors's dual qualities of vulnerability and knowingness. As a character who is able to handle her business affairs and produce and use herself as a commodity in this environment, Richardson/Ellis appears to be a tough survivor. Her assessment of events and of the people in her life is, like Dors's, not at all sentimentalized; rather, it recognizes failed expectations and contradictions. Her relationship with Cussen seems to capture her ability to cope and to get what she wants. On the other hand, her relationship with Blakely reveals her vulnerability. As the enigma at the film's center, her character raises questions about femininity but neither reduces their complexity nor explains them. As her scenes with both Cussen and Blakely dramatize, neither Ellis nor the two male characters adhere to dominant cultural expectations of masculinity and femininity. I have commented that in *Yield to the Night* the character of Jim Lancaster violates accepted notions of masculinity in a manner characteristic of social problem films. This is also the case with Cussen and Blakely. Cussen, as played by Holm and as derived from the literature surrounding the Ellis case, is a sexually ambiguous figure. He is soft-spoken and slow of speech. He retreats from the sporty world associated with Blakely. His positioning as a spectator of events (especially of Ruth's affairs) is his most marked characteristic. He is attached to her in a seemingly inexplicable fashion, follows her every movement, chauffeurs her everywhere, takes care of her son, and offers her cash and lodgings with little hope of gratification. His rivalry with Blakely for the attention and affection of Ruth's son and his curiosity about the sexual relations between Blakely and Ruth are emphasized in the film. The two men are united in their curiosity about the other's sexual activity. The film subtly hints at rather than dispelling the possibility of Cussen's complicity in the murder of Blakely, a possible complicity that did not come out until Ellis was already awaiting execution. Friends convinced her that for the sake of her children, if not for herself, she should seek a stay of execution. Persuaded, Ellis did finally request a stay, only to be denied. It was not until later, as others began to forage about in the facts of the trial, that the information about Cussen's possession of a gun, his teaching Ellis how to use it, and his accompanying her (actually driving her), to the scene of the shooting without ever dissuading her from the act came to be known. In addition, she was under the influence of liquor and tranquilizers at the time of the murder. Holm's clothing, his body movements, his stilted gestures, and his placement in the background as a spectator testify to the text's cognizance of his ambiguous persona and role. His mask of gentility is allowed to drop a few times—once when he is castigating her for leaving her child alone, another time when in rage he forces sex upon her, though she is drugged and indifferent to his demands. His investment in a relationship with Ruth's son is complex. At times, he appears to use that relationship to gain an entry into her affections; at other times he appears to be competing with her for the maternal role as well as with Blakely, using Andy as a wedge to incite Ruth against Blakely. Though rivals, both Cussen and Blakely agree in their assessment and accusation of Ruth as a bad mother.

By contrast to Cussen, Blakely has minimal pretensions to a relationship with Ellis's son, though the boy seems to prefer him to Cussen. Blakely invites the boy to the races and gives him goggles but breaks his promise to take the boy to a fair at Hampstead Heath. Ellis later attributes her final murderous rage to this broken promise. Blakely's conflicts emerge through his ambivalent connection to his class, his equally ambivalent attachment to his mother and stepfather, his failure at a career and as a racing driver—all expressed in his tempestuous and violent relationship with Ruth Ellis. The forms that his relationship with Ruth takes are as complex as Cussen's. At times, she appeals to him as the idealized mother whom he cannot do without; at other times he is attracted by her tartiness. His behavior alternates in oedipal terms between being her lover, her son, and her scourge. He seeks to rid himself of her, and yet he cannot. Physical violence is built into their interactions and is closely tied to the "fighting and fucking" paradigm. He scorns the way she "rears a child in a knocking shop." He humiliates her in public and is the major cause of her losing whatever economic independence she had. Through Ruth's relationship with him, the film builds inexorably to the anticipated climax of violence, beginning with their passion, moving on to their verbal violence, escalating to the physical violence, and culminating in the fatal shooting.

The film's abandonment of the docudrama style often attributed to social problem films is most evident in the ways in which it handles these encounters between Blakely and Ellis. At one point in the narrative, as the violence escalates, they meet on a foggy street at night in a scene reminiscent of Jack the Ripper movies or Hammer horror films. Ruth asks him how he got there, and he quips, "I followed your scent." Taunting him, she asks whether he would like to hit her again and he responds with the familiar "You ask for it."

The camera singles out a cross that she is wearing around her neck (an object not previously seen on her), and when Blakely comments that she is wearing a good luck charm, she retorts, "It's to protect me against devils and vampires." He then drags Ellis into the alley and forces her against a wall, where they engage in violent sex. In the context of the film, this scene has the effect of making an affective transition, providing an appropriate language to account for the escalation to the violence of the murder.

In using Ruth Ellis as protagonist, in creating a sense of a 1950s landscape, the film announces an investment in the past, or rather, in "popular consciousness," as Randall-Cutler has termed this history. Yet how can one assess this interest and investment in the past? The film can be read as part of a familiar commonsensical scenario, as a parable of social disintegration. The resurrection of the blonde sinner—the conventional home wrecker, an enemy, even against her will, of the family—acknowledges the much decried contemporary threat to family values that is being widely circulated through media such as films, soap operas, talk shows, political speeches, and courtroom reportage. In the context of British society, *Dance with a Stranger* recapitulates the usual British fascination and horror with class misalliance. *Dance with a Stranger* also has similarities to films of the 1980s like *Prick Up Your Ears* and *Another Country*, films that are more directly critical of heterosexual familial values and that explore same-sex relations within the context of a critique of traditional British class, national, and sexual values. *Dance with a Stranger* seems to participate in the recycling of images of violence as a rampant and mobile threat that invades and infects respectable sectors of society. The images of media in the film help to link social concerns of the 1950s to those of the 1980s, making the spectator conscious of the ubiquity of media: in the image of Ruth Ellis and in her conjuring up of certain female stars, or conversely, stars who are created in the image of Ruth Ellis, in the newsreel footage of the race at Le Mans with Zsa Zsa Gabor and Porfirio Rubirosa in the spectator box, and in the television shows that Ruth and her son watch. To put it in terms of Antonio Negri's conception of postmodernism, is the film an exercise in nostalgia, a portrait of the social antagonisms of the post-Keynesian world, or a harbinger of the creation of new subjectivities that are no longer docile?

The film invites a comparison with the numerous works that now are identified with some form of feminism or postfeminism. By using Ellis and reinforcing her relationship to a particular version of femininity, the film inevitably participates in this discourse through its focus on women's position in relation to social structures of power, on physical violence toward women, on women's representation in the media, on women's role within the family, and on women's relations to the law. The letter that Ellis writes to Blakely's mother captures a number of, the familial and juridical issues in the film. It provides information about the punishment meted out to her after the shooting. Since the film does not include a trial, it makes the last spoken dialogue in the film that of Ruth Ellis rather than the courts, which serves to problematize in a non-judgmental fashion the values she articulated and acted on. It focuses on the maternal theme, recapitulating the film's flirtation with her role as a mother and others' perceptions of this role in the final scenario. The film problematizes femininity by entertaining its constructed rather than essential nature, but it also problematizes maternity. The letter Ellis leaves Blakely's mother is given as follows:

> Dear Mrs. Cook, No doubt these last few days have been a shock to you. Please try to believe me when I say how very sorry I am to have caused you this unpleasantness. . . . The two people I blame for David's death and my own are the Findlaters. No doubt you will not understand this but before I hang. . . . I implore you to forgive David for living with me, but we were very much in love with one another. Unfortunately, David was not satisfied with one woman in his life. I have forgiven David. I only wish I had it in my heart to forgive him while he was alive. Once again, I say I am very sorry to have caused you this misery and heartache. I shall die loving your son and you should feel that his death has been repaid. Good-bye.

This letter has the same stilted and affected quality that characterizes Ellis's appearance and way of speaking. In the context of the events in the film, especially in the context of the contradictory character of Ellis, the letter portrays her as not merely a victim of femininity but as actively furthering a prescribed scenario. The letter reinforces her commitment to commonsensical notions of romantic love, maternity, crime, and retribution. Her allusions to her death as repayment for David's reinforce the sense given throughout the film that she has few illusions about her situation or about the inevitability and appropriateness of her punishment. Her plea for forgiveness from and identification with David's mother and her justification of her actions in the name of love are the staple of melodrama, revealing its basis in conventional values. This letter is not the defiant statement of an exploited woman. The only complaint expressed by Ellis involves David's friends, the Findlaters, and her only lament is David's inability to be satisfied by one woman.

Given such sentiments, the portrait of Ruth Ellis in this film raises disturbing questions about the constitution of femininity. Jacqueline Rose explores these questions in her seemingly strange juxtaposition of Ruth Ellis and Margaret Thatcher, which reverberates beyond the mere comparison of two historical female figures. Rose writes:

> In one sense there is no common point or even dialogue between these two women: from different historical moments and opposite ends of the social spectrum; they stand respectively for criminality and the law. . . . Yet Margaret Thatcher and Ruth Ellis were brought together at this historical moment in a scenario whose imaginary basis may well be what constitutes its importance and force. "Victim" and "executioner," they meet at the point of violence where the ordering of the social reveals something of the paradox on which it is based. . . . Drawing attention to themselves precisely as women, they can serve to gloss over that paradoxical and double location of violence—the perversion of the state in relation to violence can be transposed on to the perversity of the woman.[53]

Dance with a Stranger and *Yield to the Night* extend their narratives far beyond the legal question of capital punishment. In their separate ways, the films move into the more tangled web of social and psychological discourses that are embedded in gender and sexual politics. The historical pastiche that emerges from these discourses links gender and sexuality in nonessentialist terms to such social and cultural activities as social production, reproduction, work, leisure, and ethnic and national identity.

The Blonde: Violence and Value

The trajectory of the blonde bombshell is neither merely the excluded underside or binary opposite of the Angel in the House nor the negative of conformity; instead it is far more powerful as the sine qua non, as one of the very bases, of constructing social values. Ruth Ellis's line in the film, that she is in favor of "improving on nature," refers to more than her appearance. It is an index to the unnatural dimensions of life, which, in her commonsensical adherence to social values, she sees only dimly. She and the things she does are therefore "unnatural constructions" that produce social value in a number of ways and in a number of sectors. The affective value of these constructions of feminine sexuality depends heavily on their representability in a commodity form that allows them to circulate. The persistence of the transgressive blonde is as necessary as prostitution to the social construction of restraints, to the maintenance of social constraints on gender and sexuality, and to the melodramatic discourses that establish the problematic and contradictory nature of her image. Vulnerability, and knowingness, centrality and marginality are integral to the production of this form of femininity, if perhaps not to femininity generally.

Society's punishment by execution of Ruth Ellis and the affective conflicts surrounding her life and death are part of a familiar and also indispensable scenario that serves to define, legitimize, and devalue femininity at the same time that it sets it up as a necessary value. Ellis's value, like Diana Dors's value and like the value of Richardson's reenactment of Ellis, resides not in hiding her "value" but in exposing the cultural and economic relations that inhere in femininity and in making Ellis's image available for circulation in affectively economic terms by linking it to other commodities. The blonde as a source of entertainment is a commodity that begets other commodities not only in the realm of sexuality but also in the arena of entertainment, exposing connections between property, money, sexuality, and class relations. Her image produces a set of affects, clothed in common sense, that are necessary in order for this commodity to be experienced as valuable and therefore for it to exist and circulate.

Of the affects embedded in the melodramatic medium, the most striking involves the "publishing" or "advertising" of this commodity through the courts, the newspapers, the tabloids, films, star discourses, television, biographies, and even scholarly articles. The figure circulates through the culture at large. Because of its ubiquity, familiarity, and attractiveness but also because of the critical scrutiny it receives, a campy appropriation of the image or even the slightest second look will expose its representation as manufacture. In this ever present possibility of exposure lies the threat to any belief in natural qualities. The persona exists as a counterclaim to realism and to essentialism as well as to strictly binary forms of differentiation. Even the scenario of disaster that dogs the blonde sexpot has to be understood as constituted in the interests of the social value and not as a measure of fate or destiny. This intuition, this anticipation of disaster, of the "bad end"—and its realization as well—is part of the calculated scenario and is as much narratively constructed as the physical appearance of the persona is constructed. Similarly the aura of individuality and uniqueness identified with one or another attribute—breasts, hair, joie de vivre—is itself belied by comparisons, by the attributes' association with the blonde bombshell: Marilyn Monroe, Jayne Mansfield, Diana Dors, Ruth Ellis, and even Madonna.

Figures who, like Ellis, brush directly with the law are not represented as conventional victims, as lambs going submissively to the slaughter. Their threat goes far beyond the narrow retributive sense and beyond conceptions of common morality. Figures like Ellis are threatening because they endanger the very common sense they seem to embody and espouse. Despite their often articulated adherence to conventional notions of family, religion, monogamy, and maternal behavior, everything about the figures contradicts such notions. Ellis's refusal to stay within the family milieu, her frequent abortions, her work for underworld figures, her sexual promiscuity, her indifference about caring for her offspring devotedly and to the exclusion of her own pleasure, her involvement in violent sexual practices, and above all her taking revenge on her tormentors—

these all become acts that expose antagonisms between sexuality and morality, education, and the state.

No wonder that one woman at the time of Ruth Ellis's trial wanted Ellis hanged so that she could sleep better at night. Moreover the woman urged, "Let us remain a law-abiding country where citizens can walk abroad in peace and safety."[54] Ellis's admission of having paid with her life for Blakely's death reinforces this sense of the culturally necessary dimensions not only of her death but also of her transgressive life. The particular nature of the blonde sinner's role as victim and later as aggressor reinforces the sense in which the landscape of gender and sexuality involves violence, not as an excrescence but as a fundamental requirement. In affective terms, then, the element of rage as the affect that generates vengeance and violence needs further investigation, and the women's prison melodramas, specifically those dramas that address the issue of the state and capital punishment for the crime of murder, are especially sensitive to this dimension.

Thus the issue of the involvement of femininity in violence and of the perpetuation of violence against femininity by others assumes a more complicated configuration. Not only is it part of the coercive fabric attached by the culture to femininity, but it also serves to help clarify the frequent warning of coming to a bad end as a self-fulfilling prophecy that inserts the state into the civil sphere. If the law itself, as in Ruth Ellis's case, involves the state in retributive justice, that justice presupposes not merely the experience of transgression but its necessity. Ellis satisfies society's expectations and confirms its fears: that she is threatening and violent but entertaining. And since she is a member of the working class, her history doubly confirms the fear of her as feminine as well as working class. In both roles she contains the potential to challenge law and order. Both acquiescent and transgressive femininity share the same relation to the law. While the former supports the violence of the state in the name of law and order, the latter is expected to run afoul of the law and so reinforce the law. In the construction of value, what makes for the affective investment in and profitability of modes of production that seem to be valueless is that they are profoundly allied to forms of coercion that are not immediately manifest.

Like the other star narratives and films discussed above, Ruth Ellis's history is a melodrama—but not in the sense that the affect serves to conceal connections among gender, class, and sexuality and to render them depoliticized. Rather, the melodrama functions to expose how affect provides its "visible fictions." The narratives are neither escapist nor fantastic. The characters are exemplary of how antagonisms are acted out through the conjunction of media and other cultural institutions. The union of melodrama with common sense (in the Gramscian sense of residual knowledge, knowledge belonging to an earlier time that is anastomosed to present ways of thinking and behavior) is neither false consciousness nor mere ideology. It is a form of history—the history of subaltern groups—and aids reading into that history and understanding its position both as a conduit of value and as an antagonist to it. The film's uses of the past require yet another look into certain images of femininity as circulated through biography, of biography as circulated through melodrama, of melodrama as common sense, and of common sense as popular history.

The figures represented through the star biographies and the films discussed here are not static: We witness an image of femininity that, though appearing "mythic," is nonetheless closely tied to cinematic and social history (if the two can even be considered to be separate from each other). On the route from Mae West to Madonna through Diana Dors can be found the necessarily varying shapes, voices, images, and personalities, as well as the intensities relating to their pleasurable and dangerous dimensions. In discussing the particular con-figurations of Mae West's persona, Ramona Curry has argued that "West's role as prostitute in her films up to and including Klondike Annie cast her doubly as consumer object; as character within the narrative; and as fetishized star within the movie."[55] Curry argues that West's star image presented "multiple threats to the dominant order upheld by both the reform movement and the industry, which first exploited then attempted to contain and repudiate it as a powerful embodiment of transgressive female sexuality."[56] These comments apply to Dors's star image and to Ruth Ellis: "It was not West's characterization of prostitute that constituted the primary threat . . . but rather her success as star and character in the ironic and pleasurable exploitation of her own body, along with her power in herself representing a transgressive consumer of sexuality."[57]

The "successful" impersonation of femininity is dependent—to return to Candy Darling's description yet again—not only on the movie moguls and the reformers but on a more broadly shared cultural consensus that circulates among producers and consumers. The scenario of pleasure is not extricable from retri-bution; rather, it is built into the very characterization, if not prescription, of "transgressive" femininity, thereby producing and enhancing its value. The blonde tart is not exceptional in her "transgressiveness"; transgressiveness is a necessary attribute of femininity and inheres in the constitution of the affective value of this image as character, fetishized star, and carrier of the common-sensical lore of culture that helps to circulate such values. Ruth Ellis's story is not an isolated chapter in a "social history" of passive feminine victimage but a sig-nificant and productive locus and carrier of history.[58] The Ellis case, like the films devoted to it, like the reiteration of blondeness and transgression, exposes how femininity as affective value requires its visible fictions and how the British cinema is haunted by these fictions.

NOTES

1. Candy Darling, *Candy Darling* (Madras: Hanuman Books, 1992).

2. Gavatri Chakravorty Spivak, *In Other Worlds: Essays in Cultural Politics* (New York: Routledge, 1988), 166.

3. Karl Marx, *Capital*, vol. I (London: Dent, 1974), 43–44.

4. Ibid., 47.

5. Ibid., 71.

6. Antonio Gramsci, *Selections from the Prison Notebooks*, ed. Quintin Hoare and Geoffrey Nowell-Smith (New York: International Publishers, 1978), 137.

7. Ibid., 413.

8. Christine Gledhill, "Signs of Melodrama." In *Stardom: Industry of Desire*, ed. Christine Gledhill (London: Routledge, 1991), 225.

9. Darling, *Candy Darling*, 93–94.

10. Laurence Marks and Tony Van Den Bergh, *Ruth Ellis: A Case of Diminished Responsibility?* (London: Penguin Books, 1990), 134.

11. Diana Dors, *Dors by Diana: An Intimate Self-Portrait* (London: MacDonald Futura, 1981), 12.

12. Ibid., 211.

13. Ibid., 36.

14. Ibid., 32.

15. Ibid., 10.

16. Ibid., 22.

17. Mary Ann Doane, *The Desire to Desire: The Woman's Film of the 1940s* (Bloomington: Indiana University Press, 1987), 41.

18. Diana Dors, *For Adults Only* (London: W. H. Allen, 1978), 251.

19. Ibid., 180.

20. Ibid., 18.

21. Christine Gerahty, "Diana Dors." In *All Our Yesterdays: 90 Years of British Cinema*, ed. Charles Barr (London: BFI, 1986), 341.

22. Ibid., 341–42.

23. Ibid., 342.

24. David Lusted, "The Glut of the Personality." In Gledhill, ed., *Stardom*, 257.

25. Ibid., 258.

26. John Hill, *Sex, Class, and Realism: British Cinema, 1956–1963* (London: BFI, 1986), 19–20.

27. Paul Swann, *The Hollywood Feature Film in Postwar Britain* (New York: St. Martin's Press, 1987), 13–30.

28. Richard Dyer, *The Matter of Images: Essays on Representation* (London: Routledge, 1993), 100.

29. Ibid.

30. Dors, *Dors by Diana*, 21.

31. Dors, *For Adults Only*, 18.

32. Leslie Halliwell, *Halliwell's Film Guide*, 7th ed. (New York: Harper and Row, 1989), 1140.

33. Mike Prokosch, "Imitation of Life." In *Douglas Sirk*, ed. Laura Mulvey and Jon Halliday (Edinburgh Film Festival in association with the National Film Theatre and John Player and Sons, 1972), 98.

34. Jackie Byars, *All That Hollywood Allows: Reading Gender in 1950s Melodrama* (Chapel Hill: University of North Carolina Press, 1991), 121–31.

35. Dors, *For Adults Only*, 12.

36. Marks and Van Den Bergh, *Ruth Ellis*, 162.

37. Ibid., 159.

38. For example, see also Jonathan Goodman and Patrick Pringle, *The Trial of Ruth Ellis* (Newton Abbot, Eng.: David and Charles, 1974). There is also a reference to an Australian television documentary on Ellis in Marks and Van Den Bergh, *Ruth Ellis*, 198. See also Jacqueline Rose, "Margaret Thatcher and Ruth Ellis," *New Formations* 6 (1988), 3–29.

39. James Park, *British Cinema: The Lights That Failed* (London: Batsford, 1990), 159.

40. Ibid., 160.

41. Ibid., 175.

42. Ibid.

43. Ibid.

44. Mike Davis, *The City of Quartz: Excavating the Future in Los Angeles* (London: Verso, 1991), 44. Davis identifies a "major revival of noir in the 1960s and 1970s."

45. Dana Polan, *In a Lonely Place* (London: BFI, 1993).

46. David N. Rodowick, "Madness, Authority, and Ideology: The Domestic Melodramas of the 1950s." In *Home Is Where the Heart Is: Studies in Melodrama and the Woman's Film,* ed. Christine Gledhill (London: BFI, 1987), 272.

47. Vincent Canby, "Are 'New' Women's Movies Guilty of Sexism in Reverse?" *New York Times* (November 10, 1985), 162.

48. Andrew Higson, "Re-Presenting the National Past: Nostalgia and Pastiche in the Heritage Film." In *Fires Were Started: British Cinema and Thatcherism,* ed. Lester Friedman (Minneapolis: University of Minnesota Press, 1993), 128.

49. Japa, "Dance with a Stranger," *Variety* 318, no. 7 (March 13, 1985).

50. Paul Giles, "History with Holes: Channel Four Television Films of the 1980s." In Friedman, ed., *Fires Were Started,* 81.

51. Marks and Van Den Bergh, *Ruth Ellis,* 15.

52. Richard Combs, "The Social Slide," *Times Literary Supplement* (March 8, 1985), 260.

53. Rose, "Margaret Thatcher and Ruth Ellis," 9.

54. Marks and Van Den Bergh, *Ruth Ellis.* 175.

55. Ramona Curry, "Mae West as Censored Commodity: The Case of Klondike Annie," *Cinema Journal* no. 1 (Fall 1991), 78.

56. Ibid.

57. Ibid.

58. On the subject of the "feminine character," Theodor Adorno has written that it "is a negative imprint of domination. Whatever is in the context of bourgeois delusion called nature, is merely the scar of social mutilation . . . what passes for nature in civilization is by its very substance furthest from nature," *Minima Moralia* (London: Verso, 1974), 95–96.

Anton Kaes

The Presence of the Past:
Rainer Werner Fassbinder's
The Marriage of Maria Braun

The effacement of memory is more the achievement of an all-too-wakeful consciousness than it is the result of its weakness in the face of the superiority of unconscious processes. In this forgetting of what is scarcely past one senses the fury of the one who has to talk himself out of what everyone else knows, before he can talk them out of it.
—Theodor W. Adorno

I tell you all my secrets
But I lie about my past.   —Tom Waits

The arrow of memory is not poisoned, but the social body it hits seems to become more vulnerable the more it rears up and contorts itself so as not to show its vulnerability.
—André Glucksmann

The Politics of Private Life

Rainer Werner Fassbinder was found dead in his Munich apartment on June 10, 1982. He was thirty-seven years old. The epitaphs in all the world's major newspapers bear witness to the esteem he had gained for himself and for the New German Cinema. His oeuvre of forty-three films and television productions, many of which received prizes and awards, together with his uncompromising, provocatively bohemian lifestyle, won him an undisputed reputation as the "heart" of New German Cinema.[1] In the eyes of the foreign press, Fassbinder's critical view of West German reality qualified him as a reliable (because incorruptibly critical) chronicler of the Federal Republic. His films provided "information about Germany."[2] According to the conservative newspaper *The Daily Mail,* he acted as the "conscience of his nation."[3] Colette Godard began her front-page epitaph in *Le Monde* with these words: "Rainer Werner Fassbinder

Reprinted by permission of the publisher from *From Hitler to Heimat: The Return of History as Film* by Anton Kaes (Cambridge, Mass.: Harvard University Press). Copyright © 1989 by the President and Fellows of Harvard College.

represented the passionate rage of the German film, the rage of a young generation that opened its eyes in the 1960s and learned what its elders had left behind: the destruction of German identity through National Socialism."[4]

Especially outside of Germany, Fassbinder seemed to embody the West German postwar generation that grew up in the fifties during the so-called "economic miracle" and, in the sixties, revolted against parents, teachers, and the state. This is the generation of Andreas Baader (born in 1944), Gudrun Ensslin (1942), and Rudi Dutschke (1940), but also that of Peter Schneider (1942), Werner Herzog (1944), and Wim Wenders (1945). Unlike the generation of Syberberg or Kluge, born in the early 1930s, this generation did not directly experience the Third Reich, Hitler, and the war. Those born in 1945, like Fassbinder, were given the German past as an unwanted legacy.

It was a legacy that was taboo in the 1950s. The older generation had, consciously or unconsciously, banned all questions about the most recent German past. By the mid-1960s, shortly after the Eichmann trial in Jerusalem and the Auschwitz trial in Frankfurt, as the postwar children began to question their parents about their involvement in the Hitler regime, an acute, crisis developed in the relations between the generations in West Germany. No matter what justifications and excuses the parents had, the younger generation's judgment knew no mercy: their parents, now polemically called the "Auschwitz generation," were guilty. Their pride in having transformed Germany from rubble and ruins to one of the most affluent countries in the world seemed to their children merely an evasive tactic meant to divert attention from the unatoned crimes committed by them in the name of Germany.

This long-repressed hatred toward the older generation, the "generation of culprits," exploded in 1967, intensified by worldwide protest campaigns against the Vietnam War, against the new state emergency laws passed by the Bundestag, and against the right-wing mass-circulation newspapers controlled by the press baron Axel Springer. It also fed on the students' discontent with the ossified educational system and the hierarchical structure of the university. As part of an international youth culture, the so-called Woodstock generation, a movement also arose in the Federal Republic that radically altered the consciousness of the postwar generation. For the first time in the West German democracy, the students (and many others) took a stand against the state and institutional authority. The protests, most of them successful at least initially, were full of anarchic power and utopian idealism. All this revolutionary energy that galvanized politics as well as culture must have affected Fassbinder deeply. It is not a coincidence that his career began exactly in 1967, at the height of the student rebellion in West Germany. He never departed from the radical utopian-anarchic ideals of this period; they form the horizon against which the reality (and integrity) of his heroes and heroines, is measured. Not surprisingly, all of Fassbinder's films thematize the failure of these uncompromising ideals and the final shattering of illusions. They explore oppressive power relations and dependencies, melodramatic emotions, hopeless compromises, double binds, and inescapable situations that often end in suicide.

Fassbinder started out as an actor and theater director in Munich's vibrant underground theater scene. He met many of his collaborators there (for instance, Peer Raben, who wrote the scores to virtually all of Fassbinder's films) as well as many of the actors (among them Hanna Schygulla, Irm Hermann, Kurt Raab) with whom he worked for the next ten years, in the style of a small repertory theater. This working arrangement accounts in part for the remarkable speed with which Fassbinder was able to make his films and for the easily identifiable look of a "Fassbinder film." He became interested in filmmaking in 1967 when Jean-Marie Straub, whose minimalist 1965 film adaptation of a Böll novel, *Not Reconciled,* was one of the first critically acclaimed films of the New German Cinema, made a film with the *antiteater,* Fassbinder's experimental theater group in Munich. Straub's experimental short film, *Der Bräutigam, die Komödiantin und der Zuhälter (The Bridegroom, the Comedienne, and the Pimp),* took months of intensive rehearsal. Fassbinder learned a great deal in that time from Straub's controlled, self-reflexive, Brechtian use of film images. His own first films, *Liebe ist kälter als der Tod (Love is Colder Than Death)* and *Katzelmacher* (both 1969), show Straub's strong influence in both their filmic style and their dramatic structure.

In 1971 Fassbinder saw films by Douglas Sirk, the Hamburg-born Hollywood director, for the first time. Sirk had worked as Detlef Sierck for Universum–Film Aktiengesellschaft (UFA) and had made (among other films) the famous melodramas *La Habañera* and *Zu neuen Ufern (To New Shores),* starring the legendary actress Zarah Leander, before emigrating in 1937. Fassbinder was impressed by Sirk's ability to make commercially successful films with wide audience appeal without compromising a subversive, "European" sensibility and an idiosyncratic, personal style; he "adopted" the exiled German as his spiritual father, desperately wanting to be part of a tradition of German filmmaking.[5] Sirk's great melodramas of the 1950s—especially *All That Heaven Allows* (1955) and *Imitation of Life* (1958)—follow the classical style of trivial novels in concentrating on the great emotions of little people and their unrealistic aspirations. His melodramas invariably deal with people doomed to failure in a hostile social environment. In Fassbinder's eyes, Sirk depicted unbridled passions in a distinctive manner, making filmic space itself signify through high-contrast lighting, through the symbolic use of everyday objects like flowers, mirrors, pictures on the wall, pieces of furniture, and clothing, and finally through careful compositions and a dynamic mise-en-scène—most of which harked back to Sirk's beginnings as a theater director.[6] Fassbinder's *Der Händler der vier Jahreszeiten (The Merchant of Four Seasons)* (1971) and *Angst essen Seele auf (Fear Eats the Soul)* (1973) consciously evoke Sirk's style, making use of melodramatic plots, "unrealistic" lighting, obtrusive camera movements, and artificial, highly stylized decor. Overly melodramatic music breaks the illusion, and a theatrical gestural language keeps the viewer at a critical distance despite the open display of strong emotions.[7]

Sirk's influence is also visible in Fassbinder's historical films, which appeared in rapid succession after 1977: *Die Ehe der Maria Braun (The Marriage of Maria Braun*), filmed from January to March 1978; *Berlin Alexanderplatz,* filmed from June 1979 to April 1980; *Lili Marleen,* filmed from July to September 1980; *Lola,* filmed from April to May 1981; and *Die Sehnsucht der Veronika Voss (Veronika Voss),* filmed from November to December 1981. All deal with the unfulfilled and unfulfillable desires of the characters, the exploitation and exploitability of their emotions, and the destruction they bring down on themselves. These melodramatic themes provide a continuity in Fassbinder's work from his first film to the last, regardless of whether they are set in today's Germany or in the Germany of the past. Apart from the adaptations of Theodor Fontane's *Effi Briest* (1974) and of Oskar Maria Graf's *Bolwieser* (1976), Fassbinder did not explore the historical dimensions of his socially critical themes until after the mid-1970s. In 1977, however, he began work on a ten-part television series based on Gustav Freytag's 1855 novel *Soll und Haben (Debit and Credit),* in which he planned to trace the National Socialist ideology back to the nineteenth-century German bourgeoisie. Although he had to abandon this project because of network objections,[8] he was still eager to explore the past as a (pre-)history of the present—if not in a large-scale television series, then in individual films.

The period that most fascinated Fassbinder was the postwar era, the time following the rupture of 1945 in which "everything" seemed possible. The Federal Republic was not yet firmly established, and utopian hopes still existed. "Our fathers," Fassbinder said in 1978, "had the chance to found a state that could have been the most humane and freest ever."[9] Confronting the founding years of the Federal Republic meant illuminating the dominant values and illusions of the period, as well as investigating its latent dreams and longings. The postwar era coincided with Fassbinder's own lifetime; at the age of thirty, he began to look back at his and the Federal Republic's early years with a critical eye. Like many other authors of his generation, he turned in the late 1970s to his own youth in the Adenauer era, albeit less autobiographically and nostalgically than, for instance, Jürgen Theobaldy in *Sonntags Kino (Movies on Sundays)* (1978) or Angelika Mechtel in *Wir sind arm, wir sind reich (We Are Poor, We Are Rich)* (1977).[10] Fassbinder's approach is a critical one; he had little interest in "the way it really was," but rather wondered how the thoughts, feelings, and actions of his contemporaries could be explained historically.[11] Like Walter Benjamin, he wanted to deal with the constellation of past and present, with the moment of recognition in which past and present mutually illuminate each other.[12]

A further impetus for his turning to history was the crisis of Autumn 1977, which Fassbinder's generation experienced as a watershed in the political development and self-understanding of the Federal Republic. In his 26-minute contribution to the collective film *Germany in Autumn,* Fassbinder reacted spontaneously to the intellectual atmosphere of that time by playing himself— the only one of the nine filmmakers to do so. In the film he appears beleaguered, literally locked up in his own dark apartment, linked to the outside world only by a telephone. We hear a police siren and steps on the stairs, noises that cause

Fassbinder to panic. A furtive glance through the blinds shows someone crossing an empty street. Claustrophobia dominates as the camera peers into the private sphere of the controversial director whose life is surrounded by scandals. Fassbinder gives us a document of shameless self-revelation, a psychogram of his anxieties and aggressions. He intercuts the apartment scenes with an inquisitorial (scripted) interview with his own mother, who has appeared in many of his films. Scenes of radical, self-indulgent subjectivity alternate with scenes of analytical reflection. The striking disparity between Fassbinder the filmmaker, who is brought to the brink of a physical breakdown by the political situation, and Fassbinder the son, who fights with his mother about German traditions of state violence and political resistance, leaves a strong and highly disturbing impression.[13]

In the interview with his mother, the son insists on his democratic right to pursue open political discussions despite threats; anything less would mean a regression into dictatorship. His mother agrees; the current political climate reminds her "a lot of the Nazi time, when people just kept quiet to stay out of trouble."[14] Their dispute is about the freedom of opinion in times of crisis and the question of whether the law can be broken in the fight against terrorists. Fassbinder tells his mother that precisely because she lived through the Third Reich, she should have a more pronounced respect for democracy. Instead, however, she advocates a retreat from democracy: "The best thing now would be a kind of authoritarian ruler who is good and kind and orderly." Fassbinder condemns his mother for her authoritarian beliefs and her cowardice, while—and this is the dialectic behind his contribution—the camera captures those very same qualities in himself. We see him treat his mother and his gay lover in an authoritarian manner, almost sadistically. It is also clear that he does not exercise the right he demands, to take part in the public debate; instead, he withdraws from the outside world and dictates the shooting script for *Berlin Alexanderplatz,* his new film project at the time. The spectator alone must sort out these troubling contradictions.

What can a film like *Germany in Autumn* accomplish? In an interview at the end of 1977, Fassbinder said: "It can formulate anxieties. For others. If no one does that, we would retreat into a muteness in which we would soon become stupid. The film can encourage the viewer to continue to have an opinion and to express it."[15] But Fassbinder posed questions in *Germany in Autumn* that demanded a more complete answer. Following up on his interview with his mother, he planned to make another cooperative film about the older generation, called "The Marriages of Our Parents." Even though he was unable to secure financing, he did not want to relinquish this project, which, he said, would have been rich enough for an eight-hour film. Fassbinder therefore asked two professional screenwriters, Peter Märthesheimer and Pea Fröhlich, to reduce his unwieldy narrative to a conventional feature film length.[16] "The Marriages of Our Parents" thus became *The Marriage of Maria Braun,* a film that finally brought about Fassbinder's breakthrough to a mass audience both in Germany and abroad.

Coinciding with the film's premiere in February 1979, the weekly magazine *Stern* started to run a serialized novel based on Fassbinder's film, and even carrying the same title. Written by Gerhard Zwerenz, the novel more or less retold the film story and was illustrated with photographs from the film.[17] This multimedia marketing, common in the United States, was new in Germany and may have contributed to the film's commercial success. *The Marriage of Maria Braun* is the first part of Fassbinder's "BRD-Trilogie" (FRG Trilogy); it was followed by *Lola* (1981) and *Veronika Voss* (1982). All three films deal with the Federal Republic from the mid-1940s to the mid-1950s as seen from the perspective of the late seventies. When asked about the function of these historical films, Fassbinder responded:

> We didn't learn much about German history in Germany, so we have to catch up with some basic information, and as a filmmaker I simply used this information to tell a story. That means nothing more than making reality tangible. I see many things today that again arouse fear in me. The call for law and order. I want to use this film to give today's society something like a supplement to their history. Our democracy was decreed for the Western occupation zone; we didn't fight for it ourselves. Old ways of thinking, have lots of opportunity to seep in through cracks, without a swastika, of course, but with old methods of education. I am astonished how quickly the rearmament came about in this country. The attempts by the younger generation to revolt were quite pitiful. I also want to show how the 1950s shaped the people of the 1960s. How the establishment clashed with the engaged youth, which was pushed into the abnormality of terrorism.[18]

Fassbinder is obviously as much concerned with the present as with the past. The stories he tells in the FRG Trilogy—unlike Syberberg, Fassbinder loves to tell conventional stories with a beginning, middle, and end—take place in the founding years of the Federal Republic, but indirectly always refer to the present. They provide snapshots of German misery as Fassbinder understood and felt it at the end of the 1970s: the subjugation of emotions to mercenary material greed in the reconstruction years (*The Marriage of Maria Braun*); the ubiquitous corruption one had to accept in the years of opportunistic conformity (*Lola*); and the neurosis about one's own past and traumatic memories that had to be exorcised (*Veronika Voss*). The films show that the combination of economic miracle and collective denial of the past caused a potential for conflict that built up in the fifties and exploded ten years later.

Fassbinder's films on Germany do not present large-scale politics and economics directly. Instead they operate within the "micropolitics of desire,"[19] showing the hopes, aspirations, and frustrations of people in concrete historical situations. The protagonists in Fassbinder's FRG Trilogy are all women, for he believes that women are, as dramatic characters, more interesting, less predictable, and less conformist than men: "Men in this society are much more forced to play a role than women, who have a role but can break out of it much more easily or can deviate a step or two from the path."[20] Fassbinder's female protagonists shape their epoch as much as they are shaped by it. In their politically unaware private lives, they contribute to, and parabolically mirror, the dominant mentality of their time.[21] Fassbinder's films supplement official historiography with a psychological dimension, delving into everyday life and the private sphere; they show how politics is negotiated "from below."

To give an example: in a scene in *The Marriage of Maria Braun* in which Maria is visiting her relatives, the radio is turned on and Adenauer is giving a speech. "I do not want an army," we hear him say in an original sound recording, "we've had enough deaths. . . . One need only recall the fact that in Germany today there are 160 women for every 100 men" (93–94).[22] As Adenauer speaks, we see Maria and her relatives eating, commenting on the potato salad and exchanging recipes. No one listens to the radio speech, in which Adenauer vehemently opposes the rearmament of the Federal Republic. The radio voice brings a political dimension into the private family sphere, but it is ignored. Fassbinder uses this scene to illustrate dramatically the deficient political awareness of most Germans during the reconstruction period, when food was more important than politics. Toward the end of the film we hear another original recording of a radio broadcast, this time from 1954. Adenauer now advocates equally emphatically the rearmament of the Federal Republic: "We have the right to rearm—as much as we can, as much as we want" (145). It is unclear whether Maria Braun, who is eating alone in a restaurant, hears this speech with its complete about-face on the question of rearmament, but she suddenly gets up, stumbles, and vomits. The action seems to comment on the radio speech; the tension in this scene between image and sound allows Fassbinder to correlate public and private sickness, to show an extreme private reaction to what he considers a fatal development in German political history.

At regular intervals public history (*Geschichte*) breaks into the private stories (*Geschichten*). The history of the German nation from the end of the war to the so-called economic miracle of the 1950s punctuates and expands the story of Maria Braun. Political history enters the fictional frame in various forms. For instance, at the beginning of the film we hear a monotonous radio voice reading off the names and identification numbers of missing soldiers about whom information is available. The theme of searching and reunion is mirrored in public discourse: as Maria Braun looks for her husband, the state looks for its scattered subjects.

Visiting Germany in 1950, only five years after Germany's *Stunde Null* ("Zero Hour"), Hannah Arendt observed: "Everywhere one notices that there is no reaction to what has happened, but it is hard to say whether that is due to an intentional refusal to mourn or whether it is the expression of a genuine emotional incapacity."[23] Fassbinder's film reproduces this mood, in which practical survival and accommodation take precedence over the work of memory and mourning. (The camera emphasizes people's greed for simple pleasures like cigarettes or coffee through frequent, often obtrusive closeups.) At the same time Fassbinder shows the beginnings of a reemerging nationalist feeling. In the midst of a landscape of ruins someone clumsily plays a flawed version of the German national anthem on an accordion as the camera pans across destroyed buildings. Voices interrupt the street musician; someone starts singing "Deutschland, Deutschland über alles," stops, starts over, and breaks off in the middle. The dissonant, interrupted national anthem in this context stands as a sign for the half-devastated, crippled nation. The ragged singing of the anthem in the midst of ruins must be read as Fassbinder's sarcastic comment on the willed ignorance of those who do not want to admit that "Deutschland" has perished.

Historical Narration

There is always a purpose when one is talking about history.
—Alfred Döblin

"History consists of wisps of narratives," says Jean-François Lyotard in his *Instructions païennes* (1977), "stories that one tells, that one hears, that one acts out; the people do not exist as a subject but as a mass of millions of insignificant and serious little stories that sometimes let themselves be collected together to constitute big stories and sometimes disperse into digressive elements."[24] Writing history would then consist of weaving together many individual narrative threads into a "text" (in the sense of the Latin *textum*, something woven). The way in which the narrative threads are intertwined attaches a certain meaning to the historical event, which by itself has an infinite multiplicity of potential meanings. Thus Karlheinz Stierle writes: "With respect to events, history writing is a reduction. This reduction follows a direction that can be called 'the superimposition of an ideal line' (Simmel). The 'ideal line' constitutes the basic narrative relations of the story which serve to integrate the elements of the event."[25]

The narrative pattern that Fassbinder uses in his FRG Trilogy is the biography of a woman who makes her way alone through the German postwar era as an adventuress and female picaro. Less vagrant than Defoe's Moll Flanders but similarly unscrupulous when it comes to her own advantage, Maria Braun moves through the period between 1945 and 1954. *The Marriage of Maria Braun* is a densely woven text that consists of a great number of isolated small stories subordinated to the central narrative, the story of the rise and fall of Maria Braun. The life of the film persona Maria Braun is structured "like a movie": narrative and images follow the pattern of the melodramatic films of the 1940s and 1950s, which in turn had generously drawn on motifs from the popular novel of the nineteenth century. Fassbinder adopts these clichés but defamiliarizes them by multiplying, exaggerating, and accentuating them (often with the accompaniment of melodramatic musical chords). He also undercuts the conventions of the genre; thus the film does not end with a marriage but instead begins with one.

Maria weds the infantryman Hermann Braun in the last year of the war, in the middle of a bomb attack, but their marriage lasts only a single night and half a day, since Hermann has to return to the front. She waits for him and trades on the black market in order to support herself and her mother. The film carefully reconstructs the historical ambience, with scenes of returning soldiers, women picking up the rubble, and black marketeers.[26] When Hermann, believed dead, suddenly appears in the doorway—the returning soldier is a classic motif in twentieth-century German drama[27]—he surprises Maria with her lover, a black occupation soldier who is an acquaintance from an off-limits bar where she works. Mr. Bill, the GI, is presented as attractive, shy rather than aggressive. Fassbinder shows Maria's fondness for him in idyllic scenes, an unusual and provocative counterimage to the negative image of the American liberators, for instance, in Helma Sanders-Brahms's *Germany, Pale Mother* and Edgar Reitz's *Heimat*. Hermann's return is all the more shocking because he bursts in on a love scene. The two men fight, and Hermann, weakened by the long journey home from the war, is about to lose when Maria, as if in a trance, hits Mr. Bill over the head with a bottle. The GI dies. Hermann, touched by Maria's loyalty, pleads guilty in court and goes to prison in her stead. Maria promises him that their "real" life will begin upon his release. In the meantime, on her own again, she pursues a single goal: economic success. Love and emotion, her whole private life, are deferred. She holds fast to the dream of a great eternal love even when she meets Oswald, an elderly emigrant and owner of a textile factory, who falls in love with her. She takes him as her lover and rapidly rises to a leading position in his firm.

In this film Fassbinder gives us a portrait of the reconstruction period of the Federal Republic, when the decline in human values is shown to correspond directly to the increase in profit rates. "Is that how it is between people outside? So cold?" (108), Hermann asks when Maria visits him in prison and tells him that she has strictly separated business and emotions. She answers: "It's a hard time now for feelings, I think." She has become affluent and has bought a luxurious villa; now she waits for Hermann: "Our life will start again when we're together" (80). But after he is released, to Maria's puzzlement, Hermann first goes abroad, only to reappear suddenly after Oswald's death. Maria (and the viewer) do not learn about the true state of affairs until Oswald's will is read in the last minutes of the film. Oswald, his death approaching, had feared losing Maria when Hermann was released. He visited Hermann in prison and made a deal with him behind Maria's back: Hermann was to receive half of Oswald's fortune for allowing Oswald to enjoy Maria until his death. Essentially, Hermann agreed to sell Maria to Oswald. When Maria learns about this secret deal, she suddenly understands that her utopian dreams of a future "real life" have been betrayed. She realizes that she was never in control of her own destiny, which she had thought she was manipulating so masterfully. Instead, she finds herself as a mere object of exchange in a business transaction between two men. The illusion that gave her life meaning shatters completely. A gas explosion, half-consciously caused by her, blows up the villa and Maria and Hermann with it.

The film does not hesitate to reproduce the classic narrative motifs of Hollywood melodramas from the late forties and fifties—love and murder, loyalty, betrayal, yearning for an absent lover, suffering, and death—in a film *about* the forties and fifties. It elaborates on these motifs in the various subplots that cluster around the story of Maria. As in the novels of Walter Scott and the tradition of the classical historical novel, political history and personal stories interact so that the individual private stories always contribute to and illustrate general history. As Maria Braun's own story unfolds, it touches other stories, joins with them, intervenes in them.[28] Maria's life is reflected in the life stories of the people around her; even peripheral figures are granted time to speak about their lives and shed new light on Maria's. For instance, a Red Cross nurse at the train station tells Maria that when her husband fell into a mountain crevice during the war, the army as compensation sent her a mass-produced oil painting of an *ocean*, with the inscription: "They died that Germany may live" (43). This one sentence succinctly illustrates the contradiction between the cynical official distortion of history and the private experience of suffering. It also epitomizes a motif that runs through the whole film: the antagonism between private and political history. Each of the numerous miniature life stories, sometimes shown and sometimes narrated, enrich Fassbinder's portrait of the times. These life stories, these wisps of narrative threads constitute the text of history, *Geschichten* making up *Geschichte*.

The viewer comes to a double awareness of how strongly political history determines private stories and how little the subjects of history understand that relationship. "From a private perspective," a German critic said in a review of the film, "political history appears as nothing but a series of hurdles that must be overcome."[29] The characters in the film neither discuss nor reflect upon such major historical events as the founding of the Federal Republic, the final division of Germany in 1949, or the uprising in East Berlin in 1953. West Germans of the 1950s believed that thinking about politics or the most recent past would only have impeded or slowed down reconstruction.[30] All that counted was the future; everything else was deferred.

The film presents elaborate stock images of the period, first the so-called "food wave," when Germans only seemed to have eating on their minds, then their preoccupation with clothes, furniture, and travel. Fassbinder dwells on these details, which do not advance the plot but deepen our understanding of the forces determining the characters' actions. Still, the telos of the film corresponds to the dynamics of the reconstruction period. Maria Braun embodies the idea that economic success is a function of keeping one's eyes on what is coming. At one point she calls herself "an expert in matters of the future" (101).

The film consists of a dense network of fictional private stories that give us insight into how the Germans of the fifties lived and experienced their lives. This proliferation of narrative strands leads to more information than is necessary to understand the main story. But it is precisely this excess of minor characters that fosters a realistic historical effect, an illusion of authentic history. The realistic effect also results from the fact that the historical fiction of *Maria Braun* seems to unfold as a story without a narrating subject; until the final scenes it is not clear who is telling the story. The elimination of an enunciating subject is one of the conventional devices to achieve the effect of "historical realism."

In the history film this effect is produced not only by the "pluralization" of the narration but also, and primarily, by the choice of images. In *The Marriage of Maria Braun* the detailed, accurate reconstruction of the visual world of the period guarantees the veracity of the historical fiction. The faithful reconstructions, from the postwar train station to the living room decor of the fifties, from the Allied uniforms to the women's hairstyles, evoke historical time between 1944 and 1954 through visual motifs well known from old photographs and newsreels. Images, for instance, of grizzled and haggard soldiers returning home, of women in head-scarves clearing away rubble, of well-fed American soldiers and their German war brides, all carry a high recognition value. Over the years they have become conventional representations of the immediate postwar years in Germany, engraving themselves on the collective memory as the "correct" representation of this era. Fassbinder uses them almost as one might use stock footage clichés to persuade the viewer to accept the film as a historical film. The realistic historical effect thus also depends on the visual memory of the audience. Because the historical film by definition refers to a past reality known to most viewers prior to the film, either from experience or from representations, they enjoy the effect of recognition ("That's just the way it was, that's what I remember having seen before"). This extra referent, which appeals to historical knowledge (and knowledge that exists outside of the film's fictional sphere), produces an additional level of meaning and increases the meaning potential of the film. Although the historical material loses its historiographic, factual status by being absorbed within the fiction, it remains discernible as a result of the viewer's historical knowledge, which the film activates. For instance, the documentary Adenauer speeches become part and parcel of *Maria Braun*'s fictional space. At the same time they are experienced as "real," as "historical" in the sense that the sound recordings of Adenauer's speeches used in the film also exist outside of this fictional space. They are verifiable; they are not inventions or fabrications. The viewer senses, even if unconsciously, the unresolvable dual status of historical narratives, as document and fiction, authentically true and at the same time used within a freely invented story.[31]

Fassbinder's montages of sound and images became increasingly complex after 1978. That complexity corresponds to the multilayered historical subject matter of his last films, which contain diverse and stratified languages, conflicting voices, and different representational modes. His notion of film as the locus of diverse stylistic unities recalls M. M. Bakhtin's idea of "heteroglossia," a term describing the conflicting plurality of voices in the discourse of the novel. "The novel," Bakhtin says, "must represent all the social and ideological voices of its era, that is, all the era's languages that have any claim of significance; the novel must be a microcosm of heteroglossia."[32] Fassbinder tries to achieve this diversity in his historical films by an accumulation of different voices. The sheer mass of simultaneous messages, referring to one another, contradicting and mirroring one another, leads to stratified sound collages with up to four layers: music, dialogue, radio, sound effects. At the end of *Maria Braun*, for instance, as Oswald's will is being read aloud, the radio is on with the live broadcast of a soccer game, and at the same time Maria is talking to Senkenberg. This density of simultaneous acoustic signs makes it almost impossible for the viewer to follow the denouement of the story. Public and private voices intermix inseparably with one another.

The Marriage of Maria Braun is also a story about the labor of storytelling, of fabricating fictions. Maria Braun herself is the film's best storyteller. She purposely conceals, feigns, and prevaricates, lies when it is expedient, and manipulates others through her skilled self-presentation. She is an expert at pretense and disguise, the basic figures of narration. When asked why she tells different stories to different people, she answers ironically: "Because I am a master of deception. A capitalist tool by day, and by night an agent of the proletarian masses. The Mata Hari of the economic miracle!" (110). The unpredictability of Maria Braun's behavior determines the structure of the film. The narrative resembles the picaresque novel in its accidental meetings, sudden partings, coincidences, and unexpected reunions. Maria Braun adapts to each new turn of fate with skill, opportunism, and a strong belief in her own success. "I'd rather make the miracles than wait for them" (104), she says at the height of the career that has led her from poverty and unatoned murder to riches and public recognition.

The Marriage of Maria Braun is constructed around the memory of a marriage that lasted one night and half a day. This marriage is the secret center and at the same time the vanishing point of Maria's story. It legitimates her ambition, her accumulation of wealth, and her obsessive planning for the future. A growing tension between past and future that devalues the present makes her distracted and forgetful. Finally the tension between remembering and forgetting, which underlies her whole story, is compressed into a scene lasting only a few seconds. Remembering or forgetting suddenly becomes a matter of life or death. As Maria Braun takes a cigarette from the pack, she hesitates, looks at the pack, asks her husband for a match, and then goes into the kitchen, where (as we remember from an earlier scene) she has forgotten to turn off the gas. Fassbinder deliberately leaves it ambiguous as to whether she simply forgets or chooses not to remember. He sets the price of forgetting high: both protagonists die in the explosion. Maria Braun's hope for the ideal to be realized, her waiting for utopia, ends in catastrophe.

History as Trauma

Comment être encore un Allemand?
—Marguerite Duras

Several years before embarking on *The Marriage of Maria Braun*, Fassbinder had already attempted to deal in a more direct way with the German problem of forgetting and repression. However, his attempts to explore the most sensitive area of German memory, the memory of anti-Semitism and systematically planned and executed genocide, all failed. Two of his film projects were rejected, and the play *Der Müll, die Stadt und der Tod* (*Garbage, the City and Death*) was produced neither in 1976, when it was written, nor in 1985, when it was again proposed. Nonetheless, the searing debates surrounding these unrealized projects showed with shocking clarity that the relations between Germans and Jews in the Federal Republic are still far from normal.[33]

Garbage, the City and Death, written in 1975–1976, was based on the Frankfurt novel *Die Erde ist unbewohnbar wie der Mond* (*The Earth Is as Inhabitable as the Moon*) (1973) by Gerhard Zwerenz. It became Fassbinder's most controversial project. The play's central figure, a sympathetically drawn Jewish real estate speculator who is called Abraham in the novel, appears without a name in the play. Instead, Fassbinder, employing an anti-Semitic stereotype, calls him the "Rich Jew" in his published script.[34] The play was hastily written, a comic-strip tirade of hatred from the perspective of prostitutes and pimps, triggered by the ruinous redevelopment of the Frankfurt West End. "And the city turns us into living corpses, horror figures without an adequate chamber, subway people with streets which poison us,"[35] one of the prostitutes says. Fassbinder intended his play to be an indictment of the city fathers who use and exploit the figure of the "Rich Jew" for their own purposes. The Jew in fact serves the corrupt politicians as a shield, because "today, you can't say anything against the Jews"—an insidious anti-Semitic statement in itself, as Adorno had already pointed out in 1964.[36] Fassbinder thematizes the cynical instrumentalization of the problematic relationship between Jewish and non-Jewish Germans by letting his characters make statements that are clearly anti-Semitic—and meant to be that way because they are supposed to define (and implicitly criticize) the dramatic character. The utterance of anti-Semitic stereotypes by a fictional character in a play is obviously used to portray him or her as anti-Semitic; it can never mean that Fassbinder identified with everything his characters say. Still, to hear anti-Semitic language used on a German stage in the 1970s—no matter if it is Fassbinder's or a stage character's thoughts that are expressed—was shocking and justifiably called for a reaction. The danger that the play might confirm still existing anti-Semitic prejudices or create new "misunderstandings" could not be ruled out.[37] "I do not think that Fassbinder was an anti-Semite," Henryk M. Broder argues, "but I am sure that his play served as a catalyst for plenty of anti-Semitic reactions."[38] In 1976 the city of Frankfurt denied funds for the production of the play and was relieved when Fassbinder consequently resigned from his position as the controversial director of the Theater am Turm, which he had held for less than a year. The public storm of protest broke when the printed text was published by Suhrkamp early in 1976.[39] An article by Helmut Schmitz in the *Frankfurter Rundschau* of March 12 pointed out the play's anti-Semitic tendencies. A week later, Joachim Fest took up the matter and wrote a vitriolic attack on Fassbinder's play in the *Frankfurter Allgemeine Zeitung,* calling it a prime example of leftist fascism and anti-Semitism.[40] In the same week the publisher stopped distribution of the play in order to avoid "misunderstandings." Siegfried Unseld, director of the Suhrkamp Publishing House, justified the decision as follows:

The charge that the author is anti-Semitic and a leftist fascist cannot be maintained; it is unfounded and must be rejected. Like Fassbinder, we believe that we must discuss how certain groups in Frankfurt, consisting of Jewish groups and individuals, were able to change the city to the disadvantage of its citizens and what role the city government played in these events. But reader reactions show us that the text of this play is serving less the investigation of the state of affairs than the release of undesirable emotions. In fact the play can create misunderstandings for those who did not experience this period of German history. The play quite correctly attacks a taboo. But Fassbinder's undifferentiated rough-hewn style does not avoid the danger of reproducing dangerous clichés for a public burdened by German history, clichés which the play and its author wish to oppose.[41]

Considerations of "a public burdened by German history" came to the fore again in 1977, when two similar projects by Fassbinder were rejected. Plans to film Zwerenz's *The Earth Is as Inhabitable as the Moon* failed because of the objections of the Project Commission of the Film Subsidy Board (Filmförderungsanstalt). And a planned ten-part television series based on Gustav Freytag's novel *Soll und Haben* (*Debit and Credit*), a projected critical history of the nineteenth-century German bourgeoisie, raised objections among German media officials and was blocked despite a year's preliminary work. In both cases, suspicions arose that Fassbinder was using, as he had in his play, figures and motifs that could be interpreted as anti-Semitic.[42] How can Fassbinder's relentless obsession with this topic be explained?

In Freytag's infamous anti-Semitic novel *Debit and Credit*, Fassbinder thought he had found the roots not only of National Socialist ideology but also of the social order of the Federal Republic. In addition, Freytag's style offered the kind of lurid appeal and melodramatic pathos that would be effective on film. In March 1977 Fassbinder wrote an article for *Die Zeit* describing this project as part of his coming to terms with the prehistory of the Nazi period: "It is precisely the sordid parts of *Soll und Haben*—the political consciousness of its author that seems false to us, which if it didn't produce the horrors to come, at least it covered them up literarily, and with rather slight literary ambitions at that—which force us to come to terms in one of the most important ways possible with our stories and our history, with the nineteenth century, our social ancestors and ourselves. The film, with the help of television, is capable of accomplishing this."[43]

In Fassbinder's view, *Debit and Credit* tells how the bourgeoisie of the mid-nineteenth century, after the failed revolution of 1848, developed not only virtues like industry and respectability but also values inextricably bound to the "German character," so that the German bourgeoisie constantly had to define itself "in relation to the proletariat and the nobility at home, in relation to everything foreign abroad, and especially in relation to a world view of objectivity, tolerance, and humanity, which was denounced as Jewish. The values attributed to the "German character" found their way without difficulty into the National Socialist ideology of the Third Reich, but—and that is the decisive reason compelling us to come to terms with this novel—they have also survived in today's society."[44] Fassbinder's goal in his planned television series was an archaeology of German bourgeois ideology, which he held responsible for producing anti-Semitism as well as the dictatorship of the Third Reich, and which he saw—and here he violated a taboo—as continuing right up to the present. He wanted, in other words, to bring *Debit and Credit* up to date.

Fassbinder's project would have had to illuminate and probe Freytag's unquestionably anti-Semitic motifs in terms of their origin and consequences. But since film must *show* things, there was clearly a danger that, for instance, staged scenes of ghetto life might unintentionally contribute to the perpetuation of anti-Semitic stereotypes. That was the view of Friedrich-Wilhelm von Sell, director of the West German network WDR, who claimed in 1977 that using Freytag's novel to "come to terms with the historical phenomena of anti-Semitism and anti-Slavism is subject to too many risks and misunderstandings."[45] His reservations led to a protest by more than thirty German filmmakers, including Volker Schlöndorff, Peter Lilienthal, and Wolfgang Staudte.[46] Fassbinder was embittered. He believed that with this novel as a starting point, he could "present the entire history of the German bourgeoisie from the middle of the last century to the outbreak of National Socialism—and do the exact opposite of what Joachim Fest did in his *Hitler* film, which is terribly reactionary and really only the attempt of a bourgeois to free himself of guilt."[47] It seemed especially ironic that it was Joachim Fest who chastised Fassbinder for being an anti-Semite.[48] Fest's film, *Hitler: A Career*, had been publicly criticized for condensing the persecution and annihilation of the Jews by the Nazis to 2½ minutes in a two and one-half hour long film. Fassbinder responded:

> Calling me an anti-Semite is just an excuse, because what I wanted to show is how anti-Semitism comes into being. It may be that Freytag's novel is anti-Semitic, but that very fact makes it useful for a description of anti-Semitism—and Freytag is certainly not anti-Semitic in his description of life in the ghetto and the hopeless situation of the Jews, in which they had to behave in a negative way in order to survive. The best way to describe the oppression of a minority is to show what errors and misdeeds a minority is forced into as a result of that oppression.[49]

Fassbinder's complicated logic—"A film of *Soll und Haben* will be historically 'correct' when it proves false what Freytag, his figures, and his readers thought was 'correct'"[50]—demands a dialectically schooled viewer who would not blame the Jewish population for any "misdeeds" that would have to be shown, but rather would see them as the doings of the true guilty party, the German tormentors. Freytag's novel abounds with the anti-Semitic stereotypes that have been passed down through centuries and are part of a literary tradition. Fassbinder wanted to defuse those stereotypes by historicizing them and subjecting them to a dialectical process. Freytag's anti-Semitism itself would have become an object of investigation: the Jews were to appear in his film as an "ostracized group that cannot behave differently because it is not permitted to."[51] The Jews were granted, for instance, the "right" to be moneylenders, an occupation that ran counter to the bourgeois code of honor; for that reason, according to Fassbinder, they were hated. He continues:

> The bourgeoisie needed the Jews in order to stop despising its own attitudes, to be able to feel proud, important and strong. The final result of such subconscious self-hatred was the mass annihilation of the Jews in the Third Reich. It was really an attempt to weed out what people didn't want to acknowledge in themselves. This relationship means that in some way the history of the Germans and the Jews is linked for all time, not just during the period from 1933 to 1945. Something like a new original sin will be passed on to people who are born and live in Germany, a sin that is not the less weighty because the sons of the murderers now wash their hands in innocence.[52]

Fassbinder's main concern is the illumination of the relationship between "bourgeois ideology" and recent German history. At issue is the "guilt remaining in the subconscious" and the "danger of a renewed perversion of bourgeois ideology." Fassbinder wants to pierce the heart of German ideology, not only because it created the conditions that made murderous anti-Semitism possible, but also because, in his view, the soil that nourished anti-Semitism is still fertile. He sees continuities where others see rupture; he makes the system of bourgeois values itself responsible for the crimes of National Socialism. Brecht once said that fascism is "the fruit of all the centuries";[53] similarly for Fassbinder, anti-Semitism has roots that reach back for centuries.

Although Fassbinder speaks about "guilt remaining in the subconscious" and a "new original sin" with respect to the crimes of the Third Reich, he repeatedly makes use of old anti-Semitic narrative patterns and visual motifs in what he intends as a radical critique of anti-Semitism. This is not only the case in his play *Garbage, the City and Death*, which was made into a film in 1976 by Daniel Schmid, a friend of Fassbinder's, in a revised version under the title *Schatten der Engel* (*Shadow of Angels*), with Fassbinder playing the lead;[54] it is also, and especially, true in his later films, in *Veronika Voss*, *In A Year with Thirteen Moons*, and most clearly *Lili Marleen*, a film that Anni Goldmann in *Le Monde* polemically compared with Veit Harlan's *Jud Süss*, the well-known anti-Semitic propaganda film of 1940.[55] In these films the Jewish characters do not appear as oppressed victims; nor do they appear as caricatures of perfidy and immorality, as in *Der Stürmer*, the anti-Semitic Nazi periodical. Instead they are shown as privileged intellectuals or affluent businessmen who feel superior to the Germans. "The taboo," Gertrud Koch writes in her essay on the Jewish figures in Fassbinder's films, "the law forbidding contact, the shutting out from the everyday consciousness, can all be located in Fassbinder's Jews: his own coldness and distance is projected onto the Jews as an intrinsic quality. They are the ones who are untouchable, cold, aloof, unapproachable, arrogant, taking themselves for something better."[56] The victim's suffering is repressed. Instead, Koch sees Fassbinder's Jewish figures in the ambivalent position of being "judges over life and death."[57] Fassbinder aggressively turns the feelings of inhibition, guilt, and helpless shame, which the postwar generation must have felt (and still feels) in the face of the genocide their parents' generation organized, against those who gave rise to those feelings. He directs these emotions not only against the parents, the "Auschwitz generation," but against the victims as well, who seem—in his perverse logic—also responsible for the suffering that German history has caused him. In his play, one character says: "The Jew is guilty because he makes us guilty by simply being there."[58]

Fassbinder set himself the task of showing German Jewry not, as he put it, "Philo-Semitically," as noble victims, since philo-Semitism—and here he follows Robert Neumann—is nothing more than anti-Semitism in reverse.[59] His provocative and, as usual with Fassbinder, radically spontaneous opposition to this philo-Semitism completely disregarded the potential consequences and effects of his provocative stance in a concrete historical setting. Yet the reaction to his well-publicized Frankfurt play must have made him aware that he was in danger of being misunderstood either as someone who unknowingly repeats anti-Semitic stereotypes or as someone who knowingly elicits anti-Semitic sentiments for the sake of deconstructing them. It is a questionable tactic, and Fassbinder may have known the thin line he was walking when he specified in his will that the play could be premiered only in Frankfurt or New York.[60] However one interprets this strange clause, it is evidence, along with the adversarial stances taken with respect to Fassbinder in the debate on anti-Semitism that has gone on since 1976, of just how taboo-laden the post-Auschwitz "negative symbiosis" between Jews and Germans is,[61] how deeply the wound of Auschwitz festers not only in Fassbinder's awareness but in that of his entire generation.[62]

In a letter of 1946 to Karl Jaspers, Hannah Arendt wrote that the guilt Germans had placed upon themselves for the mass murders at Auschwitz could not be assuaged through the legal process, because there were no punishments appropriate for such monstrous crimes. This guilt, she wrote, "transcends and crushes any system of law. . . . There is no human, political way to deal with a guilt that is beyond crime and an innocence that is beyond good or virtue."[63] To translate this guilt onto film would exceed the limits of what can be presented, unless one proceeds as Herbert Achternbusch did in his film *Das letzte Loch* (*The Last Hole*) (1981), staging the incomprehensible as a grotesque farce and thus violating all the "rules" of traditional filmmaking (and of conventional decorum). His protagonist, Nil, insists on personally atoning for the murder of the Jews. His doctor gives him a prescription: for each murder, for each one of the six million dead, he is to drink one glass of whiskey in order to forget. The absurd calculation serves to symbolize the fact that German guilt can neither be forgotten nor cured. The surreal nature of the prescription presents the work of mourning as a helpless, hopeless, futile gesture.[64] This enigmatic film, vacillating between the grotesque and the melodramatic, ends with Nil's suicide. Full of revulsion toward Germany as the "land of mass murderers," he plunges into the Sicilian volcano of Stromboli, as Empedocles once did, with these words: "I am committing suicide because then I will belong to the charnel house of the victims. I do not want to belong to the charnel house of the self-righteous Germans."[65]

Fassbinder no less than Achternbusch suffered because of Germany. His suffering moved him to work on the German past and propelled his work forward. In mid-1977, Fassbinder contemplated emigration to Paris, New York, or Hollywood. Tabloids and foreign news magazines reported his plans, in detail, and a parliamentary deputy of the Christian Democratic Party even demanded that the government "take a position on the accusations made by film director Rainer Werner Fassbinder . . . who explained his move to the United States in terms of increasing censorship and 'less freedom' in the Federal Republic."[66] But Fassbinder abandoned those plans the very same year. He realized that only in his own country could he hold up a mirror to its faults and follies; he did not know any other country well enough, and no other country had done so much to shape him. Like Peter Schneider's Lenz, he decided to "stay here." In October 1980, an interviewer asked Fassbinder whether he was not acting like his own character Lili Marleen, the artist who did not care about the source of her money, even if it came from Hitler. Fassbinder responded: "I would say that I too live in a state whose structure I reject. Even though God knows the FRG is not comparable to Hitler's Reich. And although I can imagine a different government, this is where I do my business."[67] This antagonism toward the state is a feature in all of Fassbinder's films; his historical films especially are "counter-analyses"[68] of the present order in the Federal Republic.

The End of Utopia

The disaster is related to forgetfulness—forgetfulness with memory, the motionless retreat of what has not been treated.

—Maurice Blanchot

The career of Maria Braun was read, especially abroad, as an allegory of the Federal Republic during the economic miracle. As Jean de Baroncelli wrote in *Le Monde:* "The fate of the heroine actually parallels, point for point, the fate of Germany, conquered and reconstructed. Maria Braun not only symbolizes Germany; in Fassbinder's eyes she obviously 'is' Germany. What has become of Maria, what has become of Germany? In cynical and horrid images, Fassbinder gives the answer: a creature dressed in obviously expensive clothes that has lost its soul; a 'winner' whose head has been turned by fortune and who has courted disaster."[69] Fassbinder supports this reading by linking the history of Germany to Maria Braun's own story at the end of the film. Just as Maria Braun's utopia was betrayed, the film implies, the German nation was betrayed when Adenauer made secret deals to rearm Germany despite the painful memories of militarism and war.

As the private story of Maria Braun comes to a melodramatic end in a gas explosion, the public sphere intrudes in a live radio broadcast of the 1954 world soccer championship finals between West Germany and Hungary. The escape from private history—in the original screenplay by a conscious murder and suicide, more ambivalently in the film by a half-conscious accident—is ironically undercut by the West German team's unexpected victory. The last seven minutes of the match coincide exactly with the last seven minutes of the life of Maria and Hermann Braun. For seven minutes narrative and narrated time, fictional and "real" time are identical. The original sound recording of the sports broadcast accompanies, and at times drowns out, the fictional denouement: the reunion of Hermann and Maria Braun and the reading of Oswald's will. The rejoicing at the goal that decides the match blends into the noise of the explosion. As the final whistle blows, Herbert Zimmermann, the well-known sports announcer, screams hysterically: "Time's up! Time's up! Germany is world champion!" (*Weltmeister*—literally translated, "master of the world"), while the villa and its inhabitants go up in flames. The private story, as Fassbinder sees it, is over, but not the public one. One person's utopia disappears in rubble and ashes, but the nation "is somebody" again. The hopes for a radical new beginning were buried with the rise of Germany from the pariah of 1945 to the proud victor and "world champion" of 1954. The chances for utopia were lost.

The last images of the film are projected over the sounds of the soccer broadcast and the explosion. They consist of full-screen black-and-white negative portraits of West Germany's chancellors, projected, like still pictures in a slide show, one after the other, without commentary: Konrad Adenauer, Ludwig Erhard, Kurt Georg Kiesinger, and Helmut Schmidt, during whose term of office the film was made. This gallery of photo-portraits catapults us out of the fictional space. The flagrant anachronism suddenly confronts the viewer with the specific time when the film was made. The black-and-white negative still of Schmidt then changes to a positive; the change dates the fictional events, openly identifying the narrative as the construct of a later era. From the perspective of Helmut Schmidt's chancellorship (1974–1982), Fassbinder looks back on the first ten years of the Federal Republic, the period of rapid economic and military reconstruction in West Germany. By the late seventies the price of this "reconstruction" had become apparent.

The pictures at the end lead the viewer back to the very first image of the film: a framed painting of Hitler that falls off the wall during a bomb raid and crashes to the floor. The film itself is thus framed by pictures of German chancellors, suggesting some sort of continuity between Hitler and the postwar chancellors of the Federal Republican allusion that is more irritating than provocative because of its unhistorical superficiality. The picture of Willy Brandt, chancellor between 1969 and 1974 and the first Social Democratic chancellor since the founding of the Federal Republic, is pointedly absent from the gallery of portraits. Asked why Brandt had been omitted, Fassbinder answered: "I have the feeling that Willy Brandt's time was a hiatus, that Brandt tended to encourage self-questioning . . . leaving basic features of the government open to criticism. I just have the feeling that (what Brandt did) was something that not everyone agreed with. I see democracy as something that works like a kaleidoscope, that doesn't mean permanent revolution but rather permanent movement, the permanent questioning of premises by every generation."[70]

Anton Kaes

The idealization of Willy Brandt (who had emigrated during the Nazi era) goes back to Fassbinder's central experience, the protest movement of the mid- and late sixties. Intellectual and cultural life was strongly politicized at that time—Günter Grass, for example, campaigned extensively for the Social Democratic Party—and major reforms seemed imminent. The antifascist resistance fighter Willy Brandt stood in the eyes of Fassbinder and his generation as a symbol of this new direction in German politics, and he became the rallying point of a younger generation's hopes. The Great Coalition of December 1966, formed when Fassbinder had just turned twenty-one, had created the first political crisis of postwar West Germany because it eliminated any parliamentary opposition. The intellectuals felt called upon to assume this role outside of parliament. Hans Magnus Enzensberger warned: "The end of the second German democracy is in sight."[71] He feared that the Great Coalition also signaled the end of German literature as an oppositional, educational institution "whose goal it has been since 1945 to balance out the structural flaws of the Federal Republic with its poor powers."[72] But this opposition, consisting, in Enzensberger's self-critical view, of "belated liberals, good Social Democrats, moralists, socialists without clear ideas, antifascists without a plan for the future," no longer sufficed in 1968. "In fact, what we now need," Enzensberger wrote, "is not communism but revolution. The political system of the Federal Republic is beyond repair."[73] Fassbinder adopted this uncompromising attitude toward the Federal Republic, and, in principle, it remained his attitude for the next fifteen years. The events that occurred after 1968—the passage of the state emergency laws (under Willy Brandt), the persecution of terrorist sympathizers, the job blacklisting, and the constant attacks on Fassbinder in the Springer press—only strengthened this conviction.

Fassbinder was one of the very few among the 1968 generation to maintain his resolute radical utopianism throughout the seventies. In March 1982, three months before his death, he described himself as "a romantic anarchist."[74] For Fassbinder, anarchy meant radical independence from parties, leftist and rightist philosophies, and personal or political ties. There is an inherent utopianism in his belief that unlimited individual and national freedom could be the product of democracy correctly understood. "With the concrete utopia of anarchy in my head," he considered himself an "extreme representative of democracy":

> It's hardly permissible to say that today, that part about anarchy, because we've learned through the media that anarchy and terrorism are synonymous. But on the one hand there is the utopian idea of a nation without hierarchies, without anxieties, without aggressions, and on the other hand a concrete social situation in which utopian ideas are suppressed. A few people flipped out, understandably, and a certain dominant class wanted that, maybe on an unconscious level, in order to define itself more concretely.[75]

In his film *Die dritte Generation* (*The Third Generation*) (1979), Fassbinder settles accounts with the prevailing terrorism: terrorists of the third generation, he feels, were making common cause with the surveillance and security industries. The film demonstrates that there was little ideological difference between leftist terrorists and the rightist state. The terrorists of the first generation, Meinhof and Baader and Ensslin, had represented to him political content and an idealist utopia that had gone awry; those motives were now missing. *The Third Generation* is a film about the cynicism of modem terrorism and its disregard of human life. The film itself becomes an assault; its deafeningly aggressive soundtrack (constant radio announcements are layered over the dialogue) and its disorienting cuts (which serve to erase distinctions between terrorists and victims, pursuers and pursued) frustrate the viewer in the extreme.[76] Utopia no longer appears as even a vague possibility.

The exhaustion of utopian energies, which Jürgen Habermas considers a sign of the seventies, left its mark on Fassbinder's late films as well. Habermas writes: "Today it seems that utopian energies have been fully consumed, as if they had withdrawn from historical thinking. The horizon of the future has shrunk and, as a consequence, the spirit of the times, as well as its politics, has changed utterly. The future has negative connotations."[77] The loss of Maria Braun's private utopia, which confronts her as a shock at the end of the film, corresponds to the loss of the great utopian designs in the public sphere of the late seventies, when the film was made. More than other filmmakers of the time, Fassbinder reflects the dissolution of the dreams of 1968. In December 1977, after *Germany in Autumn* and just before filming began on *Maria Braun*, he was asked by an interviewer where he got the strength to keep on working. He answered:

> From utopia, the concrete longing for this utopia. If this longing is driven out of me, I will not do anything else; that's why as a creative person I have the feeling of being murdered in Germany, if you would please not mistake that for paranoia. I believe this recent witch-hunt, which, I think, is just the tip of the iceberg, was staged in order to destroy individual utopias. That means also to let my fears and my feelings of guilt become overpowering. If it comes to the point where my fears are greater than my longing for something beautiful, then I'll quit. And not just quit working.[78]

"You'll quit living?" he was asked. "Yes, of course. There's no reason to live without a goal."[79]

The total destruction of all the "bourgeois illusions" that we see at the end of *Maria Braun* is reminiscent of the final sequence of *Zabriskie Point* (1969). Antonioni's film about the sixties ends with the hallucinatory explosion of a nouveau-riche villa, repeated several times in slow motion. These radical endings in both films betray a helpless aggression against the "system" as a whole: what can no longer be saved should be blown up. In the negative utopia of *Maria Braun*, the explosion that occurs in 1954, at the beginning of West German rearmament, re-creates the landscape of ruins of 1945. The idea of a "Zero Hour" proved illusory; the film begins and ends with an explosion. Nothing had changed. Germany's unique chance for a radically new beginning in 1945, was, in Fassbinder's view, missed once and for all. Instead, the old capitalist ideas of property and greed and all the traditional bourgeois values were restored. The will to reform had all too soon exhausted itself.

In *Lola,* the second part of his FRG Trilogy, Fassbinder chooses a resigned rather than a violent end. The city planner, who initially exhibits moral and personal integrity, becomes vulnerable to blackmail through his love for a woman. As a consequence he gets more and more deeply implicated in the already corrupt politics of the city. But his awareness of the corruption does not lead to an explosion at the end. He accommodates himself, is "realistic," and thus becomes an accomplice.

The end of the third film in the trilogy is equally cynical and resigned. *Veronika Voss* is the story of a drug-addicted film star from the old UFA days who wallows in her memories. She is murdered, and the journalist who covers the story is led deeper and deeper into the morass of the city. He abandons his investigation at the end when he recognizes that the guilty doctor is protected by high officials, including the police. The film's ending implies that it is useless to try to expose the corruption in private and public affairs that Fassbinder considered typical of the fifties. As in *Lola,* there is no explosion of stored-up hatred of the "system"; instead the characters carry on, very much aware of inescapable moral corruption.

In principle the story in *Maria Braun* also continues after the violent exit of the protagonists. At the very moment when the explosion ends the lives of the private individuals, the rise of Germany as "world champion" begins. "We're somebody again," the Germans said proudly during the reconstruction period. This famous slogan is indicative of precisely the attitude of complacency and amnesia that Fassbinder wanted to destroy—a terrorist act that included self-destruction.

NOTES

1. The epithet is from Wolfram Schütte's obituary, "Das Herz: Die künstlerische Physiognomie Rainer Werner Fassbinders im Augenblick seines Verlustes," *Frankfurter Rundschau,* 19 June 1982.

2. See "Auskunft über Deutschland: Ausländische Reaktionen auf den Tod van Rainer Werner Fassbinder," *Frankfurter Allgemeine Zeitung,* 12 June 1982.

3. Ibid.

4. Ibid.

5. See Ernst Burkel, "Responding to What You Experience: An Interview with the Film Directors Douglas Sirk and Rainer Werner Fassbinder," in Rainer Werner Fassbinder, *The Marriage of Maria Braun,* ed. Joyce Rheuban (New Brunswick, N.J.: Rutgers University Press, 1986), 193–96, where Fassbinder speaks of Douglas Sirk: "After I had made ten films which were very personal, the time came when we said, we have to find a way to make films for the public—and then came my encounter with his films, and then with Douglas Sirk himself. That was tremendously important for me. And then—to come back to this supposed father-son relationship— it was, and is not the same thing, because most father-son relations are usually relations of conflict. I found a person who makes art in a way, as I've said, that was bound to change something in me. I'm making something.—and maybe he sees this—that takes what he made the next step" (195).

6. On Sirk's aesthetics and the function of the melodrama, see Thomas Elsaesser, "Tales of Sound and Fury: Observations on the Family Melodrama," *Monogram* 3 (1972), 2–15; Laura Mulvey, "Notes on Sirk and Melodrama," *Movie* 25 (1977–1978), 53–56.

7. See Fassbinder's 1971 analysis of Sirk films, in which he speaks directly about his own stylistic intentions: "Six Films by Douglas Sirk," in Fassbinder, *Maria Braun*, 197–207.

8. This will be discussed in greater detail later in the chapter, in the section "History as Trauma."

9. Rainer Werner Fassbinder, "Die dritte Generation," in *Rainer Werner Fassbinder: Filme befreien den Kopf, Essays und Arbeitsnotizen*, ed. Michael Töteberg (Frankfurt am Main: Fischer, 1984), 73. This sentence recurs almost verbatim in Edgar Reitz's *Heimat*.

10. See the article by Bernd Neumann, "'Als ob das Zeitgenössische leer wäre . . .': Über die Anwesenheit der fünfziger Jahre in der Gegenwartsliteratur," *Zeitschrift für Literaturwissenschaft und Linguistik* 35 (1979), 82–95.

11. Helma Sanders-Brahms's film *Germany, Pale Mother* and Jutta Brückner's *Hungerjahre* (*Years of Hunger*) present a similarly critical, although more autobiographical, view of the fifties from the perspective of the present. Edgar Reitz devotes a two-hour episode of his film cycle *Heimat* to the fifties. Here, too, despite the strong presence of nostalgic and autobiographical elements, what is called into question is the smug, repressive German society during the time of the economic miracle.

12. See Walter Benjamin, "Theses on the Philosophy of History," in *Illuminations*, ed. Hannah Arendt, trans. Harry Zohn (New York: Schocken, 1969), 255.

13. See the analysis of the Fassbinder sequence in Eric Rentschler, *West German Film in the Course of Time* (Bedford Hills, N.Y.: Redgrave, 1984), especially 191–202.

14. The dialogue is reprinted in *Rainer Werner Fassbinder: Die Anarchie der Phantasie, Gesprache und Interviews*, ed. Michael Töteberg, 214–18 (Frankfurt am Main: Fischer, 1986); here 215.

15. Fassbinder, "Ich habe mich mit meinen Filmfiguren verändert," in *Die Anarchie der Phantasie*, 128 (first published April 1978). See also his view on the social function of the cooperative film *Germany in Autumn*: "When we met then, one of the reasons we said that we had to make the film was to fight fear. So that people, who had no means of production and were perhaps even more frightened than we, shouldn't be intimidated by the feeling that was prevalent in Germany at the time, that criticism in any form was unwelcome and must be suppressed. To avoid that we wanted to say clearly, because we had the means of production at our disposal, 'You can and must keep talking, no matter what happens'" (ibid., 98).

16. See the conversation with Peter Märthesheimer, "Ein Drehbuch ist eben keine eigene Kunstform," *ARD Fernsehspiel* (January–March 1985), 46–51.

17. Gerhard Zwerenz, *Die Ehe der Maria Braun* (Munich: Goldmann, 1979). The novel reduces the film to the protagonist's love story; the political dimension, so important in Fassbinder's film, is completely missing. For a comparison between the film and its novelization, see Hans-Bernhard Moeller, "Fassbinders and Zwerenz' im deutschen Aufstieg verlorene *Ehe der Maria Braun*: Interpretation, vergleichende Kritik und neuer filmisch-literarischer Adaptionskontext," in *Film und Literatur: Literarische Texte und der neue deutsche Film*, ed. Sigrid Bauschinger et al. (Berne/Munich: Francke, 1984), 105–123.

18. "Geschichtsergänzung: Gespräch mit Rainer Werner Fassbinder," *ARD Fernsehspiel* (January–March 1985), 60. What Fassbinder says here about *Veronika Voss* is also true of *Maria Braun* and *Lola*. See also his evaluation of the fifties in "Frauen haben in dieser Gesellschaft mehr Freiheiten," *Film-Korrespondenz*, 16 March 1982, 6: "The more I work with the 1950s, the more I realize that the Third Reich was not some accident of history; it must have been inherent in the form of German society or in the way Germans live with capitalism."

19. See Félix Guattari, "Towards a Micro-Politics of Desire," in *Molecular Revolution: Psychiatry and Politics*, trans. Rosemary Sheed (Hammondsworth: Penguin, 1984), 82–107. In "Le divan du pauvre," *Communications* 23 (1975), 96, Guattari writes: "The cinema has become a gigantic machine to shape the social libido."

20. Rainer Werner Fassbinder, "Ich bin ein romantischer Anarchist," in *Die Anarchie der Phantasie*, 186.

21. On the relationship between postwar German history and Maria Braun's history, see Thomas Elsaesser, "Primary Identification and the Historical Subject: Fassbinder and Germany," in *Fassbinder: The Marriage of Maria Braun*, 248–64; Howard Feinstein: "BRD 1-2-3: Fassbinder's Postwar Trilogy and the Spectacle," *Cinema Journal* 23 (Autumn 1983), 44–56.

22. The page numbers in parentheses refer subsequently to the production script, so far published only in English: *The Marriage of Maria Braun*, ed. Joyce Rheuban (New Brunswick, N.J.: Rutgers University Press, 1986). The book also contains essays by and about Fassbinder and a bibliography. The West German publishing house of Schirmer and Mosel has announced the publication of the script for *Die Ehe der Maria Braun* in the sixth volume of its series *Fassbinder: Die Kinofilme (1987–   )*.

23. Hannah Arendt, "Besuch in Deutschland 1950," in *Zur Zeit: Politische Essays* (Berlin: Rotbuch, 1986), 44.

24. Jean-François Lyotard, *Instructions païennes* (Paris: Galilee, 1977), 39.

25. Karlheinz Stierle, "Geschchen, Geschichte, Text der Geschichte," in *Geschichte: Ereignis und Erzählung*, ed. Reinhart Koselleck und Wolf-Dieter Stempel (Munich: Fink, 1973), 532. See also Hayden White, "The Historical Text as Literary Artifact," in *Tropics of Discourse: Essays in Cultural Criticism* (Baltimore: Johns Hopkins University Press, 1978), 81–100; Reinhart Koselleck, *Futures Past: On the Semantics of Historical Time*, trans. Keith Tribe (Cambridge, Mass.: MIT Press, 1985).

26. Fassbinder himself plays one of these, in a cameo appearance. He wants to sell an edition of Heinrich von Kleist's works to Maria Braun, but she has become "realistic" through her experience of history, that is, the book burnings of 1933, and answers: "Books burn so quickly. And they don't give heat."

27. See, for instance, Bertolt Brecht's *Trommeln in der Nacht (Drums in the Night)* (1922), Ernst Toiler's *Hinkemann* (1923), or Wolfgang Borchert's *Draussen vor der Tür (The Man Outside)* (1947).

28. Significantly, we learn the least about Hermann Braun. Fassbinder consciously leaves it to the viewer to construct Hermann's story, because essentially Hermann lives only in Maria's imagination, as the idealized object of her desire.

29. Hans-Dieter Seidel, "Stationen einer Deutschen," *Stuttgarter Zeitung*, 22 February 1979.

30. Speaking in 1983 at the "International Conference on the National Socialist Seizure of Power," held in the rebuilt Reichstag in Berlin, Herman Labbe argued that to shape an identity in the period of reconstruction the Federal Republic *had* to repress the past as a matter of existential necessity. He defends the "restraint" and "discretion" of the Germans in treating their own past; only from the perspective of what he calls "theorists of repression" and "national therapists" is this "discretion" the symptom of a failure to come to terms with the past. See Lübbe, "Der Nationalsozialismus im politischen Bewusstsein der Gegenwart," in *Deutschlands Weg in die Diktatur*, ed. Martin Broszat et al. (Berlin: Siedler, 1983), 329–49. See also the critical discussion that followed his paper (ibid., 350–78) and the essay by Helmut Dubiel and Günther Frankenberg, "Entsorgung der Vergangenheit: Widerspruch gegen eine neokonservative Legende," *Die Zeit*, 18 March 1983.

31. This dual status can be seen most clearly in the criticism commonly leveled at historical films, that, for instance, the uniforms or the haircuts are not "historically accurate," which is the same as saying that the filmmaker did not do enough research or did not consult enough eyewitnesses of the period.

32. M. M. Bakhtin, "Discourse in the Novel," in *The Dialogic Imagination*, ed. Michael Holquist (Austin: University of Texas Press, 1982), 411.

33. By speaking about the "Germans" on the one hand and the "Jews" on the other, exclusion through language is perpetuated. See Henry Pachter, "On Germans and Jews: Reply to Dennis Klein," *New German Critique* 21 (Fall 1980), 143: "One does not read books or essays entitled 'Blacks and Americans,' 'Mormons and Americans' or 'Jews and Americans.'" *New*

German Critique published three special issues in 1980 (nos. 19–21) entitled "Germans and Jews." In his polemical essay "Der deutsch-jüdische Verbrüderungskitsch," *tageszeitung* (Berlin), 8 April 1986, Wolfgang Pohrt writes about this linguistic division, claiming we cannot "compare apples and fruit." On this question, see especially Max Horkheimer, "Nachwort zu Porträts deutsch-jüdischer Geistesgeschichte," in *Gesammelte Schriften*, vol. 8, ed. Alfred Schmidt and G. S. Noerr (Frankfurt am Main: Fischer, 1985), 192–93: "By the way, 'Jews' and 'Germans' seem to me to be terms on different conceptual levels . . . there are Jewish Germans just as there are Protestant, Catholic, and atheist Germans. The Jews are as little deficient as the Christians in their patriotism, that is, in their good will toward the state. . . . The terminological opposition German and Jew sounds all too current in this world that has become increasingly marked, and not to its advantage, by nationalisms and other collectivisms and in which individuals and groups that deviate from the majority have an increasingly difficult time living peacefully in the same state. It would be better to talk about Jews and Christians, the more so since in times of totalitarian barbarism, which by no means belong exclusively to the past, true Christians—note, true Christians—are threatened by the same horrors that have long been part of the Jewish fate."

34. Gerhard Zwerenz, *Die Erde ist so unbewohnbar wie der Mond* (Frankfurt am Main: März, 1973). In 1986 the novel was reprinted together with the script for the planned film. See also Gerhard Zwerenz, "Linker Antisemitismus ist unmöglich," *Die Zeit*, 9 April 1976, and "Politik mit Vorurteilen," *Vorwärts*, 22 February 1986, where he says, "No, Fassbinder's play is not anti-Semitic, but it is politically naive, easily misunderstood, and incomplete."

35. Rainer Werner Fassbinder, *Garbage, the City and Death*, in *Rainer Werner Fassbinder: Plays*, trans. and ed. Denis Calandra (New York: PAJ Publications, 1985), 186.

36. Theodor W. Adorno, "Zur Bekämpfung des Antisemitismus heute," *Das Argument* 29 (May 1964), 94.

37. A sociological study by Alphons Silbermann, *Sind wir Antisemiten? Ausmass und Wirkung eines sozialen Vorurteils in der Bundesrepublik Deutschland* (Cologne: Verlag Wissenschaft und Politik, 1982), comes to the conclusion "that between 15 and 20% of the population have strong anti-Semitic prejudices and another 30% are more or less latently anti-Semitic" (124–25). On this problem, see also the essays in *Antisemitismus nach dem Holocaust. Bestandsaufnahme und Erscheinungsformen in deutschsprachigen Ländern*, ed. Alphons Silbermann and Julius H. Schoeps (Cologne: Verlag Wissenschaft und Politik, 1986).

38. Henryk M. Broder, *Der ewige Antisemit: Über Sinn und Funktion eines beständigen Gefühls* (Frankfurt am Main: Fischer, 1986), 10.

39. The text appeared as vol. 803 (*Stüke* 3) of the series "edition suhrkamp" in the spring of 1976, but it was almost immediately withdrawn and shredded. In 1981 the play was published by a different publisher, the Verlag der Autoren; in 1996 it appeared in a second, revised edition. The English translation, *Garbage, the City and Death*, is based on the first edition; it was published by Performing Arts Journal Publications, New York, in 1985.

40. Joachim Fest, "Reicher Jude von links," *Frankfurter Allgemeine Zeitung*, 19 March 1976. Wolfram Schütte responded to Fest's accusations in the Frankfurter Rundschau of 26 March 1976.

41. Siegfried Unseld, "In dieser Form nie mehr," *Die Zeit*, 9 April 1976. Despite the fully justified fear of misinterpretation that had been voiced in 1976, Günther Rühle, the new director of the Frankfurt Playhouse, included the play in his plans for the 1985 season. Unmoved by violent press attacks, petitions, and public protest by the Jewish community and the Catholic and Protestant churches, he refused to cancel the premiere of the play scheduled for October 31, 1985. But the premiere was prevented by opponents of the play who seized the stage; further performances were canceled. The objections to the play, apart from its weak quality focused on the stereotypical presentation of the figure of a Jewish real estate speculator. The debates unleashed by the play in 1976 and again 1985–1986 involve significant issues: censorship and the autonomy of art, fictional representation and intentionality, the relationship between Jewish and non-Jewish Germans after Auschwitz, Jewish identity and memory, and German history and its terrible legacy. The controversy is extensively documented in *Die Fassbinder-Kontroverse*

oder das Ende der Schonzeit, ed. Heiner Lichtenstein (Königstein: Athenäum, 1985). See also *Deutsch-jüdische Normalität . . . Fassbinders Sprengsätze,* ed. Elisabeth Kiderlen (Frankfurt am Main: Pflasterstrand, 1985), and the heated debate in *Ästhetik und Kommunikation* 51, 52, 53/54 (1982–1983), entitled "Deutsche, Linke und Juden." See also the special issue of *New German Critique* 38 (Spring/Summer 1986) on the "German-Jewish Controversy," which contains contributions by Andrei S. Markowits, Seyla Benhabib, and Moishe Postone to a symposium at Harvard University on Fassbinder's *Garbage, the City and Death.*

42. See the documentation in *Film-Korrespondenz* 1 (16 March 1977), 1215; see also Wolfram Schütte, "Da stimmt doch was nicht," *Frankfurter Rundschau,* 12 March 1977. The text was published by Suhrkamp Verlag, ostensibly without the author's knowledge (as Fassbinder claimed in a 1977 television interview, printed in the Berlin *tageszeitung* of 21 July 1986).

43. Rainer Werner Fassbinder, "Gehabtes Sollen—gesolltes Haben: Über Gustav Freytags Roman 'Soll und Haben' und die verhinderte Fernsehverfilmung," in *Filme befreien den Kopf,* 36–37 (first published March 1977).

44. Ibid., 37.

45. Quoted in Schütte, "Da stimmt doch was nicht": "In any case it is worth considering that in our country the recent critical preoccupation with the complex of bourgeois society and anti-Semitism immediately raised the suspicion that it would result in anti-Semitism . . . so it is considered suspect and banned by those very conservatives who never said a word against the unscrupulous exploitation of the stock of Nazi films by television."

46. See the report on this in the *Frankfurter Allgemeine Zeitung,* 9 April 1977.

47. Rainer Werner Fassbinder, "Probleme nicht verdrängen, sondern sie bewusst machen," in *Die Anarchie der Phantasie,* p.88 (first published June 1977).

48. See Joachim Fest, "Linke Schwierigkeiten mit 'links': Ein Nachwort zu R. W. Fassbinder," *Frankfurter Allgemeine Zeitung,* 10 April 1976.

49. Fassbinder, "Probleme nicht verdrängen," 88. This was the direction of his "Public Statement Regarding *Garbage, the City and Death,*" *Frankfurter Rundschau,* 31 March 1976, trans. and reprinted in *West German Filmmakers on Film,* 155: "There are also anti-Semites in this play; they do not only exist in the play, though, but also for instance in Frankfurt. It goes without saying that these figures—I find it truly superfluous to repeat this—do not represent the opinion of the author, whose own stance toward minorities should have become clear enough in his previous work. Particularly some of the cheap shots in the discussion make me all the more concerned about a 'new fascism,' which was one of the reasons I wrote this play."

50. Fassbinder, "Gehabtes Sollen-gesolltes Haben," 39.

51. Ibid., 38.

52. Ibid.

53. Bertolt Brecht, *Arbeitsjournal,* vol. 1 (Frankfurt am Main: Suhrkamp, 1973), 294. The entry is dated August 1941.

54. On *Schatten der Engel,* see the telling judgment of the Working Committee for Voluntary Self-Control of the Film Industry (FSK), which considers the film "not anti-Semitic and hence not racially inflammatory in its thematic conception and its overall form," but noted the fear that certain dialogue passages "promote clichés of the Jew as a cynical, scrupulous maker of deals and confirm anti-Semitic attitudes because the film always refers to the Jewish real estate speculator as the 'rich Jew,' without a name, in a way that could lead to generalization, and because the dialogue passages in question are spoken by a man who is part of our contemporary society and does not appear, say, as an incorrigible Nazi." Quoted in Helmut Schmitz, "'So denkt es in mir': Zum Antisemitismus-Vorwurf gegen Daniel Schmids Fassbinder-Verfilmung *Schatten der Engel,*" *Frankfurter Rundschau,* 11 October 1976.

55. See Anni Goldmann, "Un nouveau 'Juif Süss': *Lili Marleen," Le Monde,* 18 May 1981. See also Thomas Elsaesser, "*Lili Marleen:* Fascism and the Film Industry," *October* 21 (Summer 1982), 115–40. In Saul Friedländer's study, *Reflections of Nazism,* Fassbinder's *Lili Marleen* serves as a prime example for the "new discourse with respect to the Third Reich," which tries to reevoke the Nazi period in all its false and dangerous glamour. On *Lili Marleen,* see especially 47–53.

56. Gertrud Koch, "Torments of the Flesh, Coldness of the Spirit: Jewish Figures in the Films of Rainer Werner Fassbinder," *New German Critique* 38 (Summer 1986), 37.

57. Ibid., 38.

58. Fassbinder, *Garbage, the City and Death*, 180. My translation follows here the original German version: "Schuld hat der Jud, weil er uns schuldig macht, denn er ist da."

59. See Benjamin Henrich's interview with Fassbinder, "Philosemiten sind Antisemiten," *Die Zeit*, 16 April 1976:

FASSBINDER: I think that the constant practice of making Jews taboo, which has existed since 1945 in Germany, can lead to an antipathy toward Jews, especially with young people who have no direct experience with Jews. As a child, whenever I met a Jew, someone whispered to me, that's a Jew, act polite, be friendly. And that continued with certain variations until I was 28 and wrote the play. I was never able to think that that was a correct attitude.

HENRICHS: So you are afraid that philo-Semitism, to which we have almost all been raised, which is a kind of rule of the game in the Federal Republic, could promote a new anti-Semitism?

FASSBINDER: Absolutely. Robert Neumann said, philo-Semites are anti-Semites who love Jews . . . I cannot say I am not unaffected about what happened to the Jews in the Third Reich. But I am absolutely more unaffected than those who are attacking me.

60. A small underground group, "Thieves' Theater," premiered the play (newly translated as *Trash, the City, and Death*) in New York's Lower East Side on April 16, 1987, with hardly any local publicity. There was no public outcry or protest in the United States. See Rainer Weber, "Der reiche Jude in Manhattan," *Spiegel* 15 (1987), 218–20.

61. See the essay by Dan Diner, "Negative Symbiose: Deutsche und Juden nach Auschwitz," *Babylon* 1 (1987), 9–21.

62. See Friedrich Knilli, "Die Judendarstellung in den deutschen Medien," in *Antisemitismus nach dem Holocaust*, ed. Silbermann and Scheops, 115–32; Ruth K. Angress, "Gibt es ein 'Judenproblem' in der deutschen Nachkriegsliteratur?" *Neue Sammlung* 26 (January–March 1986), 22–40, especially 32–40 on Schlöndorff and Fassbinder. See also Heidy M. Müller, *Die Judendarstellung in der deutschsprachigen Erzählprosa (1945–1981)* (Königstein: Forum Academicum/Hain, 1984).

63. Quoted in Diner, "Negative Symbiose," 11.

64. There were comical and grotesque filmic presentations of the Third Reich and the persecution of the Jews before Achternbusch: Charlie Chaplin's *The Great Dictator*, Ernst Lubitsch's *To Be or Not To Be*, and Lina Wertmüller's *Seven Beauties*, for instance. On this issue see Uwe Naumann, *Zwischen Tränen und Gelächter: Satirische Faschismuskritik 1933 bis 1945* (Cologne: Pahl-Rugenstein, 1983).

65. Herbert Achternbusch, *Das Haus am Nil* (Frankfurt am Main: Suhrkamp, 1981), 153. Achternbusch continues to deal with the Third Reich in his film *Heilt Hitler* (1986) and his play *Linz* (1987).

66. Wolfram Schütte, "CDU-Politiker fragt Bundesregierung, 'Warum geht Fassbinder?' . . . und Versuch einer Antwort an jemand hinterm Mond," *Frankfurter Rundschau*, 13 August 1977. The press release quoted by Schütte reads further: "In an interview with an American news magazine, Fassbinder said that the only films the Federal Republic supports are those that confirm the present situation of democracy 'with all its mediocrity.'"

67. Rainer Werner Fassbinder, "Egal, was ich mache, die Leute regen sich auf," in *Die Anarchie der Phantasie*, 169.

68. See Marc Ferro, "Film: A Counter-analysis of Society," in *Cinema and History*, trans. Naomi Greene (Detroit: Wayne State University Press, 1988).

69. Jean de Baroncelli, "Procès d'un miracle," *Le Monde*, 19 January 1980.

70. Rainer Werner Fassbinder, "Nur so entstehen bei uns Filme: Indem man sie ohne Rücksicht auf Verluste macht. Ein Gespräch mit Wolfram Schütte," in *Die Anarchie der Phantasie*, 138 (first published February 1979).

71. Hans Magnus Enzensberger, "Klare Entscheidungen und trübe Aussichten," in *Über Hans Magnus Enzensberger*, ed. Joachim Schickel (Frankfurt am Main: Suhrkamp, 1970), 229.

72. Ibid.

73. Ibid., 231.

74. Rainer Werner Fassbinder, "Ich bin ein romantischer Anarchist," in *Die Anarchie der Phantasie*, 194.

75. Rainer Werner Fassbinder, "Ich habe mich mit meinen Filmfiguren verändert," ibid., 113.

76. In the credit sequence, we read: "A comedy in six parts about social games full of tension, excitement, and logic, horror and madness, like the fairy tales we tell to children to help them bear their life until they die." Fassbinder's settling of accounts with terrorism as a "social game" was filmed at his own expense (with Fassbinder himself as cameraman).

77. Jürgen Habermas, "Die Krise des Wohlfahrtsstaates und die Erschöpfung utopischer Energien," in *Die neue Unübersichtlichkeit: Kleine politische Schriften 5*, ed. Jürgen Habermas (Frankfurt am Main: Suhrkamp, 1985), 143. In the course of his argument, Habermas criticizes this discourse about the end of utopia: "It is not that utopian energies are retreating from the historical consciousness. Rather a specific utopia has come to an end, one that in the past crystallized around the potential of the working society" (145–46).

78. Fassbinder, "Ich habe mich mit meinen Filmfiguren verändert," in *Die Anarchie der Phantaste*, 115.

79. lbid., 115–116.

Miriam Bratu Hansen

Schindler's List Is Not Shoah: The Second Commandment, Popular Modernism, and Public Memory

If there were a Richter scale to measure the extent to which commercial films cause reverberations in the traditional public sphere, the effect of *Schindler's List* might equal or come close to that of D. W. Griffith's racist blockbuster of 1913, *The Birth of a Nation*.[1] If we bracket obvious differences between the film (which are perhaps not quite as obvious as they may seem) and bracket eight decades of media history, we are tempted to make the comparison because a similar seismic intensity characterizes both Spielberg's ambition and the film's public reception Each film demonstratively takes on a trauma of collective historical dimensions; and each reworks this trauma in the name of memory and national identity, inscribed with particular notions of race, sexuality, and family. Each film participates in the contested discourse of fiftieth-year commemorations, marking the eventual surrender of survivor- (or veteran-) based memory to the vicissitudes of public history. While *The Birth of a Nation* was not the first film to deal with the Civil War and its aftermath (there were in fact dozens of Civil War films between 1911 and 1915), the film did lay unprecedented claim to the construction of national history and thus demonstrated the stakes of national memory for the history of the present. And while *Schindler's List* is certainly not the first film to deal with the German Judeocide, Spielberg's story about a Sudenten German Catholic entrepreneur who saved the lives of 1,100 Polish Jews asserts a similar place of centrality in contemporary American culture and politics.

On the level of reception, both *The Birth of a Nation* and *Schindler's List* provoked responses from far beyond the pale of industrial-commercial culture, getting attention from writers, activists, and politicians who usually don't take films seriously; it thus temporarily linked the respective media publics (emergent in the case of *The Birth of a Nation*, all-inclusive in the case of *Schindler's List*)

From *Critical Inquiry* 22 (Winter 1996). Copyright © 1996. Reprinted by permission of the University of Chicago Press and Miriam Bratu Hansen.

with the publics of traditional politics and critical intellectuals.[2] What is extraordinary about these two films is not just how they managed to catalyze contesting points of view but also how they make visible the contestation among various and unequal discursive arenas in their effort to lay claim to what and how a nation remembers not an identical nation, to be sure, but distinctly different formations of a national public. As is well known. *The Birth of a Nation* was the first film to be given a screening at the White House (after which President Woodrow Wilson's comment "it is like writing history in lightning" became part of the legend), but it was also the first film to galvanize intellectual and political opposition in an alliance of Progressive reformers and the newly formed NAACP. As is likewise known, not all intellectuals protested: *The Birth of a Nation* became the founding text for an apologetic discourse on "film art" that for decades tried to relativize the film's racist infraction.[3]

Here my comparison turns into disanalogy. For can we compare the violent and persistent damage done to African-Americans by *The Birth of a Nation* to the damage done, as some critics claim, by *Schindler's List* to the victims in whose name it pretends to speak? And can we compare the engagement for a disenfranchised community by whites and blacks, liberals and radicals, to the contemporary intellectual stance that holds all representations of the Shoah accountable to the task of an anamnestic solidarity with the dead? To what extent is the disjunction of the two films a matter of the different histories they engage and to what extent does it illustrate the profound transformation of public memory in contemporary media culture? What do we make, in each case, of the ambivalent effects of popular success? And how, finally, does popularity as such shape the critical accounts we get of the films?

In the following, I will try to trace some of the dynamics at work in the reception of *Schindler's List*. I regard the controversies over the film as symptomatic of larger issues, in particular the ongoing problematic of Holocaust remembrance and the so-called Americanization of the Holocaust, but also the more general issue of the relationship of intellectuals to mass culture, specifically to the media publics of cinema and television. I see both these issues encapsulated in the pervasive polarization of critical argument into the opposition between *Schindler's List* and Claude Lanzmann's documentary *Shoah* (1985) as two mutually exclusive paradigms of cinematically representing or not-representing the Holocaust. This opposition, I will argue, does not yield a productive way of dealing with either the films or the larger issues involved.[4]

I distinguish, roughly, among three major strands or levels in the reception of *Schindler's List*. First, there is the level of official publicity. Under this term I lump together a whole variety of channels and discourses, ranging from Spielberg's self-promotion and the usual Hollywood hype (culminating in the Oscars award ceremony) to presidential endorsements at home and abroad as well as government bannings of the film in some Near Eastern and Asian countries; from subsidized and mandatory screenings for high school students and youth groups to the largely adulatory coverage in the trades, the daily press, and television talk shows.

The second, though by no means secondary, level of reception is the mercurial factor of popular reception. While this reception is no doubt produced and shaped by official publicity, it cannot be totally reduced to intended response. The distinct dynamics of popular reception comes to the fore in precisely those moments when an audience diverges or goes away from the film, when reception takes on a momentum of its own, that is, becomes public in the emphatic sense of the word. This includes moments of failure, like the much-publicized irreverent reaction of black students at Castlemont High School in Oakland.[5] It also includes the film's enormous success in Germany, which prompted endless discussions, letters to the editor, and the discovery of local Schindlers everywhere— a development one cannot but view with amazement and ambivalence. Methodologically, this aspect of reception is the most difficult to represent, for it eludes both ethnographic audience research and textually based constructions of possible spectatorial effects; and yet it requires an approach that is capable of mediating empirical and theoretical levels of argument.

The third level of reception, on which I will focus here, is the vehement rejection of the film on the part of critical intellectuals. This includes both academics and journalists, avant-garde artists and filmmakers (among others, Art Spiegelman and Ken Jacobs in a symposium printed in the *Village Voice*), but also a fair number of liberal publicists (for example, Frank Rich, Leon Wieseltier, Philip Gourevitch, and Ilene Rosenzweig) who voiced their dissent in middlebrow publications such as the *New York Times*, the *New Republic*, and the *New York Review of Books* as well as Jewish publications such as *Forward*, *Tikkun*, and *Commentary*. Most of these critical comments position themselves as minority opinion against the film's allegedly overwhelming endorsement in the media, if not as martyrs in the "resistance" against popular taste ("there is little pleasure in being troubled by what so many have found deeply moving").[6] Accordingly, critical dissent is directed as much against the larger impact of the film—which Michael André Bernstein has dubbed "the *Schindler's List* effect"[7]—as against the film itself.

This response is no doubt legitimate and, in print at least, highly persuasive. For all I know, I might well have joined in, that is, had I seen the film in this country rather than in Germany. The kind of work the film did there, in light of a hopelessly overdetermined and yet rapidly changing "politics of memory," may arguably present a special case.[8] Seeing the film outside the context of American publicity, however, made me consider the film's textual work, if not independently of its intentions and public effects, yet still from a slightly displaced location in relation to both Hollywood global effects and its intellectual critics. Let me say at the outset that it is not my intention to vindicate *Schindler's List* as a masterpiece (which would mean reverting to the *Birth of a Nation* debate). I think there are serious problems with the film's conception, and I could have done without much of the last third, when Oskar Schindler (Liam Neeson) the opportunist, gambler, and philanderer turns into Schindler the heroic rescuer. But seen from a perspective of displacement, and considered from an interstitial space between distinct critical discourses and between disjunctive political legacies, the film did seem to have an important function, not only for empirically diverse audiences, but also for thinking through key issues involved in the representation of the Shoah and the problem of "public memory."[9] Moreover, in the way the film polarized, or was assumed to have polarized, critical and popular responses, the reception of *Schindler's List* threw into relief a particular pattern in intellectuals' positioning that rehearsed familiar tropes of the old debate on modernism versus mass culture.

Before I elaborate on this pattern, and on what it occludes in the public as well as textual workings of the film, I will first outline the intellectual critique in its key points. The following summary distinguishes, roughly, among arguments pertaining to (a) the *culture industry* (in Horkheimer and Adorno's sense); (b) the problem of *narrative;* (c) the question of *cinematic subjectivity;* and (d) the question of *representation.*

a) The first and obvious argument is that *Schindler's List* is and remains a Hollywood product. As such it is circumscribed by the economic and ideological tenets of the culture industry, with its unquestioned and supreme values of entertainment and spectacle; its fetishism of style and glamour; its penchant for superlatives and historicist grasp at any and all experience (the "ultimate statement on" or "the greatest Holocaust film ever made"); and its reifying, levelling, and trivializing effect on everything it touches. In this argument, *Schindler's List* is usually aligned with Spielberg's previous megaspectacles, especially *Jurassic Park,* and accused of having turned the Holocaust into a theme park. Since the business of Hollywood is entertainment, preferably in the key of sentimental optimism, there is something intrinsically and profoundly incommensurable about the "re-creation" of the traumatic events of the Shoah "for the sake of an audience's recreation."[10] Or, as J. Hoberman puts it so eloquently: "Is it possible to make a feel-good entertainment about the ultimate feel-bad experience of the 20th century?"[11]

This critique of *Schindler's List* links the film to the larger problem of the Holocaust's dubious mass-media currency, recalling the ugly pun of "Shoahbusiness." The interesting question here is whether Spielberg's film is merely the latest culmination of what Saul Friedlander discerned, in films and novels of the 1970s, as a "new discourse about Nazism on the right as well as on the left," a -discourse that thrived on the spectacular fusion of kitsch and death.[12] Or does *Schindler's List,* along with the success of the Washington, D.C. Holocaust museum, mark the emergence of yet another new discourse? If the latter is the case, this new discourse, whose different dynamics the film might help us understand, will have to be situated in relation to other struggles over public memorializing, concerning more specifically American traumata such as slavery, the genocide of Native Americans, and Vietnam.

b) The second and more local argument made about the film's inadequacy to the topic it engages is that it does so in the form of a fictional narrative. One emphasis in this argument is on the choice of fiction (notwithstanding the film's pretensions to historical "authenticity") over nonfiction or documentary, a form of film practice that would have allowed for a different organization of space and temporality, different sound/image relations, and therefore different possibilities of approaching the events portrayed. Attendant upon the film's fictional form—with its (nineteenth-century) novelistic and historicist underpinnings—is the claim, supported by the publicity and Spielberg's complicity with it, that *Schindler's List* does not just represent one story from the Shoah but that it does so in a representative manner—that it encapsulates the totality of the Holocaust experience.[13] If that were the case, the film's focus on the heroic exception, the Gentile rescuer and the miracle of survival, would indeed distort the proportions and thus end up falsifying the record.

Related to this charge is the condemnation of the film's choice of a particular type of narrative, specifically, the *classical* mode that governed Hollywood products until about 1960 and beyond.[14] In a technical sense, this term refers to a type of narrative that requires thorough causal motivation centering on the actions and goals of individual characters (as opposed to the "anonymous" Jewish masses who were the object of extermination); a type of narrative in which character psychology and relations among characters tend to be predicated on masculinist hierarchies of gender and sexuality (in the case of *Schindler's List*, the reassertion of certain "styles of manhood"[15] and the sadistic-voyeuristic fascination with the female body, in particular the staging of Amon Goeth's [Ralph Fiennes] desire and his violence toward Helen Hirsch [Embeth Davidtz], the Jewish housemaid); a type of narrative in which the resolution of larger-order problems tends to hinge upon the formation of a couple or family and on the restoration of familial forms of subjectivity (Schindler as a super father-figure who has to renounce his promiscuity and return to marriage in order to accomplish his historic mission, the rescue of Jewish families).[16]

A fundamental limitation of classical narrative in relation to history, and to the historical event of the Shoah in particular, is that it relies on neoclassicist principles of compositional unity, motivation, linearity, equilibrium, and closure—principles singularly inadequate in the face of an event that by its very nature defies our narrative urge to make sense of, to impose order on the discontinuity and otherness of historical experience. Likewise, the deadly teleology of the Shoah represents a temporal trajectory that gives the lie to any classical dramaturgy, of deadlines, suspense, and rescues in the nick of time, to moments of melodramatic intensity and relief. There are at least three last-minute rescues in *Schindler's List*, leading up to the compulsory Hollywood happy ending. This radically exacerbates the general problem of narrative film, which Alexander Kluge has succinctly described as the problem of "how to get to a happy ending without lying."[17] The rescue of the Schindler Jews is a matter of luck and gamble rather than melodramatic coincidence; and although the story is historically "authentic," it cannot but remain a fairy tale in the face of the overwhelming facticity of "man-made mass death."[18] Critics of the film, notably Lanzmann and Gertrud Koch, have observed that *Schindler's List* (like Agnieszka Holland's 1991 *Europa, Europa*) marks a shift in the public commemoration of the Shoah: the film is concerned with *survival*, the survival of individuals, rather than the fact of death, the death of an entire people or peoples.[19] If the possibility of *passing through Auschwitz* is the film's central historical trope, the implications are indeed exorbitant—though not necessarily, in my opinion, that self-evident and unequivocal.

Finally, as a classical narrative, *Schindler's List* inscribes itself in a particular tradition of "realist" film. This is not just a matter of Spielberg's declared efforts to ensure "authenticity" (by using authentic locations, by following Thomas Keneally's novel, which is based on survivor testimony); nor is it simply a matter of the film's use of black-and-white footage and imitation of a particular 1940s style. The film's "reality effect," to use Roland Barthes's phrase, has as much to do with the way it recycles images and tropes from other Holocaust films, especially European ones; but, as a classical narrative, it does so without quotation marks, pretending to be telling the story for the first time.[20] As Koch argues, there is "something authoritarian" in the way *Schindler's List* subsumes all these earlier films, using them to assert its own "truth claims for history" ("MMM," pp. 26, 25). The question that poses itself is whether the film's citational practice merely follows the well-worn path of nineteenth-century realist fiction, or whether it does so in the context of a postmodern aesthetics that has rehabilitated such syncretistic procedures in the name of popular resonance and success. The more interesting question, though, may be to what extent this distinction actually matters, or in which ways the event of the Shoah could be said to trouble, if not challenge, postmodernist assumptions about representation, temporality and history.

c) The third objection raised against *Schindler's List* pertains to the way it allocates subjectivity among its characters and engages the viewer's subjectivity in that process. The charge here is that the film narrates the history of 1,100 rescued Jews from the perspective of the perpetrators, the German Gentile Nazi turned resister and his alter ego, Goeth, the psychotic SS commandant. As Philip Gourevitch asserts, "*Schindler's List* depicts the Nazis' slaughter of Polish Jewry almost entirely through German eyes."[21] By contrast, the argument goes, the Jewish characters are reduced to pasteboard figures, to generic types incapable of eliciting identification and empathy. Or worse, some critics contend, they come to life only to embody anti-Semitic stereotypes (money-grubbing Jews, Jew-as-eternal-victim, the association of Jewish women with dangerous sexuality, the characterization of Itzhak Stern [Ben Kingsley], Schindler's accountant, as "king of the Jewish wimps."[22] This argument not only refers to the degree to which characters are fleshed out, individualized by means of casting, acting, cinematography, and narrative action; the argument also pertains to the level of filmic narration or enunciation, the level at which characters function to mediate the film's sights and sounds, events and meanings to the spectator, as for instance through flashbacks, voiceover, or optical point of view. As psychoanalytic film theorists have argued in the 1970s and early 1980s, it is on this level that cinematic subjectivity is formed most effectively because unconsciously.[23] If that is so (and let's for the moment, for the sake of argument, assume it is), what does it mean that point-of-view shots are clustered not only around Schindler but also around Goeth, making us participate in one of his killing sprees in shots showing the victim through the telescope of his gun? Does this mean that, even though he is marked as evil on the level of the diegesis or fictional world of the film, the viewer is nonetheless urged to identify with Goeth's murderous desire on the unconscious level of cinematic discourse?

d) The fourth, and most difficult, objection to *Schindler's List* is that it violates the taboo on representation (*Bilderverbot*), that it tries to give an "image of the unimaginable."[24] If the criticisms summarized up to this point imply by and large that the film is not "realistic" enough, this critique involves the exact opposite charge, that the film is too "realistic." So, by offering us an "authentic" reconstruction of events of the Shoah, the film enhances the fallacy of an immediate and unmediated access to the past (the fallacy of historical films from *The Birth of a Nation* to *JFK*) by posing as the "real thing" the film usurps the place, of the actual event. What is worse, it does so with an event that defies depiction, whose horror renders any attempt at direct representation obscene. Spielberg transgresses the boundaries of representability most notoriously, critics agree, when he takes the camera across the threshold of what we, and the women in the film "mistakenly" deported to Auschwitz, believe to be a gas chamber. Thus *Schindler's List,* like the TV miniseries *Holocaust,* ends up both trivializing and sensationalizing the Shoah.

Lanzmann, the most radical proponent of this critique, accuses *Schindler's List* of not respecting the unique and absolute status of the Holocaust: "unique in that it erects a ring of fire around itself, a borderline that cannot be crossed because there is a certain ultimate degree of horror that cannot be transmitted. To claim it is possible to do so is to be guilty of the most serious transgression."[25] The counterexample of a film that respects that boundary and succeeds in an aesthetic figuration of the very impossibility of representation is, for both Lanzmann and other critics of Spielberg, his own film *Shoah* (1985). Lanzmann's film strictly refuses any direct representation of the past, whether by means of fictional reenactment or archival footage. Instead, the film combines interviews featuring various types of witnesses (survivors, perpetrators, bystanders, historians) to give testimony at once to the physical, sense-defying details of mass extermination and to the *"historical crisis of witnessing"* presented by the Shoah.[26] This crisis threatens not merely the project of a retrospective, anamnestic account but the very possibility and concept of eyewitnessing and, by extension, the recording capacity of the photographic media. (This is why Lanzmann so radically distrusts Spielberg's untroubled accessing—or, as Lanzmann calls it, "fabrication"—of a visual archive: "If I had stumbled on a real SS film—a secret film, because filming was strictly forbidden—that showed how 3,000 Jewish men, women and children were gassed in Auschwitz's crematorium 2, not only would I not have shown it but I would have destroyed it.")[27]

Lanzmann's argument, like the critique of *Schindler's List* in the name of *Shoah,* is bound up with a complex philosophical debate surrounding the Holocaust, which I cannot do justice to here. Suffice it to say that the moral argument about the impossibility of representation—of mimetic doubling—is linked, via a quasi-theological invocation of the Second Commandment, to the issue of the singularity of the Shoah, its status as an event that is totally and irrecuperably Other, an event that ruptures and is ultimately outside history. What matters in this context is the further linkage, often made concurrently, between the claim to singularity and the type of aesthetic practice that alone is thought to be capable of engaging the problematic of representation without disfiguring the memory of the dead. For the breach inflicted by the Shoah has not only put into question, irrevocably, the status of culture as an autonomous and superior domain (to invoke an often misquoted statement by Adorno);[28] it has also radicalized the case for a type of aesthetic expression that is aware of its problematic status—the nonrepresentational, singular, and hermetic *écriture* to be found in works of high modernism. *Shoah* has rightly been praised for its uniqueness, its rigorous and uncompromising invention of a filmic language capable of rendering "imageless images" of annihilation (Koch paraphrasing Adorno's *Aesthetic Theory*).[29] *Schindler's List*, by contrast, does not seek to negate the representational, iconic power of filmic images, but rather banks on this power. Nor does it develop a unique filmic idiom to capture the unprecedented and unassimilable fact of mass extermination; rather, it relies on familiar tropes and common techniques to narrate the extraordinary rescue of a large group of individuals.

The critique of *Schindler's List* in high-modernist terms, however, especially in Lanzmann's version, reduces the dialectics of the problem of representing the unrepresentable to a binary opposition of showing or not showing—rather than casting it, as one might, as an issue of competing representations and competing modes of representation. This binary argument also reinscribes, paradoxically, a modernist fixation on vision and the visual, whether simply assumed as the epistemological master sense or critically negated as illusory and affirmative. What gets left out is the dimension of the other senses and of sensory experience, that is, aesthetic in the more comprehensive, Greek sense of the word, and its fate in a history of modernity that encompasses both mass production and mass extermination.[30] What gets left out in particular is the dimension of the acoustic, the role of sound in the production of visuality, especially in the technical media where sound has come to compensate for the historical marginalization of the more bodily senses. Yet, if we understand the Shoah's challenge to representation to be as much one of affect as one of epistemology, the specific sensory means of engaging this challenge cannot be ignored. The soundtrack, for example, is neither the seat of a superior truth (as Lanzmann seems to claim for *Shoah*) nor merely a masked accomplice for the untruths of the image track (as assumed in summary critiques of the classical Hollywood film), but rather the material site of particular and competing aesthetic practices.[31]

It is no coincidence that none of the critics of *Schindler's List* have commented on the film's use of sound (except for complaints about the sentimental and melodramatic music)—not to mention how few have actually granted the film a closer look. Although I share some of the reservations paraphrased above, I still would argue that *Schindler's List* is a more sophisticated, elliptical, and self-conscious film than its critics acknowledge (and the selfconsciousness is not limited to the epilogue in which we see the actors together with the survivors they play file past Schindler's Jerusalem grave). Let me cite a few, brief examples that suggest that we might imagine this film differently, examples pertaining to both the film's complex use of sound and its structuring of narration and cinematic subjectivity.

To begin with the latter point, the complaint that the film is narrated from the point of view of the perpetrators ignores the crucial function of Stern in the enunciative structure of the film. Throughout the film, Stern is the focus of point-of-view edits and reaction shots, just as he repeatedly motivates camera movements and shot changes. Stern is the only character who gets to authorize a flashback, in the sequence in which he responds to Schindler's attempt to defend Goeth ("a wonderful crook") by evoking a scene of Goeth's close-range shooting of twenty-five men in a work detail in retribution for one man's escape, closer framing within the flashback in turn foregrounds, as mute witness, the prisoner to whom Stern attributes the account. The sequence is remarkable also in that it contains the film's only flashforward, prompted by Schindler's exasperated question, "what do you want me to do about it?" Notwithstanding Stern's disavowing gesture, ("nothing, nothing—it's just talking"), his flashback narration translates into action on Schindler's part, resulting in the requisitioning of the Pearlmans as workers, which is shown proleptically even before Schindler hands Stern his watch to be used as a bribe. This moment not only marks, on the diegetic level of the film, Schindler's first conscious engagement in bartering for Jewish lives; it also inscribes the absolute difference in power between Gentiles and Jews on the level of cinematic discourse, as a disjunction of filmic temporality. Stern is deprived of his ability, his right to act, that is, to produce a future, but he can narrate the past and pass on testimony, hoping to produce action in the listener/viewer.

More often, temporal displacement is a function of the soundtrack, in particular an abundance of sound bridges and other forms of nonmatching (such as a character's speech or reading turning into documentary-style voiceover); and there are numerous moments when the formal disjunction of sound and image tracks subtends rhetorical relations of irony and even counterpoint. This disjunctive style occurs primarily on the level of diegetic sound, in particular, speech. (The use of nondiegetic music in *Schindler's List* is indeed another matter, inasmuch as it functions more like the "glue" that traditionally covers over any discontinuity and sutures the viewer into the film.)[32] But the persistent splitting of the image track by means of displaced diegetic sound still undercuts the effect of an immediate and totalitarian grasp on reality—such as is produced by perfect sound image matching in numerous World War II films or, to use a more recent example, Oliver Stone's *JFK*.

In the sequence that initiates the liquidation of the Kracòw Ghetto, disjunctive sound image relations combine with camera narration that foregrounds Stern's point of view. The sequence is defined by the duration of an acoustic event, Goeth's speech, that begins and ends with the phrase "today is history." The speech starts in the middle of a series of four shots alternating between

Schindler and Goeth shaving, which briefly makes it an acoustic flashforward. Only in the fifth shot is the voice grounded in the speaking character, Goeth, now dressed in a uniform, addressing his men who stand around him in a wide circle. In the shots that follow, the speech appears to function as a kind of voice-over, speaking the history of the Ghetto's inhabitants and the imminent erasure of this history and its subjects. But the images of the living people we see—a rabbi praying, a family having breakfast, a man and a woman exchanging loving looks—also resist this predication. So does the voice of the rabbi that competes with Goeth's voice even before we see him pray, and it continues, as an undertone to Goeth's voice, into the subsequent shots of Ghetto inabitants (so that in one shot, in which we hear the subdued synchronic voices of the family at breakfast, there are actually three different layers of sound); the praying voice fades out just before the last sentence of Goeth's speech. Not coincidentally, all the Jewish characters shown in this sequence will survive; that is, they will, as individuals, give the lie to Goeth's project. What is more, nested into this sequence is a pronounced point-of-view pattern that centers on Stern and makes him the first to witness the ominous preparations. The act of looking is emphasized by a blow-up of him putting on his glasses and turning to the window, and by the answering extreme high-angle shot that frames the window and curtain from his vantage point. This shot is repeated, after two objective, almost emblematic shots (closely framed and violating screen direction) of rows of chairs being set up by uniformed arms and hands, and then bookended by a medium shot of Stern watching and turning away from the window. The whole sequence is symetrically closed by reattaching Goeth's voice to his body, thus sealing the fate of the majority of the Ghetto population, the people not shown on the image track.

To be sure, the film's hierarchy of physicality and masculinity would never allow Stern to be seen shaving (as Schindler and Goeth are in the beginning of the sequence). But the structuring of vision on the level of enunciation establishes Stern as a *witness* for the narration, for the viewer, for posterity. By contrast, moments of subjective vision ascribed to Schindler, most notably the point-of-view shots that stage his two sightings of the little girl in the red coat, serve a quite different function, stressing character psychology rather than narrational authority. Stern's role as enunciative witness is particularly interesting in a sequence that does *not* involve optical point of view—the sequence in which Goeth kills Lisiek (Wojciech Klata), the boy whom he has made his personal servant. What is remarkable about this sequence is the oblique, elliptical rendering of the killing: we neither see Goeth shooting nor do we see the boy being hit; we only see his body lying in the background as Stern walks across the yard, and it is Stern's movement that motivates that of the camera. Even Stern's registering of the killing is rendered only obliquely, stressing the split between seeing and meaning, seeing and feeling characteristic of the concentration camp universe. Compared to the systematic way *Shoah* (in Shoshana Felman's reading) foregrounds the problematic of witnessing, such moments are perhaps marginal in *Schindler's List*, but they nonetheless deserve to be discussed in similar terms as an aesthetic attempt to engage the extreme difficulty (though not absolute impossibility) of giving sensory expression to an experience that radically defies sense.[33]

Important as the close attention to the film's textual work is, it can only provide a weak answer to the fundamental objections raised by the film's intellectual opponents. Let me repeat that I am not interested in defending *Schindler's List* on aesthetic grounds (the aesthetic narrowly understood as relating to the institution of art and its mass-mediated afterlives). Nor am I suggesting that the film's use of sound and overall narrational strategies are radical, unique, or original; on the contrary, most of these textual devices belong to the inventory of classical Hollywood cinema, from the midteens through the 1950s. Seen in light of the history of that institution up to and including commercial film production of the present, however, *Schindler's List* makes use of these devices in a relatively more intelligent, responsible, and interesting manner than one might have expected, for instance, on the basis of Spielberg's earlier work. The wholesale attack on the film not only erases these distinctions; it also misses the film's diagnostic significance in relation to other discourses, junctures, and disjunctures in contemporary American culture.

The point I'm trying to make is that the lack of attention to the film's material and textual specificity is itself a symptom of the impasse produced by the intellectual critique, an impasse that I find epitomized in the binary opposition of *Schindler's List* and *Shoah*. (Lanzmann's position in this regard is only the most extreme version of this opposition: "In [Spielberg's] film there is no reflection, no thought, about what is the Holocaust and no thought about what is cinema. Because if he would have thought, he would not have made it—or he would have made *Shoah*.")[34] It is one thing to use *Shoah* for the purpose of spelling out the philosophical and ethical issues of cinematic representation in relation to the Shoah; it is another to accuse *Schindler's List* of not being the same kind of film. For while *Shoah* has indeed changed the parameters of Holocaust representation, it is not without problems, aesthetic as well as political, nor is it sacrosanct.

More important, the attack on *Schindler's List* in the name of *Shoah* reinscribes the debate on filmic representation with the old debate of modernism versus mass culture, and thus with binary oppositions of "high" versus "low," "art" versus "kitsch," "esoteric" versus "popular." However, Adorno's insight that, to use Andreas Huyssen's paraphrase, ever since the mid-nineteenth century "modernism and mass culture have been engaged in a compulsive *pas-de-deux*" has become exponentially more pertinent in postmodern media culture.[35] "High" and "low" are inextricably part of the same culture, part of the same public sphere, part of the ongoing negotiation of how forms of social difference are both represented and produced in late capitalism. This is not to say that *Shoah* did not have to compete for funding in an unequal struggle with commercial cinema; nor that it did not have to fight for distribution and access. But once the film was released, especially in the United States, it entered the commercial circuit of the art film market and was praised by the same critics and in the same hyperbolic terms that celebrated *Schindler's List*.

Ironically, it could be argued, *Schindler's List* itself participates in the modernism/mass culture dichotomy even as it tries to overcome it. Here is where I would like to insert the concept of popular modernism (which I elaborate in greater detail elsewhere).[36] If we want to grasp the plurality and complexity of twentieth-century modernity, it is important to note the extent to which modernism was not just the creation of individual artists and intellectuals or, for that matter, avant-garde coteries, but also, especially during the interwar period, a popular and mass movement. I am thinking in particular of formations usually subsumed under labels such as Americanism and Fordism, but more specifically referring to a new culture of leisure, distraction, and consumption that absorbed a number of artistic innovations into a modern vernacular of its own (especially by way of design) and vice versa. It seems to me that Spielberg would like to go back to that moment—that he is trying to make a case for a capitalist aesthetics and culture which is at once modernist and popular, which would be capable of reflecting upon the shocks and scars inflicted by modernity on people's lives in a generally accessible, public horizon.

The reason I believe that something of that order is at stake has to do with the way *Schindler's List* refers itself to that great monument of cinematic modernism, *Citizen Kane*.[37] This argument is primarily based on striking affinities of film style—the selfconscious use of sound, low-key lighting, particular angles and compositions in frame, montage sequences, as well as the comic use of still photography early on in the film. If Spielberg tries to inscribe himself into an American film history pivoting around *Citizen Kane*, he also tries to revise the message—if one can speak of a message—of Welles's film. *Citizen Kane* traces the disintegration of its protagonist from a young man of lofty ideals to a monstrous figure of the specular, two-dimensional, and fragmented media culture he helped create. *Schindler's List* reverses the direction of this development. It presents us with an enigmatic character who starts out in the world of dazzling surfaces and glamour and who is repeatedly identified with the aesthetics of fashion, advertising, and consumption. (In the scene in which Schindler proposes to Stern what is basically a highly exploitative scheme, Stern asks: "They [the Jewish "investors"] put up all the money; I do all the work. What, if you don't mind my asking, would you do?" And Schindler replies: "I'd make sure it's known the company's in business. I'd see that it had a certain panache. That's what I'm good at. Not the work, not the work: the presentation!") But out of that cipher of a con man/grifter/gambler develops an "authentic" person, an integrated and intelligible character, a morally responsible agent. No doubt Spielberg himself has an investment in this redemptive trajectory; and if, as a number of critics have pointed out, the director strongly identifies with his protagonist, he does so in defense of a capitalist culture, of an aesthetics that fuses modernist style, popular storytelling, and an ethos of individual responsibility. Whether he succeeds in reversing *Citizen Kane*'s pessimistic trajectory, that is, in disentangling Schindler—and the story of the Schindler Jews—from the reifying effects of mass-mediated, spectacular consumer culture, is an open question, depending as much on the film's long-term public effects as on textual critique.

But perhaps this question is beside the point, as is treating the opposition of *Shoah* versus *Schindler's List* as if it were a practical alternative, a real option. For whether we like it or not, the predominant vehicles of public memory are the media of technical re/production and mass consumption. This is especially exacerbated for the remembrance of the Shoah considering the specific crisis posed by the Nazis' destruction of the very basis and structures of collective remembering. (Unlike most of the "ordinary massacres" committed in the course of the German genocidal war all over Europe, the Shoah left no *communities* of survivors, widows and children, not even burial sites that would have provided a link with a more "organic" tradition of oral and collective memory.)[38] In a significant way, even before the passing of the last survivors, the remembrance of the Shoah, to the extent that it was public and collective, has always been more dependent on mass-mediated forms of memory—on what Alison Landsberg calls "prosthetic memory."[39]

Much has been written about the changing fabric of memory in postmodern media society, in particular the emergence of new cultural practices (new types of exhibits, the museum boom) that allow the beholders to *experience* the past—any past, not necessarily their own—with greater intensity and sensuous immediacy (compare the Washington Holocaust museum).[40] We need to understand the place of *Schindler's List* in the contemporary culture of memory and memorializing; and the film in turn may help us understand that culture. This might also shed light on how the popular American fascination with the Holocaust may function as a screen memory (*Deckerinnerung*) in the Freudian sense, covering up a traumatic event—another traumatic event—that cannot be approached directly. More than just an ideological displacement (which it is no doubt as well), the fascination with the Holocaust could be read as a kind of screen allegory behind/through which the nation is struggling to find a proper mode of memorializing traumata closer to home. The displaced referents of such memorializing may extend to events as distant as the genocide of Native Americans or as recent as the Vietnam War. It is no coincidence that African-American historians have begun using concepts developed in the attempt to theorize the Shoah, such as the notion of a "breach" or "rupture," to talk about the Middle Passage.[41]

Likewise, the screen memories of the Holocaust could be read as part of an American discourse on modernity, in which Weimar and Nazi Germany figure as an allegory of a modernity gone wrong.[42] The continued currency of these mythical topoi in the popular media may indicate a need for Americans to externalize and project modernity's catastrophic features onto another nation's failure and defeat—so as to salvage modernity the American way. This would give the American public's penchant for allegories of heroic rescue (elaborated in cinematic form by D. W. Griffith) a particular historical and political twist in that it couples the memory/fantasy of having won the war with the failure to save the Jews. In any case, if *Schindler's List* functions as a screen memory in this or other ways, the pasts that it may at once cover and traverse cannot be reduced to the singular, just as the Americanization of the Holocaust cannot be explained by fixating exclusively on its ideological functions.[43] That the film touches on more than one nerve, appeals to more constituencies than a narrowly defined identity politics would have it, could be dismissed as an effect of Hollywood's marketing strategies in the blockbuster era. But it could also be taken as a measure of the film's ability to engender a public space, a horizon of at once sensory experience and discursive contestation.

No doubt *Schindler's List* could have been a different film, or many different films, even based on Keneally's novel. And different stories relating to the most traumatic and central event of the twentieth century will be and will have to be told, in a variety of media and genres, within an irrevocably multiple and hybrid public sphere. If *The Birth of a Nation* remains important to American history, it is not only for its racist inscription of the Civil War and Reconstruction periods; it is just as important for what it tells us about 1915, about the new medium's role in creating a national public, about the dynamics of cultural memory and public memorializing in a volatile immigrant society. *Schindler's List* comes at a radically different moment—in national and global history, in film history, in the history of the public sphere. To dismiss the film because of the a priori established unrepresentability of what it purports to represent may be justified on ethical and epistemological grounds, but it means missing a chance to understand the significance of the Shoah in the present, in the ongoing and undecided struggles over which past gets remembered and how. Unless we take all aspects—omissions, and distortions, displacements and possibilities—of public, mass-mediated memory culture seriously, welt remain caught in the "compulsive *pas-de-deux*" of (not just) intellectual history.

NOTES

For astute readings and suggestions on this essay, I wish to thank Homi Bhabha, Bin Brown, Michael Geyer, Alison Landsberg, and audiences at the University of Chicago, Harvard University, and the annual conference of the Society for Cinema Studies, March 1994.

1. The comparison was first suggested, in a somewhat different spirit, in Terrence Rafferty, "A Man of Transactions," review of *Schindler's List*, *New Yorker*, 20 December 1993, 132. Rafferty praises the epic significance and "visionary clarity" of *Schindler's List* by invoking James Agee's reverie about *The Birth of a Nation* as "'a perfect realization of a collective dream of what the Civil War was like, as veterans might remember it fifty years later, or as children, fifty years later, might imagine it'" (132). Obviously, such a comparison asks to be turned against itself, see Philip Gourevitch, "A Dissent on *Schindler's List*," *Commentary* 97 (February 1994), 52.

2. Another example of such boundary-crossing publicity in the recent past is Oliver Stone's *JFK* (1992). My use of the term *public*, like the distinction among various types of publicness, is indebted to Oskar Negt and Alexander Kluge, *Public Sphere and Experience: Toward an Analysis of the Bourgeois and Proletarian Public Sphere*, trans. Peter Labanyi, Jamie Owen Daniel, and Assenka Oksiloff (1972; reprint, Minneapolis: University of Minnesota Press, 1993); see also my foreword to this edition, ix–xli.

3. Woodrow Wilson, quoted in Michael Rogin, "'The Sword Became a Flashing Vision': D. W. Griffith's *The Birth of a Nation*." In *The Birth of a Nation: D. W. Griffith, Director*, ed. Robert Lang (New Brunswick, N.J.: Rutgers University Press, 1994), 251, an excellent essay

on the film's intervention in the contemporary political and ideological context. See also Janet Staiger, *"The Birth of a Nation*: Reconsidering Its Reception." In *The Birth of a Nation,* 195–213. For an earlier account, see Thomas Cripps, *Slow Fade to Black: The Negro in American Film, 1900–1942* (New York: Oxford University Press, 1977), chap. 2. On the film's devastating and lasting effects on African Americans' cinematic representation and relation to film practice, see *Black American Cinema,* ed. Manthia Diawara (New York: Routledge, 1993).

4. For a comment on the relationship between the two films, see Yosefa Loshitzky, "Holocaust Others: Spielberg's *Schindler's List* versus Lanzmann's *Shoah.*" In *Spielberg's Holocaust: Critical Perspectives on "Schindler's List,"* ed. Loshitzky (Bloomington: Indiana University Press, 1997).

5. See Kluge, "On Film and the Public Sphere," trans. Thomas Y. Levin and Miriam Hansen, *New German Critique,* nos. 24–25 (Fall/Winter 1981–1982), 206–20. For the Castlemont High School incident, see Frank Rich, "Schindler's Dissed," *New York Times,* 6 February 1994, D17, city edition, and "Laughter at Film Brings Spielberg Visit," *New York Times,* 13 April 1994, B11.

6. Michael André Bernstein, "The *Schindler's List* Effect," *American Scholar* 63 (Summer 1994), 429.

7. Ibid.

8. See Michael Geyer, "On the Uses of Shame: The German Politics of Memory." In *Radical Evil,* ed. Joan Copjec (London: Verso, 1995). See also Geyer and Hansen, "German-Jewish Memory and National Consciousness." In *Holocaust Remembrance: The Shapes of Memory,* ed. Geoffrey Hartman (Oxford: Blackwell, 1994), 175–90.

9. See Hartman, "Public Memory and Its Discontents," *Raritan* 13 (Spring 1994), 24–40. Hartman defines "contemporary public memory" in contradistinction to "traditional collective memory" (33). I am using the term in a more general and less pessimistic sense indebted to Negt and Kluge's theory of the public sphere (see n. 2). See also Hartman, "The Cinema Animal: On Spielberg's *Schindler's List,*" *Salmagundi,* nos. 106–107 (Spring/Summer 1995), 127–43.

10. Art Spiegelman, in J. Hoberman et al., *"Schindler's List*: Myth, Movie, and Memory," *Village Voice,* 29 March 1994, 27; hereafter abbreviated "MMM." See also Sean Mitchell's profile of Spiegelman. "Now, for a Little Hedonism," *Los Angeles Times,* 18 December 1994, 7, 97–98, esp. 98.

11. Hoberman, "Spielberg's Oskar," *Village Voice,* 21 December 1993, 63. See also Rich, "Extras in the Shadows," *New York Times,* 2 January 1994, 4, and Leon Wieseltier, "Close Encounters of the Nazi Kind," *New Republic,* 24 January 1994, 42.

12. Saul Friedlander, *Reflections of Nazism: An Essay on Kitsch and Death,* trans. Thomas Weyr (New York: Harper and Row, 1984), 13. Friedlander himself discusses this question in an essay scheduled to appear in *Spielberg's Holocaust.* See also Friedlander's introduction to the volume of essays, edited by him, *Probing the Limits of Representation: Nazism and the "Final Solution"* (Cambridge, Mass.: Harvard University Press, 1942), 1–21.

13. See Ora Gelley, "Narration and the Embodiment of Power in *Schindler's List,*" paper delivered at the Society for Cinema Studies annual conference, New York, March 1995.

14. See David Bordwell, Staiger, and Kristin Thompson, *The Classical Hollywood Cinema: Film Style and Mode of Production to 1960* (New York: Routledge, 1985), and Bordwell, *Narration in the Fiction Film* (Madison: University of Wisconsin Press, 1985), chap. 9. The concept of classical cinema owes much to psychoanalytic-semiotic and feminist film theory of the 1970s; see *Narrative, Apparatus, Ideology: A Film Theory Reader,* ed. Philip Rosen (New York: Columbia University Press, 1986).

15. Ken Jacobs, in "MMM," 27. See also Gertrud Koch, in "MMM," 28.

16. See Bernstein, "The *Schindler's List* Effect," 430, and Geoff Eley and Atina Grossmann, "Watching *Schindler's List*: Not the Last Word" (forthcoming in *New German Critique*).

17. Kluge, *Die Macht der Gefühle* (1983); see the script of this film and other materials published under the same title (Frankfurt am Main, 1984). See also Hansen, "The Stubborn Discourse: History and Story-Telling in the Films of Alexander Kluge," *Persistence of Vision,* no. 2 (Fall 1985), 26. On the Hollywood convention of the always-happy ending, see Bordwell, "Happily Ever After, Part Two," *The Velvet Light Trap* 19 (1982–83), 2–7.

18. See Edith Wyschogrod, *Spirit in Ashes: Hegel, Heidegger, and Man-Made Mass Death* (New Haven, Conn.: Yale University Press, 1985).

19. See Claude Lanzmann, "Holocauste, la représentation impossible," *Le Monde*, 3 March 1994, 1, 7, trans. under the title "Why Spielberg Has Distorted the Truth," *Guardian Weekly*, 3 April 1994, 14; and Koch, in "MMM," 26.

20. See Roland Barthes, "L'Effet de réel," *Communications* 11 (1968), 84–89, trans. Gerald Mead, under the title "The Realistic Effect." *Film Reader* 3 (1978), 131–35. See also Barthes, *S Z*, trans. Richard Miller (New York: Hill and Wang, 1974).

21. Gourevitch, "A Dissent on *Schindler's List*," 51. See also Jonathan Rosenbaum, "Gentile Persuasion," *Chicago Reader* 17 December 1993, 10, 26–27, and Gelley, "Narration and the Embodiment of Power in *Schindler's List*."

22. Ilene Rosenzweig, quoted in Rich, "Extras in the Shadows," 4. See Donald Kuspit, "Director's Guilt," *Artforum* 32 (February 1994), 11–12. See also "MMM," 26.

23. See, for instance, Christian Metz, "Problems of Denotation in the Fiction Film" (35–63) and "The Imaginary Signifier" (244–78); Raymond Bellour, "Segmenting/Analyzing" (66–92) and "The Obvious and the Code" (93–101); Kaja Silverman, "Suture" (219–35); Stephen Heath, "Narrative Space" (379–420); and Laura Mulvey, "Visual Pleasure and Narrative Cinema" (198–209), in *Narrative, Apparatus, Ideology*. For a critique of the cine-semiotic concept of "enunciation," see Bordwell, *Narration and the Fiction Film*, 21–26.

24. See Koch, "The Aesthetic Transformation of the Image of the Unimaginable: Notes on Claude Lanzmann's *Shoah*," trans. Daniel and Hansen, *October* no. 48 (Spring 1989), 15–24. See also Gertrud Koch, *Die Einstellung ist die Einstellung: Visuelle Konstruktionen des Judentums* (Frankfurt am Main: Suhrkamp, 1992), esp. pt. 2, "Film und Faktizität: Zur filmischen Repräsentation der Judenvernichtung," 127–84.

25. Lanzmann, "Why Spielberg Has Distorted the Truth," 14. Lanzmann makes the same argument in his critique of the TV miniseries *Holocaust*, "From the Holocaust to the Holocaust," trans. Simon Srebrny, *Telos* 42 (Winter 1979–1980), 137–43.

26. Shoshana Felman, "The Return of the Voice: Claude Lanzmann's *Shoah*." In Felman and Dori Laub, *Testimony: Crises of Witnessing on Literature, Psychoanalysis, and History* (New York: Routledge, 1992), 206.

27. Lanzmann, "Why Spielberg Has Distorted the Truth," 14.

28. Theodor W. Adorno, "Cultural Criticism and Society," *Prisms*, trans. Samuel and Shierry Weber (1967; reprint, Cambridge, Mass.: MIT Press, 1988), writes: "Cultural criticism finds itself faced with the final stage of the dialectic of culture and barbarism: to write poetry after Auschwitz is barbaric, and this corrodes even the knowledge of why it has become impossible to write poetry today" (34; trans. mod.). See also Adorno's own revision of this statement in his *Negative Dialectics*, trans. E. B. Ashton (1966; reprint, New York: Seabury, 1973), 362–63.

29. Koch, "Mimesis and Bilderverbot" *Screen* 34 (Autumn 1993), 211–22. See also Koch, *Die Einstellung ist die Einstellung*, 16ff., 123ff., and "The Aesthetic Transformation of the Image of the Unimaginable."

30. It is this sense of the aesthetic that Benjamin tries to recover against and in view of the decline and perversion of the institution of art. See Susan Buck-Morss, "Aesthetics and Anaesthetics: Walter Benjamin's Artwork Essay Reconsidered," *October* no. 62 (Fall 1992), 3–41.

31. See James F. Lastra, *Technology and the German Cinema: Perception. Representation, Modernity* (forthcoming). See also *Sound Theory, Sound Practice*, ed. Rick Atman (New York: Routledge, 1992).

32. Compare Claudia Gorbman, *Unheard Melodies: Narrative Film Music* (Bloomington: Indiana University Press, 1987), and Hanns Eisler and Adorno, *Composing for the Films* (1947; reprint, London: Athlone, 1994).

33. See Felman, "Return of the Voice."

34. Quoted in Robert Sklar, "Lanzmann's Latest: After *Shoah*, Jewish Power," *Forward*, 30 September 1994, 10.

35. Andreas Huyssen, *After the Great Divide: Modernism, Mass Culture, Postmodernism* (Bloomington: Indiana University Press, 1986), 24.

36. Hansen, "America, Paris, the Alps: Kracauer (and Benjamin) on Cinema and Modernity." In *Cinema and the Invention of Modern Life*, ed. Leo Charney and Vanessa R. Schwartz (Berkeley: University of California Press, 1995).

37. Spielberg himself claims that he was neither inspired nor influenced by any fiction film when he was working on *Schindler's List* but only watched innumerable documentaries and sifted through piles of photographs. See Hellmuth Karasek, "Die ganze Wahrheit schwarz auf weiß: Regisseur Steven Spielberg über seinen Film *Schindlers Liste*," *Der Spiegel*, 2 February 1994, 185. In the same interview, however, he acknowledges having thought of "Rosebud" to capture the enigmatic distance, the lack of clear, intelligible motivation, with which he conceived of the Schindler character. See also Annette Insdorf, in "MMM," 28. Whether or not inspired by Welles, the relative restraint and withholding of interiority in Spielberg's construction of the Schindler character, at least during the film's first half, is in my opinion much preferable to the omniscient, unrestricted access we get to Schindler's feelings and thoughts in Thomas Keneally's novel on which the film is based.

38. See the papers presented at "Per una memoria Europea dei crimi Nazisti," an international conference to commemorate the fiftieth anniversary of the 1944 massacres around Arezzo, 22–24, June 1994.

39. See Alison Landsberg, "Prosthetic Memory: The Logics and Politics of Memory in Modern American Culture" (Ph.D. diss. in progress, University of Chicago), esp. chap. 4.

40. See Huyssen, *Twilight Memories: Marking Time in a Culture of Amnesia* (New York: Routledge, 1995), esp. chaps. 1 and 12. See also Landsberg, "The 'Waning of Our Historicity'? A Closer Look at the Media of Experience" (paper delivered at the Society for Cinema Studies annual conference, New York, March 1995). For a brief survey of issues involved in American memorial culture, see Michael Kammen, *Mystic Chords of Memory: The Transformation of Tradition in American Culture* (New York: Knopf, 1991), 3–14.

41. For a recent example, see Saidiya Hartman, "Redressing the Pained Body" (paper delivered at the Chicago Humanities Institute, 17 February 1995). The terms breach and rupture refer to *Zivilisationsbruch: Denken nach Auschwitz*, ed. Dan Diner (Frankfurt am Main: Fischer-Taschenbuch Verlag, 1988). The first, quite controversial attempt to conceptualize the trauma of slavery in terms of the Shoah is Stanley M. Elkins, *Slavery: A Problem in American Institutional and Intellectual Life* (1959; reprint, Chicago: University of Chicago Press, 1968). More recently, see Paul Gilroy, *The Black Atlantic: Modernity and Double Consciousness* (Cambridge, Mass.: Harvard University Press, 1994), 213. Laurence Mordekhai Thomas, *Vessels of Evil: American Slavery and the Holocaust* (Philadelphia: Temple University Press, 1993), is a useful starting point, but he does not really engage with issues of representation and memory.

42. See Geyer and Konrad H. Jarausch, "The Future of the German Past: Transatlantic Reflections for the 1990s," *Central European History* 22 (September–December 1989), 229–59. See also Zygmunt Bauman, *Modernity and the Holocaust* (Ithaca, N.Y.: Cornell University Press, 1989).

43. In the manner of, for instance, Peter Novick, "Holocaust Memory in America." In *The Art of Memory: Holocaust Memorials in History*, ed. James E. Young (New York: Prestel, 1995), 159–65.

Sumiko Higashi

Walker and *Mississippi Burning*: Postmodernism versus Illusionist Narrative

Is history dead? In 1989, *Newsweek, Time,* and the *New York Times Magazine* featured articles about Francis Fukuyama, a state department official who heralded "the end of history" as communist regimes went bankrupt, even before Pepsi-Cola and AT&T commercials co-opted the dismantling of the Berlin Wall. Fukuyama's postmortem about the triumph of Western capitalism has since become the subject of academic discourse.[1] Charting the postmodern, Fredric Jameson informs us that since "the waning of the great high-modernist thematics of time and temporality, the elegiac mysteries of durée and memory . . . we now inhabit the synchronic rather than the diachronic . . . , our daily life . . . dominated by categories of space rather than by categories of time."[2] Albeit from opposite ends of the political spectrum, both Fukuyama and Jameson associate the eclipse of history with the triumph of late capitalism and Western-style consumerism. Jameson is particularly concerned about the way in which the rapid processing of information by the news media results in "a series of perpetual presents" and induces "historical amnesia."[3] But is not history being prematurely interred? Critics like Fredric Jameson and David Harvey, who comment on the waning of historicity in postmodernist society, do so from a modernist perspective that includes linear time and periodization, as opposed to spatial and atemporal concepts such as Foucauldian genealogy. Jameson, for example, postulates three stages of capitalistic growth—market capitalism, imperialism, and multinationalism—that correspond to cultural forms labeled realism, modernism, and postmodernism, a schematic evolution of infrastructure in relation to superstructure. Analyzing twentieth-century capitalism as a progression from assembly-line Fordism to flexible accumulation or global financial systems transcending nation-states, Harvey asserts the relevance of Marx, who "restored historical time."[4] As evidenced by the linear perspective of the very critics who are alarmed by the disappearance of the historical referent in late capitalist society, traditional concepts of history still persist. In fact, a close scrutiny of *Walker* (1987) and *Mississippi Burning* (1988), two very different films about historical events, reveals that history is still sacrosanct and that efforts to reconceptualize it provoke fractious debate.

A brief survey of recent historiographical developments, which include discourse on film as history, reveals that the historical profession is indeed very much divided.[5] Although traditional history rooted in nineteenth-century German historiography could be labeled a modernist (and thus outmoded) discipline, controversy among historians demonstrates that the field has been reconceptualized so that political history about nation-states now coexists with the "New History," a catch-all category including the social history of groups excluded from access to traditional forms of power, the new economic history or diometrics, and the new cultural and intellectual history informed by poststructuralism.[6] Primary in the canon constituting the "New History" is the work of Fernand Braudel (1902–1985), the most influential historian of the *Annales* school in Paris and a colleague of structuralist Claude Lévi-Strauss. Contrary to claims that the accelerating displacement of time by space in postmodernist consumer society means the end of history, Braudel boldly reconceptualized historical time in three tiers so that it was spatial and visual. Parallel to rapidly developing political events are social and economic patterns evolving at a slower pace and almost immobile geographical factors that can only be observed over the *longue durée.*[7] Significantly, Braudel used the language of film montage to describe how time could be manipulated and cautioned that history would "not lend itself so easily to . . . juggling with the synchronic and diachronic.[8]

Precisely the juxtaposition of synchronic and diachronic aspects of time that is so difficult to achieve in the writing of history is possible in postmodernist as opposed to illusionist representations of history in film. A consideration of *Walker* (1987), a parody about a nineteenth-century American adventurer who became president of Nicaragua, and *Mississippi Burning* (1988), an account of the events of Freedom Summer in 1964, will be the focus of this essay. As a postmodernist narrative, *Walker* is self-reflexive, ironical, and absurdist in contrast to *Mississippi Burning*, a social problem and male bonding film constructed according to genre conventions. Unfortunately, the powerful reality effect of the civil rights drama, which will be discussed later, limited public discourse on historicity to questions of the authenticity of its representation. By contrast, *Walker* cleverly exploits the cinematic apparatus that results in time compression to provoke thought about the meaning of the past and how it is constructed. Specifically, the film's representation of events is chronological and linear, but the present is superimposed on the past so that American foreign policy in Central America is informed by events of the Vietnam War and, more recently, Desert Shield and Desert Storm. In effect, the juxtaposition of contemporary military exploits with previous ones illustrates Braudel's concept of the spatialization of time that yields perspective on history viewed from a distance.[9] *Walker*, in other words, engages in a continuous dialogue about the ways in which past and present are constructed in relation to each other. Further, the synchronic and diachronic dimensions of historical experience are made visible so that the emphasis is upon continuity as well as change. Consequently, the film does not represent an endorsement of modernization as progress in a linear unfolding of time. As scriptwriter Rudy Wurlitzer concluded, "I've learned . . . about . . . the currents and cycles of history, how history is really not linear, and that it comes around with its own laws."[10]

Given Jameson's observation about the disappearance of the historical referent in late capitalist society, why does *Walker* succeed as history? As a representation of past events, the film exploits a series of contradictions, not the least of which is the concept of postmodernist cinema as history. Director Alex Cox and Wurlitzer consciously engage in a self-reflexive exercise that frustrates audience expectations with respect to genres traditionally associated with dramatizing historical events, namely, documentary, docudrama, and biopic. As a matter of fact, they eschew any attempt at illusionist narrative, play fast and loose with the facts, and collapse past and present tense by telescoping events. Further, they effect a satirical tone through a disjunction between image and sound in which voiceover narration, dialogue, and nondiegetic music are contradicted by the mise-en-scène. As Charles Jencks observes, a distanced and ironical view of the past, in which innocence is no longer possible, is the essence of postmodernist thought about time.[11] What emerges in *Walker* is thus a sense of history that runs counter to a nostalgic and romanticized construction of past events equivalent to forgetfulness. The film functions instead as a hilarious commentary on the psychosexual character of American Puritans who subordinated women and peoples of color, on the role of capital in the pursuit of Manifest Destiny, and on the relentlessness; of modernization, including a commodified media culture.

A montage of events past and present that sharpens our perspective about both, *Walker* is a representation of American spread-eagle diplomacy that ascribes capitalist exploitation of Third World peoples to institutionalized racism and sexism. Although their meeting in the film is apocryphal, industrial magnate Cornelius Vanderbilt (Peter Boyle) summons William Walker (Ed Harris), the filibusterer who was once a household word in this country and is ironically remembered today only in Nicaragua.[12] Arriving on horseback at the site of railroad construction where Chinese workers are laying tracks, a symbolic scene with reference to Manifest Destiny, Walker meets Vanderbilt underling Ephraim Squier (Richard Masur). As Squier conducts him through a series of passenger cars—a scene that is privileged as a transitional moment in the film because two men emerge outdoors where they began—Walker listens to his guide salivate about imperialistic conquest. "Central America," exclaims Squier, is "land . . . for the taking . . . [with] bare-breasted beauties under trees laden with fruit—seven to every man." A cartoonish figure seated in the midst of railroad construction, Commodore Vanderbilt echoes the business executives coded as villains in black and white as opposed to color photography in California Newsreel's *Controlling Interest* (1978). Pointing to a map of Nicaragua, dismissed as "a fucked-up little country somewhere south of here," the industrialist exclaims, "What I need is for some man to go down there and take over. I want that country stable." When

Vanderbilt fails to appeal to the ambition of his guest, who affects the dress of a clergyman, he is cunning enough to exploit his self-righteous and fanatical belief in the country's ideals. "Do you prize democracy, universal suffrage, the principles of our founding fathers? . . . Nicaragua needs democracy." Affectless throughout most of the film's tumultuous events, Walker is devastated by the sudden death of his fiancée, Ellen Martin (Marlee Matlin), decides to accept Vanderbilt's challenge, and sets sail for Nicaragua with his "Immortals." Chief among his followers is a fictional black fighter who accompanied him on an earlier filibuster in Mexico.[13] According to a convention of historical epics, documentaries, and educational film, a map is superimposed over a sailing ship as voiceover narration first announces a "new era for Nicaragua and all Central America" and then, as Walker is shot in the foreground with a cross, switches to first-person commentary inflected with ironical reference to Vietnam: "We paused at the small, unregenerated hamlet of Realejo."

Walker's complexity as a postmodernist historical film includes its representation of the politics of the "Other" as oppressed but nevertheless heterogeneous groups of people. In fact, Walker emerges victorious in Nicaragua after a disastrous series of setbacks because the country is divided by civil war between Conservative and Liberal factions. Although the Nicaraguan masses have no voice in the film, the members of the ruling class define their interests in economic rather than nationalist terms and are thus easily co-opted. Witnessing an American setback at Rivas, a Nicaraguan sympathizer rails against his countrymen's opposition: "Our American brothers came here to bring Peace, Democracy, and Liberty. . . . To improve our civilization. And strengthen our economy." Walker stumbles onto victory by accident rather than design and forms an alliance with Doña Yrena, (Blanca Guerra), a Nicaraguan aristocrat who would rather sleep with an American imperialist than embrace democratic reform. Also divided are American blacks in Walker's ragtag army, the Immortals. After staging an election to declare himself president of Nicaragua, Walker decrees slavery in order to end a labor shortage and court an alliance with the antebellum South. When he announces his intention during a zany performance of *Julius Caesar*, his black followers angrily leave the theater, but their political reactions differ. Walker's most trusted black lieutenant contests his argument that Nicaraguan Indians, like negroes, are suited for slavery by reason of their "fidelity and docility and . . . capacity for labor," but he remains a steadfast supporter. Another African-American fighter, however, contemptuously tosses his medal in the dirt and rides out of town. As his wife, who accompanied him to Nicaragua, had predicted in contemporary lingo, "Next thing you know they'll reinstitute slavery. It's the same racist, macho, sexist shit we turned our backs on." Since these events are part of a historical continuum that includes ongoing oppression of African-Americans in the United States and recent Nicaraguan struggle between Sandinistas and Contras, the elusiveness of political and socioeconomic change is underscored.

Aside from its sophisticated vision of the politics of the developing world and of ethnic minorities, *Walker* reverberates with echoes of feminist discourse on the filmic representation of women. The heroines who are romantically or sexually linked with Walker are, not coincidentally, unable to communicate in English and thus represented as constructs of different forms of language. Unfortunately, not much is known about Walker's brief relationship with Ellen Martin, a hearing-impaired Southern woman who succumbed to yellow fever.[14] Condemning Manifest Destiny as "a cover-up for slavery," she quickly emerges as the moral center of the film. Despite her inability to speak and hear, Ellen reduces Walker to despair during a quarrel sparked by his refusal to convey her political sentiments to Squier, a smug expansionist. She signs to him, "You never represent me. You're always paraphrasing everything I say. Censoring me. . . . I don't trust you." Walker is photographed against a painting of a fertile landscape and next to a model of a sailing ship when he swears, "I'll never leave again." Since the film's cinematography and editing contradict the sound track, Ellen's hearing impairment questions speech or utterance as symbolic of the diachronic in favor of mise-en-scène as visual evidence of the synchronic. When Ellen suddenly dies of yellow fever, Walker accepts Vanderbilt's offer to invade Nicaragua, only to succumb to the influence of yet another strong-willed woman, Doña Yrena.

Unlike Ellen, the Nicaraguan aristocrat is a completely fictional construct: but a necessary one in that sexual politics is symbolic of colonialist expansion. Again, sexual difference, complicated in this instance by cultural difference, is conveyed by the woman's lack of access to the language spoken by male imperialists. Doña Yrena disguises her ability to speak English, decreed the official language of Nicaragua, so that her Spanish dialogue is subtitled on the screen. Although Walker is repeatedly photographed in foreground and at low angle, Doña Yrena, who is sexually aggressive, observes his slight physical stature and reassures him that his performance in bed is "not great, but for a gringo good enough." Walker's decision to execute General Ponciano Corral, the legitimist leader, and to torch the centuries-old city of Granada are vindictive reactions to Doña Yrena's defiance. She contemptuously dismisses him as "a dog's asshole." The representation of territorial conquest as sexual imperative is nothing new, but the film's sex role reversals and irreverent tone provide more than a little amusement.

Perhaps most telling in *Walker*'s juxtaposition of past and present to emphasize the continuity of capitalist exploitation is the use of twentieth-century icons in the narrative of a nineteenth-century adventurer. When Doña Yrena escapes from Granada with two Nicaraguan legitimists, her companions are reading *People* and *Newsweek*, both featuring cover stories about Walker, self-styled "Gray-Eyed Man of [Manifest] Destiny." As they discuss the politics of "those crazy gringos" in a horse-drawn carriage, a Mercedes overtakes them on the dirt road. During an interview with a news reporter, Walker asserts that the ends, which he has admittedly forgotten, justify the means. As the two men walk down a stretch of beach in an extreme long shot, in the foreground are icons of multinational corporate dominance, an American with a Coca-Cola bottle and a pack of Marlboros. Undoubtedly most disturbing in the film's anachronistic mise-en-scène is the presence of a computer terminal signifying the information age and Foucauldian panoptic surveillance in Vanderbilt's quarters. At the conclusion, when Walker and his men retreat during the burning of Granada, World War II air raid sirens are heard on the sound track and a helicopter, the quintessential symbol of the Vietnam War, descends in front of the Palacio Nacional to rescue men who can produce American passports. Finally, as the credits roll, a video monitor on screen right shows President Ronald Reagan reassuring the public, "Let me say to those who invoke the men of Vietnam . . . there is no thought of sending American combat troops to Central America." But the newsreel footage shows American men involved in maneuvers and lifeless bodies of Nicaraguan victims. An instance of yet another juxtaposition between past and present tense to achieve historical consciousness, the transition from film to television as a medium for reporting news events, especially military intervention abroad, is particularly apt in representing an era dominated by the small screen.

Despite "the evaporation of any sense of historical continuity and memory" attributed to the postmodern condition by critics like David Harvey, *Walker* demonstrates that postmodernist cinema can indeed be compelling as history. Clarification of this argument requires a focus on the narrower issue of modernization because critics are by no means in agreement about definitions of postmodernism versus modernism, or the extent to which these are overlapping and continuous cultural practices. Andreas Huyssen, for example, argues that poststructuralism is "primarily a discourse of and about modernism," whereas Brook Thomas aligns such discourse with the postmodern and thus construes it as existing in tension with the new historicism. Complicating critical discourse even further, T. J. Jackson Lears points out that literary critics and historians do not agree on definitions of modernism, a phenomenon that he labels antimodernism for the purposes of his argument. In addition, critics have expressed disagreement regarding the issue of postmodernism in relation to history. Marshall Berman, for example, critiques both structuralism and postmodernism, which in some instances he equates with modernism, as essentially ahistorical. Linda Hutcheon argues, on the other hand, that contrary to Jameson's observation about the waning of historicity, postmodernist writing characterized by self-reflexivity and parody is indeed rooted in the historical world. Given these disagreements, I focus on the more limited subject of *Walker* as discourse on the issue of modernization as a significant aspect of modernity. Although Berman indicts social scientists for splintering discussions of modernity into compartmentalized subjects such as industrialization, market formation, urbanization, and nation-states, these issues are significant precisely because historians, not all of whom claim to be social scientists, have traditionally studied processes of political, economic, and social change.[15]

As a historical film *Walker* is an interesting amalgam because it calls for a critique of American economic domination, in both its imperialistic and multinational corporate phases, and of modernization, albeit in an innovative postmodernist form. Are we then to assume that the film as modernist narrative reconceptualizes history? *Walker* does constitute a departure in that it exemplifies Linda Hutcheon's discussion of "historiographic metafiction" as writing that foregrounds both history and fiction as constructs and employs this awareness to rework the "forms and contents of the past." Yet despite the privileging of multiple voices in response to American hegemony, *Walker* is ultimately limited in rethinking history because it focuses on such traditional issues as nationhood, diplomacy, and military conquest. *Annales* historians, it should be remembered, shifted the terms of debate about modernization and rejected as peculiarly Western the notion that the experience of a modern industrialized society should serve as a yardstick by which to measure the history of the rest of the world.[16] Given this perspective, *Walker* remains traditionalist in its subject matter despite elements of satire, irony, and absurdist humor. Suppose the history of Walker's exploits had been represented instead as Doña Yrena's autobiography or memoir, a Nicaraguan perspective that contradicts and overlaps with American accounts including those written by the filibusterer.[17] Such a representational strategy would produce disjunction resulting from differences in terms not only of culture but of gender.

Walker, to be sure, remains an interesting departure, but reconceptualizing history provokes resistance, as an analysis of its reception demonstrates, because traditional concepts based on empiricism, objective truth, and linear progress are still dominant in bourgeois culture. As historical reenactment, *Walker* does not conform to the legacy of public images of history validated by realistic representation in mainstream cinema. A film that begins with voiceover narration associated with documentaries and a title proclaiming "THIS IS A TRUE STORY"—only to show battle scenes recalling Sam Peckinpah westerns to the tune of festive Latin rhythms—does not qualify as history. Filmgoers stayed away from the box office, and film critics focused on questions of authenticity and unconventional form. *Newsweek*'s David Ansen, for example, listed several factual errors in the film and concluded, "Wurlitzer's script offers a tinny, underground-commix view of history. What a waste. The real story of Walker . . . would make a great epic." As a matter of fact, *Walker* questions the adequacy of the historical epic as a representation of the past in its parodic staging of *Julius Caesar*. *Variety*'s critic objected that *Walker* was "completely unconvincing in its presentation of events" and faulted "surrealist anachronisms that have been woven into the visual fabric . . . to emphasize the modern parallels." The *Wall Street Journal* described *Walker* as a "convoluted—and generally silly—spoof" like *Saturday Night Live*. Apparently without humor, Michael Wilmington warned in the *Los Angeles Times* that some audiences "may conclude the movie makers have gotten confused about what century they're in."[18]

Walker did receive more appreciative notices from Richard Schickel in *Time*, David Sterritt in the *Christian Science Monitor*, and Stanley Kauffmann in the *New Republic*. Vincent Canby of the *New York Times* liked its "hip, cool, political satire" and observed that its "neo-Brechtian believe-it-or-not inventory of character and events . . . must strike most Americans as outlandishly unbelievable, while many Central Americans may simply nod their heads in recognition." In fact, the *Los Angeles Times* reported that contrary to its reception in the United States, *Walker* played to packed houses in Managua, Nicaragua, despite the fact that the price of a ticket exceeded the daily earnings of an average worker. Although Nicaraguan reviewers, like their American counterparts, tallied up factual errors in the film and did not always appreciate farcical humor, filmgoers in Managua reportedly broke into laughter over the juxtaposition of past and present events.[19] Apparently, postmodernist film as history does speak to the "Other" in multiple voices.

The fact that most reviewers objected to *Walker*'s collapsed temporality, presentism, and ironical sense of time, not to mention its absurdist humor, is instructive regarding the public's definition of historical film. A consideration of critical as well as audience reception, in other words, that postmodernist reading strategies are in effect addressed to insiders willing to consider a historiographic representation in which history as opposed to subject matter becomes the focus. Director Alex Cox evidently misread moviegoers because his intention was "to steer the film away from a drab 'Masterpiece Theater' presentation" and to "reach a broader audience, not just the people who go to the art houses." On the contrary, *Walker* is the sort of release that would be exhibited in art film theaters rather than in shopping malls. The negative reception of film critics demonstrates that postmodernist historical narrative is unacceptable to a public still invested in realistic representations of the past as opposed to discourse on the nature of those very representations. Consequently, the commercial and critical success of *Mississippi Burning* is quite revealing because its powerful realism focused debate on questions of authenticity, as did the postmodernist approach of *Walker*, but not on the issue of history itself as a construct. Coincidentally, director Alan Parker, like his British countryman Cox, also denigrated public television broadcasting because he wanted to reach a mass audience. Unlike Cox, he succeeded.[20]

In contrast to *Walker*, *Mississippi Burning* is an illusionist narrative constructed according to the conventions of the social problem film as well as of the detective and male buddy genres. One reviewer dubbed it "Dirty Harry beats dirty laundry."[21] The precredit and credit sequences establish the film's concern with racial injustice: as black spiritual music wails on the sound track, a white man and a black boy drink from separate water fountains, and a building torched by the Ku Klux Klan goes up in flames. Civil rights workers modeled on Andrew Goodman, Michael Schwerner, and James Cheney are stopped at night on a lonely country road and murdered by white southern rednecks. Assigned to head investigation of the crime are two FBI agents, Alan Ward (Willem Dafoe), a punctilious eastern bureaucrat who is ineffectual, and Rupert Anderson (Gene Hackman), a rumpled but savvy southerner who eventually convinces his sidekick to resort to KKK tactics. Aside from ignoring procedure and playing rough, Anderson shrewdly observes the local citizenry and exploits Mrs. Pell (Frances McDormand), the lonely and sensitive young wife of the deputy sheriff. At the beginning of the film, Ward and Anderson sit in their car and observe a small town shortly after their arrival in Mississippi. What appear to be casual street scenes photographed in extreme long shot and in soft focus reveal potential sources of information to the southern agent. A symbol of white conscience, Mrs. Pell eventually betrays her husband and discloses to Anderson where the civil rights workers are buried. In fact, the location of the burial site was revealed by an informant who collected a thirty-thousand dollar reward.[22]

Switching into high gear, the two FBI agents lead a team, including an African-American agent, who trick and terrorize the guilty. Accelerating events lead to a montage of men being arrested and subsequently leaving a courthouse with black and white still shots that identify each convicted man by name and jail sentence. Unfortunately, this last tactic, as well as the documentary-style interviews of local denizens voicing their opinions about race relations, tends to historicize events and fuel controversy about the film. At the conclusion, a tracking shot of a cemetery stops to focus on the vandalized tombstone of the black civil rights worker. But this image of persistent racism is undercut by the film's characterization of black men as essentially passive and impotent, a representation that attests to white paranoia expressed in the myth of the black stud and a history of lynching. Consistent with the precredit sequence in which both an African-American boy and a white adult man drink water from segregated fountains, the only fearless black male in the film is a child. A significant aspect of the narrative strategy of *Mississippi Burning* as a buddy film is to displace irreconcilable racial division onto categories of males, both black and white civil rights workers and FBI agents, who are characterized as either macho or impotent. Further, the appeal to male camaraderie provides a means of resolving a particularly heinous crime in the civil rights era. To put it another way, the film achieves narrative closure by encoding a pattern of social organization based on male bonding that cuts across class and racial lines. Such camaraderie, however, is in reality restricted to rituals like professional athletics because macho codes are not only elitist but also sexist. Anderson is able to exploit Mrs. Pell, for example, because she is socially isolated; as a consequence of her betrayal, she is savagely beaten by her husband in the presence of Klansmen.

The reception of *Mississippi Burning,* a release that received far more attention than *Walker,* provides evidence of what the public construes as a legitimate historical film. Distributed in December 1988 according to a phased release schedule involving only nine screens nationwide, the film required strong reviews, especially in New York, for a successful run. As the result of a *Time* cover story, several *New York Times* articles, and a *CBS This Morning* report, *Mississippi Burning* became the subject of controversy that led to brisk box-office business and primed the audience for a wide release in January and a video release in July.[23] Despite a disclaimer that the film was a fictionalized account based on true events, its strong reality effect influenced reviewers to react in terms of conventional views about history. Put simply, such views equate history with objectivity and truth. *Variety*'s critic wrote, "Approach is fictional, but . . . [the] script captures much of the truth in its telling of the impact of a 1964 FBI probe into the murders of three civil rights workers." But several reviewers objected to two gross distortions in the film: the blatant repression of black activism in the civil rights movement and the glorification of FBI agents who had in actuality thwarted rights workers. Pauline Kael, sounding a note of disagreement among New York critics, claimed, "Alan Parker is essentially putting blacks at the back [of the bus] again." Similarly, Abbie Hoffman responded to Stuart Klawans's positive review in the *Nation*, by asserting that "the idea that the FBI brought an end to a segregated South is about as ludicrous as saying that noble elements inside the joint Chiefs of Staff were essentially responsible for ending the war in Vietnam."[24]

Clearly, controversy about the historical authenticity of this film was based on concern that filmgoers, unable to differentiate between fact and fiction, would accept Parker's representation of the civil rights struggle. Claims to historical truth are vigorously debated because competing visions of the past are invoked to influence social attitudes and to shape public policy. At least since the controversial premiere of *The Birth of a Nation* (1915), film as history has been subject to debate because it is based on realistic representation. As Jack E. White asserted in the *Time* cover story, "Many viewers, whose ability to discern a whopper . . . has been obliterated by an age of TV docudramas, . . . leave the theater believing a version of history so distorted that it amounts to a cinematic lynching of the truth." Significantly, reviewers who defended the film resorted to the strategy of downplaying the importance of historical accuracy. Vincent Canby, for example, asserted that social issues were best represented in documentaries but claimed that "nothing . . . seriously damages the film's validity as a melodrama or as an evocation of recent history." Canby later argued in a convoluted defense of his views that *Mississippi Burning* was such a powerful indictment of racism that it could only be undermined by "finding reasons not to believe the film." Attempting to minimize objections to the film on the grounds of its lack of credibility, he questioned the value of objectivity and was not above firing salvos at *We Are Not Afraid*, Seth Cagin's and Philip Dray's monograph about the Freedom Summer murders.[25]

Discourse on *Mississippi Burning* was not restricted to newspapers, magazines, and trade journals but also appeared in scholarly publications. Robert Toplin gave a detailed summary of factual errors in the film in *Perspectives*, the newsletter of the American Historical Association. Why did academics not simply dismiss *Mississippi Burning* as just another movie? Sundiata K. Cha-Jua argued in *Radical History Review* that for most moviegoers, especially youth who were not old enough to recall the civil rights movement, the film might be their only source of information and, moreover, obscured a public television series such as *Eyes on the Prize*. Similarly, Thomas Doherty expressed concern about the impact of the film on teenaged audiences in *Cineaste*, a journal whose editors condemned Parker's "egregious inversion of historical facts." Ultimately, the argument provoked by the film in the popular press, if not in scholarly publications, probably cost it Academy Awards—though not nominations. Despite a formidable campaign launched by distributor Orion to counteract negative publicity, the film won an Oscar in only one of seven categories, editing. Nevertheless, *Mississippi Burning* earned respectable figures at the box office even though it could not compete with star-studded blockbusters like *Rain Man* (1988) or *Twins* (1989), also released during the Christmas season. When the film last appeared on *Variety*'s charts, its cumulative gross receipts during a period of 178 days totaled more than thirty-four million dollars. Additionally, when *Mississippi Burning* was released in video format, it remained on the list of top-ten rentals for more than two months and was more popular than *Twins*.[26]

Controversy about *Mississippi Burning* demonstrates that traditional conceptualizations of history are still widely held, not only among professional historians but among film reviewers and their readership. Peter Novick defines the concept of historical objectivity as follows: "The assumptions on which it rests include a commitment to the reality of the past, and to truth as correspondence to that reality; a sharp separation between knower and known, between fact and value, and, above all, between history and fiction." Although most filmgoers are obviously not trained as historians, they would most likely agree with this formulation because it dovetails with their educational experience and ideological beliefs. As Fukuyama stresses, history deteriorates into antiquarianism unless it is enlisted in a larger cause.[27] Despite his belief that the triumph of Western capitalism signaled the end of history, discourse on historical representation in film, most recently the contentious reception of *JFK* (1991), demonstrates that the public is still invested in traditional concepts about the past. As for the historical profession, Lawrence Stone has observed that despite serious challenges mounted by the "new history," political history based on empiricist research is still dominant in the discipline.[28] Critics' proclamation of a new postmodernist age notwithstanding, traditional history remains as one of the bulwarks of modernist thought in which the individual is still constituted as an autonomous subject, however beleaguered, as opposed to being reduced to a textual construct. The epistemological divide between critical theorists and historians, in other words, is underscored to a significant extent by debate on the issue of human agency as opposed to the privileging of reified texts.[29] Whether repeated calls for the historicizing of texts, on the one hand, and greater attention to history as a construct, on the other, will lead to more frequent cross-disciplinary dialogue that will affect future historiography remains a matter of speculation.

A final word about the argument provoked by *Mississippi Burning* is in order. Ultimately, public discourse on the film's authenticity reinforced belief in linearity, progress, and the ability of Americans to accomplish social engineering. The very fact that the film had been made was cited as a sign of improved race relations despite statistics to the contrary.[30] Controversy, however, did not move beyond questions of veracity to include a consideration of either history itself or the ideological function of history. *Walker,* on the other hand, provokes thought about the relationship between past and present through its lack of verisimilitude and its spatialization of time so that the result is cyclical rather than teleological. Progress is not equated with linear development in a patriotic celebration of American civic virtues, as is the case in *Mississippi Burning*. Despite its limitations, *Walker* does provoke thought about the nature of historical representation as a construct that often validates nationalism and patriotism. As such, it succeeds, whereas *Mississippi Burning* does not. But it was the latter film that found favor with most critics, made millions of dollars at the box office and video rental shops, and garnered Golden Globe awards and Oscar nominations. The lesson is that not only is postmodernist historical representation unacceptable for a public still invested in traditional notions about history; so too are the sweeping generalizations of critics about the waning of historicity itself.

NOTES

I wish to thank Ronald Gottesman, Robert Rosen, Vivian Sobchack, and Charles Wolfe for comments on previous drafts read at the Society for Cinema Studies conference in Los Angeles in 1991 and at the American Studies annual meeting in Costa Mesa in 1992.

1. Otis L. Graham, Jr., "Premature Reports: "The 'End of History,'" *OAH Newsletter* 18 (May 1990), 3, 23; James Atlas, "What Is Fukuyama Saying?" *New York Times Magazine*, 22 October 1989, 38–42; Alan Ryan, "Professor Hegel Goes to Washington," *New York Review of Books*, 26 March 1992, 7–13; and Peter Fritzsche, "Francis Fukuyama, *The End of History and The Last Man*," *American Historical Review* 97 (June 1992), 817–19. See also Francis Fukuyama, *The End of History and the Last Man* (New York: Free Press, 1991).

2. Fredric Jameson, "Postmodernism, or, the Cultural Logic of Late Capitalism," *New Left Review* 146 (July–August 1984), 64; reprinted in *Postmodernism, or, The Cultural Logic of Late Capitalism* (Durham, N.C.: Duke University Press, 1991). See also Jameson, "Reification and Utopia in Mass Culture," *Social Text* 1 (Winter 1979), 130–48; "Postmodernism and Consumer Society." In Hal Foster, ed., *The Anti-Aesthetic: Essays on Postmodern Culture* (Port Townsend, Wash.: Bay Press, 1983), 111–25; "Progress vs. Utopia; or, Can We Imagine the Future?" In Brian Willis, ed., *Art after Modernism: Rethinking Representation* (New York: New Museum of Contemporary Art, 1984), 239–52; and "Nostalgia for the Present," *South Atlantic Quarterly* 88, no. 2 (Spring 1989), 517–37. See also Michael Walsh, "Postmodernism Has an Intellectual History," *Quarterly Review of Film and Video* 12, nos. 1–2 (1990), 147–61.

3. Jameson, "Postmodernism and Consumer Society," 125.

4. Jameson, "Postmodernism, or, the Cultural Logic of Late Capitalism," 77–78; David Harvey, *The Condition of Postmodernity: An Inquiry into the Origins of Cultural Change* (Cambridge: Basil Blackwell, 1989), part 2, 273.

5. See Robert A. Rosenstone, "History in Images/History in Words: Reflections on the Possibility of Really Putting History onto Film," *American Historical Review* 93 (December 1988), 1173–85. For critical theorists on historical film, see Vivian Sobchack, "'Surge and Splendor': A Phenomenology of the Hollywood Historical Epic," *Representations* 29 (Winter 1990), 24–49; and Janet Staiger, "Securing the Fictional Narrative as a Tale of the Historical Real," *South Atlantic Quarterly* 88 (Spring 1989), 393–412.

6. See "AHR Forum: The Old History and the New," *American Historical Review* 94 (June 1989), 654–98. Essays read at the AHA annual meeting in December 1987 include Theodore S. Hammerow, "The Bureaucratization of History"; Gertrude Himmelfarb, "Some Reflections on the New History"; Lawrence W. Levine, "The Unpredictable Past: Reflections on Recent American Historiography"; Joan W. Scott, "History in Crisis? The Others' Side of the Story"; and John E. Toews, "Perspectives on 'The Old History and the New': A Comment."

7. On the *Annales* school, see Lynn Hunt, "French History in the Last Twenty Years: The Rise and Fall of the Annales Paradigm," *Journal of Contemporary History* 21 (April 1986), 209–24; and Hunt, *The New Cultural History* (Berkeley and Los Angeles: University of California Press, 1989), 1–22. See also Georg G. Iggers's introduction, "The Transformation of Historical Studies in Historical Perspective," to Georg G. Iggers and Harold T. Parker, eds., *International Handbook of Historical Studies: Contemporary Research and Theory* (Westport,

Conn.: Greenwood Press, 1979), 1–14. On Braudel's concept of structure, see Samuel Kinser, "Annaliste Paradigm? The Geohistorical Structuralism of Fernand Braudel," *American Historical Review* 86 (February–December 1981), 63–105. On the *Annales* school critique of narrative history, see Hayden White, "Narrative in Contemporary Historical Theory." In *The Content of Form: Narrative Discourse and Historical Representation* (Baltimore: Johns Hopkins University Press, 1987), 31–32.

8. Fernand Braudel. "Time, History, and the Social Sciences," trans. Siam France. In Fritz Stern, ed., *The Varieties of History* (New York: Vintage Books, 1973), 424–25. Originally published as "Histoire et sciences sociales: La Longue durée," *Annales* 13 (1958), 725–53.

9. Kinser, "Annaliste Paradigm?" 99.

10. Rudy Wurlitzer, *Walker* (New York: Harper and Row, 1987), 41.

11. Charles Jencks, *Post-Modernism: The New Classicism in Art and Architecture* (New York: Rizzoli, 1987), 20–21.

12. For a brief account of Walker's filibusters, see Karl Berman, *Under the Big Stick: Nicaragua and the United States since 1948* (Boston: South End Press, 1986), 51–102. A standard account is William O. Scroggs's aptly titled *Filibusters and Financiers: The Story of William Walker and His Associates* (New York: Russell and Russell, 1916). Walker wrote an account of his adventures in third person, *The War in Nicaragua* (Mobile, Ala.: Goetzel, 1860).

13. A Broadway musical entitled *Nicaragua, or, General Walker's Victories* that opened in New York in 1856 included a character named Ivory Black, "a superior nigger." See Karl Berman, *Under the Big Stick,* 76.

14. She was actually Helen Martin. See Scroggs, *Filibusters and Financiers,* 14.

15. Andreas Huyssen, "Mapping the Postmodern," *New German Critique* 33 (1984), 37–38, reprinted in *After the Great Divide: Modernism, Mass Culture, Postmodernism* (Bloomington: Indiana University Press, 1986), 178–221; Brook Thomas, "The New Historicism and Other Old-fashioned Topics." In H. Aram Veeser, ed., *The New Historicism* (New York: Routledge, 1989), 182–203; T. J. Jackson Lears, *No Place of Grace: Antimodernism and the Transformation of American Culture, 1880–1920* (New York: Pantheon, 1981), xix; Marshall Berman, *All That Is Solid Melts Into Air: The Experience of Modernity* (New York: Simon and Schuster, 1982), 33–34; and Linda Hutcheon, *A Poetics of Postmodernism: History, Theory, Fiction* (New York: Reutledge, 1998), 5. See also Thomas, *The New Historicism and Other Old-Fashioned Topics* (Princeton: Princeton University Press, 1991).

16. Hutcheon, *A Poetics of Postmodernism,* 5; quoted in Iggers, "The Transformation of Historical Studies," 9. On Marxism and the *Annales* school, see Hunt, "French History in the Last Twenty Years" and *The New Cultural History.*

17. See, for example, Natalie Zemon Davis, *The Return of Martin Guerre* (Cambridge, Mass.: Harvard University Press, 1983), which was made into a film. See also Staiger, "Securing the Fictional Narrative."

18. David Ansen, "A Yankee Devil's Manifest Destiny: History as a Bad Joke," *Newsweek,* 7 December 1987; "Walker," *Variety,* 2 December 1987; untitled review, *Wall Street Journal,* 3 December 1987; Michael Wilmington, "'Walker' Dramatizes Bizarre Historical Exploit Gone Awry," *Los Angeles Times,* 4 December 1987; in *Walker* clipping file, Margaret Herrick Library, Academy of Motion Picture Arts and Sciences, Los Angeles, Calif.

19. Richard Schickel, "Bananas Republic," *Time,* 7 December 1987; David Sterrit, "'Walker': History as Tragedy . . . and Farce," *Christian Science Monitor,* 7 January 1988; "Stanley Kauffman on Film," *New Republic,* 28 December 1987; Vincent Canby, "Film: 'Walker,' Starring Ed Harris," *New York Times,* 4 December 1987; "'Walker' Is an Amusing Hit in Nicaragua," *Los Angeles Times,* 5 March 1988, in *Walker* clipping file, Margaret Herrick Library, Academy of Motion Picture Arts and Sciences.

20. Quoted in Patrick Goldstein, "Hollywood Invades Nicaragua," *Los Angeles Times Calendar,* 10 April 1987, 17; Wayne King, "Fact vs. Fiction," *New York Times,* Arts and Leisure section, 4 December 1988, 20. According to *Variety, Straight to Hell* and *Walker* "convinced Hollywood [that Cox] . . . couldn't be trusted; as a renegade the director has been making films in Mexico." See "Missing Persons," *Variety,* 8 June 1992, 83.

21. Richard Corliss, "Fire This Time," *Time*, 9 January 1989, 58.

22. Also cited as an example of blatant racism is the fact that James Cheney, the black civil rights worker, was driving, rather than sitting in the back seat as shown in the film. See Seth Cagin and Philip Dray, *We Are Not Afraid: The Story of Goodman, Schwerner, and Cheney and the Civil Rights Campaign for Mississippi* (New York: Macmillan, 1988).

23. "Orion Giving 'Mississippi' Straight Promo Push, Avoids Controversy," *Variety*, 18–24 January 1989, 13. According to *Variety*'s "Weekend Box Office Report," a weekly feature of the trade journal, the film remained on the charts from the time that it was released in December until June 1989. Released in video format in July, the film ranked no. 12 among the top fifty video rentals in 1989. See "Top Video Rentals 1989," *Variety*, 24 January 1990. The film even spawned a television docudrama called *Murder in Mississippi* that was aired on CBS in February 1990 and received an Emmy nomination for best comedy-drama special.

24. "Mississippi Burning," *Variety*, 30 November 1988, 12; Pauline Kael, review of *Mississippi Burning*, *New Yorker*, 26 December 1988, 74; letters, *Nation*, 13 February 1989, 182.

25. *Time*'s own Richard Schickel had written earlier that the film's "power finally sweeps away one's resistance to the film's major improbabilities." See "The Fire in the South," *Time*, 5 December 1988, 90; Vincent Canby, "Alien Visions of America," *New York Times*, Arts and Leisure section, 18 December 1988, 14; and Canby, "Taking Risks to Illuminate a Painful Time in America," ibid., 8 January 1989, 13.

26. Robert Brent Toplin, "*Mississippi Burning* Scorches Historians," *Perspectives* (April 1989), 20; Sundiata K. Cha-Jua, "*Mississippi Burning:* The Burning of Black Self-Activity," *Radical History Review* 45 (1989), 132–35; Cha-Jua argues that depiction of Klansman as rednecks (more than half the men eventually indicted held white-collar positions) fails to show that racism transcends class and that repressing black activism in favor of FBI heroics precludes an exploration of the economic base of racial injustice; Thomas Doherty, "*Mississippi Burning*," *Cineaste* 17 (1989), 48; editorial, ibid., 2; "Weekend Box Office Report," *Variety*, 7–13 June 1989, 8; "Who Benefits from the Academy Awards Promo Campaigns?" *Variety*, 22–28 March 1989, 5; "Top Fifty Video Titles," *Variety*, 20–26 September 1989, 43. *Rain Man*, starring Dustin Hoffman and Tom Cruise, and *Twins*, starring Arnold Schwarzenegger and Danny DeVito, had earned $160 and $110 million, respectively, at the time *Mississippi Burning* disappeared from *Variety*'s charts.

27. Fritzsche, "Francis Fukuyama," 817.

28. Peter Novick, *That Noble Dream: The "Objectivity Question" and the American Historical Profession* (Cambridge: Cambridge University Press, 1988), 1–2; Lawrence Stone, "Resisting the New," *New York Review of Books*, 17 December 1997, 59–62.

29. See my "Ethnicity, Class, and Gender in Film: DeMille's The Cheat." In Lester Friedman, ed., *Unspeakable Images: Ethnicity and the American Cinema* (Urbana: University of Illinois Press, 1991), 112–39.

30. Ansen, "A Yankee Devil's Manifest Destiny," 73.

History, Fiction, and Postcolonial Memory

Naomi Greene

Empire as Myth and Memory

One of the most striking phenomena in recent French cinema is, certainly, the number and range of works devoted to France's colonial past. In this essay, I would like to concentrate on two films that deal less with the actual history of that past than with memories of it—in particular, with memories of the traumatic era of decolonization in Algeria. I am speaking now of Pierre Schoendoerffer's *Le Crabe-tambour* (*The Drummer Crab*) (1977) and Brigitte Rodan's *Outremer* (*Overseas*) (1991). Although seemingly very different from one another, both films filter the era that marked the end of French rule in Algeria (although *Le Crabe-tambour* also deals with Indochina) through the memories of two social groups who were deeply affected by these events: that is, the military (*Le Crabe-tambour*) and the Pieds-Noirs, or French settlers, in Algeria (*Outremer*).

In embracing a perspective that is clearly partial and subjective, these films raise several vital issues. Most obviously, perhaps, they suggest some of the ways in which the memories of individuals are shaped, transformed—indeed, created—by a shared vision of the past, driven by its own logic and desire. At the same time, the opaque and private shapes assumed by memories in these films indicate some of the difficulties involved in remembering, or mourning, one of the most divisive wars in French history. And these issues, in turn, lead into broader considerations concerning the very nature of memory—especially the memories of social groups such as those represented here—in the contemporary world.

In looking at the intensely private and coded nature of the memories evoked in *Le Crabe-tambour* and *Outremer*, it is important to keep in mind just how difficult it has been to remember, or discuss, France's long struggle to retain Algeria. In fact, the difficulties of "remembering" the Algerian war constitute the subject of a series of essays found in an important historical work, *La Guerre d'Algérie et les Français*, published in 1990. In one of these essays, Robert Frank notes that "although the wars of Indochina and Algeria were the longest and the most recent of the four wars France has fought in the twentieth century, they appear the most forgotten. Despite the fact that the Algerian war has left burning traces in our memory, or perhaps because of this, the process of commemoration has taken place in the most difficult manner."[1] If France's humiliating defeat is one reason commemoration has been difficult, the unpopularity of the Algerian war is certainly another. It was an unpopular war for a variety of reasons. While only a minority of French people actively sympathized with the Algerians' struggle for independence, many more saw the army's routine use of torture as a chilling reminder of Nazi atrocities. Moreover, while Algeria was technically French, to most French people on the mainland the fields of battle seemed distant and unknown, devoid of emotional resonance. Deemed a "phantom" war or a "war without a name" because of de Gaulle's refusal to admit that France could be at war with one of its own *départements*, it was, above all, a struggle without a clear and compelling message. And to come back to the question of memory, how could one mourn or commemorate a struggle without such a message? "The survivors," to cite Robert Frank once again, "could celebrate the fact that they did not die for nothing. But by honoring the memory of their fallen comrades, they would implicitly be asking the terrible and, by definition, the most taboo of questions: why did they die? . . . It is because this question is basically unbearable that this war is uncommemorable."[2]

Given the divisiveness of the war, the fact that it has still to find a place in national memory, it is hardly surprising that only those directly involved—like the army or the Pieds-Noirs—should retain vivid memories of it. Memories all the more vivid, perhaps, since the vast majority of their countrymen and women wanted so clearly to forget. But it is also true that these groups do, indeed, have much to remember. After years of anguish and struggle, the Pieds-Noirs—many of whom were small farmers or businessmen—were forced to flee to France, to a "mother country" many had never seen. Not only did these refugees lose home and country but they often found little sympathy or understanding awaiting them when they arrived in France. Blamed for an unpopular war, they were frequently cast in the role of the "Other," a role that they had always assigned to Arabs. Small wonder that the rage many continue to feel has helped fuel the extreme Right in France or that, as *New York Times* commentator Marlise Simons phrased it in 1992, many still "ached for Algeria thirty years after the war."[3]

In the case of the army, feelings of bitterness and betrayal went, perhaps, deeper still. Enlisted men and professional soldiers may have viewed the war differently—a "dirty war" for the former, for the latter it was a defeat that could have been avoided—but both, as historian Isabelle Lambert notes, felt "abandoned and rejected" by their country.[4] Moreover, the professional army—which often included men who had served in Indochina as well as Algeria—may well have been the sector of the French population, as historian Pierre Nora suggests, most deeply attached to the idea of a national empire. "In the end," observes Nora, "the overseas army is the only sector of the national community to have lived the colonial problem as a national problem."[5] And the resentment of the professional military was exacerbated by the conviction that Algeria was but a terrible replay of Indochina. Professional soldiers felt that they had been mice betrayed by the government's vacillations and lack of resolve. "It was in fact during the conflict in Indochina," says historian Alain Ruscio, "that the 'army's malaise' began, an army betrayed by the civilian population, by politics, by defeatists."[6] When de Gaulle finally signed the treaties ending the Algerian war, this "malaise" erupted into violence: disaffected veterans attempted an aborted coup d'état, or putsch, against the Republic and rallied to the OAS (Organisation de l'armée secrète), a "secret army" that resorted to terrorist tactics in Algeria and on the mainland in its continuing efforts to bring down the civilian government, which, the veterans felt, had abandoned them and betrayed the best interests of France.

In light of these events, it is not difficult to see why many Pieds-Noirs as well as many veterans should have been haunted by what happened in Algeria long after the war itself had ended, long after most of the settlers, in particular, had established new lives for themselves in France. Events that barely touched many of their compatriots determined the course that lives would take, the shapes that identities would assume. But if memories remained vivid, so, too, did they remain difficult to express. Denied entry into a shared past, imbued with the guilt and unease surrounding the war, they became even "guiltier" as the social and cultural climate changed. As the very project of colonialism became imbued with opprobrium, memories of the colonial past—and, especially, memories infused with nostalgia for a colonial order now recognized as unjust—became less "admissible" than ever before.

It is precisely this dilemma—that is, both the need, and the difficulty, of remembering and representing a past imbued with guilt—that seems to have inspired the particular shapes and impulses assumed by memory in *Le Crabe-tambour* and *Outremer*. Neither film leaves any doubt that the past remains vivid and alive: permeated by a sense of intense melancholy and nostalgia, these films depict survivors for whom time has stopped, men and women who continue to live in the past. But at the same time this past with all its weight of guilt and unease has been transformed by memory. That is, while the precise historical context that gave rise to the melancholy that is felt here is not hidden, its exact outlines remained blurred. Assuming an intensely private and subjective cast, memory leads us away from the continuities of history and into an atemporal zone marked by the absolute cast of dreams at once collective and individual. Drawn away from the clearings and explanations of history, we enter an ambiguous world of private symbols and allusions, a mysterious world marked by the displacements and repetitions of dreams. It is a world where the most troubling and "guilty" aspects of the colonial past—particularly the scandal at its heart, that is, the relationship between oppressed and oppressor are consistently obscured or erased. Drawn into the undertow of memory, we enter a world dominated by a melancholy nostalgia that, unable to represent the true object of its desire, takes the form of existential longings for a dreamlike moment of youth and innocence, for a world before the fall from grace. Historical trauma is veiled and disguised even as forgetting is no longer a passive process but instead, to borrow a phrase from Michel de Certeau, an "action directed against the past."[7] Here, as critic Alain-Gérard Slama has written in regard to several novels dealing with Algeria, nostalgia impels memory not to "confront" but rather to "reject" history.[8]

————————

While both *Le Crabe-tambour* and *Outremer* "reject" history, they do so in different ways. In contrast with *Le Crabe-tambour*, which takes us into the realm of collective dreams and myth, *Outremer* pulls us into the narrow tunnel of the individual psyche, into the subjective and intensely private landscape of haunted dreams. This essential difference, in turn, may well be linked to what is the most obvious point of contrast between the two films: that is, while the world of *Outremer* is dominated by women, that of *Le Crabe-tambour* is almost exclusively masculine. Reflecting Schoendoerffer's own experience in the military in Indochina (where he was made a prisoner of war at the time of the decisive French defeat at Dien Bien Phu), *Le Crabe-tambour* focuses on the career officers who fought in France's last colonial wars.

The three principal protagonists of *Le Crabe-tambour* are, in fact, present or former naval officers. As the film opens, two of them are crossing the Atlantic aboard a vessel of the French merchant marine. One, who narrates much of the film, is the ship's doctor; the other, a man whose mortal illness ensures that this will be his last journey, is her captain. Slowly, they become friends as they reminisce about their experiences, as they do so, remembered flashbacks disrupt the present and transport us to the past that so obsesses them. It was a past, we gradually learn, dominated by a former comrade of theirs, Wilsdorf. Presently captain of a fishing boat, Wilsdorf served with the doctor in Indochina and with the captain in Algeria. As fragments of the past are brought to life, we learn of the bleak and traumatic moment that dramatically altered the captain's life, as well as that of Wilsdorf. This critical moment—which, significantly, is never seen—was that of the aborted putsch in Algeria. At that time, the paths of the captain and Wilsdorf diverged radically: unlike the captain, Wilsdorf chose to join those comrades who rebelled against the civilian government, an act that led to imprisonment and expulsion from the navy. While the captain refused to join the rebels' ranks, the sympathy he obviously felt for Wilsdorf and his cause prompted him to promise the latter that whatever the outcome of the putsch, he would resign from the navy. His subsequent failure to keep this promise—a failure that he sees as a kind of betrayal—has troubled him ever since. On this, his last voyage, he wants nothing more than to bid his former comrade-in-arms a final adieu. In what is probably the film's climactic moment, the captain's wish is granted when, for a brief instant, his ship passes Wilsdorf's fishing vessel on the high seas and the two men speak, from afar, one last time.

Even this brief summary suggests, surely, some of the deep-seated emotional currents—of honor and betrayal, of melancholy and decline—associated with the memories of former military men. The protagonists embody those veterans who became known as *les soldats perdus* (lost soldiers), whose lives were shattered by their experiences in Indochina, and especially Algeria. Prisoners of a traumatic past, they suffer from a sense of lost hopes and futile sacrifices. As if in limbo, these eternal nomads now spend their days in endless journeys from one end of the globe to another. Reading from his cherished Bible, the captain repeats the question that haunts them all. "What have you done with your gifts?" he sadly intones. Still, guided by the codes of honor and stoicism, of bravery and solidarity, that held sway in the military, they do battle against that most elemental of foes: the sea. A long and beautiful sequence of the ship's prow breaking up ice floes embodies the harshness of their struggle against freezing temperatures, gales, and high seas. At the helm of his ship, the captain is in his element, for he is a master of waves and tides, a lover of the sea who will return to land only to die.

Like the captain, few of these restless adventurers would exchange their lonely and harsh existence for the ease of life on land. This is a sentiment that Schoendoerffer appears to share, for the single view of Paris afforded by *Le Crabe-tambour* depicts a desolate city peopled by prostitutes and marked by ugly posters and seedy bars. And the sense of decline implicit in this sequence—a decline associated by the military with the end of Empire—reverberates throughout the film. It is no accident that the men are bringing mail and medical assistance to the rocky promontory of St. Pierre off the Canadian coast: one of France's last colonies, this snow-clad coast is a barren reminder of a lost empire that once extended throughout North America.[9] Neither is it mere happenstance that the broadcasts that issue forth from their radio describe the last spasms of another doomed colonial struggle—that of the war in Vietnam.

But the bleaker the present, the more the past seems to assume the glowing intensity of a lost paradise. Significantly, perhaps, of all the films dealing with this period, it is *Le Crabe-tambour*—which springs from what historian Claude Liazu calls the most "impossible" of memories or discourses concerning the war—that does most to transform the past. (For Liazu, the military discourse is so "impossible" precisely because it contracts the nation's "conscience and its historical imaginary.")[10] In no other film is the contrast between past and present so stark, the loss of youth and hope, of grace and innocence, so absolute. We are reminded of it each time a flashback takes us from the harsh gray seas of the North Atlantic to the lush greens and oneiric mists of Asia, from the ice and cold of the present to the warmth and beauty of the past. Seen through the lens of an all-powerful and all-transforming memory, Asia is not a war zone of enemy ambushes, of mud and grenades, but a dreamlike land of soft mists and hazy rivers. "All these wars," writes director Schoendoerffer revealingly in a 1969 novel, "are sadly always the same: we slogged through the mud, we waited forever, we shot, they died. That is what war is. . . . But the wind has blown away the odor of the corpses and all that remains in our memory is the blaze of youth."[11]

But the ugly, realities of war—as well as the terrible moment of the putsch—are not, of course, the only ones that vanish in the "blaze of youth" conferred by memory. Telling omissions and ambiguities work to erase the most troubling recollections of the past. Some of the most subtle of these involve the film's depiction of native peoples. For, like the "odor of corpses," these people too—people whose very presence serves as a reminder of the historical scandal at the heart of colonialism—have also disappeared from a remembered past. They appear in fact in only two scenes—scenes that say far more about Schoendoerffer's taste for myth and legend (including the racial stereotypes they often contain) than about his taste for historical realities. In one of these scenes, Wilsdorf is captured by a Black tribe after a shipwreck off the coast of Africa. At first he is their helpless prisoner, exhibited in a cage like a prized and rare specimen. But at a critical moment he becomes their talismanic leader when he teaches them how to aim their guns and kill their enemies. If this scene hints at the myth of White supremacy (Wilsdorf is a far better warrior than the natives), the other encounter raises the specter of Asian barbarism. Here, Wilsdorf visits a native village, only to suddenly discover that some of the faces he sees around the fire belong to decapitated heads, which are leering at him from spikes.

A reminder of Asian "Otherness," this last scene also seems a deliberate echo of a similar episode in Joseph Conrad's *Heart of Darkness*. (Interestingly, this sequence from *The Heart of Darkness* also inspired similar scenes in Malraux's 1930 novel *La Voie royale* and in another film that does much to turn a divisive war—that of Vietnam—into myth: that is, Francis Ford Coppola's *Apocalypse Now*.) And, indeed, *Le Crabe-tambour* says far more about Schoendoerffer's love for the mythic adventures told by writers of the last century— by Conrad and Melville, and by Jules Verne—than about the recent historical past. Wilsdorf himself is hardly an ordinary mortal. Instantly set apart from the others by dress and demeanor—in the first scene he is seen in gleaming white holding a black cat—his character was, in fact, based on a legendary French soldier who was imprisoned at the time of the putsch. A kind of romantic adventurer, a latter-day T. E. Lawrence who has put home and country far behind him, he cries out, "Old Europe, to hell with you," as he prepares to sail a Chinese junk halfway around the world. Endowed with as many lives as his mysterious cat, he has performed deeds admired by seamen all over the globe. Indeed, whenever his name is mentioned, someone has yet another exploit to recount, another tale to add to his legend. In fact, if this way of describing his life—that is, through flashbacks remembered by different people—forces us to decipher and reconstruct the past as we would a dream, so too, as French critic François de la Bretèque has astutely observed, does it create the sense that we are watching a legend unfold. Since each character recalls a different moment in Wilsdorf's past, notes de la Bretèque, we learn about his life "in a fragmented and indirect way rather than in a strict chronological order. This remarkable *procédé* gives him a mythic aura and transforms the search for him into a symbolic quest. He incarnates the past of each of the protagonists and, beyond that, of colonial France herself."[12]

While the daring figure of Wilsdorf dominates *Le Crabe-tambour*, other aspects of the film clearly reinforce its epic cast, the way in which memory transforms history into myth. Shot in beautiful color by master cameraman Raoul Coutard, the film has the temporal and spatial sweep of an epic as it takes us from youth to old age and from one end of the globe to the other. As de la Bretèque goes on to note, the very fact that the same few characters repeatedly meet one another in totally different parts of the world creates the sense of a ritualistic drama that takes the entire globe for its stage. In this sense, the current journey portrayed in the film—a journey that takes the men from the Old World to the New even as it leads to the final act in the captain's life, that is, the meeting with Wilsdorf—takes on symbolic resonance. As compelling as the search for the great white whale in *Moby Dick* or the terrifying trek into the heart of darkness taken by Conrad's protagonist, this voyage takes place not in the zone of history but in that of myth. When the captain finally meets Wilsdorf, the legendary being who has haunted him for so many years, everything in the scene—the movement of the waves, the distance that still separates the two ships—heightens the epic cast of their encounter. Even Wilsdorf's ship, which bears two painted eyes upon its prow in the Asian manner, appears to be a fabulous sea creature as it slowly comes into the captain's line of vision. Although their final adieu cannot help but recall the political events that drove a wedge between former comrades, those events are submerged by the haunting mood of the scene. Imbued with all the melancholy of approaching separation and death, their meeting speaks, above all, of failed hopes and brave sacrifices, of exile and memory, of life and death. Here, human fife, seen against the boundless and eternal landscape of the sea, is as brief as the greetings exchanged by passing ships.

Like *Le Crabe-tambour*, *Outremer* was also inspired, in part, by memories drawn from the life of its director.[13] And, no less than Schoendoerffer's film—in which remembered flashbacks constantly eclipse the present—the very structure of *Outremer* bears witness to the power of such memories and the spell they cast upon the present. In *Outremer*, three separate narratives draw us into the past obsessively and insistently, for each successive narrative returns to moments and events evoked by the preceding one. Each time, these moments are seen from a different perspective, since each narrative is focused on one of three Pied-Noir sisters living in Algeria at the time of *les événements* (as the Algerian struggle for independence was euphemistically called). Almost invariably, the moments and events depicted involve deep-seated currents of passion and longing, of love and desire. Even as this intensely subjective focus, as well as the repetitions inherent in the tripartite structure, confer a dreamlike sense upon the moments depicted, the elliptical and partial nature of each narrative gives rise to mysterious ambiguities and omissions. Once again, the past we encounter resembles a dream that must be painfully deciphered and reconstructed. Only gradually, with difficulty and uncertainty, do we begin to understand the complex psychological mechanisms that govern the sisters' inner lives.

The first narrative reflects the perspective of the oldest sister, Zon, who has married a naval officer. Devoted to husband, home, and children, she seems to lead the most conventional life of the three. But soon it is clear that disturbing emotional currents lie below the surface. Consumed by longing for her husband—who is absent much of the time—she is unable to accept his death when he is declared missing in action. (She makes a melodramatic and disturbing bargain with God: she will give up her children, she declares, if only he will return her husband to her.) Before long, she herself is taken ill with cancer and, in a very strange and troubling deathbed scene, she dons her husband's uniform and writhes in spasms of agony (which have a strange sexual cast) on the bed they have shared before falling, lifeless, to the ground.

After Zon's death, the film's focus shifts to the second sister, Malène. Once again, on the surface all is well: Malène has made a "good" marriage with a wealthy man who adores, her. But he is an ineffectual dreamer and so, despite herself, she must play the "man": that is, make all the decisions and do all the work on the beloved farm they own. Ultimately, her refusal to leave this farm leads to her death: while doing an errand in the car she is killed by an Arab bullet that was probably intended for her husband.

Only the third and youngest of the sisters, Gritte, refuses to follow the conventional path taken by her sisters. Spurning eligible and attractive suitors, she takes an Arab rebel as a lover. But she is not immune to violence and death: she loses not only her sisters but also her lover, who is shot by French soldiers when he is on his way to see her one night. The psychic toll of all the horror she has endured is made very clear in the final scene of the film. In a dramatic temporal ellipse, a shot of Gritte about to leave Algeria is followed by one of her standing, years later, in a Parisian church, where she is about to be married. As the camera explores the vast hall, the past comes to life: the whispering voices of her dead sisters are heard and, soon, their ghostly faces are seen superimposed on the stone walls. In this haunted atmosphere, all the death and violence Gritte has experienced seem to reach out into the present and smother it. For when she is asked to take the marriage vows she hesitates, unable—it seems—to begin life anew, to put down new roots to replace those so brutally severed in the past. She remains mute, paralyzed, as the camera backs away; the credits appear on the screen while the voices of little girls are heard singing the ditties of childhood.

The film ends, then, on the same note of terrible nostalgia and melancholy that permeates *Le Crabe-tambour*. Like Wilsdorf and his comrades, Gritte is a survivor, condemned to spend what remains of her life in limbo. While Schoendoerffer's film is haunted by the "blaze of youth," *Outremer* looks still further back in time—to the innocence and joy of a paradisaical childhood. Once again, we enter a world where time loses its precise chronology and gives way, instead, to the wrenching contrast between past and present, between a luminous "before" and a dark and somber "after." If the children's songs that are heard at the end of *Outremer* recall the innocence and joy of a world before the fall, the final scene embodies the powerful charge of loss and exile at the heart of Pied-Noir memory.

In an attempt to discover the general shapes taken by this memory, more than a quarter of a century after the end of the Algerian war a French historian, Anne Roche, conducted a series of interviews with former Pieds-Noirs. The responses of those with whom she spoke leave little doubt that the terrible contrast between past and present—the contrast that is so dramatically embodied in *Outremer*—continues to haunt the vast majority of Pieds-Noirs. "The interviews as a whole," observes Roche, "clearly bring to fight the creation of a 'before' and an 'after' which . . . always function in the, same way. . . . 'Before' is strongly valorized and the subject of nostalgia; 'after' is seen pejoratively."[14] Nor, according to Roche, was this the only dimension of Pied-Noir memory that finds a powerful echo in *Outremer*. Compelling resemblances link the memories voiced by Roche's subjects to those embodied in the film in two other vital domains. One concerns the ways in which the history of the war itself has been remembered; the other bears upon the all-important relationship between Arabs and Pieds-Noirs.

In the course of her interviews, Roche was struck by the ambiguities and omissions that seemed to cloud the memories of her subjects (most of whom were women) whenever it came to these domains. She notes, for example, that her subjects appeared to repress the precise outlines of the convulsions that had overtaken Algeria. While most of them displayed a "myopic concentration" on the details of daily life in Algeria, their recollections of historical and political events were hazy and confused. Most notably, she observes, they lacked a sense of the "different phases of the way [and] a synthesizing view of the forces at work."[15] Along with this refusal to confront what had happened went a continuing need to repress the memory of social injustice, the enormous social gap that existed between them and the Arabs. Hence they remembered Algeria as a "paradise without colonial sin," a land where everyone, Arabs and Europeans, lived in harmony and plenty. When confronted, however, with the obvious discrepancy between these happy memories of an "idyllic world" and the brutal facts of rebellion and war, they tended to establish a dichotomy between a few individual "good" Arabs (who bore witness that French rule was a benevolent one) and Arabs seen as an "undifferentiated, confusing, and probably manipulated mass."[16]

It is, precisely, in these two critical areas that *Outremer* reveals the same complicated mechanisms of repression and denial as those displayed by Roche's interviewees. Indeed, virtually every aspect of this film works to draw us away from the shared realm of history—a realm marked by temporal markers and clear outlines—into the subjective realm of memory and dream. As suggested earlier, the obsessive repetitions inherent in the tripartite narrative structure as well as the elliptical and mysterious nature of each narrative all suggest a world composed of primal moments of longing and desire. Shifting perspectives and temporal gaps, mysteries that are not always elucidated by a subsequent narrative, all conspire to disorient us, to keep us off balance, to deny us the sense of ordered chronology necessary to a historical overview. The convulsions of history may be felt in the violence that invades the sisters' very bodies, but the historical context for this private violence never comes into focus. Instead, we are led into psychic crevices where desires and feelings condition perception itself. Even time is subject to the play of emotions, the pull of fear or desire. "Sometimes," writes critic Jacques Siclier, "time is suspended in illusions, sometimes it stretches out due to the effect of precise dangers and changes in the relationship of French and Arabs."[17]

This intensely subjective realm is one in which vivid and fragmented images assume the private codes, the symbolic resonances, of those in dreams. All of this is dramatically announced in the film's disorienting and mysterious opening sequence, which, repeated at critical junctures throughout the film, becomes a kind of leitmotiv. A shot of barbed wire seen through the credits is followed by one of three young women in a small boat waving to someone. Abruptly, this gives way to the closeup of a man in a white uniform. But, contrary to all expectations, as the next shot reveals, he is not the person to whom they were waving. Instead of establishing us in space and time, this opening has left us with a series of questions. Who and where are these women? To whom am they waving and why? Although we must wait before these questions are answered, from the first it is clear that the dreamlike images of the opening embody the deeply felt emotions that run throughout the film: a sense of limbo (the open sea); of claustrophobia (the barbed wire); of lost innocence (the dim young girls in the boat); of exile and separation (the sea).

Marked, as this sequence suggests, by the logic of dreams, *Outremer* is, significantly, at its most mysterious, its most ambiguous and elliptical, when it comes to the darkest areas of memory: that is, in those scenes that reflect the vital relationship between Arabs and Pieds-Noirs. It is here where the director's vision appears to merge with that of her protagonists—that we enter the most troubling zones of the film, the underlying strata of ambivalence and denial. Not surprisingly, it is also here that the gap between the different layers of the film—between attitudes that are voiced and overt and those embodied at a deeper, formal level— is most intense.

On the surface, of course, the film appears to criticize Pied-Noir attitudes toward Arabs. Not only does it appear to mock the sisters' racist remarks but it also depicts a love affair—between a European woman and an Arab—that breaks one of the most fundamental taboos of the colonial system. Still, when it comes to what we see rather than what we hear or are told, disturbing ambiguities and omissions begin to make themselves felt. The sisters' view of Arabs may appear ludicrous; but when Arabs themselves are seen they invariably correspond to Pied-Noir stereotypes: shadowy and menacing, they suddenly materialize from nowhere and mutter among themselves in a conspiratorial fashion. It might be argued, of course, that we are seeing them from a Pied-Noir perspective: that is, they *appear* menacing to the sisters and other Europeans. But the film gives no indications that the view we are seeing of the Arabs is the view through the sisters' eyes—above all, through their fears. Without such indications, the power of film is such that we tend to believe in the reality of what is shown. In this case, this means that we too see the Arabs as faceless members of a conspiratorial and frightening group or (as Roche has it) an "undifferentiated mass."

The suspicion that this portrayal of Arabs reflects the director's own ambivalence(s)—be they conscious or unconscious—is confirmed, moreover, by several critical scenes. In one such scene, the Arab laborers on the farm owned by the middle sister and her husband—a farm to which she is passionately attached— begin to mutiny as one after another expresses discontent when handed his meager wages. Faced with their anger, the sister expresses great surprise; she can do nothing, she says, because it is her husband who determines their wages. Our first reaction is to believe her and to sympathize with her plight: she is the main character, with whom we tend to identify. But with reflection come disturbing questions. After all, the film has clearly established that she, and not her husband, runs the farm. Why, then, does she immediately blame him? Since she appears to be genuinely shocked and distressed, it is difficult to take her response as a calculated and self-protective be. But that leaves only one conclusion: she believes in her professed innocence precisely because she desperately wants to ignore, to repress, the terrible truths of social injustice. Like those interviewed by Roche, she too wants to believe that everyone in Algeria, including the Arabs on her farm, lived in harmony and plenty. And doesn't the profoundly ambiguous nature of this scene—which somehow invites us to believe that she is telling the truth—suggest that the director herself shares this thirst for innocence?

In this respect, it is telling that the scenes depicting the forbidden love affair between the youngest sister, Gritte, and the Arab rebel are the most ambiguous and elliptical of the entire film. True, all the men in *Outremer* are vague figures. But each of the other men—be he a suitor or a husband—has a clearly marked identity, a psychological profile. Not so the Arab. Mute and spectral, he is but an icon of passion, the embodiment of European desires as well as, perhaps, fears. Silent, rough, and grimy, in what appears to be their second encounter (although even this is not made clear), he suddenly appears on the road next to Gritte and wordlessly pulls her toward him as if he meant her bodily harm. After this episode, they are seen together for the briefest of sequences. Since Gritte's sisters have been depicted with their husbands in intimate moments, this omission is disquieting. Does it mean that even the director cannot imagine how an Arab and a Frenchwoman would behave together? Or what they would talk about? Or does the silence of the film reflect the taboos that cling to the affair? Furthermore, it is odd that in a film which dissects the slightest tremor of the psyche, the motives for their affair remain opaque: Is her passion for him mixed with rebellion? With guilt? And his love for her is even more mysterious. Is it motivated by revenge? By the color of her skin? Such questions must remain unanswered because they never interact as a couple and because the Arab is deprived of those traits that would bring him to life not only as a lover but as a human being.

The mysteries and ambiguities that envelop this affair provide a vivid illustration of the denials and repressions at work in Pied-Noir memory. The way these scenes are depicted suggest that, perhaps despite herself, the director cannot confront the darkest zones of the past, the most inadmissible of historical truths. In this sense, the silence that shrouds Gritte's doomed and passionate affair corresponds to the absence of the putsch in *Le Crabe-tambour*. In both instances, the most troubling and guilty zones of the past—those involving rebellion (if not treason) and racism—are those that cannot be represented. In their refusal to confront these zones, both films point to the extent of the divide between the brutal facts of history and the transformations wrought by memory.

There is no doubt, as suggested at the beginning of this essay, that this divide is particularly acute in *Le Crabe-tambour* and *Outremer* because both portray memories of a "taboo" war, memories that have been rendered even more "inadmissible" with the passage of time. But an important and influential essay by historian Pierre Nora suggests that the divide between history and memory that is felt here may well reflect broader social impulses. Titled, significantly "Entre Mémoire et histoire" (Between Memory and History), Nora's essay serves as the introduction to *Les Lieux de mémoire*, a highly influential collection of essays devoted to the ways in which the memories invested in *les lieux*—whether these "places" be physical (as in the case of archives and museums) or symbolic (as are, for example, holidays and emblems)—both reflect and influence changing perceptions, of history.

At the heart of Nora's essay is his conviction that the decline of traditional, largely rural societies has entailed a radical transformation in the form and function of memory and, especially, in its relationship to history and to the individual. In the past, he asserts, memory was largely a collective phenomenon—linked, especially, to the nation-state and to its history. Transmitted from one generation to the next, memory provided a powerful existential link with the past—a link connecting people to their ancestors and, beyond them, to the "undifferentiated time of heroes, origins, and myth."[18] But, continues Nora, the "acceleration" of history, the dislocations of the modern world, have hastened the demise of traditional societies and radically altered the role and nature of memory. Just as the collective (and frequently religious) idea of a unified "nation" has given way to that of "society" (with, one supposes, its connotations of diversity and secularism), so too has collective memory largely been replaced by the more "private" memories (*la mémoire particulière*) of different social groups. Like the two social groups represented in *Le Crabe-tambour* and *Outremer,* such groups share common loyalties by virtue of a shared heritage, or culture, or religion. "The end of history-memory," observes Nora, "has multiplied individual memories (*'les mémoires particulières'*) which demand their own history."[19] More limited in scope than collective memory, these "private" memories are also, asserts Nora, different in kind. And it is here, where Nora elaborates upon these critical differences, that one begins to sense the affinities between *la mémoire particulière* as described by Nora and the social memories represented in *Le Crabe-tambour* and *Outremer*. For what he sees as the defining characteristics of *la mémoire particulière*—that is, its deeply psychological and private nature and the distance it establishes between past and present—are precisely those traits that give these films their special cast.

It is Nora's contention that these traits started to make themselves felt, and to alter the very nature of memory, toward the end of the last century—during the era, significantly, of Proust and Bergson. As the rural world began to collapse, and memory was displaced from the central role it had played in the life of the nation-state, it also underwent a dramatic shift from the "historical to the psychological, from the social to the individual, from transmissive to subjective, from repetition to commemoration. . . . The total psychologization of contemporary memory has led to a conspicuously new economy in the identity of the self, in the mechanisms of memory, and the relationship to the past."[20] This "new economy," continues Nora, manifests itself in several distinctive ways. Whereas collective memory was a spontaneous phenomenon, private social memories must be consciously cultivated and protected by individuals if they are to preserve their very identity. The "obligation to remember" thus assumes "an intense power of internal coercion. The psychologization of memory gives everyone the feeling that salvation ultimately depends upon repaying this impossible debt."[21] Spurred on by the force of this "obligation to remember," groups and individuals seek to preserve every shred or fragment of the past, to establish archives and museums to keep memories alive. But now a paradox arises. For these very efforts to entomb and preserve the past create a distance between past and present. The lived and spontaneous link with the past that characterized traditional societies—where memory was passed down from one generation to the next and the past was relived in the present (as in the rituals of earlier peoples)—has vanished. Discontinuity, not continuity, reigns. "The past," writes Nora, "is seen as radically other; it is the world from which we are forever cut off. And it is by showing the extent of this separation that memory reveals its essence."[22] Hence, not only is modern memory lived as a "duty" (or "obligation") and embodied in the "archive" but—paradoxically—it is "distanced" from the very past it strains to embrace. Historical memory (*mémoire-histoire*) has thus become, declares Nora, archival (*mémoire-archive*), obligatory (*mémoire-devoir*), and distanced (*mémoire-distance*).

"Distance"; "archive"; "obligation." It would be difficult, I think, to find terms better suited to describe the memories represented in *Le Crabe-tambour* and *Outremer*. The protagonists of these works cling to memory with a determination that bespeaks, certainly, a kind of inner "coercion." They desperately need to remember the past because it offers them not only the warmth and life lacking in the present but a sense of their very identity as well. At the same time, however, in re-creating a world forever lost, such memories emphasize not the link between past and present but, instead, the absolute discontinuity. Marked by its "distance" from history, in these films memory seeks less to recapture the past than to re-create it; it wants not to confront the ghosts of history but rather to establish a place where they may flourish forever. If the private and coded memories of these films suggest the difficulties of remembering a "taboo" war, the force of desire embedded in them, the rupture they establish between past and present, as well as the distance that separates them from history, all point to impulses that transcend any particular war, any single experience.

Which leaves "archive"—a word central not only to Nora's essay but, indeed, to the entire project of *Les Lieux de mémoire*. And it may well be a word that goes to the heart of these films. For like an archive, don't these works preserve the memories of distinct social groups? If, as Nora observes, an archive or (more generally) a "place of memory" is designed to "stop time and block the work of memory," don't the images of these films accomplish precisely that by creating a changeless and compelling past? Distinguishing between history (or historical memory) and memory, Nora tells us that "places of memory do not have referents in reality. Or, rather, they are their own referent: pure, self-referential signs. This is not to say that they are without content, physical presence, or history: quite the contrary. But what makes them places of memory is that, precisely, by which they escape from history."[23] It is, I think, precisely this "escape" that is effected in these film. Pulling us into the timeless world of myth and dream, they create "places of memory" for those whose "impossible" memories have been excluded from history—that is, from a shared national past. Muted and silenced, history gives way to a remembered world in which time has stopped and the past has absorbed the present.

NOTES

1. Robert Frank, "Les Troubles de la mémoire française." In *La Guerre d'Algérie et les Français*, ed. Jean-Pierre Rioux (Paris: Fayard, 1990), 603.

2. Ibid., 607.

3. Marlise Simons, "Still Aching for Algeria, Thirty Years after the Rage," *New York Times*, 20 July 1992.

4. Isabelle Lambert, "Vingt ans après." In Rioux, *La Guerre d'Algérie et les Français*, 557.

5. Pierre Nora, *Les Français d'Algérie* (Paris: Julliard, 1961), 71.

6. Alain Ruscio, "French Public Opinion and the War in Indochina: 1945–1954." In *War and Society in Twentieth-Century France*, ed. Michael Scriven and Peter Wagstaff (New York and Oxford: Berg, 1991), 119.

7. Michel de Certeau, "Psychanalyse." In *La Nouvelle Histoire*, ed. Jacques LeGoff, Roger Chartier, and Jacques Revel (Paris: Retz ,1978), 477.

8. Alain-Gérard Slama, "La Guerre d'Algérie en littérature ou la comédie des masques." In Rioux, *La Guerre d'Algérie et les Français*, 597.

9. I am grateful to Jim Hannon for this telling observation.

10. See Claude Liazu, "Le Contingent entre silence et discours ancien combattant." In Rioux, *La Guerre d'Algérie et les Français*, 513.

11. Pierre Schoendoerffer, *L'Adieu au roi* (Paris: Grasset, 1969), 21.

12. François de la Bretèque, "L'Indochine au coeur d'une oeuvre: L'Illiade et l'Odyssée de Pierre Schoendoerffer," *Cahiers de la cinémathèque* no. 57 (Oct. 1992), 76.

13. Some of the autobiographical elements in *Outremer* are discussed by director Brigitte Roüan in an interview with *France Magazine* (Winter 1991), 43.

14. Anne Roche, "La Perte et la parole: Témoignages oraux de Pieds-Noirs." In Rioux, *La Guerre d'Algérie et les Français*, 527.

15. Ibid., 531.

16. Ibid., 532.

17. Jacques Siclier, *Le Cinéma français* (Paris: Ramsay, 1991), 2:205.

18. Pierre Nora, "Entre Mémoire et histoire." In *Les Lieux de mémoire*, ed. Pierre Nora (Paris: Gallimard, 1984), xviii.

19. Ibid., xxix.

20. Ibid., xxx.

21. Ibid., xxx–xxxi.

22. Ibid., xxxi –xxxii.

23. Ibid., xli.

Ismail Xavier

Black God, White Devil:
The Representation of History

Accusations of "formalism" are often addressed to films in which the work of narration, rather than being effaced, is made present and visible. Such films foreground their own narrative operations; the discursive operations of the text come to the surface and, as a result, the usual immersion in a fictive universe is rendered difficult or impossible. While conventional films allow the spectator to witness the unfolding of an imaginary world that gradually takes on the density of the "real," *Black God, White Devil* offers no such satisfaction. An adequate analysis of the film, therefore, must go beyond the represented fiction (the diegesis) if it is to account for the wealth of significations. The film cannot be reduced to the subjective whims of an auteur, nor to simplistic labels such as the "baroque," presumably expressing some hypothetical Brazilian "essence." This reading focuses, therefore, on the complex play of relations between the fictional world posited by the film and the work of narration that constitutes that world. The film's densely metaphorical style virtually pleads for allegorical interpretation even while its internal organization frustrates and defies the interpreter searching for a unifying "key" or implicit "vision of the world." And this resistance to interpretation is by no means incidental; it structures the film and constitutes its meaning.

The "fable" of *Black God, White Devil* is organized around a peasant couple, Manuel and Rosa. The film speaks of their social condition, their hopes and representations, and their links to two forms of contestation: messianic cults and what Hobsbawm calls "social banditry" (*cangaço*). We can identify, and the narrator clearly distinguishes, three stages in their evolution. In the first stage, the cowherd Manuel lives with his wife Rosa and his mother on a backwoods plantation. He takes care of the local landowner's cattle in exchange for a small portion of the herd. Rosa, meanwhile, cultivates the crops necessary to their survival. The first "break" in this stage occurs when Manuel, cheated out of his due allotment of cattle, kills the landowner (Colonel Morais) whose henchmen pursue him and murder his mother. Hounded by the powerful and seeing his mother's death as a sign from heaven, Manuel joins the followers of Sebastião, the miracle-working saint (*beato*), the black God. In the second stage Manuel, ignoring Rosa's objections, places his destiny in Sebastião's hands. To prove his devotion, he performs the necessary purification rites. Sebastião's cult, meanwhile, begins to preoccupy both the local landowners and the Catholic Church. Together, they call on Antônio das Mortes—"killer of *cangaceiros*"— to repress the movement. The break in this stage occurs when Antônio, das Mortes agrees to exterminate the *beatos*. At the same moment that Antônio massacres the *beatos*, Rosa slays Sebastião, ending his domination of Manuel. In the final stage, blind singer Julião leads Manuel and Rosa, the lone survivors of the massacre, to Corisco, survivor of another massacre, that of the *cangaceiro* Lampião and his band. Manuel transfers his faith to Corisco, whom he sees as another divine emissary. He and Corisco discuss the role of violence in the struggle to master destiny. A poetic "challenge" (*desafio*) revolves around the relative grandeur of Sebastião versus Lampião, an argument that comes to absorb all the protagonists: Manuel, Rosa, Corisco, and Dadá, his mate. The final break occurs when Antônio das Mortes fulfills his promised mission of eliminating Corisco. With both the black God (Sebastião) and the white Devil (Corisco) slain, the *sertão* opens up to the headlong flight of Manuel and Rosa.

The three phases outlined here do not occupy equal intervals in the temporal development of the narrative. The first is relatively short, suggesting a kind of prologue. Already in this phase, however, the film develops its central procedure: the synthetic representation of social existence. This procedure distinguishes *Black God, White Devil* from films like *Vidas Secas* whose scenic conventions derive from the Neo-Realist tradition. The "prologue" of *Black God, White Devil* already "condenses" ordinary activities and situations, making them emblematic of a mode of existence. This process occurs, for example, in the scenes beginning with Manuel's return to his farm when he tries to communicate the shock caused by his first encounter with Sebastião and that ends with his traversal of the small-town corral to meet Colonel Morais. At the same time, this scene, by its precise way of preparing the spectator to grasp the dramatic significance of the dialogue with Colonel Morais, fully demonstrates a style of narration announced in the prologue and reasserted throughout the film.

The film's credits—superimposed over shots of the arid *sertão*—announce the narrative style. The crescendo of Villa-Lobos's "Song of the *Sertão*" coincides with images (two close shots of the decomposing skull of an ox) emblematic of the drought afflicting the region. Contrasting in scale with the preceding long shots, these images are still reverberating in our mind when we first see Manuel. These brief shots, then, concentrate a dramatic charge of information concerning the drought and the precarious conditions of *sertão* life. The drama erupts, and dissolves, rapidly. The synthetic style and the information-laden shock-image condensing a broad range of significations already anticipate the film's constant modulation of contrasts and energetic leaps.

This modulation becomes clearer in the sequence of dialogue with Colonel Morais. Rather than evoke tension through a conventional play of shot–reaction shot, Rocha exploits composition within the frame and the slow movement of the actors. The tension is primarily created by the dilatation of the scene over time, especially in the long hiatus preceding the conflict's resolution. Manuel's violence responds to the colonel's violence; it discharges the accumulated tension, finding resonance in the montage as long takes give way to a rapid succession of short duration jump-cut shots. The narration "short-hands" the struggle between Manuel and the colonel, the chase by a cavalcade of *jagunços*, and the exchange of gunshots leading to the death of Manuel's mother. At the same time, coincident with this discontinuous visual montage, silence gives way to a saturated soundtrack that superimposes the sounds generated by the action with the music of Villa-Lobos. This aural saturation is proleptically "triggered" by the stomping hooves of the cavalcade, heard even before the colonel's death. This rush of sounds and events then give way to the prolonged shot in which Manuel, after closing the eyes of his murdered mother, slowly rises while looking back at the house. Complete silence, broken only by the singer's hushed lament, translates the pensive immobility of the character. Within this sequence, then, dilated time, relative immobility, and silence "frame" a more contracted time of multiple actions and crucial decisions in a contrastive scheme typical of the entire film. Rosa's mounting exasperation with Manuel's idolization of Sebastião, for example, transforms itself into a scream that "cues" Antônio's exuberant entrance into the film.

The sequence in which Manuel performs penance by carrying a boulder up an interminable slope brings dilation to the exasperation point. At the altar, Sebastião quietly tells Manuel to bring his wife and child to the sacrifice. The film opposes the interior of the chapel, space of ceremonial silence and equilibrium, to the exterior, space of hysteria and agitation, evoked by the permanently gyrating handheld camera and the strident cries, amplified by the blowing wind, of the *beatos*, in the same dialectic of rarefaction–excess that commands the narrative as a whole. In the chapel, the ritual evolves in a silence marked by fixed glances and stylized gestures. The itinerary of the camera's glance, meanwhile, gradually transforms the central instrument of the rite (the dagger) into the center of the gravity of the composition. The hieratic disposition is broken only with Rosa's slaying of Sebastião and the fall of icons and candles from the altar, the clatter of which "signals" the eruption of gunfire and cries originating from the scene of the massacre. Extremely brief shots render the agitation and fall of the devout under the relentless fire of an Antônio das Mortes multiplied in a montage effect that recalls Eisenstein's *October* and even "quotes" images from the Odessa steppes sequence of *Potemkin*. The massacre completed, the film reverts to slow camera movements over the victims, as shots of a pensive Antônio install a new phase of reflection.

This dialectic of scarcity and saturation marks the temporality of *Black God, White Devil* as a whole. On a semantic level, this narrative organization might be seen as metaphorizing the psychology of the characters, here taken as typical representatives of the peasant class. The exasperating passivity, the verbal awkwardness, the atmosphere of hesitant rumination, alternating with sudden explosions of violence, characteristic of peasant life, thus find resonances within the narrative style. This metaphor could be extended to the environmental conditions of the *sertão* with its rude challenges to human survival, where drought alternates with deluge. More important than these plausible homologies between character and milieu, however, is the conception of temporality, historical in one of its dimensions, inherent in this modulation. The narrative, in its very texture, molds time so as to privilege disequilibrium and transformation. What seems immobility is in fact accumulation of energy, moments of apparent stasis that mask and express hidden forces. The slow passages are not neutral moments of pure extension; they engender the strong moments and the qualitative leaps. The internal movement of the narrative, in its swift changes and irreverent lack of measure, asserts the discontinuous but necessary presence of human and social transformation.

Functionally, this modulation opens "breaches" for the diverse interventions of the narrative voices, creating space for explicit commentary on the imaginary world represented in the film, and making possible the autonomous development of sound and image tracks. What guides the movement of the images, apart from the unifying "stage" of Monte Santo, is the contrasting articulation of Sebastião's messianic discourse versus Rosa's disbelief. We accompany the play of questions and answers on the soundtrack; it matters little that a sentence spoken during one scene is completed in a different scene. The same criteria operate in the *cangaceiro* episodes. The film emphasizes the rhetorical elaboration of Corisco's argument; the changes of tonality are always subordinated to the discourse rather than to the action.

Black God, White Devil is dotted with ritual stagings of its own central ideological debate. The succession of phases weaves an overall movement of reflexion, and everything in the film—the mise-en-scène, the montage, the singer-narrator, the dialogue, the discursive use of image and sound—foregrounds this movement. Although the film speaks of historical struggles, it never reproduces those events through naturalistic spectacle. The film is not preoccupied with the reconstitution of appearances, or with showing events as they actually transpired. Unlike spectacular, expensive, dominant cinema, it does not seek "legitimacy" in the illusory transfer of the "real" life of another epoch to the imaginary universe of the screen. In its refusal of the dominant industrial esthetic, *Black God, White Devil* affirms the basic principles of "the esthetic of hunger." The film attunes its style to its own conditions of production and thus marks its esthetic and ideological opposition to the colonizing discourse of the film industry. Its very texture expresses the underdevelopment that conditions the film, transforming its own technical precariousness into a source of signification. And within this multiple operation, it adds a crucial element: it uses as the mediating figure of the discourse, the central narrative instance of the film, a poet from the oral tradition, a personage belonging to the same universe that constitutes the film's object of reflection.

This mediation, if not the only source of the film's cavalier attitude toward historical data, at least partially explains the fact that the film speaks of Corisco, Lampião, Antônio Conselheiro, and Padre Cícero without seeking any rigorous fidelity to the official history of dates and documents. The "figural" method of the film transforms history into a referential matrix covered with layers of imaginary constructions. The mediation operates as a kind of permeable membrane that allows passage only to selected fragments and transfigured characters. This precipitate of the popular imagination takes the form of exemplary tales whose purpose is not fidelity to fact but rather the transmission of a moral. The historical process is represented as a parable that retains only what the narrator sees as essential, in a style reminiscent, in its criteria of selection and its narrative poetics, of *cordel* literature. In the film, this tradition is embodied by the singer-narrator, although it would be simplistic to see the narration as merely the expression of his values. Popular poetry is but one of the multiple mediations that inform *Black God, White Devil,* for the film exploits all the parameters of the medium. The material of its representation (industrialized sound and image) is not homogenous to the material of oral literature and its conditions of production are not those of the *cordel* tradition. To state the obvious, *Black God, White Devil* is a film, with all that this fact implies. The mediation of *cordel* literature, resulting from an impulse of identification with popular art, interacts with the other processes involved in the film's construction, and this interaction generates the displacements that render the discourse ambiguous. The story of Manuel and Rosa "transfigures" the accumulated experiences of the peasant community. These experiences, schematized and encapsulated within an individual linear trajectory, are mediated by a narrative instance that constantly shifts its position. In this sense, the film constitutes a decentered and problematic reflection on history itself, in which the memory of peasant revolts is both revealed and questioned from diverse points of view.

The singer's narration, the work of the camera, and the musical commentaries of *Black God, White Devil* are not always in accord. In the sequence of Manuel's first encounter with Sebastião, for example, the image of the sky coincides with the singer's first chord on the guitar. While the camera pans vertically to frame Sebastião, the singer begins his song. He presents the characters and anticipates the special character of the encounter. The initial camera movement seems to define a unity of perspectives: sound and image define the saint as blessed by God. As Manuel approaches on horseback, however, the voice of the singer is stilled and the visual composition interprets the encounter in a way that anticipates the subsequent unmasking of Sebastião. Manuel excitedly circles Sebastião and his followers, staring at the saint. The play of shot/countershot, however, underlines Sebastião's indifference to Manuel. The subjective camera shows that the saint does not look at Manuel, who becomes present to him only when Manuel places himself directly before the saint's impassive eyes. This treatment helps characterize Manuel by discrediting in advance his account of the incident in the following scene. At the same time, the image does not support the singer's description of Sebastião ("goodness in his eyes, Jesus Christ in his heart"). There is a total divorce between the actor and the camera, and the distance that characterizes the play of glances only becomes more pronounced as the film progresses. In these encounters, Sebastião remains an enigma as the camera identifies more and more with the perspective of Rosa, the focus of skepticism. Sebastião, for his part, stimulates this skepticism by his vain air of aristocratic indifference and by a certain sadistic touch in his ministering of the ceremonies. His behavior culminates in an inglorious, almost cowardly, death, the ordinary humanness of which contrasts with his former haughtiness and definitely unmasks him in our eyes. Only minutes before Rosa's attack, after all, had not this same man resolutely murdered a child?

This process of demystification, however, hardly exhausts the film's account of the social phenomenon of messianism. Manuel's "surrender" to Sebastião is constructed so as to celebrate a religious force capable of uniting the peasant masses. The camera anticipates Manuel and Rosa climbing the mountain up to Sebastião's domain, thus providing a rare moment of apotheosis. Processions of banners and symbols outlined against the sky and agitated by the wind find an echo in the symphonic music of Villa-Lobos. The solemn grandiosity of the scene comes, interestingly, not from the *cordel*-singer's voice but rather from the music of a non-regional "universal" composer. Even here, however, the figure of Sebastião is treated with great subtlety, since the camera emphasizes the pomp and circumstance surrounding him, ignoring his "good eyes" in order to emphasize the collective force of religious ecstasy. The following sequence points up the hysterically repressive side of this same religion by showing ritual humiliations and flagellations. The violent confrontation between the *beatos* and the larger society is rendered in a kind of strident shorthand, and the critique of messianism implicit in this passage is subsequently confirmed by the extended sequences on Monte Santo, locus of retreat and contemplative longing. Metaphorically exploring the topography of the mountain, the narration crystallizes the idea of proximity to heaven and imminent ascension, of retreat to a kind of antechamber to Paradise (the island that constitutes Sebastião's fundamental promise). In this privileged space, detached from the earth and its sordid involvements, the possibility of direct intervention in the world ceases to be a goal. Messianic rebellion takes the peasants out of the process of production and distances them from the official church. It frees them from the domination of landlord and boss, but in their place proposes only the passivity of prayer and the initiatory rituals that will define them as elect in the moment of cataclysm.

After the massacre, Manuel continues to be faithful to Sebastião. The saint's demystification takes place within the work of narration, without the knowledge of the characters. With the appearance of Corisco, however, the mise-en-scène changes significantly. An element from within the diegesis now becomes the focus of critical reflection. As master of ceremonies, Corisco's reflection is directly addressed both to us as spectators and to Manuel within the fiction. From this point on, the extended passages of rarefied action involve the characters' discussion of their own experience, a discussion in which Corisco collaborates. A new kind of dialogue appears with the insertion of the singer himself, or of his double, within the scene. At the same time, image and sound, by repeating similar elements within apparently opposite conditions, suggest that Sebastião and Corisco are merely two sides of the same metaphysic; in the symmetry of their inversions lies a deeper unity.

The same voice (Othon Bastos) delivers the words of both Sebastião and Corisco. And the same Villa-Lobos music consecrates Sebastião's triumph on Monte Santo and Manuel's initiation—by castrating the *fazendeiro*—into *cangaço* violence. The same metaphor marks the horizon of their practice: "The *sertão* will become sea, and the sea *sertão*." Both speak in the name of Good and Evil. The unity that underlies their contradictions is expressed in symmetrical presentations; Corisco too is announced as a kind of advent ("as fate would have it") in versification similar to that of the beginning of the film.

At the same time, there are significant inversions; the vertical pan from sky to earth associated with Sebastião becomes a creeping horizontal pan over the *sertão* with Corisco. This inversion opposes Corisco's rootedness in the "lower" world of "that devil Lampião" to the "elevated" world of the saint. The *beatos'* straight-lined progression toward Monte Santo, furthermore, is replaced by the back and forth movements of Corisco's violent rituals. In long shot, he promises vengeance, as his circular movements underline the clearly limited space of his action on the close-cropped *sertão*. The perspectival view of his stage, staked out by his immobile henchmen, project on his figure the shadow of a closing and an absence of horizons that will only be reaffirmed and rendered explicit as the film progresses.

In its theatricality, the *cangaceiro* phase of the film takes on the tone of a ritual of the living dead, of survivors without hope or prospect. While Manuel lives the experience as an optimistic present, Corisco stages the events in a very different spirit, as the accomplice of the very forces that condemn him. More than once it is he who defines this condition of living death. In the metaphor of the two heads (one killing, the other thinking) he sees himself as a repetition of Virgulino, as the vestige of an historically condemned practice that he carries to its foredoomed conclusion. Corisco himself represents the limitations of social banditry on his backlands stage. His most daring strokes seem like ritual expositions of a doctrinaire solution, without practical consequence but relived symbolically as a hymn of praise to violence as a form of justice. This violence involves no program beyond "turning things upside down," and its loyalties and vengeance are based only on circumstance and personal connection. They become legitimate only when enlisted in the service of "Good" and "Evil." Corisco sees himself as the agent of Good and the figure of the just avenger (he is Saint Jorge, the people's saint, versus the dragon of wealth) and as the agent of Evil in the figure of the condemned man, who, when confronted with the greater indignity of death by starvation, chooses violence. He takes on his destructive task in the name of justice, knowing that it involves, by the ironic economics of destiny, his own condemnation. His discourse is caught in self-defeating circularity; it creates a short circuit of means and ends, an alternation of revolt and accommodation with the enemy. The exuberant rhetoric with which Corisco demystifies Sebastião (Manuel's myth) implies the demystification of Virgulino (his own myth).

In its simultaneous praise and demystification of both Sebastião and Corisco, the narration discredits messianism and *cangaço* as practices likely to generate a more just human order. The underside of the metaphysic of Good and Evil is exposed in the equivocal expression of its rebellion. The film clearly favors the willed defeat and exemplary revolt of the White Devil to the radical alienation of the Black God, whence the similarity between Corisco's discourse and that of Antônio das Mortes, figure of infallible efficacy. Like Corisco, Antônio defends his own violence as a kind of euthanasia—the people must not die of hunger. He defines himself, furthermore, as the condemned agent of destiny within the same logic of "kill and be killed" proposed by Corisco. But while Corisco exposes his contradictions in a frenetic back-and-forth movement, Antônio is enigmatic and laconic, mysterious in his physical presence and contradictory in his words. His hesitation in accepting the task proposed by the priest and the colonel implies that he understands the conversation on some other level ("it is dangerous to meddle with the things of God"). When he accepts with the words "Sebastião is finished," his tone of voice, suggesting both power and resignation, impresses solemnity on the moment. And in the conversation with blind Julião he posits once and for all the larger meaning of his acts, a meaning that his conscience intuits but that he never really explains.

Our task now is to reflect on this "larger order" affirmed by the symbolic recapitulation of the peasant revolts and their religious ideology, along with its narrative elaboration. By foreseeing the outcome of the encounter between Manuel and Sebastião, the singer suggests the idea of Destiny. The beato enters Manuel's life without Manuel having done anything to provoke the encounter. At the same time, Manuel's revolt is perfectly explicable in more earthly terms—the material conditions of his life, the social relations of his work, his visionary tendencies, Rosa's despair. To explain Manuel's violence, one need only assume a minimal notion of right and wrong and an elementary aspiration to justice. Angered by an obvious fraud and frustrated in a very precise hope (the possession of land), Manuel fails to understand the structural nature of his oppression, and therefore invokes metaphysical entities to explain his adversity and justify his revolt. Sebastião's presence in this moment of revolt encourages Manuel to adopt the saint's interpretive system. Manuel attributes the tragedy to a divine plan that requires his devotion to the saint, an option that placates his guilty conscience and protects him from police pursuit.

The singer's authority remains ambiguous, not only because he says nothing about the destiny supposedly manifest in these events, but also because image and sound reveal situations that hardly require supernatural stratagems to explain them. The providential presence of Sebastião remains the focus of this ambiguity; he offers Manuel, at precisely the right moment, the option for which his consciousness is prepared. It is the narrator, admittedly, who brings Sebastião to Manuel, but Manuel must also play his part for destiny to be fulfilled.

It this coincidence, this complexity, which triggers movement and concretizes the first moment of rupture in the film.

In the second major rupture, the intervention of Antônio, also a stranger to the devout world of Monte Santo, coincides with Rosa's act of violence. Her act too is explicable in terms of her own situation. She does not kill the saint to serve some transcendent design, but rather in her own name. Antônio's intervention, already ambiguous in itself, becomes doubly ambiguous by this precise coincidence with Rosa's violence. In the two moments of rupture, external forces and human actions converge to create a turnabout that projects the characters into a new phase of life. Transformation arises from this correspondence, which marks a double determination: the narrative creates a situation in which the characters, unconscious of the stratagems mounted against them, and moved by both personal and extra-personal motives, act at the right time, participating actively in a process controlled by these same stratagems. Everything moves toward a goal that remains unthinkable for Manuel and Rosa but that is palpably clear to the spectator.

In reality, events do not evolve according to Manuel's expectations. The narration works, in fact, to discredit his interpretation, suggesting instead the existence of a pre-ordained end. After the Monte Santo massacre, the projection of the singer (blind Julião) into the fiction, visibly conducting Manuel and Rosa, makes palpable the presence of the agents of the grand plan behind the whole arrangement. In his first dialogue with Julião at the crossroads, Antônio explains that he allowed Manuel and Rosa to survive so they could "tell their story." He thus reinforces the notion that he collaborates with the larger order that controls individual destinies. He makes the protagonists the spokesmen of his own legend, bastions of the oral tradition that organizes the film. He hints, then, at the very level at which the narration is engendered, for it is in the nature of the narratives to organize themselves within a certain teleology. *Black God, White Devil* "confesses" this condition and comments on it, even as it fulfills it.

The *cangaceiro* phase inaugurates a new system. Corisco arrives via the voice of the singer, and the couple comes to Corisco via blind Julião. Manuel, after the encounter, has his reasons for carrying out the predetermined: he joins the *cangaço* in order to avenge Sebastião. Prepared for violence, he sets out on a new trajectory of equivocations, in which his actions follow one design (that of a dimly glimpsed teleology) while his consciousness imagines another (based on the very metaphysic being discredited). Without knowing it, Manuel completes a circle; he descends from his messianic flight only to return to the down to earth practicality of Rosa. At this point, however, a subtle dislocation distances Manuel and Rosa from the central events of the fable. Although they remain present to the end of the film, their survival is determined by Antônio ("I didn't kill once, and I won't kill again"). In the final sequence, the most relevant fact within the larger order is the duel between Corisco and Antônio; the song makes no reference to Manuel and Rosa. For the couple, survival marks a new opening and the reassertion of immediate natural bonds. Their conscious future consists in liberation from both Sebastião and Corisco in favor of the life-oriented immediacy of Rosa.

If Manuel initially shows capacity for revolt, the Manuel of the end shows only minimal initiative. Corisco gains strength, paradoxically only in so far as he participates in the ritual representation of his own inevitable defeat. Antônio das Mortes, despite his infallibility, relinquishes all personal ambition, seeing himself as merely the doomed agent of a predestined scheme. None of the characters in the film consciously make their own history and the film advances no project for taking control of destiny. The narration moves in the opposite direction, from initial ambiguity toward explicit definition of a teleology. Initially, this teleology is merely suggested by the singer and by the mise-en-scène, while the characters retain some initiative. With the dialogue between blind Julião and Antônio, however, this teleological scheme, implicit in Corisco's style of representation, becomes explicit. Antônio, by his infallible action, consummates the scheme; his revelatory word evokes the final term of the overall movement: "the great war, without the blindness of God and the Devil." His own behavior, furthermore, favors this progression from implicit to explicit teleology. His slaying of the *beatos* is explicable, on one level, by his earthly code of money, but his enigmatic attitude hints at more transcendent considerations. His duel with Corisco is not commercially motivated—killing *cangaceiros* is simply his destiny. The film refers only to his commitment to the future whose teleology leads to a great war whose preparation is the only motive proposed for Antônio's action. The overall development of the film, and Antônio's specific course, suggests that progress is not determined by human beings. In this sense, the film moves toward a determinism whose focus is outside of the characters whose consciousness is completely alienated, at worst, and capable, at best, only of vague intuitions of a more comprehensive order. And it is precisely Antônio who most clearly professes this radical agnosticism.

There are, then, two major crisscrossing movements in the film: the questioning of a dualistic metaphysic in the name of the liberation of human beings as the subjects of history is superimposed on the gradual affirmation of a "larger order" that commands human destiny. This coexistence does not develop along parallel paths, but rather through a fundamental interdependence: the very person who furthers liberation and humanistic values is also the fated agent of a dim larger order. Antônio, incarnating this short circuit of alienation–lucidity, constitutes the nucleus of both movements, in which History advances along the correct path thanks to ambiguous and equivocal figures. Antônio's repressive violence is not an unfortunate incident but a basic necessity, not a despite but a through by which History–Destiny weaves itself. Messianism and *cangaço* are moments through which human consciousness moves toward lucid acknowledgment of human beings themselves as the source, the means, and the end of transforming praxis. This ascension to consciousness does not take place, however, within the perspective of the protagonists. There is a hiatus between their experience and the final term, the revoluntionary telos around which the narrative organizes its lesson. Manuel need not complete this trajectory because he does not liberate himself alone; he is not the center of his own trajectory. The horizon of History is not delineated by Manuel or even by Rosa; the "larger order" requires that the certainty of the end be affirmed through incompletion.

The dominant voice in the fable of *Black God, White Devil* is that of the narrator. He composes the story as a propedeutic recapitulation of a historical process (peasant revolts) that the narrator understands as propedeutic, as incorporating the movement toward the "great war," an essential subterranean movement that the recapitulation, by its symbols, tries to make clear and palpable. This "making palpable" is realized by the transfiguration of the Marxist idea of "historical necessity" into the idea of "Destiny"—a version of "necessity" familiar to popular oral traditions and to *cordel* literature. The carrying out of the revolutionary telos is a certainty, but its mechanisms remain ambiguous. The crucial point is that, under the form of Destiny, the film paradoxically affirms the apparently opposite principle of human self-determination.

This paradox is clearly inscribed in the final sequence. Antônio arrives at the duel, observing Corisco without being seen. He easily aims his rifle, but before shooting, he hesitates. It is only with the beginning of the singer's ballad that Antônio resumes his arbitrarily frozen gesture. His raising of the rifle is synchronized with the words "surrender, Corisco!" in the song. From this point on, the montage schematizes the diegetic action in such a way as to make it illustrative—by its rhythm and tonality, and by its chivalric style—of the song. *Cordel* literature dominates the representation. The singer draws the moral of his own story: "this world is ill-divided—it belongs to Man, and not to God or the Devil." He affirms a conception of change that places history in the hands of human beings themselves, thus confirming Antônio's allusions to the "Great War" and completing the demystification of the metaphysical based on both Black God and White Devil. The hope of transformation, or rather its certainty, is reasserted by the refrain: "the *sertão* will become sea, and the sea *sertão*." Manuel and Rosa's headlong *corrida* toward the sea—the first straight-lined vector within a trajectory marked by a constant circling of glances, movements, and even thoughts—reinforces the projection toward a dimly glimpsed future. The narrative discourse, however, does not end with their *corrida*. It offers one last reversal by celebrating revolutionary certainty in such a way as to challenge the secular humanism implicit in the singer's final words. By an imagistic leap, the narration visually realizes the metaphor of transformation used by both Sebastião and Corisco: the surf invades the screen; the *sertão* becomes the sea. The ritual sounds and voices of the Villa-Lobos music elaborates the transformation. The waves break again and again, connoting omnipresence, domination. The image strengthens and renders actual the telos that guides the entire film, lending to Manuel's *corrida* on the level of immediate appearance nothing more than a blind flight across the *sertão*—a note of hope.

The discontinuity between this narrative leap and Manuel's trajectory situates the certainty of transformation on the level of the Universal ("Man") and reaffirms the hiatus between his lived experience and his meaning as a figure within the frame of the stratagems of destiny. His trajectory constitutes an oblique, transfigured representation of the certainty, just as Antônio's "repression," finally, both liberates and represents this same certainty. Everything in *Black God, White Devil* denies the possibility of thinking in terms of lost trails, irrecoverable detours, or insurmountable gaps. The redemptive power of its teleology is radical. The story evolves as the fulfillment of Destiny, at the same time that it grants humanity the condition of subject. Everything in the story only reaffirms this problematic condition, as it is expressed in the contradictory movement of the film.

The winds of History are ubiquitous. Its modulations are palpable in moments of violence, and there is no doubt about its final direction. But who or what impels it? *Black God, White Devil* gives no univocal response to this question, and it would be obtuse to require one, for what is fundamental in the film is the very heterogeneity of its representations. The interaction of voices renders ambiguous the principle of its revolutionary lemon, thus creating an unresolved tension, deriving from the criss-crossing movements in which "Man" and "Destiny" struggle for primacy. There is no definitive answer concerning the knowledge that sustains this certainty because the mediations in the film mark the debate with different systems of interpretation of the human experience within history.

Crystallizing an esthetic and ideological project that affirms popular forms of representation (as a focus of cultural resistance, and a logos where national identity is engendered) and striving for social transformation, on the basis of a dialectical vision of history, the film neither idealizes nor downgrades popular culture. Rather than dismiss popular forms in the name of ideological correctness, Rocha uses them even as he questions the traditional character of their representation. Cinema Novo confronted this task—of reelaborating popular traditions as the springboard for a transformation-oriented critique of social reality—in diverse ways. *Black God, White Devil* is a key film because it incorporates within its very structure the contradictions of this project. It avoids any romantic endorsement of the "popular" as the source of all wisdom, even as it discredits the enthnocentric reductionism that sees in popular culture nothing more than meaningless superstition and backward irrationality, superseded by bourgeois progress and rationalism. Adopting the didactic formula, *Black God, White Devil* decenters the focus of its lesson and, contrary to the "edifying" and dogmatic discourse of the "models for action" school, challenges us with an aggressive fistful of interrogations. Rather than offer, in a single diapason, an insipidly schematic lesson about class struggle, it encourages reflection on the peasantry and its forms of consciousness, and more important, on the very movement of History itself.

Mbye Cham

Official History, Popular Memory: Reconfiguration of the African Past in the Films of Ousmane Sembène

I would like to begin my presentation by quoting the words of a griot. His name is Diali Mamadou Kouyaté; he performed the Sundiata epic, which has been transcribed by Djibril Tamsir Niane. The griot starts his performance with these words:

> I am a griot. . . . we are the vessels of speech, we are the repositories which harbor secrets many centuries old. The art of eloquence has no secrets for us; without us, the names of kings would vanish into oblivion, we are the memory of mankind. . . . History has no mystery for us . . . for it is we who keep the keys to the twelve doors of Mali. . . . I teach kings the history of their ancestors so that the lives of the ancients might serve them as an example. For the world is old, but the future springs from the past. [1]

The last two decades in Africa have yielded a significant crop of films devoted primarily to a critical engagement with the African past as a way of coming to terms with the many crises and challenges confronting contemporary African societies. This current preoccupation with history, and its implications for the present, underlies a number of films which have been produced during these past two decades. Ousmane Sembène, of course, led the way with *Emitaï, Ceddo,* and more recently, *Camp de Thiaroye.* This is also a strain that has pretty much defined many of the films of Med Hondo of Mauritania, more specifically, a film he produced in 1978 entitled *West Indies,* which is an adaptation of a play with the same title by a Martinican playwright, Daniel Boukman, and Hondo's latest film, entitled *Sarraounia,* which came out in 1986. Also in this category is a recent film produced by a young filmmaker from Guinea-Bissau, whose name is

From *Ousmane Sembène: Dialogues with Critics and Writers,* ed. Samba Gadjigo, Ralph Faulkingham, Thomas Cassirer and Reinhard Sander. Copyright © 1993 by Five Colleges, Inc. Reprinted with permission of The Five College African Studies Council.

Flora Gomes. The title of the film is *Mortu Nega,* and it is a reconstruction of the recent history of Guinea-Bissau during and after the armed liberation struggle against Portuguese colonialism. There is also a young Malagasy filmmaker, Raymond Rajaonarivelo, who in 1988 came out with another film that reconstructs an event that took place in the context of the Second World War in the Malagasy Republic, and the title of that film is *Tabataba.* We also have two recent films from Ghana. One is by a young Ghanaian filmmaker who is currently residing in London. His name is John Akomfrah; his 1988 film entitled *Testament* looks at the Nkrumah era in Ghana. The other one, *Heritage Africa,* also a 1988 film, is by Kwaw Ansah.

So dominant is this current in contemporary African filmmaking that one is reminded of a statement made by Jorge Fraga, a Cuban filmmaker and member of the Cuban Film Institute: "Cuban filmmakers are always viewing things from a historical perspective because 'we can't help it.'"[2] Judging from the recently finished films, as well as a number of projects that are currently in production, it seems that African filmmakers too cannot help but look at things from a historical perspective. The necessity of looking at the present in the past is made urgent by the fact that the histories of former colonies have been characterized by arbitrary fictions, fictions such as the White Man's Burden, Manifest Destiny, Hegel's Africa beyond the pale of history, repeated by Hugh Trevor-Roper's notion of history in Africa as only the history of Europeans in Africa, and so on and so forth. And because of these fictions, African filmmakers and other artists have taken on the task of purging their histories of these imposed remembrances. In turning to the pre-colonial and colonial past, many contemporary African filmmakers repeat, with a significant difference of course, the gestures of an earlier generation of African artists, who in their various ways responded to prevailing Western fictions and orthodoxies about Africa and Africans by effecting a return to the sources in the form of counter-accounts and reconstructions of Africa before the arrival of Europeans.

Early in this century—in the twenties, thirties, and forties—some African poets and novelists developed Négritude and other cognate rallying cries and ideologies as a framework for delving into the African past in order to intervene in and alter dominant Eurocentric versions of Africa and Africans by introducing different African versions of Africa and Africans. I don't wish to explore here how authentic these Négritude versions of Africa and Africans were, but the point I am interested in is the act of looking back as a means of coming to terms with current prevailing beliefs and orientations and challenges in Africa. While the contemporary African filmmaker repeats the historical moves of his Négritude predecessor, he does so with a different set of ideologies and orientations, a different conception of history and tradition, and under a different set of social, political, and cultural circumstances. Given these differences, what emerges in recent African film is a radical revision and representation of the African past in ways which not only purge it of imposed European and other foreign remembrances, but which also foreground the relevance of the new reconstructed histories to the present challenges of postcolonial African societies.

It is not an exaggeration to claim that the principal force behind this orientation in African film is Ousmane Sembène, whose films, especially *Emitaï*, *Ceddo*, and more recently, *Camp de Thiaroye*, constitute some of the most compelling and indeed radical filmic revisions and reinterpretations of history in Africa. Particularly noteworthy in these new film versions of history are:

a) The recovery and deployment of popular memory to recompose past events.
b) The radical reconstruction of Euro-Christian as well as Arab-Islamic histories and how these are implicated in African history.
c) The conflation of Euro-Christianity and Arab-Islam as two sides of the same colonial coin.
d) The national as well as the pan-African nature and dimension of these histories.
e) The recovery and reconstitution of African women's histories—from a male point of view, of course.

I had wanted to consider these and related issues as well as their modes of representation in *Ceddo*, *Emitaï*, and *Camp de Thiaroye*, but because of the limitation of time, I am going to focus only on *Ceddo*. I would like to echo here the words of Diali Mamadou Kouyaté, which I have quoted at the beginning, with the words of another noted African elder and intellectual from Mali, whose name is Amadou Hampathé Bâ. Amadou Hampathé Bâ has stated the following:

> The fact that it has no system of writing does not in itself deprive Africa of a past or of a body of knowledge. . . . Of course, this body of inherited knowledge that is transmitted from the mouth of one generation to the ear of the next may either grow or wither away. . . . The African body of knowledge is vast and varied, and it touches on all aspects of life. The "knowledge expert" is never a "specialist" but a generalist. . . . The African body of knowledge is thus a *comprehensive* and living knowledge, and that is why the old men who are its last trustees can be compared to vast libraries where multifarious bookshelves are linked to each other by invisible connections which are the essence of the "science of the invisible."[3]

It was in reference to the urgency of recovering and deploying the knowledge and wisdom of this last generation of great depositories, this living memory of Africa, that Hampathé Bâ made his now canonical statement that in Africa an old person who dies is a library that burns. The filmic reconstruction of history, in the work of Ousmane Sembène, rests solidly on this heritage of oral tradition and memory. From this base, with the true griot as a model, Sembène enters into a battle for history and around history. Official versions of the past, Western as well as Arabic, are contested, revised, and/or rejected, and new, more authentic histories are put in their place.

Sembène's films may partly be seen as undertaking what Teshome Gabriel has labeled "a rescue mission," to the extent to which their recourse to popular memory aims to recover, privilege and articulate the historical significance and the contemporary, as well as future, implications of what official histories insist on erasing. My conception of the notions of popular memory and official history owes a great deal to Teshome Gabriel's elaboration of these concepts:

Official history tends to arrest the future by means of the past. Historians privilege the written word of the text—it serves as their rule of law. It claims a "center" which continuously marginalizes others. In this way its ideology inhibits people from constructing their own history or histories.

Popular memory, on the other hand, considers the past as a political issue. It orders the past not only as a reference point but also as a theme of struggle. For popular memory, there are no longer any "centers" or "margins," since the very designations imply that something has been conveniently left out.[4]

Then, echoing a widely articulated Third World view, Teshome Gabriel has argued that

Popular memory, then, is neither a retreat to some great tradition nor a flight to some imagined "ivory tower," neither a self-indulgent escapism, nor a desire for the actual "experience" or "content" of the past for its own sake. Rather, it is a "look back to the future," necessarily dissident and partisan, wedded to constant change.[5]

Ceddo, Emitaï, and *Camp de Thiaroye,* each in its own way, embody the spirit of popular memory. *Ceddo* is a film that re-creates the structures of power and power relations in the nineteenth-century Wolof state of Joloff, on the eve of its demise at the hands of Islam, in competition at times with Christianity and its ally, French commercial and secular power. The privileged point of view in this film is clearly the *ceddo*'s, and it inscribes itself in popular memory. Foregrounding this hitherto repressed point of view results in the explosion by Sembène of a solidly entrenched official version of history of Islam in Senegal. According to this version, Islam is Senegalese. In other versions that concede its non-Senegalese origins, it is posited that Islam's mode of entry into Senegal was all peaceful. Another aspect of this official version states that Islam was voluntarily espoused by the Senegalese, who were won over by exponents of redemption and salvation. In *Ceddo,* therefore, the term "official" takes on a new meaning, beyond its usual designation of that which is French or French-derived, which is the dominant conception of what is official in Senegal and also in many other African countries. It is no longer a monopoly of the French.

In the same breath, Sembène also enlarges the field of foreign colonial actors in Senegal beyond the French, as is the case in *Emitaï* and *Camp de Thiaroye,* to expose the other equally significant and deadly force which has succeeded in passing itself off as Senegalese, namely Islam. Unlike a good number of his fellow Senegalese, who tend to subscribe to Islam's claim to indigenous antiquity in Senegal, Sembène presents Islam in *Ceddo* as one of the forces—the other being Euro-Christianity, of course—responsible for what Wole Soyinka refers to as "Africa's enforced cultural and political exocentricity."[6] Customs, beliefs, values, and practices, hitherto presented and taken as Senegalese or African, are examined and shown to be of Arab-Islamic origin by Sembène in *Ceddo.* Moreover, the process by which these Arab-Islamic customs, beliefs, values, and practices came to take root in Senegal is presented as insidious and violent, not unlike the ways in which Euro-Christian slavery, colonialism, and imperialism bulldozed their way into Senegal. Thus, Sembène counteracts the official Senegalese-

Islamic version of the West as the sole source of Africa's cultural contamination and degradation with a new version which splits Islam's roots away from Senegalese soil, casts Islam as heavily infused with Arab culture, and conflates it with Euro-Christianity. *Ceddo* is therefore the most irreverent rewriting of Islam in Senegal by a Senegalese artist. It reconstructs its history in Senegal in ways that radically destabilize and undo the dominant Islamic myth espoused by the Muslim elite and their followers, who happen to be the majority of the Senegalese.

In *Ceddo*, the image of Islam that is portrayed is not a beautiful one at all. The Muslims are presented as scheming, violent fanatics with little regard for the principles of self-determination and religious and cultural freedom. Their belief in the supremacy of Islam is translated into a series of highly studied moves, which systematically eliminate the rival Christian mission, the traditional secular power structure, and a significant number of the *ceddo* and their belief systems. This project culminates in the establishment of a regime of rule based on principles of Islam, with the imam as the head. The designs of the imam on the society are progressively made clear in the course of the narrative in *Ceddo*. His initial litany of verbal attacks on the persistence of pagan practices among the *ceddo* is indirectly pointed at the Wolof secular authority, the King, who is now a convert, yet who tolerates the presence of such infidels, as he calls them, in his society. These attacks become more pointed as the militancy of the Muslims intensifies and as the imam's vow to undertake a *jihad* against all non-Muslims in the society looms closer to execution. To the King's question as to why the imam never addresses him by the title "King," the imam replies that for him there is only one king, and that king is Allah. To the *ceddo*'s complaint about the growing harassment from the Muslims, and to their question as to whether religion is worth a man's life, the imam, usurping the prerogative and power of the King, shouts blasphemy and renews his threats against them. This attitude defines the relationship of the imam to the society around him, and it sets the stage for embarking on a jihad to bring about the rule of Allah. The Muslims burn down the Christian mission and kill the white missionary and the trader, from whom they had obtained their weapons. Next, the news is announced that the King has died from a snake bite; as a consequence the *ceddo* we subdued and forcibly converted to Islam. Into the power vacuum created by the death of the Wolof king steps the imam. Thus, Sembène reconstructs the origin of, and the reasons for, the absence of traditional secular power figures and structures, and the hegemonic status and power of Muslim marabouts and brotherhoods in Senegal today.

In *Ceddo*, the imam's ascension to power marks the beginning of what Sembène conveys in the film as one of the most radical and intolerant projects of cultural transformation in Senegalese history. The imam institutes as law most of the spiritual and social conduct hitherto adhered to by only a tiny minority. Among the practices of the *ceddo* that are prohibited under the new Muslim theocracy are the consumption of alcohol, the reproduction of human forms in art, and former modes of worship. The Islamic regime of five daily prayers, the shahada, and koranic education become mandatory. The griot of the erstwhile royal court, together with his cronies, is unceremoniously dismissed and replaced by the koran-toting disciples of the imam. The high point of this process of social and cultural change comes in the mass conversion sequence of the film, where the *ceddo* are subdued and submitted to a ritual of purification as a prerequisite for assuming new Muslim identities. They have their heads shaved clean and their *ceddo* names are replaced by new Arab or Arab-derived names, such as Hadidiatou, Fatoumata, Mamadou, Souleymane, Babacar, and Ousmane. Historical reconstruction in *Ceddo*, then, privileges a non-Muslim perspective, one that is repressed in official accounts of Islam in Senegal. It explores a deeply ingrained myth in Senegalese society. Sembène's own attitude towards this myth is most graphically defined in the final sequence when Dior Yacine, the princess, heir to the throne, kills the imam with a shotgun, in full view of his disciples and the new converts. Thus Sembène rewrites and represents, in a radically different view, a much neglected aspect of the historical role of women in African history. In *Ceddo*, Princess Dior is posited as a figure of resistance and liberation. The amount of screen time that she occupies in the film is rather limited, and we only hear her voice in relatively few sequences. However, in spite of these physical absences, Princess Dior is the overwhelming presence in the film. The narrative turns and moves around her captivity. And it is she who emerges from her position of royalty—captured royalty nevertheless—to rekindle and put in action the *ceddo* spirit of resistance and refusal of domination. This is captured symbolically in the final sequence of the film which ends—and I put "ends" in quotes here, because the film never actually ends—in a halfshot freeze-frame, with her occupying the larger portion of the screen.

Historical reconstruction, then, in *Ceddo*, aims to explore deeply ingrained myths in Senegalese society. *Ceddo* may be unique in Senegalese artistic perceptions of Islam and the history of Islam, in terms of its tone, its tenor, and its uncompromising view of the religion. But it is indicative of a growing current of thought, both in African literature and in African film. One is reminded of the equally caustic savaging of Islam in Yambo Ouologuem's *Le devoir de violence*, Ayi Kwei Armah's *Two Thousand Seasons*, and elsewhere in Chancellor Williams's *The Destruction of Black Civilization*.

NOTES

1. T. Niane, *Sundiata: An Epic of Old Mali*, trans. G. D. Pickett (London: Longman, 1965), 1.

2. Quoted in Luis H. Francia, "The Other Cinema," *Village Voice*, 17 May 1983, 63.

3. Amadou Hampathé Bâ, *Aspects de la civilisation africaine* (Paris: Présence Africaine, 1972), 22, 26.

4. Teshome Gabriel, "Third Cinema as Guardian of Popular Memory: Towards a Third Aesthetics." In *Questions of Third Cinema*, ed. Jim Pines and Paul Willemen (London: British Film Institute, 1989), 53–54.

5. Ibid., 54.

6. Wole Soyinka, *Myth, Literature and the African World* (Cambridge: Cambridge University Press, 1976), 99.

History and Television

Mary Ann Doane

Information, Crisis, Catastrophe

The major category of television is time. Time is television's basis, its principle of structuration, as well as its persistent reference. The insistence of the temporal attribute may indeed be a characteristic of all systems of imaging enabled by mechanical or electronic reproduction. For Roland Barthes, the *noeme* of photography is the tense it inevitably signifies—the *"That-has-been"* which ensures both the reality and the "pastness" of the object photographed.[1] The principal gesture of photography would be that of embalming (hence Barthes's reference to André Bazin). In fixing or immobilizing its object, transforming the subject of its portraiture into dead matter, photography is always haunted by death and historicity. The temporal dimension of television, on the other hand, would seem to be that of an insistent "present-ness"—a *"This-is-going-on"* rather than a *"That-has-been,"* a celebration of the instantaneous. In its own way, however, television maintains an intimate relation with the ideas of death and referentiality Barthes finds so inescapable in his analysis of the photograph. Yet, television deals not with the weight of the dead past but with the potential trauma and explosiveness of the present. And the ultimate drama of the instantaneous—catastrophe—constitutes the very limit of its discourse.

According to Ernst Bloch, "Time *is* only because something happens, and where something happens, there time is."[2] Television fills time by ensuring that something happens—it organizes itself around the event. There is often a certain slippage between the notion that television covers important events in order to validate itself as a medium and the idea that because an event is covered by television—because it is, in effect, deemed televisual—it is important. This is the significance of the media event, where the referent becomes indissociable from the medium. The penetration of everyday life by the media is a widely recognized phenomenon. But it is perhaps less widely understood that television's conceptualization of the event is heavily dependent upon a particular organization (or penetration) or temporality which produces three different modes of apprehending the event—information, crisis, and catastrophe. Information would specify the steady stream of daily "newsworthy" events characterized by their regularity if not predictability. Although news programs would constitute

From *Logics of Television: Essays in Cultural Criticism*, edited by Patricia Mellencamp. Copyright © 1990. Reprinted by permission of Indiana University Press.

its most common source, it is also dispersed among a number of other types of programs. Its occasion may be politics, science, or "human interest." Information is noteworthy but is not shocking or gripping—its events are only mildly eventful, although they may be dramatized. The content of information is ever-changing, but information, as genre, is always *there*, a constant and steady presence, keeping you *in touch*. It is, above all, that which fills time on television—using it up. Here time is flow: steady and continuous.

The crisis, on the other hand, involves a condensation of temporality. It names an event of some duration which is startling and momentous precisely because it demands resolution within a limited period of time. Etymologically, crisis stems from the Greek *krisis*, or decision, and hence always seems to suggest the necessity of human agency. For that reason, crises are most frequently political—a hijacking, an assassination, the takeover of an embassy, a political coup, or the taking of hostages. There is a sense in which information and catastrophe are both subject-less, simply there, they *happen*—while crisis can be attributed to a subject, however generalized (a terrorist group, a class, a political party, etc.). The crisis compresses time and makes its limitations acutely felt. Finally, the catastrophe would from this perspective be the most critical of crises for its timing is that of the instantaneous, the moment, the punctual. It has no extended duration (except, perhaps, that of its televisual coverage) but, instead, happens "all at once."[3]

Ultimately, the categories of information, crisis, and catastrophe are only tenuously separable in practice. There are certainly phenomena which seem to annihilate the distinctions between them—a flood, for instance, which has elements of both the crisis (duration) and the catastrophe (it takes many lives), or an assassination which, although it may be experienced as a catastrophe, is a political action which must be attributed to a subject. But what is more striking in relation to this inevitable taxonomic failure is that television tends to blur the differences between what seem to be absolutely incompatible temporal modes, between the flow and continuity of information and the punctual discontinuity of catastrophe. Urgency, enslavement to the instant and hence forgettability, would then be attributes of both information and catastrophe. Indeed, the obscuring of these temporal distinctions may constitute the specificity of television's operation. The purpose of this essay is to investigate the implications and effects of this ambivalent structuration of time, particularly in relation to the categories of information and catastrophe.

Television overall seems to resist analysis. This resistance is linked to its sheer extensiveness (the problem of determining the limits or boundaries of the television text has been a pressing one), its continual barrage of information, sensation, event together with its uncanny ability to assimilate, appropriate, or recuperate all criticisms of the media. A story on the March 7, 1988, *CBS Evening News* detailed how the presidential candidates of both parties produced increasingly provocative or scandalous commercials in order to generate additional television coverage. The commercials would be shown several times in the regular manner and then, depending upon the level of their shock quotient, would be repeated once or more on local or national news, giving the candidates, in effect, free publicity. CBS News, in airing the metastory of this tendency, demonstrates how television news reports on, and hence contains through representation, its own exploitation. Its recuperative power is immense, and television often seems to reduce and deflate, through its pervasiveness and overpresence, all shock value.

Televisual information would seem to be particularly resistant to analysis given its protean nature. Not only does television news provide a seemingly endless stream of information, each bit (as it were) self-destructing in order to make room for the next, but information is dispersed on television among a number of genres and forms, including talk shows, educational/documentary type programs such as *Nova, National Geographic* specials, and *Wide, Wide World of Animals*, "how-to" programs such as *The Frugal Gourmet, This Old House*, and *Victory Garden*, news "magazines" such as *60 Minutes* and *Chronicle*, children's shows (*Sesame Street*), sports, etc. Furthermore, even the two generic forms which are most consistently associated with the concept of information—news and the educational/documentary program—exhibit diametrically opposed formal characteristics. Documentary programs such as *Nova* tend to activate the disembodied male voiceover whose authority has long ago lapsed in the realm of the cinema (it is a voice which, as Pascal Bonitzer points out, has irrevocably "aged").[4] News programs, on the other hand, involve the persistent, direct, embodied, and personalized address of the newscaster. Information, unlike narrative, is not chained to a particular organization of the signifier or a specific style of address. Antithetical modes reside side by side. Hence, information would seem to have no formal restrictions—indeed, it is characterized by its very ubiquity. If information is everywhere, then the true scandal of *disinformation* in the age of television is its quite precise attempt to *place* or to *channel* information—to direct its effects. Even if it is activated through television, it uses broadcasting in a narrowly conceived way. Disinformation loses credibility, then, not only through its status as a lie but through its very directedness, its limitation, its lack of universal availability. The scandal is that its effects are targeted. Disinformation abuses the system of broadcasting by invoking and exploiting the automatic truth value associated with this mode of dissemination—a truth value not unconnected to the sheer difficulty of verification and the very entropy of information.

Yet, in using the concept of information, I am accepting television's own terms. For the concept carries with it quite specific epistemological and sociological implications associated with the rise of information theory. As Katherine Hayles points out, the decisive move of information theory was to make information quantifiable by removing it from the context which endowed it with meaning and, instead, defining it through its own internal relations. According to Hayles, this results in what is, in effect, a massive decontextualization: "Never before in human history had the cultural context itself been constituted through a technology that makes it possible to fragment, manipulate, and reconstitute informational texts at will. For postmodern culture, the manipulation of text and its consequently arbitrary relation to context *is our* context."[5]

From this point of view, television could be seen as *the* textual technology of information theory. Insofar as a commercial precedes news coverage of a disaster which in its own turn is interrupted by a preview of tonight's made-for-TV movie, television is the preeminent machine of decontextualization. The only context for television is itself—its own rigorous scheduling. Its strictest limitation that of time, information becomes measurable, quantifiable, through its relation to temporality. While the realism of film is defined largely in terms of space, that of television is conceptualized in terms of time (owing to its characteristics of "liveness," presence, and immediacy). As Margaret Morse notes, television news is distinguished by the very absence of the rationalized Renaissance space we have come to associate with film—a perspectival technique which purports to *represent* the truth of objects in space.[6] Instead, the simultaneous activation of different, incongruous spaces (the studio, graphics, footage from the scene, interviews on monitor) is suggestive of a writing surface and the consequent annihilation of depth. Television does not so much *represent* as it *informs.* Theories of representation painstakingly elaborated in relation to film are clearly inadequate.

Conceptualizing information in terms of flow and ubiquity, however, would seem to imply that it lacks any dependence whatsoever upon punctuation or differentiation. Yet even television must have a way of compensating for its own tendency toward the leveling of signification, toward banalization and non-differentiation—a way of saying, in effect, "Look, this is important," of indexically signaling that its information is worthy of attention. It does so through processes that dramatize information—the high seriousness of music which introduces the news, the rhetoric of the newscaster, the activation of special effects and spectacle in the documentary format. Most effective, perhaps, is the crisis of temporality which signifies *urgency* and which is attached to the information itself as its single most compelling attribute. Information becomes most visibly information, becomes a televisual commodity, on the brink of its extinction or loss. A recent segment of *Nova*, "The Hidden Power of Plants," chronicles the attempt to document the expertise of old medicine men who, when they die, take their knowledge with them (it is "worse than when a library burns down," the anonymous voiceover tells us). Similarly, the numerous geographic specials demonstrate that the life of a particular animal or plant becomes most *televisual* when the species is threatened with extinction. The rhetoric of impending environmental doom is today applicable to almost any species of plant or animal life given the constant expansion and encroachment of civilization on territory still designated as "natural." In this way, television incessantly takes as its subject matter the documentation and revalidation of its own discursive problematic. For information is shown to be punctual; it inhabits a moment of time and is then lost to memory. Television thrives on its own forgettability. While the concept of information itself implies the possibilities of storage and retrieval (as in computer technology), the notion of such storage is, for television, largely an alien idea. Some television news stories are accompanied by images labeled "file footage," but the appellation itself reduces the credibility of the story. Reused images, unless carefully orchestrated in the construction of nostalgia, undermine the appeal to the "live" and the instantaneous which buttresses the news.

The short-lived but spectacular aspect of information is revealed in the use of special-effects sequences where the drama of information is most closely allied with visual pleasure. In a *National Geographic* special entitled "The Mind," an artist's conception of the brain curiously resembles the mise-en-scène of information theory. The brain is depicted as an extensive network of neurons, synapses, and neurotransmitters regulating the flow of information. In one cubic inch of the brain there are 100 million nerve cells connected by 10,000 miles of fibers (laid end to end, the voiceover tells us, they would reach to the moon and back). The amount of information is so enormous that cells must make instantaneous decisions about what is to be transmitted. The sequence is organized so that music announces the significance of these data, and an almost constantly moving camera suggests the depths of the representation. The camera treats what is clearly a highly artificial, technologically produced space as the experienced real, while the voiceover provides verbal analogues to real space (the fibers which reach to the moon and back, the pinch of salt in a swimming pool which helps one to grasp what it would be like to look for a neurotransmitter in the brain). Yet, there is no pretense that an optical representation of the brain is adequate—it is simply *necessary* to the televisual discourse. The voiceover announces, "If it could be seen, brain cell action might look like random flickering of countless stars in an endless universe. Seemingly an infinite amount of information and variety of behaviors in an unlikely looking package," while the visuals mimic such a sight with multicolored flickering lights. Television knowledge strains to make visible the invisible. While it acknowledges the limits of empiricism, the limitations of the eye in relation to knowledge, information is nevertheless conveyable only in terms of a *simulated visibility*—"If it could be seen, this is what it might look like." Television deals in potentially visible entities. The epistemological endeavor is to bring to the surface, to expose, but only at a second remove—depicting what is not available to sight. Televisibility is a construct, even when it makes use of the credibility attached to location shooting—embedding that image within a larger, overriding discourse.

The urgency associated with information together with the refusal to fully align the visible with the dictates of an indexical realism suggests that the alleged value of information, like that of television, is ineluctably linked with time rather than space. And, indeed, both information and television have consistently been defined in relation to the temporal dimension. According to Walter Benjamin, the new form of communication called information brought about a crisis in the novel and in storytelling: "The value of information does not survive the moment in which it was new. It lives only at that moment; it has to surrender to it completely and explain itself to it without losing any time. A story is different. It does not expend itself. It preserves and concentrates its strength and is capable of releasing it even after a long time."[7] Information must be immediately understandable, graspable—it is "shot through with explanation."

Meaning in storytelling has time to linger to be subject to unraveling. It has "an amplitude that information lacks."[8] This tendency to polarize types of discourses with respect to their relation to temporality is evident also in Jonathan Culler's activation of Michael Thompson's categories of transience and durability: "We are accustomed to think—and tradition urges us to think—of two sorts of verbal, visual compositions: those which transmit information in a world of practical affairs—utilitarian and transient—and those which, not tied to the time or use value of information, are part of the world of leisure, our cultural patrimony, and belong in principle to the system of durables."[9] Benjamin might say that the loss of aura associated with electronic reproduction is a function of its inability to *endure*. In other words, there are things which last and things which don't. Information does not. It is expended, exhausted, in the moment of its utterance. If it were of a material order, it would be necessary to throw it away. As it is, one can simply forget it.

Television, too, has been conceptualized as the annihilation of memory, and consequently of history, in its continual stress upon the "nowness" of its own discourse. As Stephen Heath and Gillian Skirrow point out, "where film sides towards instantaneous memory ('everything is absent, everything is *recorded*— as a memory trace which is so at once, without having been something else before'), television operates much more as an absence of memory, the recorded material it uses—including the material recorded on film—instituted as actual in the production of the television image."[10] This transformation of record into actuality or immediacy is a function of a generalized fantasy of "live broadcasting." Jane Feuer pursues this question by demonstrating that a certain ontology of television, defined in terms of a technological base which allows for instantaneous recording, transmission, and reception, becomes the ground for a pervasive ideology of "liveness."[11] Although, as she is careful to point out, television rarely exploits this technical capability, minimalizing not only "live" transmission but preservation of "real time" as well, the ideology of "liveness" works to overcome the excessive fragmentation within television's flow. If television is indeed thought to be inherently "live," the impression of a unity of "real time" is preserved, covering over the extreme discontinuity which is in fact typical of television in the United States at this historical moment.

From these descriptions it would appear that information is peculiarly compatible with the television apparatus. Both are fully aligned with the notion of urgency; both thrive on the exhaustion, moment by moment, of their own material; both are hence linked with transience and the undermining of memory. But surely there are moments which can be isolated from the fragmented flow of information, moments with an impact which disrupts the ordinary routine— moments when information bristles, when its greatest value is its shock value (in a medium which might be described as a modulated, and hence restrained, series of shocks). These are moments when one stops simply *watching* television in order to *stare*, transfixed—moments of catastrophe. But what constitutes catastrophe on television? And what is the basis of the widespread intuition that television exploits, or perhaps even produces, catastrophe? To what extent and in what ways is the social imagination of catastrophe linked to television?

Etymologically, the word "catastrophe" is traceable to the Greek *kata* (over) plus *strephein* (turn)—to overturn. The first definition given by *Webster's* is "the final event of the dramatic action esp. of a tragedy" (in this respect it is interesting to note that the etymology of the term "trope" also links it to "turn"). Hence, although the second and third definitions ("2. a momentous tragic event ranging from extreme misfortune to utter overthrow or ruin; 3. a violent and sudden change in a feature of the earth") attempt to bind catastrophe to the real, the initial definition contaminates it with fictionality. Catastrophe is on the cusp of the dramatic and the referential, and this is, indeed, part of its fascination. The etymological specification of catastrophe as the overturning of a given situation anticipates its more formal delineation by catastrophe theory. Here, catastrophe is defined as unexpected discontinuity in an otherwise continuous system. The theory is most appropriate, then, for the study of sudden and unexpected effects in a gradually changing situation. The emphasis upon suddenness suggests that catastrophe is of a temporal order.

The formal definition offered by catastrophe theory, however, points to a striking paradox associated with the attempt to conceptualize televisual catastrophe. For while catastrophe is designated as discontinuity within an otherwise continuous system, television is most frequently theorized as a system of discontinuities, emphasizing heterogeneity. Furthermore, the tendency of television to banalize all events through a kind of leveling process would seem to preclude the possibility of specifying *any* event as catastrophic. As Benjamin pointed out in a statement which seems to capture something of the effect of television, "The concept of progress is to be grounded in the idea of catastrophe. That things 'just go on' *is* the catastrophe."[12] The news, in particular, is vulnerable to the charge that it dwells on the catastrophic, obsessed with the aberrant, the deviant. According to Margaret Morse, "The news in the West is about the *a*normal. It is almost always the 'bad' news. It is about challenges to the symbolic system and its legitimacy."[13] Furthermore, in its structural emphasis upon discontinuity and rupture, it often seems that television itself is formed on the model of catastrophe.

Given these difficulties, is it possible to produce a coherent account of events which television designates as catastrophe? What do these moments and events have in common? One distinctive feature of the catastrophe is that of the *scale* of the disaster in question—a scale often measured through a body count. By this criterion, Bhopal, the Detroit Northwest Airlines crash of August 1987, and the Mexican earthquake could all be labeled catastrophes. However, other events which are clearly presented as catastrophic—Chernobyl, the explosion of the *Challenger*—do not involve a high number of deaths, while wartime body counts (Vietnam, the Iran–Iraq war), often numerically impressive, do not qualify as catastrophic (undoubtedly because war makes death habitual, continual). Evidently, the scale which is crucial to catastrophe is not that of the quantification of death (or at least not that alone).

Mary Ann Doane

Catastrophe does, however, always seem to have something to do with technology and its potential collapse. And it is also always tainted by a fascination with death—so that catastrophe might finally be defined as the conjuncture of the failure of technology and the resulting confrontation with death. The fragility of technology's control over the forces it strives to contain is manifested most visibly in the accident—the plane crash today being the most prominent example. Dan Rather introduced the CBS story about the August 1987 Detroit Northwest Airlines crash with the rhetoric of catastrophe—the phrase "aftershocks of a nightmare" accompanying aerial images of wreckage strewn over a large area. The inability of television to capture the precise moment of the crash activates a compensatory discourse of eyewitness accounts and animated reenactments of the disaster—a simulated vision. Eyewitnesses who comment upon the incredible aspects of the sight or who claim that there were "bodies strewn everywhere" borrow their authority from the sheer fact of being there at the disastrous moment, their reported presence balancing the absence of the camera. What becomes crucial for the act of reportage, the announcement of the catastrophe, is the simple gesture of being on the scene, *where* it happened, so that presence in space compensates for the inevitable temporal tag. Hence, while the voiceover of the anchor ultimately organizes the event for us, the status of the image as indexical truth is not inconsequential—through it the "story" touches the ground of the real. Nevertheless, the catastrophe must be immediately subjected to analysis, speculation, and explanation. In the case of the airplane crash, speculation about causes is almost inevitably a speculation about the limits and breaking points of technology (with respect to Northwest flight 255, the history of the performance of the engine was immediately a subject of interrogation).

As modes of transportation dependent upon advanced and intricate technologies become familiar, everyday, routine, the potential for catastrophe increases. The breakdown of these technologies radically defamiliarizes them by signaling their distance from a secure and comforting nature. As Wolfgang Schivelbusch points out, this was the case for the railroad in the nineteenth century, its gradual acceptance and normalization subjected to the intermittent shock of the accident:

> One might also say that the more civilized the schedule and the more efficient the technology, the more catastrophic its destruction when it collapses. There is an exact ratio between the level of the technology with which nature is controlled, and the degree of severity of its accidents. The preindustrial era does not know any technological accidents in that sense. In Diderot's *Encyclopédie*, "Accident" is dealt with as a grammatical and philosophical concept, more or less synonymous with coincidence. The preindustrial catastrophes are natural events, natural accidents. They attack the objects they destroy from the outside, as storms, floods, thunderbolts, hailstones, etc. After the industrial revolution, destruction by technological accident comes from the inside. The technical apparatuses destroy themselves by means of their own power. The energies tamed by the steam engine and delivered by it as regulated mechanical performance will destroy that engine itself in the case of an accident.[14]

In the late twentieth century, the potential for technological collapse is more pervasive, characterizing catastrophes as diverse as Bhopal, Chernobyl, the *Challenger* explosion, earthquakes which science and technology fail to predict, as well as railway and plane crashes. But this massive expansion is perhaps not the decisive difference. After the Detroit crash, airport authorities spray-painted the burned-out grass green in order to conceal all traces of the accident and enable other travelers to avoid the traumatic evidence. Yet, this action was then reported on radio news, indicating that what is now at stake in the catastrophe, for us, is *coverage*. While the vision of catastrophe is blocked at one level, it is multiplied and intensified at another. The media urge us now to obsessively confront catastrophe, over and over again. And while the railway accident of the nineteenth century was certainly the focus of journalistic inquiry, its effects were primarily local. Television's ubiquity, its extensiveness, allows for a global experience of catastrophe which is always reminiscent of the potential of nuclear disaster, of mass rather than individual annihilation.

Catastrophe is thus, through its association with industrialization and the advance of technology, ineluctably linked with the idea of Progress. The time of technological progress is always felt as linear and fundamentally irreversible—technological change is almost by definition an "advance," and it is extremely difficult to conceive of any movement backward, any regression. Hence, technological evolution is perceived as unflinching progress toward a total state of control over nature. If some notion of pure Progress is the utopian element in this theory of technological development, catastrophe is its dystopia, the always unexpected interruption of this forward movement. Catastrophic time stands still. Catastrophe signals the failure of the escalating technological desire to conquer nature. From the point of view of Progress, nature can. no longer be seen as anything but an affront or challenge to technology. And so, just as the media penetrate events (in the media event), technology penetrates nature. This is why the purview of catastrophe keeps expanding to encompass even phenomena which had previously been situated wholly on the side of nature—earthquakes, floods, hurricanes, tornadoes. Such catastrophes no longer signify only the sudden eruption of natural forces but the inadequacy or failure of technology and its predictive powers as well.

On the *ABC Evening News* of September 15, 1988, Peter Jennings stood in front of a map tracking the movements of Hurricane Gilbert for the first fifteen minutes of the broadcast. A supporting report detailed the findings of a highly equipped plane flying into the eye of the hurricane. The fascination here was not only that of the literal penetration of the catastrophic storm by high technology but also that of the sophisticated instruments and tracking equipment visible inside the plane—a fetishism of controls. Our understanding of natural catastrophe is now a fully technological apprehension. Such incidents demonstrate that the distinction made by Schivelbusch between preindustrial accidents (natural accidents where the destructive energy comes from without) and postindustrial accidents (in which the destructive energy comes from within the technological apparatus) is beginning to blur. This is particularly the case with respect to nuclear technology which aspires to harness the most basic energy of nature itself—that of the atom. And in doing so, it also confronts us with the potential transformation of that energy into that which is most lethal to human life.

While nuclear disaster signals the limits of the failure of technology, the trauma attached to the explosion of the *Challenger* is associated with the sheer height of the technological aspirations represented by space exploration. The *Challenger* coverage also demonstrates just how nationalistic the apprehension of catastrophe is—our own catastrophes are always more important, more eligible for extended reporting than those of other nations. But perhaps even more crucial here was the fact that television itself was on the scene—witness to the catastrophe. And the played and replayed image of the *Challenger* exploding, of diverging lines of billowing white smoke against a deep blue Florida sky—constant evidence of television's compulsion to repeat—acts as a reminder not only of the catastrophic nature of the event but also of the capacity of television to record instantaneously, a reminder of the fact that television was *there*. The temporality of catastrophe is that of the instant—it is momentary, punctual, while its televisual coverage is characterized by its very duration, seemingly compensating, for the suddenness, the unexpected nature of the event.

A segment of Tom Brokaw's virtually nonstop coverage on NBC contained a video replay of the explosion itself, a live broadcast of the president's message to the nation, Brokaw's reference to an earlier interview with a child psychiatrist who dealt with the potential trauma of the event for children, Chris Wallace's report of Don Regan's announcement and the press's reception of the news during a press briefing, a mention of Mrs. Reagan's reaction to the explosion as she watched it live on television, Brokaw's speculation about potential attacks on Reagan's support of SDI ("Star Wars"), and Brokaw's 1981 interview with one of the astronauts, Judy Resnick. The glue in this collection of disparate forms is Brokaw's performance, his ability to *cover* the event with words, with a commentary which exhausts its every aspect and through the orchestration of secondary reports and old footage.[15] Brokaw is the pivot, he mediates our relation to the catastrophe. Furthermore, as with television news, it is a direct address/appeal to the viewer, but with an even greater emphasis upon the presence and immediacy of the act of communication, with constant recourse to shifters which draw attention to the shared space and time of reporter and viewer: terms such as "today," "here," "you," "we," "I." Immediately after a rerun of the images documenting the *Challenger* explosion, Brokaw says, clearly improvising, "As I say, we have shown that to you repeatedly again and again today. It is not that we have a ghoulish curiosity. We just think that it's important that all members of the audience who are coming to their sets at different times of the day have an opportunity to see it. And of course everyone is led to their own speculation based on what happened here today as well." The "liveness," the "real time" of the catastrophe is that of the television anchor's discourse—its nonstop quality a part of a fascination which is linked to the spectator's knowledge that Brokaw faces him/her without a complete script, underlining the alleged authenticity of his discourse. For the possibility is always open that Brokaw might stumble, that his discourse might lapse—and this would be tantamount to touching the real, simply displacing the lure of referentiality attached to the catastrophe to another level (that of the "personal" relationship between anchor and viewer).

There is a very striking sense in which televisual catastrophe conforms to the definition offered by catastrophe theory whereby catastrophe represents discontinuity in an otherwise continuous system. From this point of view, the measure of catastrophe would be the extent to which it interrupts television's regular daily programming, disrupting normal expectations about what can be seen and heard at a particular time. If Nick Browne is correct in suggesting that, through its alignment of its own schedule with the work day and the work week, television "helps produce and render 'natural' the logic and rhythm of the social order,"[16] then catastrophe would represent that which cannot be contained within such an ordering of temporality. It would signal the return of the repressed. The traumatic nature of such a disruption is underlined by the absence of commercials in the reporting of catastrophe—commercials usually constituting not only the normal punctuation of television's flow but, for some, the very text of television.

That which, above all, cannot be contained within the daily social rhythms of everyday life is death. Catastrophe is at some level always about the body, about the encounter with death. For all its ideology of "liveness," it may be death which forms the point of televisual intrigue. Contemporary society works to conceal death to such an extent that its experience is generally a vicarious one through representation. The removal of death from direct perception, a process which, as Benjamin points out, was initiated in the nineteenth century, continues today:

> In the course of the nineteenth century bourgeois society has, by means of hygienic and social, private and public institutions, realized a secondary effect which may have been its subconscious main purpose: to make it possible for people to avoid the sight of dying. Dying was once a public process in the life of the individual and a most exemplary one. . . . There used to be no house, hardly a room, in which someone had not once died. . . . Today people live in rooms that have never been touched by death.[17]

Furthermore, the mechanization of warfare—the use of technologically advanced weapons which kill at a greater and greater distance—further reduces the direct confrontation with death. Consistent with its wartime goal of allaying the effects of death and increasing the efficiency with which it is produced, technology also strives to hold death at bay, to contain it. Hence, death emerges as the absolute limit of technology's power, that which marks its vulnerability. Catastrophe, conjoining death with the failure of technology, presents us with a scenario of limits—the limits of technology, the limits of signification. In the novel, according to Benjamin, death makes the character's life *meaningful* to the reader, allows him/her the "hope of warming his shivering life with a death he reads about."[18]

What is at stake in televisual catastrophe is not meaning but reference. The viewer's consuming desire, unlike that of the novel reader, is a desire no longer for meaning but for referentiality, which seems to have been all but lost in the enormous expanse of a television which always promises a contact forever deferred. Death is no longer the culminating experience of a life rich in continuity and meaning but, instead, pure discontinuity, disruption—pure chance or accident, the result of being in the wrong place at the wrong time.

And it is not by coincidence that catastrophe theory, on an entirely different level, seeks to provide a means of mapping the discontinuous instance, the chance occurrence, without reducing its arbitrariness or indeterminacy. Catastrophe theory is based on a theorem in topology discovered by the French mathematician René Thom in 1968. Its aim is to provide a formal language for the description of sudden discontinuities within a gradually changing system. The points of occurrence of these discontinuities are mapped on a three-dimensional graph. In 1972, E. D. Zeeman developed an educational toy called the "catastrophe machine" to facilitate the understanding of Thom's theory. (The appeal of this toy is that you can make it yourself with only two rubberbands, a cardboard disk, two drawing pins, and a wooden board.) The point of the catastrophe machine is the construction of an apparatus which is guaranteed to *not* work, to predictably produce unpredictable irregularities. For catastrophe theory is, as one of its proponents explains, "a theory about singularities. When applied to scientific problems, therefore, it deals with the properties of discontinuities directly, without reference to any specific underlying mechanism."[19] It is, therefore, no longer a question of explanation. Catastrophe theory confronts the indeterminable without attempting to reduce it to a set of determinations. Thom refers to "islands of determinism separated by zones of instability or indeterminacy."[20] Catastrophe theory is one aspect of a new type of scientific endeavor which Lyotard labels "postmodern"—a science which "by concerning itself with such things as undecidables, the limits of precise control, conflicts characterized by incomplete information, 'fracta,' catastrophes, and pragmatic paradoxes—is theorizing its own evolution as discontinuous, catastrophic, non-rectifiable, and paradoxical. It is changing the meaning of the word *knowledge*, while expressing how such a change can take place."[21]

Television is not, however, the technology of catastrophe theory, or if it is, it is so only in a highly limited sense. The televisual construction of catastrophe seeks both to preserve and to annihilate indeterminacy, discontinuity. On the one hand, by surrounding catastrophe with commentary, with an explanatory apparatus, television works to contain its more disturbing and uncontainable aspects. On the other hand, catastrophe's discontinuity is embraced as the mirror of television's own functioning, and that discontinuity and indeterminacy ensure the activation of the lure of referentiality. In this sense, television is a kind of catastrophe machine, continually corroborating its own signifying problematic—a problematic of discontinuity and indeterminacy which strives to mimic the experience of the real, a real which in its turn is guaranteed by the contact with death. Catastrophe thrives on the momentary, the instantaneous, that which seems destined to be forgotten, and hence seems to confirm Heath's and Skirrow's notion that television operates as the "absence of memory." But because catastrophe is necessary to television, as the corroboration of its own signifying problematic, there is also a clear advantage in the somewhat laborious construction and maintenance of a memory of catastrophe. The spectator must be led to remember, with even a bit of nostalgia, those moments which are preeminently televisual—the explosion of the *Challenger,* the assassination of John F. Kennedy (the footage of which was replayed again and again during the time of the recent twenty-fifth anniversary of the event). What is remembered in these nostalgic returns is not only the catastrophe or crisis itself but the fact that television was there, allowing us access to moments which always seem more real than all the others.

Catastrophe coverage clearly generates and plays on the generation of anxiety. The indeterminacy and unexpectedness of catastrophe seem to aptly describe the potential trauma of the world we occupy. But such coverage also allows for a persistent disavowal—in viewing the bodies on the screen, one can always breathe a sigh of relief in the realization that "that's not me." Indeed, the celebrity status of the anchorperson and of those who usually appear on television can seem to justify the belief that the character on the screen—dead or alive—is always definitively *other,* that the screen is not a mirror. Such persistent anxiety is manageable, although it may require that one periodically check the screen to make sure. But this is perhaps not the only, or even the most important, affect associated with catastrophe coverage.

Something of another type of affective value of catastrophe can be glimpsed in Slavoj Zizek's analysis of the sinking of the *Titanic* and its cultural and psychical significance. At the end of the nineteenth century, "civilized" Europe perceived itself as on the brink of extinction, its values threatened by revolutionary workers' movements, the rise of nationalism and anti-Semitism, and diverse signs indicating the decay of morals. The grand luxury transatlantic voyage incarnated a generalized nostalgia for a disappearing Europe insofar as it signified technological progress, victory over nature, and also a condensed image of a social world based on class divisions elsewhere threatened with dissolution. The shipwreck of the *Titanic* hence represented for the social imagination the collapse of European civilization, the destruction of an entire social edifice—"Europe at the beginning of the century found itself confronted with its own death."[22] The contradictory readings by the right and the left of the behavior of first-class "gentlemen" with respect to third-class women and children corroborate this reading of a social imagination seized by the shipwreck and treating it as an index to the maintenance or collapse of former class differences.

But Zizek goes on to claim that there must be something in excess of this symbolic reading. For it is difficult to explain satisfactorily the contemporary fascination with images of the wreck at the bottom of the sea: "The mute presence of wrecks—are they not like the congealed residue of an impossible *jouissance*? . . . One understands why, notwithstanding technical problems, we hesitate to raise the wreckage of the *Titanic* to the surface: its sublime beauty, once exposed to daylight, would turn to waste, to the depressing banality of a rusted mass of iron." It would be problematic to bring the *Titanic* too close—it is there to be watched in its "proper" grave, to be regarded as a monument to catastrophe in general, a catastrophe which, in its distance, makes you feel real. According to Zizek, the two aspects of the *Titanic*—the "metaphorical one of its symbolic overdetermination and the real one of the inertia of the thing, incarnation of a mute *jouissance*"—represent the two sides of the Freudian symptom. For although the symptom can be interpreted as a knot of significations, it is also always more than that. There is a remainder, an excess not reducible to the symbolic network (in the words of Jacques-Alain Miller, one "loves one's symptom like oneself"). This is why, according to Zizek, "one remains hooked on the real of one's symptom even after the interpretation has accomplished its work."[23]

It is this remainder, this residue, which televisual catastrophe exploits. The social fascination of catastrophe rests on the desire to confront the remainder, or to be confronted with that which is in excess of signification. Catastrophe seems to testify to the inertia of the real and television's privileged relation to it. In the production and reproduction of the metonymic chain—the body-catastrophe-death-referentiality—television legitimates its own discourse. This is why it is often difficult to isolate and define catastrophe, to establish the boundary which marks it off from ordinary television. Information and catastrophe coexist in a curious balance. According to Susan Sontag, "we live under continual threat of two equally fearful, but seemingly opposed, destinies: unremitting banality and inconceivable terror."[24] Television produces both as the two poles structuring the contemporary imagination.

This relation to catastrophe is by no means an inherent or essential characteristic of television technology. Rather, it is a feature which distinguishes television and its operations in the late capitalist society of the United States where crisis is produced and assimilated as a part of the ongoing spectacle—a spectacle financed by commercials and hence linked directly to the circulation of commodities. What underlies/haunts catastrophe but is constantly overshadowed by it is the potential of another type of catastrophe altogether—that of the economic crisis. According to Schivelbusch, "If the nineteenth century perceives the cause of technological accidents to be the sudden disturbance of the uncertain equilibrium of a machine (that is, the relationship between curbed energy and the means of curbing it), Marx defines the economic crisis as the disruption of the uncertain balance between buying and selling in the circulation of goods. As long as buying and selling work as a balanced and unified process, the cycle goes on functioning, but as soon as the two become separated and autonomous, we arrive at a crisis."[25] Of course, economic crisis does not appear to meet any of the criteria of the true catastrophe. It is not punctual but of some duration, it does not kill (at least not immediately), and it can assuredly be linked to a notion of agency or system (that of commodity capitalism) if not to a subject. Yet, for a television dependent upon the healthy circulation of commodities, the economic crisis can be more catastrophic than any natural or technological catastrophe.

Ironically, for this very reason, and to deflect any potentially harmful consequences, it must be disguised as catastrophe and hence naturalized, contained, desystematized. The economic crisis as catastrophe is sudden, discontinuous, and unpredictable—an accident which cannot reflect back upon any system.

In comparison with the lure of referentiality associated with catastrophe "proper," the economic crisis confronts us as an abstraction. Yet, the abstraction of catastrophe is difficult since catastrophe seems to lend itself more readily to an account of bodies. Hence, the reporting of the Wall Street crash of October 1987 strives to restore the elements of catastrophe which are lacking—the iconography of panic becomes the high-angle shot down at the milling crowd of the stock exchange, bodies in disarray. An interviewee claims, "It's fascinating, like a bloodbath." Furthermore, a catastrophe which seems furthest removed from the concept of a failure of technology is rebound to that concept through the oft-repeated claim that a major cause of the crash was computer trading gone awry. Economic crisis is also tamed by naturalizing it as a cyclical occurrence, like the change of seasons. This is a containment of a catastrophe which, unlike the others, potentially threatens television's own economic base, its own mechanism for the production of commodity-linked spectacle. And perhaps this is why catastrophe has become such a familiar, almost everyday, televisual occurrence. According to Ernst Bloch, "the crisis of the accident (of the uncontrolled things) will remain with us longer to the degree that they remain deeper than the crises of economy (of the uncontrolled commodities)."[26] The depth which television accords to the catastrophes of things is linked to the lure of referentiality which they hold out to us. Catastrophe makes concrete and immediate, and therefore deflects attention from, the more abstract horror of potential economic crisis. For the catastrophe, insofar as it is perceived as the *accidental* failure of technology (and one which can be rectified with a little tinkering—O-rings can be fixed, engines redesigned), is singular, asystematic—it does not touch the system of commodity capitalism.

The concept of crisis is linked to temporal process, to a duration of a (one can hope) limited period. This is why the time of crisis can coincide with that of politics, of political strategy. Crisis, *krisis,* is a decisive period insofar as it is a time when decisions have to be made, decisions with very real effects. The televisual representation of catastrophe, on the other hand, hopes to hold onto the apolitical and attach it to the momentary, the punctual. Here time is free in its indeterminacy, reducible to no system—precisely the opposite of televisual time which is programmed and scheduled as precisely as possible, down to the last second. Television's time is a time which is, in effect, wholly determined. And this systematization of time is ultimately based on its commodification (time in television is, above all, not "free"). As both Stephen Heath and Eileen Meehan point out, what networks sell to advertisers is the viewing time of their audiences.[27] Here the commodification of time is most apparent (and perhaps this is why, in the reporting of catastrophes, there are no commercials).

The catastrophe is crucial to television precisely because it functions as a denial of this process and corroborates television's access to the momentary, the discontinuous, the real. Catastrophe produces the illusion that the spectator is in direct contact with the anchorperson, who interrupts regular programming to demonstrate that it can indeed be done when the referent is at stake. Television's greatest technological prowess is its ability to be there—both on the scene and in your living room (hence the most catastrophic of technological catastrophes is the loss of the signal). The death associated with catastrophe ensures that television is felt as an immediate collision with the real in all its intractability—bodies in crisis, technology gone awry. Televisual catastrophe is thus character-ized by everything which it is said not to be—it is expected, predictable, its presence crucial to television's operation. In fact, catastrophe could be said to be at one level a condensation of all the attributes and aspirations of "normal" tele-vision (immediacy, urgency, presence, discontinuity, the instantaneous, and hence forgettable). If information becomes a commodity on the brink of its extinction or loss, televisual catastrophe magnifies that death many times over. Hence, catastrophe functions as both the exception and the norm of a television practice which continually holds out to its spectator the lure of a referentiality perpetually deferred.

NOTES

1. Roland Barthes, *Camera Lucida: Reflections on Photography*, trans. Richard Howard (New York: Farrar, 1981), 77.

2. Ernst Bloch, *A Philosophy of the Future*, trans. John Cumming (New York: Herder, 1970), 124.

3. The time proper to catastrophe might be thought of as compatible with that of the digital watch where time is cut off from any sense of analogical continuity, and the connection between moments is severed. One is faced only with the time of the instant—isolated and alone.

4. Pascal Bonitzer, "The Silences of the Voice." In *Narrative, Apparatus, Ideology*, trans. Philip Rosen and Marcia Butzel, ed. Philip Rosen (New York: Columbia University Press, 1986), 328.

5. N. Katherine Hayles, "Text out of Context: Situating Postmodernism within an Infor-mation Society," *Discourse* 9 (Spring/Summer 1987), 26.

6. Margaret Morse, "The Television News Personality and Credibility: Reflections on the News in Transition." In *Studies in Entertainment*, ed. Tania Modleski (Bloomington: Indiana University Press, 1986), 70.

7. Walter Benjamin, "The Storyteller." In *Illuminations*, ed. Hannah Arendt, trans. Harry Zohn (New York: Schocken, 1969), 80.

8. Benjamin, "The Storyteller," 89.

9. Jonathan Culler, "Junk and Rubbish," *Diacritics* 15.3 (Fall 1985), 10.

10. Stephen Heath and Gillian Skirrow, "Television, a World in Action," *Screen* (Summer 1977), 55–56.

11. Jane Feuer, "The Concept of Live Television: Ontology as Ideology." In *Regarding Tele-vision: Critical Approaches—An Anthology*, ed. E. Ann Kaplan (Frederick, Md.: Publications of America, and the American Film Institute), 13–14.

12. Walter Benjamin, "Central Park," trans. Lloyd Spencer, *New German Critique* 34 (Win-ter 1985), 50.

13. Morse, 74

14. Wolfgang Schivelbusch, *The Railway Journey: Trains and Travel in the 19th Century*, trans. Anselm Hollo (New York: Urizen, 1979), 133.

15. This performance could also be seen as a masculinist discourse which attempts to reestablish control over a failed masculinized technology. In this sense, catastrophe is feminized insofar as it designates the reemergence of the nature technology attempts to repress and control. Brokaw's performance is thus a discursive management of catastrophe. Such a reading is problematic insofar as it equates nature and the feminine, technology and the masculine, but gains a certain amount of historical force from an influential mythology. It was, after all, a woman (Pandora) who unleashed catastrophe upon the world.

16. Nick Browne, "The Political Economy of the Television (Super) Text." In *Television: The Critical View*, ed. Horace Newcomb, 4th ed. (New York: Oxford University Press, 1987), 588.

17. Benjamin, "The Storyteller," 94–95.

18. Ibid., 101.

19. T. Saunders, *An Introduction to Catastrophe Theory* (Cambridge: Cambridge University Press, 1980), 1.

20. René Thom, "Topological Models in Biology," *Topology* 8 (1969), quoted in Michael Thompson, *Rubbish Theory: The Creation and Destruction of Value* (Oxford: Oxford University Press, 1979), 142.

21. Jean-François Lyotard, *The Postmodern Condition: A Report on Knowledge*, trans. Geoff Bennington and Brian Massumi (Minneapolis: University of Minnesota Press, 1984), 60.

22. Slavoj Zizek, "Titanic-le-symptôme," *L'Ane* 30 (April–June 1987), 45.

23. Ibid.

24. Susan Sontag, "The Imagination of Disaster." In *Against Interpretation* (New York: Dell, 1969), 227.

25. Schivelbusch, 134.

26. Quoted in ibid., 131.

27. See Eileen R. Meehan, "Why We Don't Count: The Commodity Audience," in *Logics of Television: Essays in Cultural Criticism*, 117, and Stephen Heath, "Representing Television," in *Logics of Television: Essays in Cultural Criticism*, 267.

Richard Dienst

History, the Eternal Rerun:
On *Crime Story*

*The past can be seized only as an image which flashes up
at the instant when it can be recognized and is never seen
again.*
——Walter Benjamin

Is it possible to think about history and television at the same time? Have you
ever seen the two of them together? It is one thing to place television in (a) history, to treat television as an historical object belonging to a particular moment;
it is another to talk about the way television represents history, how history
becomes a set of objects for televisual transmission. Which one frames the other?
And what if we cannot assume that these two terms name different orders, an
order of forces and events over here and an order of representations over there?
How can we place television in a "historical context" once we understand (via
contemporary Marxism and/or poststructuralism) that history can be made visible only as a textual production? (That the notion of history's "textuality" is in
no way diminishing, simplifying, or debilitating should be obvious from Jameson's *The Political Unconscious* and Derrida's *Of Grammatology*—to cite only
two well-elaborated arguments.) Despite these difficulties, we may still reassert
the familiar nineteenth-century concept of historical thinking as such, in which
the prodigious representational and temporal effusions of television would be
viewed as a limited deformation of a larger scheme of events that remains finally
comprehensible in outline. But if television participates not only in how history
is *figured* but in how it *happens*—thereby mixing the terms, obscuring old lines
of sight and making new kinds of events possible—it is not enough to analyze
how history appears on television; we must address another problem, which is
always there, concerning the fragile constitution of historical sense itself. Here,
then, in order to ask about the appearance of history on television, we will have
to speak of its apparent disappearance there.

The issue turns on how a new technology of representation dissolves or
betrays earlier figural devices in the process of inventing new ones. Although

From *Still Life in Real Time*, pp. 69–78. Copyright © 1995 by Duke University Press. All rights
reserved. Reprinted with permission.

television seems simply to destroy history—through what might be called inaccuracies, indistinctions, and forgettings—it also constructs its own kind of historical material, precisely by projecting new lines of linkage and new speeds of reference. Rather than chart all the ways in which television either cancels or reasserts the possibility of seeing history, I offer a modest demonstration of how one television series—a tenuous narrative here isolated from the programming matrix that carried it—repeatedly encounters blockages that it can "solve" only by breaking its course and starting elsewhere.

Crime Story, a serial broadcast in the United States by NBC from 1986–1988, traversed a number of different historical and dramatic situations in its short two-year run. According to its initial press releases, it was designed to trace a decades-long battle between an incorruptible cop (Michael Torello), a liberal lawyer (David Abrams), and a hoodlum-turned-gangster (Ray Luca) from a Chicago neighborhood to Las Vegas and beyond. Many smaller narrative units inhabit this serial story structure, but their relationship to the general plot changes over time, becoming less tangential and more tributary. In broad outline, the Chicago episodes treat the relationship between crime and order in terms of organic social groups: each character belongs to a distinct familial and ethnic milieu, so that conflicts within and between milieux have to be mediated by an outsider, who is in turn caught in another set of conflicts. This interlocking system—in which criminals, cops, and lawyers share the same space—dissolves when Luca becomes a manager for a Jewish organized crime family and when Torello and Abrams move from the city to the federal level of the justice system. At that point, in the middle of the first season and about twelve hours into the series, the scene shifts to Las Vegas.

Crime Story sets out, at least in its own publicity, on a grand scale: not exactly a historical "period" piece that would remain in place, nor a miniseries that neatly crosses and closes down its historical span, but a historical retelling that simply starts "in the past" without any clear destination except, perhaps, the present. It cannot therefore be easily subsumed under the category of "nostalgia film," which Fredric Jameson has identified as a dominant form in postmodern cultural production.[1] At least, it would have to be a different kind of nostalgia from that practiced by cinema, one that takes advantage of a specifically televisual made of production that allows the historical material of the older narrative forms to be recast precisely as a series of stories whose very shape and scale can change in the telling. It would reflect a nostalgia not only for the objects of a given style gathered into various period ensembles or "moments"—which are typically synchronic frames—but for the dynamic of style itself, the buzz that comes from things happening, replayed as an inexorable process of errant metamorphosis. As a result of this historical drive, *Crime Story* must force itself through several different cataclysms so that it can reset its narrative gears and restock the environment with stubborn signifiers of the past.

In the beginning, *Crime Story* measured time in several registers at once. There is a generational time marked by conflicts within organizations (criminal and legal). On one side, the old ethnic identities of the gangsters are supplanted by the corporate identity of the next generation; on the other side, the old-style cops come under the control of federal technocrats of the RFK stamp. The time scale is inscribed in surrounding spaces, as the dark alleyways and glittering sky-lines of Chicago give way to the neon frenzy and desert stretches of Las Vegas. (In another code: from Mies to Venturi.) Old, inhabited space becomes new, kinetic space: Torello moves from a high-rise apartment building to a motel, and Luca moves from a neighborhood social club to an immense casino. Of course a whole layer of glaring historicity informs the clothes, the cars, and the background music.[2] In spite of all the momentum built up in the move to Vegas, the official time of the story remains 1963, as if this whole range of uneven developments, ruptures, and displacements could be compressed into a brief fictional sequence. "Our 1963 never really existed," said Michael Mann, the show's executive pro-ducer, neatly summing up what goes without saying.[3]

Already in the first season, another kind of time scale—what I call generic time—begins to frame the other elements. At various points, the "story" in *Crime Story* crosses through various postwar fictional genres, allowing their distinc-tive character types and story patterns to take over and run their course. Generic events—the big heist, the civil rights trial, the car chase, the hostage standoff—are established within a limited rhythm and duration; by the same token, larger generic paradigms—the hardboiled detective investigation, the reporter's cru-sade, the deposing of a crimelord—can be defined by the way they pace the exchange between transgression and punishment. *Crime Story* cites all of these generic traits and more, treating them as historical artifacts in their own right, a sequence of limit-situations that the main characters live through and over-come on the way to some other fate. Thus there must always be time tags in the operation of a generic presentation: first, if it will work at all it must operate at once, so that its point of departure is as conventional and familiar as possible; then, unfolding, it may offer divergences that break the chain of expectations holding the paradigm together. (This is why the notion of a genre always implies an improbable contract between visible images on one hand and a hypothetical public memory on the other.) In *Crime Story*'s multilayered generic time, his-torical periods (specifically the Forties and Fifties) are reconstructed through their own narrative conventions, only to be then dismantled. Characters are killed off and situations are wrecked without completing their distinctive des-tinies, foreclosing certain narrative options when their animating energies, hopes, and struggles have become obsolete.

The shifting from one time scale to another gathers speed toward the end of the first season: as Luca's crimes mount, so does Torello's determination to bring him down. In the season's final episode (broadcast before the network had decided whether to renew the series), the vicious cat-and-mouse game leads to a nighttime shootout on the Vegas strip. But just when the whole story seems to come down to a one-on-one battle to the death, Luca is rescued by his side-kick Pauli Taglia. There is a freezeframe of Torello on his knees in the street, shooting wildly. Then it is daybreak, Luca and Taglia are in a shack in the desert. Luca, wounded but beginning to relax, notices a marking on the furniture:

GROUND ZERO. He shouts at Taglia, they scramble out the door, and begin to drive away—then a white flash on the screen and stock A-bomb footage rolls until the closing credits. This image of the A-bomb blast raises several interpretive possibilities, some of them false starts or dead-ends. All questions about the meaning of the image have to be suspended until we know whether the story will continue.

With the prescribed enactment of justice blocked, events shift to a level beyond the moral economy of the story up until that point. The bomb blast is both an arbitrary, accidental fate and a reminder of some vast and terrible order of events that (for the moment) remains obscure. it breaks several contextual frames at once: the generic traits, the symbolic scale, the contested scene of action. From a crime story to a cynical apocalypse: the series casts a black comic negation over its whole course up to that point.

But how final could any such "conclusion" be? Can this image, because of its "extremity," seal the story? An absolute end would mean that the series halted itself by turning its historical project into an eschatological one.[4] If only the blast is big enough, the story would really be over, a genuine end would be imaginable above and beyond mere resolutions and score settlings. Certain political and religious scenarios would be confirmed as never before. Insofar as any moral reading of this episode, even a cynical or oppositional one, relies on this closure to seal a meaning, the image of the Bomb must also spell the halt of televisual representation: nothing else must happen, no other event or image can join the story and send it in a new direction. Interpretation would have to know how to stop itself at just the right moment, turn off the television, and appeal to some other authority, some other narrative. If the bomb blast seems to insist on the possibility of finishing a story, it does so in the name of something else, something outside the televisual domain, something like a non-narrativizable History. I am not yet speaking of the logic of nuclear deterrence, which as Derrida points out also speaks in the name of something else, "that which is worth more than life, that which, giving its value to life, has greater value than life."[5]

For the image of the Bomb has its own history. It has functioned in the global rhetoric of deterrence as an absolute simulation, a perfect and whole replacement for apocalypse. It is the image of an impossible end, an end without end, an end that waits. The image preserves not so much a memory of a past event (testing) but the prospect of a future one (aggression): indeed, it was not the effectiveness of the bomb being tested in the desert, but the effectiveness of the images of the Bomb. And so, even while they evoke a long tradition of apocalyptic discourse, the images also speak an undeniable realism: we (the audience, the world) need to believe that an atomic bomb destroys utterly whatever happens to be under and around it. Only through that belief and this fear can armament and disarmament take place. And if we believe there is any truth to the nuclear image, *Crime Story* must now be finished. Ray Luca, like Hiroshima, Nagasaki, Bikini, and elsewhere, becomes a sacrifice to the "reality" of nuclear weapons, yet again attesting to the possibility of representing that reality.

If, on the other hand, Ray Luca could survive that explosion, if the image of Luca in one instant can be distanced from the image of the mushroom cloud in the next, if that image does not refer always to the end of all lives and all stories, if it is possible for the show to continue, then televisual narrative proves that it can survive even the Bomb (if only for a second). After all, the image of destruction will always be insufficient to destroy anything: it can appear only on the way to destruction, or on the way toward an end. It is only through certain linkages, especially narrative ones, that this image can come to serve a strategy (like all images, it can never speak for itself). To reproduce this image in a story without end is to reserve the threat of finality within the power of visuality. Nuclear deterrence operates through deferral of an end, just as narrative deferral of closure deters the stabilization of meaning: both share the same kind of inertia.

Yet in an unexpected way, *Crime Story* reinstates a claim to history through its stylized evocation of the end of history. By risking its story in the cultural imaginary of doom, the show reintroduces historical distance at the crucial moment. turning apocalypse itself into an item of nostalgia. Note that the key images of the explosion are in fact "historical" footage. In its day, it was possible for such footage to signify (ironically and iconically) the end of the world (as in *Dr. Strangelove*) or just the end of the story (as in *Kiss Me Deadly*). For us this scrap of footage refers also to that moment—precisely, 1963—when an image of the end could still have been imagined as the final one. Once the apocalyptic tone has been struck and surpassed, the sense of ending becomes merely formal, and the enclosure of the past dissolves into the openness of the present.

Undaunted by Luca's fate, the network (NBC) renewed *Crime Story* for another season. After several episodes, Luca and Taglia are revealed to be alive and recovering from their radioactive burns in Mexico. Luca tells his boss, Manny Weisbord, that the blast has changed him. He is "only looking at big pictures now. International enterprise, that's our future, Manny. Governments become our partners. We go worldwide." Out of the atomic flames, Luca has been reborn as the very soul of neocapitalism. He no longer acts as an individual force; rather, he becomes a nexus, variably passive and reactive, almost an empty relay point in a vast power system, the managing angel. This functional transformation of Luca corresponds to another generic switch. The movement from street hoodlum to organized crime boss goes only so far (as *Bugsy* shows); there remains another story, another tier that reaches from organized crime to multinational enterprise legitimated and served by political power. The site of criminality migrates from urban neighborhoods to enterprise zones to offshore operations. from onscreen to off. Luca and Weisbord no longer just skim the till in Vegas or operate a national telecom bookie scheme: they ship weapons to "insurgents" in Guatemala, bringing back drugs for the American market. The weekly narrative no longer keeps up with the details of the criminal schemes. Now the only course of progress or continuity—and a very slow and stubborn one at that—belongs to the cops. As the story approaches the present, its trajectory begins to lose the sharp turns of historical fiction, taking on the force of an unstoppable fate.

Nowhere is this divergence of history and story more apparent than in an episode titled "Femme Fatale," in which Luca tries to help an agent from the People's Republic of China secure uranium for an H-bomb, in exchange for permission to fly smuggling planes in and out of the Golden Triangle. In the course of the episode, the deal is foiled, severing the expected connections to the historical "facts" of the Chinese bomb and American drug smuggling operations in Southeast Asia. By allowing the logic of episodic narrative to obstruct the unfolding of a more or less "established" history, *Crime Story* refuses to offer a reassuring "secret history" (the way familiar things "really happened") but instead selects and rearranges diverse historical elements in a structure of possibilities, thereby producing combinations that range from the historically necessary to the transitory lost chance. But "Femme Fatale" is overdetermined in another way: the episode has its own generic reference points and visual style distinct from other episodes in the series. It happens that the Chinese agent is a young woman who suddenly appears on Torello's doorstep in distress, shadowed in seductive foreboding. That is the least of the clues: each element of the storytelling apparatus participates in a complex reconstruction of film noir. The first half of the story unfolds through Torello's weary voiceover narration, just up until the point where Luca's plan to hand over the uranium fails, the woman's deception is revealed, and the storyline veers towards an espionage thriller. The logic of conflict shifts all at once: hazy emotional attachments are overwhelmed by resolute national allegiances. More remarkable, however, is the episode's color texture: through manipulation of the light and color levels, the scenes have exactly the look of a black and white film that has been colorized. Neither a simulation of film noir in black and white nor a remake done with the full lushness of the contemporary palette, the "look" of this episode suggests that the representation of history has become essentially a matter of translating images from earlier media technologies into later ones.

In the case of television, such representation can be a matter of rewriting images from one part of the programming matrix into the terms of another, so that images thought to belong to the immediate present (news reports) are displaced into an explicitly fictionalized and historicized framework. *Crime Story* produces this echo effect by making television part of its (hi)story. As the second season winds down, Torello orchestrates a televised Senate hearing, where he hopes to embarrass government officials into confessing their connections to Luca. But the wall of complicity appears unassailable, and one witness after another refuses to crack. The déjà vu may be overwhelming—everything recalls the Iran-Contra hearings, detail by detail, which had occupied the screen less than a year before this episode aired. The parallels are played out until Colonel Danz, the Oliver North link in Luca's drugs-for-arms trade, blurts out the whole story. Torello is about to obtain indictments for Luca's gang, and all at once this becomes a utopian version of the 1980s: in the spectacle of a hearing, the bright clarity of the images, and the distilled moment of revelation, the Sixties quiver and evaporate. Suddenly history, or at least the history of American foreign policy, appears disconcertingly cyclical: that time Guatemala, that time Laos, this time Iran, or Iraq, or Guatemala all over again. A structure of allusion, operating on the level of images but tagged by proper names, sketches an elliptical political memory. Except for one new element: the cycle will now be broken, the crimes will be admitted and judgment handed down at last—an imaginary resolution to real corruptions.

At just this moment, just when *Crime Story* almost produces a televisual narrative of historical justice, another kind of televisual history overtakes it, precisely the history of television as a spectacular disruption. The hearing is dramatically interrupted by an announcement: "The North Vietnamese have fired on our ships in the Gulf of Tonkin." Everybody rushes from the room. There will be no climax, no verdict. Torello and his crew look bewildered. "Vietnam?" What's that?

It is not Vietnam that halts the narrative, it is television, or more precisely, a specifically televisual event. In submitting itself to this moment of chaos, *Crime Story* dramatizes the birth of media politics and media history: the original force of television is revealed in the way one media event can interrupt another, the new event randomizing the old horizon of references and suspending the procedures of truth. Now, instead of offering a mimetic proximity to current events, a dense historical distance drops down, punctuated only by television's faulty memory of itself. On that plane, the pre-Vietnam moment is literally prehistoric, before television assumed the task of producing a constant stream of instant history To situate all of *Crime Story* back then, back when this prolonged televised horror had not yet begun, is to dispel all of its accumulated historical resonance, sending it back to another era. Vietnam, a dreadful future collapsed to the intensity of a single moment, cuts off the narrative drive, stopping it far short of the present and moving the story elsewhere.

Yet the second season does not end here: Luca and his entourage fly to an unnamed Latin American country, where he quickly takes direct control of local drug production, deposes the president, and installs his own puppet leader. Torello and his men follow, seeking a more or less illegal kind of vengeance. The scene is a composite Third World where power is exercised according to different rules—which is, after all, what is supposed to define the otherness of the place. But the change of scenery is neither a "return" to some prior stage of history, nor an escape somewhere "outside" the force field of the United States. On the contrary, this path is the logical opposite of any judicial resolution: now the story follows the genealogy of the "crime," a chase back along the chain of production to expose the general social arrangements that support the criminal enterprise pyramid. A reverse movement like this, however, carries a cost: the characters who perform the "return" become disposable as soon as their purely figural function has been exhausted. Luca and Torello can appear as opposing structural elements only as long as they remain at their stations of individualized power; once they surrender those sites of economic concentration and political command, they no longer serve as significant participants in the "story" they have carried this far. Their fate thus becomes a matter of purely generic interest once the genuine "crime story"—now revealed as the gradual but aggressive creation of a new criminal/capitalist world order—has reached its triumphant completion with the commercial recolonization of the Third World. Any genuinely unclosed historical narrative will always dissolve the privilege of its fictional representatives by returning them at last to our common fate, oblivion and death, so that the drift of historicity can be attached to other figures. So it goes with Luca and Torello: when we last see them, they are fighting hand-to-hand in a plane that crashes into the ocean. Nothing depends on them any longer: even if they were to "survive" this perfect cliffhanger, they would have to be miraculously reconstructed and repositioned before they could again serve as bearers of this story. But they will not survive. The network numbers have long since doomed them.

More explicitly than most, but no more totally than any other, this series projects its historical materials into televisual rhythms. It advances fitfully over the breaks of transmission, turning its moments of suspense and temporary closure into emblems of an uneven historical time. *Crime Story* mobilizes a vast matrix of historical devices—iconic, temporal, textural—to bring various chronologies into instant adjacency. if on one plane televisual texts are always cutting each other up, on another level they all become figurative extensions of each other. Thus any text duplicates the work of television as a whole, which can only ever produce an image of history as an assemblage of dissembled distances from the instantaneous present. Televisual flux emits a new kind of History—jumbled, familiar, open—which is never yet *ours*.

NOTES

1. See Fredric Jameson, "The Existence of Italy," *Signatures of the Visible* (New York: Routledge, 1990), esp. 217–29; also "The Cultural Logic of Late Capitalism" and "Nostalgia for the Present," in *Postmodernism: or, the Cultural Logic of Late Capitalism* (Durham, N.C.: Duke University Press, 1991), esp. 19–25.

2. On-screen music offers a different twist: when Luca and Abrams listen to Miles Davis in a club, they do not hear the late-bop Miles of the early sixties, but the wrinkled electric Miles of the late eighties, who happens to be right there in the smoky lounge, looking even more like a time traveller than usual.

3. " 'Crime' Pays on City Streets," Kay Gardella, *New York Daily News*, August 20, 1987. Mann is best known for the television series "Miami Vice," which introduced the word "nihilism" into the lexicon of television reviewers, and the film *Thief*, another allegory of crime and capitalism that exposes the anarchist underbelly of the American Dream myth.

4. For more on apocalypse, catastrophe and television, see Patricia Mellencamp, ed., *Logics of Television: Essays in Cultural Criticism* (Bloomington: Indiana University Press, 1990), especially the essays by Meaghan Morris, Margaret Morse, Mary Ann Doane, and Patricia Mellencamp. See also Joyce Nelson, *The Perfect Machine: TV in the Nuclear Age* (Toronto: Between the Lines, 1987).

5. Jacques Derrida, "No Apocalypse, Not Now (full speed ahead, seven missiles, seven missives)," trans. Catherine Porter and Philip Lewis, *Diacritics* 14:2 (Summer 1984), 30. Also see "On an Apocalyptic Tone Recently Adopted in Philosophy," trans. John P. Leavey, Jr., *Oxford Literary Review* 6 (1984). There Derrida raises the question that an apocalyptic horizon hangs above the "program" of the West.

Taylor Downing

History on Television:
The Making of *Cold War,* 1998

The first point to make about history on television is that there is a lot more of it about today than ten or twenty years ago. This article argues that through the medium of television, history documentaries have come a long way—that history on television has come of age and a generation of "television historians" have emerged. I will also explain a little about the background to the making of *Cold War,* a major series that is of special interest to readers of this journal.

There are some magnificent examples of history film making that precede the television era, for instance two pioneering compilation films Esther Schub made in the Soviet Union in the late 1920s, *The Fall of the Romanov Dynasty* and *The Great Road.* During World War II, history was used by most combatants in the production of propaganda films to justify the wartime struggle—in propaganda terms most effectively by Frank Capra and his team in the *Why We Fight* series. In the postwar era there were some outstanding historical documentary films, such as Alain Resnais's *Night and Fog* and *Hiroshima Mon Amour.* However, overall, the small number of these historical documentaries is striking—and this is not referring to historical dramas or period melodramas, which have been popular since the early days of the cinema. This is referring to the historical documentary, usually a compilation using news film or newsreel as its source material. Indeed, to make a point, Jay Leyda's study of the compilation film *Films beget Films* is a very slim volume indeed—little more than a hundred pages.

Interestingly, Jay Leyda's study of the historical compilation film was first published in 1964—the year in which history documentaries on television really began to take over from history documentaries made for the cinema. In the United States, the long-running NBC series *Victory at Sea* was a landmark project that had already rated highly; in Britain, in 1964, the BBC produced the first of the history mega-series for television, *The Great War*—twenty-six episodes to mark the fiftieth anniversary of the outbreak of World War I and to help launch a new channel in Britain—BBC2.

The Great War set the tone for the heavyweight television history documentary—a rousing title sequence with dramatic music, a powerful commentary

Reprinted from *Historical Journal of Film, Radio and Television* 18:3 (August 1998), by permission of Carfax Publishing.

sonorously read by Michael Redgrave, the dramatic use of archive material and the selection of hardhitting, firsthand testimony from eyewitnesses and survivors. Moreover, the archive film was, for the first time in a popular television series, step-printed to slow down the action from the silent speed at which most of it was shot to the sound speed at which all the film was then run. This device meant that people walked, moved and went over the top at normal speed rather than at the jerky and slightly silly speed which was associated then with the slapstick of the silent cinema.

Although *The Great War* showed the strengths of this type of television, it also illustrated its weaknesses. For instance, the film makers freely intercut feature film footage with the limited documentary material actually shot at the front. And, to heighten the drama, they felt the need to ensure that the British, French and allies should always advance left to right, whilst the Germans, Austrians and the other side should always advance right to left—so whenever the material did not record the action this way it was flopped over, in order not to confuse the audience!

On British television, *The Great War* remained a high spot of historical documentary making for a decade. Although there were one or two other documentary series, they lacked the impact of *The Great War* and the simple fact remains that there was not much television history on the small screen.

In the mid-1970s came *The World at War*. This time it was not good old "Auntie" BBC who told people what to think about the past, but their supposedly down-market, brash, commercial rivals, Thames Television. Not only did *The World at War* win immense critical acclaim (it won awards galore and the honour of being recommended by teachers and academics) and not only was it so popular with audiences that it has been repeated almost continuously ever since (on cable in the United States, as soon as it finishes its 26-week run, it starts showing again), but it also made stacks of money for Thames Television. It has been continuously bought by broadcasters throughout the world for more than twenty years. *The World at War* demonstrated that history on television could be high quality, attract a large popular audience and make a great deal of money. After *The World at War*, the rest, as they say, is history.

The World at War established the classic pattern for history television—the breaking up of historical events into smaller, accessible story-lines that can be well told using archive film and interviews with eyewitnesses. This will occasionally be supplemented by the use of location shooting to establish atmosphere and to fill a gap where archive film did not exist.

Today on British television there is an abundance of history programming—although, it has to be said, rarely achieving the excellence of *The World at War*. Both channels of the BBC feature history programmes regularly. The latest major series from the BBC, *People's Century*, was first shown on the popular, mass-market channel, BBC1. The ratings for the BBC's history flagship series, *Timewatch*, frequently make it one of the top factual strands on the minority channel, BBC2. Channel 4 includes history programming at all times of the day and night—one-off documentaries, regular strands like *Secret History* and countless series. As if all this is not enough, there is a channel on the cable and satellite service, BSkyB, devoted to nothing but history. The very existence of The History Channel, transmitting several hours a day, it could be argued, is evidence that television history has grown up. There is enough programming to run a schedule day after day, week after week, month after month, with nothing else. The programming is, in the main, of good quality. And people watch it.

This growth of television history is not, of course, a uniquely British phenomenon. History programmes sell throughout the world. And as the end of the century approaches, there are more in production now than ever before. The History Channel in the United States, which is the parent of the United Kingdom channel, currently has an extraordinary 43 million subscribers—and it is still growing. Siblings of this parent history channel, owned by the Arts and Entertainment Network, are to be found in Brazil and France and will soon hit the screens in Italy, Germany and Scandinavia. In addition, in the United States, the public broadcasting stations, most notably WGBH in Boston and KCET in Los Angeles, but many others besides, have produced some superb history programmes over recent years despite the cutbacks and funding crises in the public broadcasting sector. In Europe there has even been a fund, financed through the Media Programme from Brussels, offering independent producers across Europe loans to develop history programmes (Memorie Archiv Programmes [MAP-TV], based in Strasbourg). What more powerful illustration can there be of the acceptability of television history than the existence of a Brussels Euro-fund?

In some ways, of course, the spread of television history reflects the popularity of factual programmes in general. Despite the dire predictions of those who have been saying for decades that the "documentary is dead," there are more hours of documentary on British television today than ever before. Some of these additional hours are in the cheap and cheerful world of the specialist satellite and cable market. Here there has been a growth of niche channels devoted to subjects such as motoring, food, leisure and computing as well as history. The Discovery Channel as a stand-alone, factual channel has carved its own distinctive place in the scheduling map. Discovery Communications (including the American, European, and Asian arms) is now the largest single producer of documentaries in the world.

But if this profusion of television history is good television, it begs one central question—is it good history? At the heart of most historical documentaries is archive film. Probably everyone reading this has their own story about what can be called the "horrors of the howlers"—archive film that has been misused so appallingly that it is difficult to take anything in the programme seriously after that. Jerry Kuehl has written extensively about this. He has some marvellous stories to tell. One of my favourites is the film of the sinking of the Austro-Hungarian battle-cruiser, the *Svent Istvan*. This unfortunate ship was sunk on 10 June 1918 in a hit and run raid by Italian torpedo boats. The dramatic shots of the hull keeling over and of sailors running to escape across the sinking hull, was taken by an escort vessel. These images are used to illustrate countless episodes at sea—from the battle of Jutland to Pearl Harbor. It might be suggested that there should be an IAMHIST award given for the most "creative" use of the footage of the sinking of the *Svent Istvan*!

History programmes that rely upon the use of archive film certainly bring their own problems. What people have chosen to point their cameras at over the last 100 years are not always the things that today are regarded as significant. And if there is no archive footage of something, does it mean that the subject cannot be covered by television historians? There are countless examples. For instance, only now is it becoming apparent how vital was the work of the code breakers and the decypherers at Bletchley Park just outside London, in winning the war. There is virtually no authentic archive film to illustrate this hush-hush, supremely top secret work. Another example, at the core of the Arab-Israeli conflict, is the flight of nearly 750,000 Palestinians in the spring and summer of 1948, many of them expelled from their homes at the time of the creation of the state of Israel. There is no archive film of this tragic refugee exodus. In a third example, it is now known how the North Korean leader, Kim Il Sung, pleaded with Stalin to let him invade South Korea for two years before Stalin finally gave the go-ahead in the spring of 1950, unleashing the Korean War. There is no archive film to illustrate these secret meetings and the intense diplomatic activity between Pyongyang and Moscow.

Does this mean that producers of history programmes cannot deal with subjects such as the intelligence war, the history of the Arab-Israeli conflict or the causes of the Korean War? Do not believe this is the case. It is an obvious point, but archive film is only one ingredient in the mix that goes into a history programme. There is a serious flaw in the argument that history made for television has to rely exclusively upon archive film—otherwise the logic would be that there could be no television history on subjects before the early twentieth century. Ken Burns showed in his epic series *The Civil War* how marvellously creative it is possible to be with a supply of faded photographs, a cache of letters, and a few good songs. Producers have to be inventive. More and more programmes which combine archive film and talking heads (the classic duopoly of television history) extend the use of location filming into simple reconstructions to create a sense of an event—feet walking down a corridor inside a government building, fingers tapping on a typewriter, officers looking out from the bridge of a ship. This should not be a problem—as long as reconstructions are clearly labelled as such. The producer who intercuts reconstruction with archive film and pretends there is no difference between them is as flawed as the producer who claims that a shot of an Austro-Hungarian battle-cruiser sinking in June 1918 is in fact HMS *Repulse* or the *Prince of Wales* being sunk by the Japanese air force off the coast of Malaya in January 1942. Some facility houses can now generate telecine scratches on specially shot film to make it look like decaying archive film. This might be amusing in a commercial for beer, but it most certainly will not do in a proper history documentary.

There is a strong belief that there is much fascinating footage that has never been reused since it was originally shot, edited and screened. New footage, in the words of the ubiquitous Television History Press Release, is constantly being "discovered." For instance, a few years ago there was an upsurge of interest in home movies. Some marvellous programmes were made. *Cinememo* was a European-wide collection of films using amateur footage. The series helped give birth to INEDITS, the European Association of Amateur film. And, in Hungary, the films of Péter Forgács used home movies in an extraordinarily powerful way to paint a picture of the gulf between the public and private faces of a people living under communism. Recent programmes in Britain on the cultural history of food, the social history of the motor car and the history of the secretary in the workplace have all been archive-based series that have used new and unusual archive film in a challenging, fresh way. One look at *Footage: The Worldwide Moving Image Sourcebook* (1997) will show just how many extraordinary films there are available that have not been reworked by television historians.[1]

"The power of the image" is something television historians have the ability to use which most academic historians rarely take advantage of. It can be argued that the image can convey a multitude of meanings and, in the detail of dress, uniform, facial expression and attitude, can help give understanding to an event in a completely different way to that of a dozen documents. The central role of all historians in using documents to establish an understanding of the past cannot be denied. What could be said is that historians frequently undervalue the "power of the image" to capture the mood, atmosphere and attitude of a moment in time. And, of course, in newsreels, public information films, works of propaganda or television newscasts, film frequently not only captures an impression of what an event looked like but gives a topical and often revealing interpretation of that event, which is, in its own way, a historical document itself. Television historians must use the image accurately and sensitively but when used intelligently and effectively it can have the impact of 1000 words.

The other element in the conventional "duopoly" of television history is, of course, what television makers call "the talking head." Historians have rightly been suspicious of oral history as a means of understanding past events. Memories can only too easily become blurred with the years—it is surprising how many rosy accounts of wartime experiences are heard about events that must have been sheer hell to live through at the time. And, of course, oral history can easily be used to argue a point of view, present a selective account of an event, give a partial interpretation or even deliberately mislead. But, of course, the same could be said about any personal letter, diary or memoir. And historians are perfectly accustomed to dealing with them. Oral history needs to be used carefully and intelligently and since the 1970s historians have increasingly come to realise how personal testimony, when used critically, can contribute to an understanding of history. The large oral history seminars and conferences that have been set up in recent years to consider events such as the Cuban missile crisis or the war in Vietnam, with policy makers from both sides recounting what they were thinking and doing at the time, have revealed fascinating new insights into how and why events unfolded the way they did.

Television historians too often use interviewee recollections uncritically—there is no doubt of this. However, when used intelligently, with a personal account of going over the top at the Somme, arriving by train at Auschwitz, being in the room when Stalin met Mao Tse Dung, or hearing Kennedy's speech in the main square in Berlin in June 1963, the memories of these moments can powerfully convey an account of an event with impact, emotion and with levels of meaning that no one should ignore. Television historians must be aware of the need to question the memories of their interviewees; nothing should be taken as gospel. Many television historians do interrogate the evidence they record from oral history and use it intelligently to convey a powerful impact about past events. It is possible to see, on all channels and in great abundance, programmes in which the ubiquitous "talking heads" are used with power and effect to help understand not only what it was like to live through events (itself a perfectly honourable historical objective) but also how and why events were shaped the way they were.

Cold War 1998

One of the biggest television documentary history series in production at the present time is the *Cold War* series. *Cold War* is being produced by Jeremy Isaacs Productions for Turner Broadcasting and the BBC. It is due for screening in the United States and Europe in the autumn of 1998. The *Cold War* series is the brainchild of Ted Turner himself. The story goes that he was at the closing ceremony of the Goodwill Games in Leningrad in 1994, when he first had the idea of making a major series about the history of the Cold War. Ted Turner's all-time favourite historical documentary series is *The World at War,* of which he is a passionate admirer and he instructed his head of production to contact the man who had made *The World at War* and to tell him to make the *Cold War* series. The executive producer of *The World at War* was Jeremy Isaacs. He had gone on to a distinguished career in British television, as controller of programmes at Thames Television and then as founder and chief executive in the early 1980s of Britain's Channel 4 Television. His Channel 4 was and remains one of Britain's most unique cultural achievements. However, by the time Ted Turner's people contacted him he had left the world of television and was doing something far more difficult—he was running the Royal Opera House in Covent Garden. The task of trying to reconcile the impossibly conflicting problems of lack of public money with the demands of one of the world's finest opera houses, was captured in the fly-on-the-wall documentary series *The House,* which was recently shown in both Britain and the United States.

When Jeremy Isaacs was tracked down in Covent Garden, he initially expressed no interest whatsoever in returning to television. However, slowly he was persuaded that the challenge of turning the Cold War into a television history series was irresistible—a series covering nearly fifty years of world history that we have all just lived through and which in one way or another has affected all our lives. He gathered a small group of historians, programme makers and writers together to brainstorm in his office every Friday evening and to kick around different ideas for ways of making a series about the Cold War. The brief from Ted Turner was simple—to tell the full story of the Cold War, not just as a confrontation between two superpowers but how it went on to affect science, the space race, sport, culture and most of the world and not to present the history in any way as a triumphalist celebration of America's final victory in the Cold War.

With this in mind, Isaacs's concept for *Cold War* was to tell the history chronologically rather than thematically, so that, over a long run of programmes covering so many decades, the viewer would know where he or she was in history and to break the subject into episodes, each one of which could be viewed as a self-contained historical story. For the viewer who stayed with the series, each programme would, like building blocks placed one around another, add more and more to an overall understanding of the years of the Cold War.

During this development phase, whilst ideas were formulating, the team were privileged to hear the views of three great historians who became the central panel of advisors for the series—John Lewis Gaddis, one of the most prominent American historians of the Cold War, now at Yale; the brilliant young Russian historian Vladislav Zubok, who is at the forefront of opening up the archives of the former Soviet Union; and Lawrence Freedman, who runs the Department of War Studies at Kings College in London. Episodes of the series would later benefit from the contributions of several other distinguished historians, such as David Ellwood, whose knowledge of the rebuilding of Europe in the late 1940s greatly helped the making of the episode in *Cold War* on the Marshall Plan. The series also benefited enormously from the wholehearted support and assistance of the Cold War International History Project based at the Woodrow Wilson International Centre in Washington, D.C. Students of the Cold War have been helped by the project's pioneering work in getting into the archives of not only the former Soviet Union and the East European countries, but also their work in China and Vietnam. This research has enabled historians to reassess and rework their understanding of much of the Cold War. In addition the National Security Archive in Washington, D.C. supported *Cold War*, where, again, fantastic work has been done in prying material out of the U.S. Government archives and in rewriting the narrative of the Cold War in the light of the abundant new evidence that is available.

On the *Cold War* series, the team established close working relationships with their historical advisors. They saw and commented on the initial treatments, rough cuts, fine cuts and commentary scripts for each and every programme. A great deal is being learnt from them. At the end of the development phase of *Cold War*, a detailed outline was submitted to Ted Turner explaining how the team wanted to approach the subject. Most people on the broadcast side know how long it takes television organisations to make decisions about commissioning major projects. Not only is there an important editorial commitment to make, but there are the slots in the schedule to be found and, of course, the money to be raised. A countless range of television executives and planners have to be brought into the decision-making loop. So, it was expected not to hear from Ted Turner for many months. However, Jeremy Isaacs received a call from Ted Turner after only nine days, committing Turner Original Productions to the entire project and instructing him to put a team together and to start production in a matter of weeks. Never in the history of television production has so much been committed by so few, so quickly. Production offices were found and a team started work, led by Martin Smith, the immensely experienced documentary maker who also had acted as consultant to the setting up of the permanent exhibitions at the National Holocaust Museum in Washington, D.C. Later, at a memorable dinner in Atlanta, Ted Turner insisted that Jeremy Isaacs make more than the original 20 programmes and the series was finalised at 24 episodes.

The film researchers on *Cold War* found an astonishing array of new footage which it is hoped will surprise, shock and enchant when the programmes are screened. New colour footage was discovered of events that before now had only been "seen" in black and white. Stunning images from the former Soviet and East European archives, ranging from experiments in rocket technology to scenes of Muscovites going shopping or Poles playing cards on the sidewalk, provide a revealing insight into the lives and conditions of millions of citizens denied the luxuries of consumer goods taken for granted in the West. Early television material that even the American networks did not know they had, along with public films capturing the anti-Red fervor in American society that have somehow slipped through the net of the National Archives in Washington, were also found.

The programme researchers obtained interviews with not only those who themselves shaped events, such as American presidents and senior officials and top Soviet and European officials, but also with those who lived through events. Interviews have been recorded with people who witnessed walls going up or down, who fought in armies or guerrilla organisations, who served in government agencies or in private companies, who watched events and felt frightened for themselves and their children or who shared in the triumphs and tragedies of 45 years of the Cold War. Altogether, there is approximately six hundred hours of videotaped interview material recorded for *Cold War*.

What this paper has tried to argue is that television history has now achieved great popularity on terrestrial channels and has a long shelf-life in the cable and satellite markets. Companies such as Turner Broadcasting who have not been in the history business before are now commissioning new history programming. The History Channel is seen in nearly one-third of all homes in the United States. In Britain and Europe, there are more history programmes on television than ever before. Many people around the world who will never pick up a history book will derive most of their views about the past and about life in a century that is nearing its end from television programmes. Television history has indeed grown up. There is an awesome responsibility on those inside the world of television production to produce programmes to the highest and the most rigorous standards. The veracity of personal testimony must be constantly examined and archive documents—film and photographs either as stock shots or as original recordings—be used rigorously. This is what must be done if television history is to be taken seriously. There is now a generation of television historians who approach their documents with rigour and with specific critical skills that have been built up over the last couple of decades. In the next phase of the future of television history, the pressure will be on to reduce budgets and cut comers. The highest possible historical standards must be maintained. This is the continuing challenge for the producers of television history—the television historians.

NOTES

I am grateful to James Welsh and Salisbury State University, Salisbury, Md., for making possible this paper which was first delivered as the keynote address at the July 1997 IAMHIST Congress.

1. Rick Gell, Editor in Chief, *Footage: The Worldwide Moving Image Sourcebook*, 195 (New York: Second Line Search, 1997), Fax 212-787-3454; e-mail: footage@filmclip.com.

Gary Edgerton

Ken Burns's Rebirth of a Nation: Television, Narrative, and Popular History

Striking a Responsive Chord

I don't think [the story of the Civil War] can be told too often. I think surely it ought to be retold for every generation.
— Ken Burns, 1990[1]

It's been nearly four years since the phenomenon of *The Civil War* premiered over five consecutive evenings (September 23–27, 1990), amassing a level of attention unsurpassed in public television history. Ken Burns's 11-hour version of the war between the states acted as a kind of lightning rod for a new generation, attracting a spectrum of opinion that ranged from rapturous enthusiasm to milder interest in most segments of the viewing public, to outrage over Yankee propaganda in a few scattered areas of the south, to both praise and criticism from the academy.[2] Burns employed twenty-four prominent historians as consultants on this project, but understandably, not all of these scholars agreed with everything in the final series. With so many experts, and with a subject the size and scope of the Civil War as the historical terrain, a certain amount of controversy was unavoidable.[3]

One historian even concluded his analysis of *The Civil War* by calling the series "a flawed masterpiece," thus evoking the customary judgment of D. W. Griffith's *The Birth of a Nation* (1915) that's been repeated in literally dozens of general film histories over the past fifty years.[4] This analogy only goes so far, however, making more sense on the grounds of shared cinematic brilliance than because of any similarities in outlook and sensibility. Indeed, one of Burns's stated intentions was to amend the "pernicious myths about the Civil War from *Birth of a Nation* to *Gone with the Wind*," especially in regards to racial stereotyping and the many other bigoted distortions in plot and imagery.[5]

Still *Birth of a Nation* and *The Civil War* were similarly indicative of mainstream public opinion during their respective eras. For example, Russell Merritt

From *Film and History* 22:4 (December 1992). Reprinted with permission of the editors.

has argued convincingly that the racist aspects of *Birth of a Nation* were anything but the ravings of some "isolated crackpot," but rather representative of white America at the time. According to Merritt, Griffith "attracted his audience . . . because the drama itself was one . . . Americans wanted to see."[6] As a result, *Birth of a Nation* was embraced by an estimated ten percent of the U.S. population in its original release, making it the preeminent box-office success in silent film history.[7]

The widespread reaction to *The Civil War* was likewise lavish and record-setting. The initial aim of this essay, in fact, is to examine the unprecedented response to this series, focusing specifically on why *The Civil War* struck such a spirited chord with a contemporary mass audience. A second and related priority, moreover, is to analyze Ken Burns's approach to doing history, assessing both the historiography of *The Civil War* as well as the filmmaker's relationship to the practices and goals of traditional scholarship. More than anyone before him, Ken Burns has transformed the historical documentary into a popular and compelling form through the apt though unexpected forum of prime-time television.

The Public Broadcasting System actually achieved its highest ratings when 39 million Americans tuned into at least one episode of *The Civil War,* averaging more than 14 million viewers each evening.[8] Interestingly, the viewership "skew[ed] older, male and upscale," while nearly half the audience would not have been watching at all if it had not been for this program.[9] These inclinations were also reflected in the range of published responses to *The Civil War,* even including political pundits who rarely, if ever, attend to the opening of a major motion picture or television series. George Will, for example, wrote: "Our *Iliad* has found its Homer . . . if better use has ever been made of television, I have not seen it."[10] David Broder and Haynes Johnson weighed in with similar praise.[11]

Film and television critics from across the country were equally effusive. *Newsweek* reported "a documentary masterpiece"; *Time* "eloquen[t] . . . a pensive epic"; and *U.S. News & World Report* "the best Civil War film ever made."[12] David Thomson in *American Film* declared that *The Civil War* "is a film Walt Whitman might have dreamed."[13] Tom Shales of the *Washington Post* remarked: "This is not just good television, nor even just great television. This is heroic television."[14] And Monica Mullins of *The Boston Herald* informed her readers that "to watch 'The Civil War' in its entirety is a rare and wonderful privilege." She then urged: "You have to keep in mind that the investment in the program is an investment in yourself, in your knowledge of your country and its history."[15]

Between 1990 and 1992, accolades for Ken Burns and the series took on institutional proportions. He won "Producer of the Year" from the Producers Guild of America; two Emmys (for "Outstanding Information Series" and "Outstanding Writing Achievement"); a Peabody; a duPont–Columbia Award; a Golden Globe; a D. W. Griffith Award; two Grammys; a People's Choice Award for "Best Television Mini-Series"; and eight honorary doctorates from various American colleges and universities, along with many other recognitions.[16] As Burns remembers,

I was flabbergasted! I still sort of pinch myself about it . . . it's one of the rare instances in which something helped stitch the country together, however briefly, and the fact that I had a part in that is just tremendously satisfying . . . I don't really know how to put my finger on it. A generation ago as we celebrated, or tried to celebrate the centennial, we seemed focused on the battles or the generals, and the kind of stuff of war, but here we seemed to respond to the human drama and maybe it just resonated in a particular way with how we are. I feel a tremendous sympathy for this country and somewhere along the line that sympathy must line up with where we are now and whatever the subject is.[17]

The Civil War became a phenomenon of popular culture. The series was mentioned on episodes of *Twin Peaks, Thirtysomething,* and *Saturday Night Live* during the 1990–1991 television season. Ken Burns appeared on *The Tonight Show;* and he was selected by the editors of *People* magazine as one of their "25 most intriguing people of 1990." The series also developed into a marketing sensation as the companion volume by Knopf, *The Civil War: An Illustrated History* became a runaway bestseller; as did the accompanying Warner soundtrack and the nine episode videotaped version from Time-Life.

The Civil War has continued to fascinate Americans for more than 130 years. James M. McPherson, the 1988 Pulitzer Prize–winning author of *The Battle Cry of Freedom* estimates that the literature "on the war years alone . . . totals more than 50,000 books and pamphlets."[18] Reader interest had actually been increasing in the five years preceding the debut of *The Civil War;* 520 of the 1,450 titles that were still in print in September 1990 had only been published since 1986. After the premiere of the series, however, fixation with the war became "higher . . . than it has ever been."[19]

Several interlocking factors evidently contributed to this extraordinary level of interest, including the quality of *The Civil War* itself, its accompanying promotional campaign, the momentum of scheduling Sunday through Thursday, and the synergetic merchandising of its ancillary products. Most significantly, though, a new generation of historians had already begun addressing the war from the so-called "bottom-up" perspective, underscoring the role of African-Americans, women, immigrants, workers, farmers, and common soldiers in the conflict. This fresh emphasis on social and cultural history had revitalized the Civil War as a subject, adding a more inclusive and human dimension to the traditional preoccupations with "great men," transcendent ideals, and battle strategies and statistics. The time was again propitious for creating another rebirth of the nation on film which included the accessibility of the "bottom-up" approach. In Ken Burns's own words, "I realized the power that the war still exerted over us."

Shelby Foote was the first contemporary writer to liken the Civil War to the *Iliad* in the third volume of his trilogy, *The Civil War: A Narrative* (1974); and his intent was to emphasize how "we draw on it for our notion of ourselves, and our artists draw on it for the depiction of us in the same way that Homer and the later dramatists—Aeschylus, Sophocles, Euripides—drew on the Trojan war for their plays."[20] Much of the success of Ken Burns's *The Civil War* must be equated in kind to the extent to which his version makes this nineteenth century conflict immediate and comprehensible in the 1990s. The great questions of race and continuing discrimination, of the changing roles of women and men in society, of big government versus local control, and of the individual struggle for meaning and conviction in modern life, all remain. The Civil War fascinates because its purposes continue; Americans are as engaged as ever in the war's dramatic conflicts. As Burns summarizes,

> there is so much about *The Civil War* that reverberates today . . . a developing women's movement, Wall Street speculators, the imperial presidency, new military technology, the civil rights question and the contribution of black soldiers . . . there are also approximations and that sort of thing. You have to cut stuff out. I would have loved more on the congressional sort of intrigues during the Civil War. I would have loved to do more on women and more on emancipation and more on Robert E. Lee and more on the western battles, but limitations of photographs or just time or rhythm or pacing, or whatever it is, conspired against those things. And they were there, but they were taken out to serve the demands of the ultimate master, which is narrative.

The Filmmaker as Popular Historian

Television has become more and more the way we are connected to the making of history.
—Ken Burns, 1992[21]

Academia has taken away the idea that the word history is mostly made up of the word story. . . . I would like to suggest that television can become a new Homeric mode. What other form would allow such powerful emotions of the war to come forward, would allow you to follow the spear carriers as well as the gods?
—Ken Burns, 1990[22]

Narrative is a particular mode of knowledge and means of relaying history. It is a historical style that is dramatic and commonly literary, although *The Civil War* does indicate that it can be ideally adapted to film and television as well. In selecting the Homeric mode, Ken Burns drew certain narrative parameters which are epic and heroic in scope. The epic form tends to celebrate a people's national tradition in sweeping terms; a recurring assertion throughout Ken Burns's filmic history is how the Civil War gave birth to a newly redefined American nation. The final episode, "The Better Angels of Our Nature," for example, begins with three commentaries on nationhood which rhetorically sets the stage from which the series will be brought to its rousing conclusion:

> Strange is it not that battles, martyrs, blood, even assassination should so condense a nationality.
> —Walt Whitman

It is the event [the Civil War] in American history in that it is the moment that made the United States as a nation.

—Barbara Fields

Before the war it was said the United States are, grammatically it was spoken that way and thought of as a collection of independent states, and after the war it was always the United States is as we say today without being self-conscious at all—and that sums up what the war accomplished: it made us an is.

—Shelby Foote

These remarks are then immediately followed by the bittersweet and tragic lament that serves as the series's anthem, "Ashokan Farewell," thus reinforcing the overall heroic dimensions of the narrative. Heroism, honor, and nobility are related Homeric impulses that permeate this series, shaping our reactions to the "Great Men" of the war, such as Abraham Lincoln, Frederick Douglass, and Robert E. Lee, along with the many foot soldiers whose bravery often exceeded the ability of their officers to lead them, resulting in the appalling carnage recounted in episode after episode.

The series's most celebrated set piece, in fact, the eloquent and poignant voiceover of Major Sullivan Ballou's parting letter to his wife before being killed at the first battle of Bull Run (and again accompanied by the haunting strains of "Ashokan Farewell"), foregrounds why there has been a degree of criticism lodged at *The Civil War* by some professional historians. This scene, which lasts approximately three and one-half minutes, concludes episode one, "The Cause," thus rendering the preceding 95 minutes with an air of melancholy, romance, and higher purpose. Poetic license is used throughout the scene, as Ballou's declaration of love is heard over images that have nothing factually to do with Sullivan Ballou, but evoke the emotional texture of his parting sentiments, including photographs of the interior of a tent where such a letter might have been written; a sequence of pictures portraying six other Civil War couples; and three static filmed shots of Manassas battlefield as it looks today in a pinkish twilight.

The impact and effectiveness of this section, entitled "Honorable Manhood," was apparent immediately as Ken Burns recalls:

> Within minutes of the first night's broadcast, the phone began ringing off the hook with calls from across the country, eager to find out about Sullivan Ballou, anxious to learn the name of Jay Ungar's superb theme music ("Ashokan Farewell"), desperate to share their families' experience in the war or just kind enough to say thanks. The calls would not stop all week—and they continue still.[23]

Several historians, in contrast, took a closer and more analytical look at the Ballou letter, raising serious questions about its authenticity, and the number of different versions that do indeed exist. Burns himself expresses

> [Poetic license] is that razor's edge between fraud and art that we ride all the time. You have to shorten, you have to take shortcuts, you have to abbreviate, you have to sort of make do with, you have to sometimes go with something that's less critically truthful imagery-wise because it does an ultimately better job of telling the larger truth, but who is deciding and under what system becomes the operative question.

Here Burns raises the two fundamental differences between his own approach to documentary film structure as history and the goals of more critically-based historians. First, Ken Burns is more concerned with the art of storytelling than detailed accuracy, although he is careful and meticulous in marshaling the "facts" of history as his stated goal of capturing an "emotional truth" warrants. He continues:

> the historical documentary filmmaker's vocation is not precisely the same as the historian's, although it shares many of the aims and much of the spirit of the latter. . . . The historical documentary is often more immediate and more emotional than history proper because of its continual joy in making the past present through visual and verbal documents.[24]

Second, Ken Burns is not as self-reflexive about historiography as the professional historian. He is aware that there are "systems" to history, but there are times when he is chided for stressing narrative instead of analysis.

> I am primarily a filmmaker. That's my job. I'm an amateur historian at best, but more than anything if you wanted to find a hybridization of those two professions, then I find myself an emotional archeologist. That is to say, there is something in the process of filmmaking that I do in the excavation of these events in the past that provoke a kind of emotion and sympathy that remind us, for example, of why we agree against all odds as a people to cohere.

At first blush, this final statement might appear to confirm the assessment offered in a 1992 *American Quarterly* essay, "Videobites: Ken Burns's 'The Civil War' in the Classroom," which suggests that "'The Civil War' stands as a new nationalist synthesis that in aims and vision can be most instructively compared to James Ford Rhodes's histories of the Civil War (written at the end of the nineteenth and in the early twentieth centuries)."[25] A 1991 appraisal in *American Historical Review* similarly takes the filmmaker to task:

> Burns used modern historical techniques, at the level of detail and anecdote, to create an accessible, human-scale account of the Civil War. But, when it comes to historical interpretation, to the process by which details coalesce to make events meaningful, *The Civil War* is vintage nineteenth century.

The severity of these judgments is encapsulated by the same author in a final dismissal: "[*The Civil War*] is the visual version of the approach taken by generations of Civil War buffs, for whom reenacting battles is a beloved hobby."[26]

Historical documentaries should certainly be subject to evaluation and criticism, especially if they are to be viewed by audiences of tens of millions on television or in theaters, and subsequently used as teaching tools in our nation's schools. *The Civil War*, for example, was licensed after its premiere telecast to over sixty colleges and universities for future classroom use; and Ken Burns reports that he's "received over 6,000 letters and cards from secondary school teachers alone, grateful for the series, pleased with how well it works."[27] There

is clearly a responsibility to assess any film being employed for educational purposes to such a widespread degree. Both of these articles, in fact, do raise important questions of interpretation and detail that are useful and edifying. It is a
welcome development that historians are increasingly attending to the validity
of films and television programs.

These reviews, on the other hand, concurrently demonstrate the academy's
longstanding and persistent tendency to underestimate yet another motion picture or television series which, in turn, shortchanges *The Civil War* as a classroom supplement. One of the primary goals of scholarship is to create new
knowledge and be "cutting edge." No more thorough indictment exists, according to this frame-of-reference, than to reject a text for its obsolete conception
and design; in this case, banishing it to the dustbin of the nineteenth century. *The
Civil War*, however, deserves a more measured examination than merely being
dismissed as the stuff of "Civil War buffs."

In his widely acclaimed book, *That Noble Dream* (1988), Peter Novick has
skillfully examined the controversies that have fundamentally affected the historical discipline over the last generation.[28] Current debates continue in the
literature and at conferences over the relative merits of narrative versus analytic
history, synthetic versus fragmentary history, and consensus versus multi-
cultural history. Lawrence Levine suggests that all of these historiographical
exchanges make

> sense only when it is seen as what, at its root, it really is: a debate about the extent
> to which we should widen our historical net to include the powerless as well as the
> powerful, the followers as well as the leaders, the margins as well as the center,
> popular and folk culture as well as high culture.[29]

The Civil War is similarly a product of this intellectual climate. In this
respect, it is not enough to focus exclusively on the eleven hours of *The Civil
War* without also considering Ken Burns's ideological bearings alongside the
scope of his "historical net." This more comprehensive unit-of-analysis does,
in fact, reveal fragments of a nationalist approach to historiography as the afore-
mentioned reviewers suggest. *The Civil War*, moreover, evinces elements of the
romantic, progressive, "new" social history, and consensus schools as well. As
Burns explains,

> in narrative history you have this opportunity, I believe, to contain the multitude
> of perspectives. You can have the stylistic, and certainly my films have a particu-
> lar and very well known style. You can involve yourself with politics, but that's not
> all there is. And that's what I'm trying to do, is to embrace something that has a
> variety of viewpoints.

The Civil War is essentially a pastiche of assumptions derived from a number of schools of historical interpretation. As just mentioned, the series is nationalistic in its apparent pride in nation building, but without the nineteenth
century arrogance that envisioned America as the fulfillment of human destiny,

The Civil War is romantic in its narrative, chronological, and quasi-biographical structure, but it lacks the unqualified, larger-than-life depictions of the unvarnished "Great Men" approach. *The Civil War* is progressive in its persistent intimation that the war was ultimately a struggle to end slavery and ensure social justice, although this perspective too is tempered by passages, such as Barbara Fields's assertion in the final episode that the Civil War "is still to be fought, and regrettably, it can still be lost."

The Civil War is also informed by social history with its attention to African-Americans, women, laborers, farmers, and especially firsthand accounts in each of the nine episodes by two common soldiers (Elish Hunt Rhodes, a Yankee from Rhode Island, and Sam Watkins, a Confederate from Tennessee), but the series is nowhere near as purely representative of the "bottom-up" view as are the "new" histories. In Burns's own words, "I try to engage, on literally dozens of levels, ordinary human beings from across the country—male and female, black and white, young and old, rich and poor, inarticulate and articulate."[30]

What Ken Burns is annunciating is the liberal pluralist perspective where differences of ethnicity, race, class, and gender are kept in a comparatively stable and negotiated consensus within the body politic. Consensus history is marked more by agreement than is the multicultural or diversity model which grounds the "new" social history. The preservation of the Union, and an emphasis on its ideals and achievements, are fundamental to consensus thinking; they are also some of Burns's primary themes throughout *The Civil War:*

> It's interesting that we Americans who are not united by religion, or patriarchy, or even common language, or even a geography that's relatively similar, we have agreed because we hold a few pieces of paper and a few sacred words together, we have agreed to cohere, and for more than 200 years it's worked and that special alchemy is something I'm interested in. It doesn't work in a Pollyannaish way . . . we corrupt as much as we construct, but nevertheless, I think that in the aggregate the American experience is a wonderful beacon . . . and I think the overwhelming response to *The Civil War* is a testament to that.

Rather than being ideologically stuck in the nineteenth century, Ken Burns and the audience for *The Civil War* are instead very much of the 1990s. The tenets of liberal pluralism have understandably been challenged and qualified in the academy since the mid-1970s, but the consensus outlook remains the most prevalent view on the streets of contemporary America. Popular metaphors, such as the "quilt" or the "rainbow" or to a lesser degree, the old-fashioned "melting pot," are still widespread images used by public figures across the political spectrum to evoke a projection of America that is basically fixed on agreement and unity, despite whatever social differences may exist. By realizing this outlook on film, Ken Burns has, moreover, usurped one of the foremost goals of social history, which is to make history meaningful and relevant to the general public. *The Civil War* brilliantly fulfills this objective as few books, or motion pictures, or television series, or even teachers, for that matter, have ever done.

The Historical Documentary and the Academy

My job is to convey history to people. No film, however
well done, can ever replace that task.
—Barbara Fields, 1990[31]

We have begun to use new media and new forms of expres-
sion—including films and television—to tell our histories,
breaking the strangle hold the academicians exercised over
this discipline for the last hundred years.
—Ken Burns, 1991[32]

The mutual skepticism that sometimes surfaces between the historian and the historical documentary filmmaker is understandable and unfortunate. Each usually works with different media (although some professional historians now make films and videotapes); each tends to place a dissimilar stress on the respective roles of analysis versus storytelling in relaying history; and each tailors a version of history which is designed for disparate though overlapping kinds of audiences. These distinctions are certainly real enough. Still the scholar and the filmmaker, the professional historian and the amateur, complement each other more than is sometimes evident in the expressions of suspicion, defensiveness, and even on occasion, scorn, that are too often apparent in published remarks.

Ken Burns's *The Civil War,* for example, conveys some genres of knowledge better than books or lectures ever will, such as the empathetic and experiential aspects of history that are generally communicated best through the electronic media (or in a much different way on field trips); Burns's series render the people of the 1860s accessible to contemporary audiences in a direct and intimate way. As the filmmaker explains,

> we wanted you to believe you were there . . . there is not one shot, not one photo-
> graph of a battle ever taken during the Civil War. There is not one moment in which
> a photographer exposed a frame during a battle, and yet you will swear that you saw
> battle photography. . . . You live inside those photographs, experiencing a world as
> if it was real inside those photographs. . . . Once you've taken the poetry of words
> and added to it a poetry of imagery and a poetry of music and a poetry of sound, I
> think you begin to approximate the notion that the real war could actually get
> someplace, that you could bring it back alive.

Burns accordingly eschews detailed analysis by stressing "poetry and emotion" above all else. His series has a tendency to present contradictory points-of-view as if to suggest their eventual reconciliation in the renewal of America. Ken Burns has even stated that *The Civil War* was meant "to emphasize the story in history, avoiding the contentions of analysis."[33] In the "Was It Not Real?" segment of the final episode, for example, there is a montage of three commentaries presenting both corroborating and conflicting opinions about the lasting meaning of the Civil War. Barbara Fields, who previously had suggested that Lincoln was actually a moderate on the issues of race in comparison to his contemporaries, begins by observing that "the *slaves won the war* [my emphasis] and they lost the war because they won their freedom, that is the removal of slavery, but they did not win freedom as they understood freedom."

Next James Symington provides a different slant on the issue by declaring that "the significance of *Lincoln's life and victory* [my emphasis] is that we will never again enshrine [slavery] into law," while affirming Fields with "let's see what we can do to erase . . . the deeper rift between people based on race . . . from the hearts and minds of people." Stephen Oates then ends this section by shifting the focus to the survival and triumph of popular government, ending with the assertion that the Civil War is "a testament to the liberation of the human spirit for all time." Oates's conclusion has little to do with the specific substance addressed in the previous statements by either Fields or Symington, although coming where it does, his testimony cannot help but soften the references to racial injustice that preceded it.

More importantly, this specific sequencing of remarks establishes the liberal pluralist consensus: in other words, different speakers might clash on certain issues (such as what degree of freedom was actually won in the Civil War and by whom), but disagreements ultimately take place within a broader framework of agreement on underlying principle. In this case, the larger principle is Oates's evocation of popular government, which is understood to guarantee the democracy and human rights needed to eventually eradicate racial inequality and disharmony. Historical narrative, therefore, does not merely record what happens; it interprets events and shapes the presentation of the subject at hand.

Furthermore, this particular example illustrates that the historical documentary is not a particularly useful instrument for in-depth analysis (as opposed to scholarly publication or classroom discussion and debate, for instance). The expert testimonies and first-person reports that Burns employs do provide shifting angles-of-vision that sometimes agree and, at other times, differ and contrast with each other. These multiple voices, however, form a cultural consensus because of both the filmmaker's liberal pluralist orientation, and in Burns's words, "the power of film to digest and synthesize."[34]

The limitation of the liberal pluralist perspective resides in its belief and aspiration that all outlooks and disagreements are ultimately reconcilable in consensus. As Ken Burns proposes,

> we have begun to speak of a synthesis of the old and the new histories, a way to combine the best of the top down version, still inspiring even in its "great man" addiction, with the bottom-up version, so inspiring too at times, with the million heroic acts of women, minorities, labor, ordinary people.[35]

In contrast, new historians, social and ideological, would argue that the "Great Men" and "bottom-up" approaches are fundamentally incompatible since any combining of the two perspectives is destined to be incomplete and uneven. The Achilles' heel of liberal pluralism is the way that it subordinates all differences, such as race, class, ethnicity, and gender, to a consensus which in the end preserves the present power relations in society essentially as they are. Some groups do indeed benefit from current conditions, while other subordinated constituencies are left silent and outside the supposed consensus. In this way, *The Civil War* does have its limits in interpretation, but its strengths as a teaching tool far outweigh any weaknesses.

By any standard that has gone before, *The Civil War* is a masterful historical documentary. Its liberal pluralist framework can serve as a topic for discussion and analysis, along with the multiple responses that a classroom full of students are bound to have to the series or one of its episodes. In many ways, Ken Burns is the ideal filmmaker for this period of transition between generations, bridging the sensibilities of the people who came of age during World War II along with his own frame of reference as a babyboomer. He agrees that his perspective was shaped by both

> the fifties and sixties because I think that maybe all of that stimulus from the centennial celebration of the Civil War, to the mythology that still pertained, not only got fixed, but then got challenged in the sixties. And I think that those two things going in opposite directions, probably accounts for why we're all drawn to [*The Civil War*] right now.

Burns similarly contends, "the Civil War compelled me to do the film." enabling him to establish "a dialogue with the past." As Barbara Fields reminds us in the final episode of the series: "the Civil War is in the present as well as in the past." In this sense, at least, all history is contemporary. We can never escape our own time or set of ideological predispositions; and within this context, no one has ever done a better job of "bringing [the Civil War] back alive" to more Americans through the power and reach of television than Ken Burns.

NOTES

1. Matt Roush, "Epic TV Film Tells Tragedy of a Nation," *USA Today*, 21 September 1990, 1.

2. See Lewis Lord, "'The Civil War': Did Anyone Dislike It? *U.S. News & World Report*, 8 October 1990, 18; "Ken Burns," *People*, 31 December 1990–7 January 1991, 47; *Civil War Illustrated*, July/August 1991; and *Confederate Veteran*, January–February 1991, March–April 1991, and July–August 1991.

3. Some of the more prominent critiques of *The Civil War* focus on errors in detail, the way the series abridges the origins of the war and later the matter of reconstruction, and the condensing of other complex issues, such as policymaking and the formation of public opinion. For additional disagreements in interpretation, see Jerry Adler, "Revisiting the Civil War," *Newsweek*, 8 October 1990, 62; David Marc and Robert J. Thompson, *Prime Time, Prime Movers* (Boston: Little, Brown, 1992), 307; Jane Turner Censer, "Videobites: Ken Burns's "'The Civil War' in the Classroom," *American Quarterly* 44:2 (June 1992), 244–54; Ellen Carol DuBois, "The Civil War," *American Historical Review* 96:4 (October 1991), 1140–42; A. Cash Koeniger, "Ken Burns's 'The Civil War': Triumph or Travesty?" *The Journal of Military History* 55 (April 1991), 225–33; Hugh Purcell, "America's Civil Wars," *History Today* 41 (May 1991), 7–9; and Mark Wahlgren Summers, "The Civil War," The *Journal of American History* 77:3 (December 1990), 1106–1207.

4. Koeniger, "Ken Burns's 'The Civil War': Triumph or Travesty?" 233. Like many film scholars before him, Louis Giannetti writes, "Birth is a diseased masterpiece, steeped in racial bigotry," in *Masters of the American Cinema* (Englewood Cliffs, N.J.: Prentice-Hall, 1981), 67.

This critical ambivalence about *The Birth of a Nation* in general film histories dates back to Terry Ramsaye, *A Million and One Nights* (Now York: Simon & Schuster, 1926), Benjamin Hampton, *A History of the Movies* (New York: Covici, Friede, 1931), and Lewis Jacobs, *The Rise of the American Film* (New York: Harcourt, Brace, 1939).

5. John Milius, "Reliving the War Between Brothers," *New York Times*, 16 September 1990, Sect. 2, pp. 1, 43.

6. Russell Merritt, "Dixon, Griffith, and the Southern Legend: A Cultural Analysis of *Birth of a Nation*." In *Cinema Examined: Selections from Cinema Journal*, ed. Richard Dyer MacCann and Jack C. Ellis (New York: Dutton, 1982), 167, 175.

7. Ibid., 166.

8. "Learning Lessons from 'The Civil War,'" *Broadcasting*, 8 October 1990, 52–53; Richard Gold, "'Civil War' Boost to Docu Battle," *Variety*, 1 October 1990, 36; Bill Carter, "'Civil War' Sets an Audience Record for PBS," *New York Times*, 25 September 1990, C17; Jeremy Gerard, "'Civil War' Seems to Have Set a Record," *New York Times*, 29 September 1990, 46; and Susan Bickelhaupt, "'Civil War' Weighs In With Heavy Hitters," *Boston Globe*, 25 September 1990, 61, 64.

9. "CBS, PBS Factors in Surprising Prime Time Start," *Broadcasting*, 1 October 1990, 28.

10. George F. Will, "A Masterpiece on the Civil War," *Washington Post*, 20 September 1990, Sect. A, 23.

11. David S. Broder, "PBS Series Provides a Timely Reminder of War's Horrors," *Sunday Republican* (Springfield, Mass.), 30 September 1990, B–2; Haynes Johnson, "An Eloquent History Lesson," *Washington Post*, 28 September 1990, Sect. A, 2.

12. Harry F. Waters, "An American Mosaic," *Newsweek*, 17 September 1990, 68; Richard Zoglin, "The Terrible Remedy," *Time*, 24 September 1990, 73; and Lewis Lord, "The Civil War, Unvarnished," *U.S. News & World Report*, 24 September 1990, 74.

13. David Thomson, "History Composed with Film," *Film Comment* 26:5 (September/October 1990), 12.

14. Tom Shales, "The Civil War Drama: TV Previews The Heroic Retelling of a Nation's Agony," *Washington Post*, 23 September 1990, Sect. O, 5.

15. Monica Collins, "A Victory for 'Civil War,'" *The Boston Herald*, 21 September 1990, 43.

16. Ken Burns has received honorary degrees from the following eight institutions: LHD (hon.), Bowdoin College, 1991; Litt.D. (hon.), Amherst college, 1991; LHD (hon.), University of New Hampshire; DFA, Franklin Pierce College; Litt.D. (hon.), Notre Dame College (Manchester, N.H.); Litt.D. (hon.), College of St. Joseph (Rutland, VT.); LHD (hon.), Springfield College (Illinois); and LHD (hon.), Pace University.

17. Ken Burns, Personal Interview, 18 February, 1993. These comments by Ken Burns, and the many unfootnoted ones that follow, are from an extended telephone interview with the author.

18. James M. McPherson, *Battle Cry of Freedom* (New York: Oxford, 1988), 865.

19. Edwin McDowell, "Bookstores Heed Call on Civil War," *New York Times*, 1 October 1990, D10.

20. Shelby Foote, *The Civil War, A Narrative: Red River to Appomatox*, Volume 3 (New York: Random House, 1974), 1064; and Lynne V. Cheney, "A Conversation with . . . Civil War Historian Shelby Foote," *Humanities* 11:2 (March/April 1990), 8.

21. Ken Burns, "In Search of the Painful, Essential Images of War," *New York Times*, 27 January 1991, Sect. 2, p. 1.

22. Milius, "Reliving the War Between Brothers," 43.

23. Ken Burns, text of speech, "Mystic Chords of Memory," delivered at the University of Vermont, 12 September 1991, 14.

24. Cathryn Donohoe, "Echoes of a Union Major's Farewell," *Insight* 6:45 (5 November 1990), 54–55; and Susan Bickelhaupt, "Civil War Elegy Captivates TV Viewers," *Boston Globe*, 29 September 1990, 1, 5.

25. Censer, "Videobites," 245.

26. DuBois, "The Civil War," 1140–41.

27. Dylan Jones and Dennis Kelly, "Schools Use Series to Bring History to Life," *USA Today*, 1 October 1990, 4D; and Burns, "Mystic Chords of Memory," 16.

28. Peter Novick, *That Noble Dream: The "Objectivity Question" and the American Historical Profession* (Cambridge: Cambridge University Press, 1988).

29. Lawrence W. Levine, *The Unpredictable Past: Explorations in American Cultural History* (New York: Oxford, 1993), 5.

30. *"The Civil War:* Ken Burns Charts a Nation's Birth," *American Film* 15:12 (September 1990), 58.

31. Adler, "Revisiting the Civil War," 61.

32. Ken Burns, "Thoughts on Telling History," *American History Illustrated,* Volume 26, number 1, March–April 1991, 27.

33. Robert Hunto, "War Stories: Ken Burns' Epic-length *Civil War* Moves From the Home Front to the Front Lines In Its Exhaustive Coverage," *The Riverfront Times* (St. Louis, Missouri), July 11–17, 1990, 19.

34. Bernard A. Weisberger, "The Great Arrogance of the Present Is to Forget the Intelligence of the Past," *American Heritage* 41:6 (September/October 1990), 99.

35. Burns, "Mystic Chords of Memory," 6.

Shawn Rosenheim

Interrotroning History:
Errol Morris and the
Documentary of the Future

Truth isn't guaranteed by style or expression.
Truth isn't guaranteed by anything.

—Errol Morris

Is there hope for television's representation of history? The answer to this question may at first seem obvious, for television has probably never been more intensely bound up with the representation of historical events than in the last few years. In 1991, for example, Ken Burns's twelve-part *The Civil War* became the most widely watched show in the annals of PBS, and the video of the series sold millions of copies. With its mawkish score and star-driven narration, I take *The Civil War* as an example of the intellectual poverty of historical documentaries on television. Television has also played a complex role in the production of recent history. In the live broadcasting of the 1992 Los Angeles riots that followed the acquittal of police in the Rodney King–beating trial, television images of looting and burning became a feedback loop intensifying the events themselves. Local viewers were not only informed by live broadcasts, but, in ways unintended by the producers, were also spurred to action, told by implication where to go and what to do. Similarly, when O. J. Simpson was visually apprehended by helicoptered television crews following his white Ford Bronco, all three national networks forsook their scheduled programming to capture events as they unfolded. Despite broadcasters' attempts to maintain objectivity, here too the presence of television itself irrevocably altered events (would the L.A.P.D. have so respectfully followed Simpson's Bronco without the escort of the media?).

As historical representations, it seems clear that *The Civil War* and television coverage of such popular historical events as the Reginald Denny or O. J. Simpson trials are antithetically defective. In its manipulative way, *The Civil War* presents a romantic history that demands a continual empathy from its viewers. Caught in the trap of Burns's nostalgia, viewers feel, rather than think, the

From *The Persistence of History: Cinema, Television, and the Modern Event*, edited by Vivian Sobchack (New York: Routledge, 1996), pp. 219–234. Copyright © by Shawn Rosenheim. Reprinted with permission from the author.

meaning of the war, experiencing pity, fear, but above all, a self-congratulatory affirmation of loss and redemptive nationhood that ennobles Northerner and Southerner alike. The media frenzy over Simpson represents an inverse situation. Despite the massive television coverage (and such ancillary creations as the CNN interactive CD-ROM, *The People Versus O. J. Simpson*), the crime and its consequences have remained shapeless and badly told, as journalists have attempted to master the situation through repetition, meaningless updates, and mutual self-reference. Though such coverage was in its way often riveting, the reporting of Simpson's case only rarely interpreted the real issues of race, gender, and celebrity the case has raised. Due in no small part to the televisual ideology of presentness, the live coverage has often threatened to dissolve into a meaningless collection of factoids, stereotypes, and possible scenarios.[1]

But television need not only have to choose between and chronicle and sentimental myth. In what follows, I would like to consider such an alternative, a proposed documentary series which might fairly be described as *mentalité* TV. The weekly series analyzes not only what happened in particular criminal cases, but also the texture of historical experience that so frequently allows justice to be perverted or confused. Simultaneously modernist and postmodernist, the series—entitled *Errol Morris: Interrotron Stories*—insists on the importance of "what happened" even as it exposes normative histories as tissues of myth. The agent for such revelations is in large part an interviewing device called the Interrotron. Why this bit of technology should have such resonant historical implications will be the burden of this essay.

Here's how the pilot begins. (Since *Interrotron Stories* has not yet been aired, I will describe the opening of the first episode in some detail.) Lights up on a television studio. A chair is perpendicular to the viewers, facing a camera setup. To thrumming drums and horns, a man strides onto the set and sits. The camera pans right, past the cameraman, past another technician, to an identical camera and chair setup. Cut to a medium shot of the man—now visible as Errol Morris—peering at the snow on a video monitor and then to an asymmetrical shot of a television monitor, on which Morris's face appears. As Morris speaks, the camera cuts between tilting close-ups of his face, the monitor image, and its distorted, blue-black reflection on a perpendicular glass surface. "What do you do when someone kills somebody and there's nothing You can do about it? Where if you say anything, they may come to kill you, too. Where nobody cares. And nobody wants to know. Meet John Shows, the man who spent almost forty years hunting the killer. And meet Diane Alexander, the woman who finally heard the truth." As Morris says "the truth," the camera cuts to an extreme close-up of his right eye, the eyebrow raised in emphasis. The music builds to its climax. A logo: *Errol Morris: Interrotron Stories*. Cut to black.

Mixing high-tech studio interviews, news footage, and dramatic re-creations, the *Interrotron Stories* are designed to upset the prevailing conventions of reality TV. Although ABC, for whom Morris originally developed the series, has not yet purchased it, the network has paid for an additional pilot episode, as has Fox Television. (As this essay goes to print, Fox has just announced plans to air five hours of *Interrotron Stories* in the Fall of 1995.)[2] Morris's plan was to create a format based on his quirky sensibility, treating news stories ranging from national scandals to far more obscure incidents that engaged his imagination. Each episode was to be narrated wholly by participants in the case. Central to the series's conceit is the Interrotron, an interview device that allows subjects to look directly into the lens of the camera, instead of off to one side at an interviewer. Essentially a series of modified teleprompters, the Interrotron bounces a live image of Morris onto a glass plate in front of the interviewee, just as the director—"off in a booth somewhere, like the Wizard of Oz—addresses a video image of his subject. In the same way, interviewees respond to an image of Morris that floats directly in line with the camera. The result is "the birth of true first-person cinema," as subject and interviewer stare at each other down the central axis of the lens.[3] Such direct contact intensifies each interview: larger-than-life, chiaroscuroed faces stare from the television with an unnerving intimacy, warily focused on the roving camera's lens. For Morris, "every look takes on a completely different significance. The inclination of the head suddenly takes on enormous dramatic power."[4]

On one level, the Interrotron is merely a gimmick, a device to give the series a memorable profile. The 1950s science fiction–sounding name recalls earlier instances of television auteurism, such as *Alfred Hitchcock Presents* and *Rod Serling's Night Gallery*.[5] Morris himself admits that he "still can't tell whether the Interrotron is a joke or something truly wonderful." But in either case, the Interrotron offers "one more technique in a whole arsenal of techniques that you can bring to bear on nonfiction," and one that provides a remarkable means for visually dynamizing on-camera interviews. The formal originality of Morris's filmmaking has always centered on his treatment of the interview. From his first film, *Gates of Heaven* (1978), Morris practiced a reticent style of interviewing designed to eclipse his relation to the camera. During interviews, most shot with a fixed-focus 25-mm Zeiss high-speed camera, Morris would sit listening with his head pressed to the side of the camera lens, interrupting his subjects as little as possible. The resulting sense of his subjects' effortless self-revelation was heightened by editing that removed Morris's questions, even as the filmmaker's invisible hand produced a foreboding sense of overdetermined worlds. The Interrotron refines this process, allowing Morris to dissolve completely into the cinematic apparatus, thereby closing the dynamic circuit between camera and viewer and intensifying the viewer's cathexis to the screen. The device intensifies the psychoanalytic valence of the film camera, operating as the equivalent of the impassive analyst in classical Freudianism.

We may take the Interrotron as an exaggerated figure for the documentarization of the world. Docudramas, The Discovery Channel, amateur pornography, *TV Nation*—as cable channels proliferate, one increasingly encounters forms of nonfiction programming.[6] Yet if the documentary camera is ubiquitous today, it is also less tethered to direct visual perception. Any number of miniaturized, digitized, or magnetic image technologies are shattering the Newtonian scale that has always dominated the cinema. *Interrotron Stories* demonstrates a social corollary of this fact, as we see that human relations, too, are deeply inflected by our reliance on machines. The truth it reveals is not an empirical claim about the world, but a social fact, produced by the interaction between the camera, the studio setting, and the interview subject. Faced with the lens's interrogative eye, most subjects feel pressed to fill the dead time with words until something surprising is unintentionally revealed. In *Interrotron Stories*, speeches are not relational acts between people, but between a subject and the film apparatus. The Interrotron's mediatory system of cameras and monitors qualifies the truth of direct vision, particularly when—as in the re-creations—such vision originates in odd, anxiety-producing angles, or epistemologically dubious points of view. Such effects are enhanced by the Interrotron's disturbing mobility. With their nervous, tilting cameras, misleading dramatic reenactments, and monomaniacal narrators, the completed *Interrotron* episodes produce an effect Morris likens to "a real-life *Twilight Zone.*"

Like the dioramic worlds built for *A Brief History of Time* (1992), the Interrotron is part of a shift in Morris's work toward extreme artifice. Just as Stephen Hawking and his friends and colleagues were filmed not in their real homes or offices but in imaginary domestic environments built on a London soundstage, so the idea for *Interrotron Stories* was "to bring people to Boston, construct sets in Boston, and do all of the interviews in studio."[7] Morris originally created the Interrotron out of a longstanding interest in "the possibility of being very, *very* close to someone, and see them speaking absolutely naturally, and yet directing their primary attention to the camera." Given his earlier filmmaking practice, such drastic close-ups were not possible, since they would have magnified the angle between the camera's lens and Morris's face, wrecking the cinematic illusion of first person address. The Interrotron was developed during a series of commercial shoots, working out the mechanics of the piece by trial and error (as a mark of his success, Morris is now hotly sought after by companies interested in the device's distinctive visual signature).[8] At first, the Interrotron work was "very much like all the interviews I've done in the past," with a static, locked-down camera. But then it gradually became apparent that "if I'm no longer seated next to the camera, the camera can really do anything," including panning, tilting, and clutching. The resulting material

> enabled interviews to be edited in a way I've never seen anything edited before. I could essentially put together a seamless piece of interview, that might have a hundred cuts in it. Obviously the cuts are there, but because everything is dutched with respect to everything else, you don't notice them. You have the benefit of montage without having to interrupt what someone's saying, or resorting to jump cuts.

The Interrotron represents Morris's version of Dziga Vertov's *kinoglaz*, a cinema eye that insists on the necessity of mediation and manipulation.[9] Morris enacts this through the constant iteration of eyes and unusual viewpoints and above all in the "dutching" of the series as a whole, which takes a canted approach to its own narration. Here, no authority asserts itself; no clear narrator emerges to resolve the truth of each episode. In this sense, the artifice of *Interrotron Stories* represents, if not *cinema vérité*, then the psychological *vérité* of cinema.

While the aesthetic implications of the Interrotron are interesting in themselves, they become even more so in light of the difficulties Morris has had getting *Interrotron Stories* on the air, suggesting the extent to which television circumscribes the possible relations of documentary to historiography. Having perfected his Interrotron technique, Morris shopped his series to various networks. At ABC, the director screened a rough cut of "Stalker," the story of a postal supervisor who was blamed when a former employee went on a murder spree in a Michigan post office. "People were just speechless," the filmmaker remembers. "I don't think anybody knew what to make of it." ABC ordered a pilot. But just as he was about to begin filming the final dramatic re-creations, the network's office of Standards and Practices issued a hold on the production, claiming it violated a policy not to film any subject in which litigation was pending.

With "Stalker" blocked, Morris was asked to submit new episode ideas. ABC picked "Digging Up the Past," a tale of the deathbed murder confession of an Alabama Klansman. Set in the past, it was plainly less risky material. Yet while Deborah Leoni, ABC vice president for Dramatic Series Development, described the show as "riveting," the series was not picked up, partly because of a conflict with *Turning Point*, a new ABC news show, and partly for fear that future episodes would raise similar legal tangles.[10] Leoni explained that while the news division is allowed to present particular points of view on current stories. "We weren't and aren't the News. We at Drama are not allowed that same liberty." "Interrotron Series"—true stories filmed to feel neither exactly like fact, nor exactly like fiction—was deemed too dramatic for news and too real for drama.

Morris next took *Interrotron Stories* to Fox, which ordered its own pilot, "The Parrot." Yet Fox also had difficulties in placing the series. Though Fox executives said that the problem was one of timing, according to Morris the real problem was the show's excessive novelty.[11] Television viewers, Morris remembers an unnamed Fox executive saving, "don't want twenty percent, twenty-five percent new. They want at most ten to fifteen percent new. Now what we have here, Errol, this looks to me like forty percent new. This might be even fifty percent new. There's just too much new here." The irony is striking: while certain of Morris's films, including *Gates of Heaven, Vernon, Florida* (1981), and *The Thin Blue Line* (1988), helped to invent reality programming, networks, threatened by the formal innovation of his series, left the filmmaker caught in a programming no-man's land.[12]

The debate over *Interrotron Stories* had less to do with Morris's choice of stories than with the stylistic ambiguity of their telling. By revealing the confusion, self-deception, and ambiguity clouding these murder cases, these episodes explicitly destabilize our perception of what counts as televisual history. To an audience used to the pieties of *The Civil War*, there is something troubling about the indeterminacy of these cases, particularly when the episodes invoke the finesse and closure of fictional TV programming. As Stu Smiley, a former Fox executive, puts it, the series represents "reality TV with a real dramatic narrative. It's reality as fiction. Which sounds crazy, but that's what Morris does best."

For all their interest in the bizarre and the grotesque, the *Interrotron* plots are the stuff of tabloids. "The Parrot" tells the story of Jane Gill, a penniless real-estate agent posing as a wealthy developer, who was apparently strangled by a business partner named as the beneficiary of her life-insurance policy. On its face an ordinary story of murder for profit, "The Parrot" turns unexpectedly when the defense produced as a key witness Max, an African grey parrot, who observed his owner's murder, and whose cries of "Richard! No! No! No!" were taken by the defense as evidence of the innocence of its client, Gary Rasp, and the possible guilt of Richard Mattoon, a close friend of Jane Gill. Morris further twists the tale by leaving open the question of the bird's evidentiary capacity. The audience remains unsure of whether the parrot's throttled "Richard! No!" represents a traumatic repetition of the murder or just a memory of the bird's previous owner reprimanding his two-year-old son.

"Stalker" recounts the celebrated case of Tom McElvaine, the fired Michigan postal worker who killed six of his fellow employees. It gives the story a surprise point of view, narrating the event from the perspective of Bill Kingsley, the killer's former supervisor, whose career was shattered after he was first stalked by the disgruntled McElvaine and then blamed by the press for pressuring McElvaine to violence. Kingsley is a brilliant natural narrator, who, seen in the tight close-ups Morris favors, fixes viewers with his stern, brooding eyes and hyperarticulate speech, as he recounts his story in a stream of words too fast to process. We tour Kingsley's face, shot against a series of scrims, too close for a comfortable televisual relation. The camera staggers and halts, stutters in panning across faces, as voices out of synch with the action precede or follow the images. Kingsley is an electronic Ancient Mariner, a troubled face staring out of the screen directly at our eyes, buttonholing viewers.

And then there's "Digging Up the Past," which recounts the alleged confession of a Klansman named Henry Alexander to the 1963 murder of Willie Edwards, a black truck driver from Detroit who was forced by four members of the KKK to jump from a bridge to his death. (Edwards emerges as a metaphorical cousin to Randall Adams, the man wrongly accused in *The Thin Blue Line*, another victim of malign chance. Having stopped his truck to buy a soda, Edwards—who was making his very first trip through the South—was mistaken for another man.) The drama of the episode develops out of gradual revelation of Henry Alexander's participation in the 1963 murder. This process of discovery culminates after Alexander's death, when, following his instructions, his wife Diane digs up a buried chest of Klan memorabilia, including yellowed clippings about the murder of Willie Edwards, thus bringing the crime to a partial, if extrajudicial, resolution.

In its re-creation of a racial crime from the height of the Civil Rights period, "Digging Up the Past" is the most historically situated of the existing episodes.

It is also a mosaic of different kinds of documentary evidence, including reproduced photographs, newspaper articles, location footage, and so on.

Interrotron Stories distinctively engages historical narration on four levels. The first two are long-established conventions of documentary film. First the series includes such familiar documentary images as photographs, newspaper articles, location footage, and other factual representations of aspects of the case at hand. Second, *Interrotron Stories* uses new documentary footage concerning the past, generated by the filmmaker through his interviews with subjects who participated in some way in the original narrative.

Third, *Interrotron Stories*, like *The Thin Blue Line*, also includes dramatic re-creations of events based on interview testimony. While such re-creations are anathema to most documentarians, Morris's willingness to incorporate such scenes suggests that he recognizes how what might be called a *tabloid* interest in dramatic verisimilitude and sensational representations of scandal forms a crucial element in the popular understanding of history. Here, too, *The Thin Blue Line* serves as Morris's model, because from its opening dissolves between maps of Dallas and aerial shots of that city, the film exploits the uncertain distance between events in the world and their documentary representations. As the record of an investigation into the trial of Randall Dale Adams, an out-of-town worker sentenced to death for the 1976 killing of a Dallas policeman, *The Thin Blue Line* powerfully indicates how, through their reluctance to prosecute a local teenager named David Harris, the Dallas police and judiciary effectively conspired to put an innocent man on death row. Crosscutting between a judge's memories of his father's work with the FBI and an old feature about Dillinger, Morris provides an objective correlative for the judge's thoughts, even as he shows how our impressions of guilt are filtered and shaped by the American media machine. Nor, as Morris recognizes, is *The Thin Blue Line* exempt from this same process of manipulation. The film's concluding scenes are built around a montage, combining David Harris's confession, his reminiscences of his brother (drowned at age three), and childhood photographs of Harris swimming with his brother, in which Morris seems to suggest that Harris's sociopathy stems from his guilty failure to save his sibling. But the artifice of these scenes (in their color coordination and repeated use of water imagery), like Harris's sense of being *prompted*, reveal psychoanalysis as just another model for making sense of Harris's life. Far from explaining the mystery of Harris's violence, these formal and thematic elements work to expose the audience's hunger for narrative logic and dramatic order.

Unlike *The Thin Blue Line*, however, *Interrotron Stories*'s fourth level of historical narration contextualizes all these different levels within the dialectical frame represented by Morris's opening and closing remarks, where he comments on the episode. While such commentary might initially sound like the naturalizing narrators of *911* or *Eyewitness Video*, by mixing Morris's direct address to the audience with his skewed, Max-Headroomish presence on the teleprompters, *Interrotron Stories* carries its dialectical use of narrative levels even into its surrounding framework.

The evidence mustered in "Digging Up the Past" functions both as an important element in Morris's thickly textured visual form, and as a baseline account of the story's presence in the world. But the evidence such documents provide quickly proves tainted or inconclusive. *Interrotron Stories* is built on the dissonance between the story told in the documentary record and that adduced by Morris's interview subjects in the present. Morris dramatizes Diane Alexander's story both through re-creations of the night on the bridge and by intercutting into his interviews reenactments of Alexander walking through the woods, digging, and then unearthing the chest. The metaphor of the buried past is old, even stale, with its implied archaeology of guilt as past crimes are brought into the light. In "Digging," Diane Alexander responds to the crisis of her husband's guilt first with her own grief, and then (in an excerpt borrowed from a *Donahue* show) in a scene in which Alexander meets and embraces Willie Edwards's widow, as tears stream down their faces. The dénouement seems familiar: social ills resolved through sentimental expiation, true to the form of daytime television.

But more is at stake in these reenactments than is apparent through a casual viewing. Despite the way that Morris's dramatic re-creations seem to conform to a cheesy televisual logic (the Klan members are cartoon backwoods racists, and the twangy. *Deliverance*-style banjoes of the score are used to signify "danger in the South"), all three episodes denaturalize their representations through excessive or anomalous camera work. As Willie Edwards jumps to his death, Morris cuts from a shot of the killers on the bridge to an underwater shot of Edwards's body knifing into the water, years later, when the body is discovered, the camera swoons blurrily toward the skull, its jaw yawed open in death. The very staginess of the KKK re-creations should remind us that these scenes are faked.

In "The Parrot," the audience is treated to a literal bird's eye view of the murder, as we watch Jane Gill through the parrot's green-tinted vision. Such an outlandish perspective is complemented by very intimate close-ups of the parrot's eyes: looking through the transparent lens of the bird's eyeball into the dark pool of the iris, we see the instrument of our seeing. There is a striking inverse relation between the hyperreal clarity of the bird's appearance and the filtered, tinted shots representing the bird's point of view—an implicit admission that the technologies of storytelling inflect the unverifiable rhetoric of narration. Like Morris's use of the stylistic *cinema verité* now ubiquitous in television, it is a way of keeping reality claims at bay—warding off presumptions to direct representation. Such shots belie the verisimilitude implicit in the bland, saturated color and high-key lighting that many of Morris's re-creations share with network television.

Further, the very staginess of the KKK re-creations should remind us that these scenes are faked. Like *The Thin Blue Line*, *Interrotron Stories* reveals its director's training as a former private investigator and as a graduate student of philosophy obsessed with issues of criminal evidence. In a procedure diametrically opposed to that of other reality shows, Morris uses his re-creations not to show "what really happened," but to illustrate the slipperiness of memory. Insisting that "such scenes are not *evidence* for anything," Morris employs his mini-dramas as "ironic commentaries" on his narrators, which call our attention to the fact that what we see may be a lie" or only one of many possible interpretations of an event. "If you use a reenactment, the main thing that you need to do is articulate to the audience right away that you're showing them a lie." Otherwise, documentary film is simply a way of easing the audience out of the work of interpretation.

In "Digging Up the Past," the reenactments are not literally false—Diane Alexander really *did* dig up the evidence of her husband's crime—but they are nonetheless misleading. That is because the episode isn't really about tracking down a smoking gun; it isn't really a tale about the locatability—and hence expiability—of guilt. Indeed, Diane Alexander's behavior in her interviews offers an object lesson in the structure of self-deception, as her common-law husband's power (Henry Alexander was a prominent local businessman) and her weakness conspire to corrupt the historical record. This logic of self-justification, in which only the victors are allowed to write history, comes to a breathtaking head when, as we listen to Diane Alexander's voice observe the similarities between Henry Alexander and Willie Edwards, Morris cuts from a shot of Edwards's decrepit wooden grave to Alexander's marble stone, prominently engraved with the single word "SAVED." The juxtaposition of the shots returns us to the realm of metahistory, as Morris's camera captures the way in which Henry Alexander used his wealth and racial privilege to rewrite his life into a fiction of Christian salvation.

Morris is drawn to murder cases because they precisely illustrate the limits of historical narration and the operations of law and justice. Murder investigations are, he claims, "a model of historical inquiry," and one which, postmodern narratology notwithstanding, has at its heart a concrete (if not necessarily knowable) set of events. In the words of Henry David Thoreau, "some circumstantial evidence is very strong, as when you find a trout in the milk."[13] Just so with murder: faced with a body shot in the back, one may generally presume a crime. Obviously, not all historical narratives can be definitely resolved: in the case of events dispersed in time and place, like the rise of Hitler or the sources of the Great Depression, no single explanation will be satisfactory or final. And even murder cases often turn less on a particular action than on the interpretation of motive and context: knowing who fired the gun, we still must ask about provocation, self-defense, and other extenuating circumstances.

Far from doing away with the difficulty of adjudication, murder cases reveal the stakes involved in the interpretation of seemingly unambiguous events. This approach is largely responsible for the curious mixture of stylistic elements within Morris's films. In their play of referential levels, frequent quotation and allusion, and lack of originating authority, Morris's films are thoroughly postmodern. Perhaps the most oddly memorable shot in *The Thin Blue Line* is an extreme close-up of a chocolate shake, thrown by a police officer caught off guard in her patrol car as her partner was shot down. Pirouetting slowly through the air, glopping heavily on the pavement, the shake partakes of a hyperreal post-modernity, mesmerizing us in excess of its status as an index of the police-woman's confusion. But the film's implicit hermeneutics mark Morris off as the last modernist, obsessively concerned with controlling his complex, ironic, but essentially coherent authorial intention. Morris's films are confident that there is a there out there: a world in which Randall Adams *or* David Harris killed the Texas state trooper, in which Gary Rasp *or* Richard Mattoon killed Jane Gill, but not one in which the problem can be given up with a shrug or by apportioning blame equally to everyone involved. The problem, the film and the series suggest, is that while an objective physical world does exist, we have no secure way of judging the way in which "the lenses that we are," to use Ralph Waldo Emerson's phrase, are warped, dirty, or otherwise flawed.

In *The Thin Blue Line* it seems necessary to grant Morris the validity of his old-fashioned claims to knowability and consequence. If that film holds up the police and legal systems for derision (on the grounds of their culpable self-deception) it is not a postmodern parable of the detective caught in his own web, in the manner of Paul Auster or Jorge Luis Borges. When the evidence (which culminates with a chilling taped confession by the actual killer) is properly researched and weighed—a task Morris undertook both in the film itself and in his own private researches—the conclusion that Adams is innocent becomes nearly unavoidable, and to attack it on rhetorical grounds ("What about the suppressed homoeroticism?" critics have asked, for example, as if the chance that Adams was cruising Harris made him complicit in the murder) is to collude with the Dallas authorities in sending an innocent man to jail.

The same logic holds true in *Interrotron Stories*. Sometimes, as in "The Parrot," Morris struggles to pack too much information and too many characters into the twenty-two minutes of each episode. But when the scale is right, as in "Stalker," whatever is lost in intricacy is made up by the vividness of these fables of miscarried justice. Although "Digging Up the Past" ends with the suggestion that Alexander died tormented by his crimes of long ago, this seems more a rhetorical convenience than a conclusion suggested by the evidence of the episode. The real story is not Diane Alexander's repudiation of her husband's past, but her own complicity. As Alexander recounts it, having heard suspicions of her husband's involvement in the crime, she "made a pact with God" that He would send a sign if Alexander was guilty. With no sign forthcoming, she went ahead with the marriage. It was, says Morris, "a pact with God to be self-deceiving," a kind "which I'm not sure you can find precedent for in the Bible."

Not only does Alexander's testimony reveal her convenient willingness to absolve her husband of his possible crimes but, as the episode makes clear, she is *still* protecting the last living member of the KKK posse involved in the murder, out of fear of retribution. Alexander's refusal to identify a certain Sonny Kyle Livingston as the fourth suspect explodes the sentimental conclusion which *The Donahue Show* and other journalists tacked on to Alexander's story. In Morris's version, by contrast, "the whole thin is really dreamlike. It's the ultimate faux-redemptive ending—the search for some overarching principle of justice or God." In his Interrotron coda, Morris directly involves the audience in the interpretation of the story just seen. Framed askew in the monitor, a video image of Morris's face asks: "What do *you* think? *Was* Henry Alexander ever punished for his crimes? Were there other people on the bridge that night? I'm Errol Morris, and this is *Interrotron Stories*. Good night, and [big smile] sleep well." Only the bad sleep well, Morris implies; despite Morris's own efforts and those of lawmen before him, Sonny Kyle Livingston still walks the streets a free man.

In its treatment of the Edwards murder, "Digging Up the Past" bears out Linda Williams's comments on Morris's filmic practice, that "while there is very little running after the action, there is considerable provocation of action." In *The Thin Blue Line*,

> The preferred technique is to set up a situation in which the action will come to [Morris]. In this privileged moment of *vérité* (for there finally are moments of relative *vérité*) the past repeats. We thus see the power of the past not simply by dramatizing it, or reenacting it, or talking about it obsessively (though these films do all this) but finally by finding its traces, in repetitions and resistances, in the present.[14]

In its direct address to the viewer, as in its refusal of external "expert" discourses (no judges or trial lawyers testify here), "Digging Up the Past" continues Morris's practice from *The Thin Blue Line*, where he requires his viewers to act for themselves as historical interpreters, detectives sifting the evidence not for a simple verification of guilt, but for the ramifying ways in which acts like Edwards's murder are written into the daily fives of those near the crime, rendering them, too, a part of its lies.

Though Walter Benjamin's "The Work of Art in the Age of Mechanical Reproduction" has long been a chestnut for film studies, just how much of the essay is concerned with the documentary value of film (what Benjamin calls "actuality") has gone relatively unnoticed. Benjamin brilliantly captures how the aesthetics of a documentary realism in film depends upon the effacement of technology: "The equipment-free aspect of reality here has become the height of artifice; the sight of immediate reality has become an orchid in the land of technology." For man today, Benjamin adds, "the representation of reality by the film is incomparably more significant than that of the painter, since it offers, precisely because of the thoroughgoing permeation of reality with mechanical equipment, an aspect of reality which is free of all equipment."[15]

Morris's series represents something like the fulfillment of Benjamin's prediction, where the permeation of mechanical equipment permits not the direct representation of reality, but the presentation of the *rhetoric* of direct reality. The series establishes a dialectical relationship between its opening sketch of the Interrotron, Morris's direct address to the audience, and the transparent realism of the re-created scenes that have effaced technology just as Benjamin has described. The interviews represent a median point between these modes, since although they provide the direct address to the audience by the "real figures," the illusionist lighting, the canting camera, and the swirling scrims behind the interviews remind us of televisual mediation. To his credit, this does not mean that Morris has sacrificed his films' claims on the world. The specificity of evidence he adduces and the way he puts his storytelling skills into the service of his version of each tale remind us that the peculiar charge of nonfiction filmmaking still lies in the privileged claims it can make about the world.

Interrotron Stories stands as both a symptom of and a response to the crisis now taking place within the domain of historical documentary. While postmodern historiography has long proclaimed the death of objectivist history popular culture now reflects this same conclusion in various ways, including the general loss of what might be called a historical sense. Yet historical fictions still matter, and increasingly these partake of documentary or pseudodocumentary modes of representation. Besides such resonant traditional documentaries as the PBS series *Eyes on the Prize* or Barbara Kopple's *American Dream* (1989), one can also name more formally innovative or personal films such as *Who Killed Vincent Chin?* (Renée Tajima and Chris Choy, 1988) or Michael Moore's *Roger and Me* (1989), to say nothing of the way that a filmmaker like Oliver Stone has adapted documentary rhetorics and styles in films as different as *Platoon* (1986), *JFK* (1991), and *Natural Born Killers* (1994). Stone has, of course, come in for a great deal of criticism for *JFK*, for the historical liberties he takes with his material, for his megalomania, and for his taste for conspiracies. Much of the hostility seems to have been generated by his freehand mixing of documentary, feature, and pseudo-documentary footage, as for example in his intercutting of Gary Oldman as Lee Harvey Oswald with real Oswald footage in such a way as to be almost undetectable without recourse to a videorecorder on slow. In a world in which large numbers of people will turn to films like *JFK* for much of their historical sensibility, Morris knows that it is pointless to ask for a stylistic purity or representational austerity in documentary filmmaking. Hence the Interrotron foregrounds the seductive and manipulative powers of the camera, even as the omnibus stylistic mixture of the *Interrotron* episodes becomes both a source of pleasure and a way of acknowledging the contingency of representation.

For many viewers today, I suspect that the epistemological and ethical distinctions between features and documentaries have almost completely dissolved. Raised on MTV's *The Real World,* this generation simply does not find the *propriety* of documentary rhetoric to be much of an issue. Which is another way of saying that the historical configuration of the documentary as, in Bill Nichols's admirable words, a "discourse of sobriety," of high-minded, voiced-over authority, may have largely come to an end.[16] While we cannot do without myths of history, *Interrotron Stories* suggests an alternative to the queasy sentimentalism and self-absorption that has characterized the television handling of such celebrated cases as Simpson's almost endless trial. Morris's series constitutes a remarkable double-critique of history, interrogating both the reductive accounts of human behavior offered by the popular press and the hegemonic accounts offered by *The Civil War* and kindred films, and leaving viewers instead with the uncertain testimonies of the filmmaker's subjects, struggling to understand their own and others' behavior—accounts that necessarily precede attempts to write grander social or national histories.

In the end, then, Morris is able to put the Interrotron to good social-historical use, because the psychoanalytical dimensions of the device are subordinated to the production of a *mentalité*-style history which refuses to treat traditional narrative histories as a natural category. The series represents a televisual analog to such works of cultural history as Carlo Ginzburg's *The Cheese and the Worms*, which recounts the life of Menocchio, the sixteenth-century miller who is ultimately executed for his blasphemous belief that the earth was born out of a mass of rotting cheese.[17] Like Morris, Ginzburg trains his considerable analytical powers on the behaviors of the marginal and the bizarre as a way of obliquely illuminating the zeitgeist of a given moment. It is worth stressing that for Ginzburg the case of Menocchio is especially compelling because of the way the challenge posed by this harmless eccentric mobilized the power structure of the Roman Catholic Church—a fact at least as telling about the Renaissance as anything Menocchio himself invented. Just so, *Interrotron Stories* are also profoundly tales of the dysfunction of the law, of the discrepancy between our prurient interest in scandal, outrage, and crime, and of the narrative models available to the law to adjudicate such behaviors.

If I claim *Interrotron Stories* as the documentary of the future, it is because the series forgoes the conventions of authority predicated on the neutrality and objectivity of the camera. *Interrotron Stories* represents historical filmmaking for the MTV generation, in which what is at stake is not the authority of the camera (its pretense towards autonomy and objectivity), but its implicative dexterity and seductive force. By incorporating the interview subject into the televisual apparatus. *Interrotron Stories*'s self-reflexive text simultaneously sutures the viewer to television and reveals how that suturing occurs. Long after the particulars of the Willie Edwards case are reduced to a paragraph in the history of civil rights, "Digging Up the Past" and its companion pieces might conceivably represent a moment in which television faced up to its enormous role in our cultural imaginary. In so doing, the show negotiates a shift worth pondering—from a conception of television as a forum for delivering more or less inadequate historical representations. to one in which we can begin to reckon with the convoluted ways in which television itself forms so large a part of the history of our time.

NOTES

My epigraph is taken from "Truth Not Guaranteed: An Interview with Errol Morris," *Cineaste* 17 (1989), 17. Thanks to Vivian Sobchack and to Cassandra Cleghorn for expertly reading earlier versions of this essay.

1. The CNN CD-ROM is particularly bad in this respect, repeatedly describing Nicole Simpson as "the blond in the convertible," and illustrating its text with Quick-time video clips not of Simpson, but of a half-dozen *other* Los Angeles blonds in convertibles, who generically substitute for Nicole herself.

2. Britain's Channel Four is also negotiating to buy the existing pilots.

3. Philip Gourevitch, "Interviewing the Universe," *New York Times Sunday Magazine*, August 9, 1992, 53.

4. From an interview with the author, September 25, 1994. Unless otherwise noted, all quotations by Errol Morris come from this interview.

5. From a telephone conversation with Deborah Leoni, Vice President for Dramatic Development, ABC, October 7, 1994.

6. According to Leoni, "the appetite for reality material has diminished." Despite critical acclaim, *TV Nation*, the Michael Moore nonfiction series, was not renewed by NBC, and *Cops*, one of the venerable originators of reality programming, hovers near last place in the Nielsen ratings.

7. The Interrotron is further removed from ordinary documentary provenance by its origin in television commercials. For the last several years Morris has largely made his living as a director of commercials, primarily because of his difficulty in financing his feature-length projects. His ongoing projects include *Fast, Cheap, and Out of Control*, an omnibus film shot partly by Robert Richardson, Oliver Stone's cinematographer, and *Honeymoon in Auschwitz*, a portrait of the electrocutioner and Holocaust revisionist, Fred Leuchter.

8. Morris's *Interrotron* commercials include spots for 7–11, American Express, and Ford.

9. On *kinoglaz* and related subjects, see Dziga Vertov, *Kino-Eye: The Writings of Dziga Vertov*, ed. Annette Michelson (Berkeley: University of California Press, 1984), especially the introduction by Michelson, and 32–64.

10. In a fitting case of irony, *Turning Point* was cancelled in November, 1994.

11. According to Stu Smiley, a former Fox executive, by the time Fox received "The Parrot," "the pilot season was already winding down." Telephone conversation, October 4, 1994.

12. Ari Emmanuel, Morris's agent, describes the series in conflicted terms that are interesting in this context: "I don't think this is reality TV. Errol Morris is not reality. Somebody's gotta get the vision that this is not reality TV. This is the next generation. Essentially, you've got the filmmaker that created reality television, and now he's taking it to the next generation." Telephone conversation, September 30, 1994.

13. Ralph Waldo Emerson, "Thoreau," quoted in *American Literature*, vol. 1, ed. Emory Elliot, et al. (Englewood Cliffs, N.J.: Prentice Hall, 1991), 1453.

14. Linda Williams, "Mirrors Without Memories: Truth, History, and the New Documentary," *Film Quarterly* 46:3 (Spring, 1993), 15.

15. Walter Benjamin, "The Work of Art in the Age of Mechanical Reproduction." In *Illuminations*, trans. Hannah Arendt (New York: Shocken Books, 1969), 233.

16. Bill Nichols, *Representing Reality: Issues and Concepts in Documentary* (Bloomington: Indiana University Press, 1991), 3.

17. Carlo Ginzburg, *The Cheese and the Worms: The Cosmos of a Sixteenth-Century Miller*, trans. John and Anne Tedeschi (New York: Penguin Books, 1982). Writing of Menocchio's complex relation both to the elite written and the oral peasant culture, Ginzburg observes that "an investigation initially pivoting on an individual, moreover an apparently unusual one, ended by developing into a general hypothesis on the popular culture (more precisely, peasant culture) of preindustrial Europe, in the age marked by the spread of printing and the Protestant Reformation" (xii). In much the same way, through their combined involvement both with the American legal system and with television, the eccentric subjects of the *Interrotron Stories* become representatives of much larger and more diffuse cultural processes.

Select Bibliography

Aldgate, Tony. *Cinema and History, British Newsreels and the Spanish Civil War*. London: Scolar Press, 1979.

Allen, Robert C., and Gomery, Douglas. *Film History: Theory and Practice*. New York: Alfred A. Knopf, 1985.

Anderegg, Michael, ed. *Inventing Vietnam: The War in Film and Television*. Philadelphia: Temple University Press, 1991.

Balibar, Etienne and Immanuel Wallerstein. *Race, Nation, Class: Ambiguous Identities*. London: Verso, 1991.

Bann, Stephen. *The Clothing of Clio: A Study of the Representation of History in Nineteenth-century Britain and France*. Cambridge: Cambridge University Press, 1984.

———. *The Invention of History: Essays on the Invention of the Past*. Manchester: Manchester University Press, 1990.

Barthes, Roland. *Camera Lucida: Reflections on Photography*. Richard Howard, Trans. New York: Farrar, 1981.

Benjamin, Walter. "The Storyteller." *Illuminations*, ed. Hannah Arendt, trans. Harry Zohn. New York: Schocken, 1969.

Berman, Marshall. *All That Is Solid Melts Into Air: The Experience of Modernity*. New York: Viking, 1988.

Bondanella, Peter, ed. *The Eternal City: Roman Images in the Modern World*. Chapel Hill and London: University of North Carolina Press, 1987.

Burgoyne, Robert. *Film Nation: Hollywood Looks at U.S. History*. Minneapolis: University of Minnesota Press, 1997.

Carr, E. H. *What Is History*. New York: Knopf, 1965.

Chow, Rey. *Primitive Passions: Visuality, Sexuality Ethnography in Contemporary Chinese Cinema*. New York: Columbia University Press, 1995.

Dalle Vacche, Angela. *The Body in the Mirror: Shapes of History in Italian Cinema*. Princeton: Princeton University Press, 1992.

Deleuze, Gilles. *Cinema 1: The Movement-Image,* trans. Hugh Tomlinson and Barbara Habberjam. Minneapolis: University of Minnesota Press, 1986.

———. *Cinema 2: The Time-Image,* trans. Hugh Tomlinson and Robert Galeta. Minneapolis: University of Minnesota Press, 1989.

Derrida, Jacques. *Archive Fever: A Freudian Impression,* trans. Eric Prenowirtz. Chicago: University of Chicago Press, 1996.

Diawara, Manthia, ed. *Black American Cinema*. New York: Routledge, 1993.

Dixon, Wheeler Winston. *Disaster and Memory: Celebrity Culture and the Crisis of Hollywood Cinema*. New York: Columbia University Press, 1999.

Dyer, Richard. *The Matter of Images: Essays on Representation*. London: Routledge, 1993.

Elsaesser, Thomas. *Fassbinder's Germany: History Identity Subject*. Amsterdam: Amsterdam University Press, 1996.

———. "Film History as Social History: The Dieterle/Warner Brothers Bio Pic." *Wide Angle* 8:2 (1986), 15–31.

———. "Tales of Sound and Fury: Observations on the Family Melodrama." *Monogram* 33, (1972), 2–15.

Fanon, Frantz. *The Wretched of the Earth,* trans. Constance Farrington. New York: Grove Press, 1968.

Ferro, Marc. *Cinema and History.* Detroit: Wayne State University Press, 1988.

Foucault, Michel. *Logic, Counter-Memory, and Practice: Selected Essays and Interviews,* ed. Daniel F. Bouchard. Ithaca, N.Y.: Cornell University Press, 1977.

Fraser, George MacDonald. *A Hollywood History of the World: From One Million B.C. to Apocalypse Now.* New York: Fawcett Columbine, 1988.

Friedlander, Saul. *Reflections of Nazism: An Essay on Kitsch and Death,* trans. Thomas Weyr. New York: Harper & Row, 1984.

Friedman, Lester, ed. *Fires Were Started: British Cinema and Thatcherism.* Minneapolis: University of Minnesota Press, 1993.

Gabriel, Teshome. "Third Cinema as Guardian of Popular Memory: Towards a Third Aesthetics." *Questions of Third Cinema,* ed. Jim Pines and Paul Willemen. London: British Film Institute, 1989, 53–54.

Geyer, Michael. "On the Uses of Shame: The German Politics of Memory." *Radical Evil,* ed. Joan Copjec. London: Verso, 1995.

Geyer, Michael, and Miriam Hansen. "German-Jewish Memory and National Consciousness." *Holocaust Remembrance: The Shapes of Memory,* ed. Geoffrey Hartman. New York: Oxford, 1994. 175–90.

Gibbons, Luke. *Transformations in Irish Culture.* Notre Dame: University of Notre Dame Press, 1996.

Gilroy, Paul. *The Black Atlantic: Modernity and Double Consciousness.* Cambridge, Mass.: Harvard University Press, 1994.

Ginzburg, Carlo. *Clues, Myths, and the Historical Method,* trans. John and Anne C. Tedeschi. Baltimore: Johns Hopkins University Press, 1989.

Gledhill, Christine, ed. "Signs of Melodrama." *Stardom: Industry of Desire.* London: Routledge, 1991.

Gramsci, Antonio. *Selections from the Prison Notebook,* ed. Quintin Hoare and Geoffrey Nowell-Smith. New York: International Publishers, 1978.

Greene, Naomi. *Landscapes of Loss: The National Past in French Postwar Cinema.* Princeton: Princeton University Press, 1999.

Grindon, Leger. *Shadows of the Past: Studies in the Historical Fiction Film.* Philadelphia: Temple University Press, 1994.

Hall, Stuart. "Encoding/Decoding." *Culture, Media, Language,* ed. Stuart Hall. London: Hutchinson, 1980.

———. *Hard Road to Renewal: Thatcherism and the Crisis of the Left.* London: Verso, 1988.

Harper, Sue. *Picturing the Past: The Rise and Fall of the British Costume Drama.* London: BFI, 1994.

Hayles, N. Katherine. "Text out of Context: Situating Postmodernism within an Information Society." *Discourse* (Spring/Summer 1987), 26.

Hutcheon, Linda. *A Poetics of Postmodernism: History, Theory, Fiction.* New York: Routledge, 1988.

Huyssen, Andreas. *After the Great Divide: Modernism, Mass Culture, Postmodernism.* Bloomington: Indiana University Press, 1986.

———. *Twilight Memories: Marking Time in a Culture of Amnesia.* New York: Routledge, 1995.

Jameson, Fredric. *Postmdernism or, the Cultural Logic of Late Capitalism.* Durham, N.C.: Duke University Press, 1991.

Kaes, Anton. *From Hitler to Heimat: The Return of History as Film.* Cambridge, Mass.: Harvard University Press, 1989.

King, John, Ana M. Lopez, and Manuel Alvarado, eds. *Mediating Two Worlds: Cinematic Encounters in the Americas.* London: BFI Publishing, 1993.

Kracauer, Siegfried. *From Caligari to Hitler: A Psychological History of German Film.* Princeton: Princeton University Press, 1947.

Landy, Marcia. *Cinematic Uses of the Past.* Minneapolis: University of Minnesota Press, 1996.

Leab, Daniel. "The Moving Image as Interpreter of History—Telling the Dancer from the Dance." *Image as Artifact: The Historical Analysis of Film and Television,* ed. John E. O'Connor. Malabar, Fla.: Robert E. Krieger, 1990. 69–95.

Levine, Lawrence W. *The Unpredictable Past: Explorations in American Cultural History.* New York: Oxford, 1993.

Lyotard, Jean-François. *The Postmodern Condition: A Report on Knowledge,* trans. Geoll Bennington and Brian Massumi. Minneapolis: University of Minnesota Press, 1984.

Marx, Karl. *The Eighteenth Brumaire of Louis Bonaparte.* New York: International Publishers, 1963.

Nichols, Bill. *Representing Reality: Issues and Concepts in Documentary.* Bloomington: Indiana University Press, 1991.

Nietzsche, Friedrich. "On the Uses and Disadvantages of History for Life." *Untimely Meditation,* trans. R. J. Hollingdale. Cambridge: Cambridge University Press, 1991.

Nora, Pierre. *Realms of Memory: Rethinking the French Past,* trans. Arthur Goldhammer. New York: Columbia University Press, 1996.

Novick, Peter. *That Noble Dream: The "Objectivity Question" and the American Historical Profession.* Cambridge: Cambridge University Press, 1988.

Petrie, Duncan, ed. *Screening Europe: Image and Identity in Contemporary European Cinema.* London: BFI, 1992.

Petro, Patrice. *Fugitive Images, from Photography to Video.* Bloomington: Indiana University Press, 1995.

Rentschler, Eric. *The Ministry of Illusion: Nazi Cinema and Its Afterlife.* Cambridge, Mass.: Harvard University Press, 1996.

Rosenstone, Robert. *Visions of the Past: The Challenge of Film to Our Idea of History.* Cambridge, Mass.: Harvard University Press, 1995.

———, ed. *Revisioning the Past: Film and the Construction of a New Past.* Princeton: Princeton University Press, 1995.

Said, Edward W. *Orientalism.* London: Penguin, 1985. First published 1978.

Shohat, Ella and Robert Stam. *Unthhinking Eurocentrism: Multiculturalism and the Media.* London: Routledge, 1994.

Sobchack, Vivian, ed. *The Persistence of History.* New York: Routledge, 1996.

Staiger, Janet, "Securing the Fictional Narrative as a Tale of the Historical Real." *South Atlantic Quarterly* 88 (Spring 1989), 393–412.

Straw, Will. "The Myth of Total Cinema History." Ron Burnett, ed., *Explorations in Film Theory: Selected Essays from Ciné-Tracts.* Bloomington: Indiana University Press, 1991. 237–46.

Thompson, E. P. *Visions of History.* New York: Poultheon Books, 1984.
Vidal, Gore, *Screening History.* London: Abacus, 1993; Harvard University Press, 1992.
White, Hayden. *Metahistory: The Historical Imagination in Nineteenth-Century Europe.* Baltimore: Johns Hopkins University Press, 1973.
———. *Tropics of Discourse.* Baltimore: Johns Hopkins University Press, 1978.

Contributors

MBYE CHAM is Associate Professor of African Studies at Howard University. Cham is the co-author of *Wolof Grammar and Textbook* (1981) and the co-editor of *Blackframes: Critical Perspectives on Black Independent Cinema* (1988) and *African Experiences of Cinema* (1996). Cham's work has appeared in journals such as *Research in African Literatures, Africa: Revue de l'Institut Africain International, A Current Bibliography on African Affairs, Africana Journal: A Bibliographic Library Journal and Review Quarterly, Ba Shiru: A Journal of African Languages and Literature,* and *Présence Africaine: Revue Culterelle du Monde Noir.* Cham's work has also been included in collections such as *Faces of Islam in African Literature* (1991) and *Ousmane Sembène: Dialogues with Critics and Writers* (1993).

GEORGE CUSTEN is Professor of Communications, Theatre, and American Studies at the College of Staten Island–CUNY and The Graduate School–CUNY. He is the author of *Bio/Pics: How Hollywood Constructed Public History* (1992) and *Twentieth Century Fox: Darryl F. Zanuck and the Culture of Hollywood* (1997), for which he was awarded a John Simon Guggenheim Fellowship in 1995. He is the series editor of the Rutgers Series in Communication, Media, and Culture. His work has appeared in journals such as *Cineaste* and in collections such as *Film/Culture: Explorations of Cinema in Its Social Context* (1982) and *Queer Representations: Reading Lives, Reading Cultures: A Center for Lesbian and Gay Studies Book* (1997).

RICHARD DIENST is Associate Professor of English at Rutgers University. He is the author of *Still Life in Real Time: Theory After Television* (1994). He is the co-editor of *Reading the Shape of the World: Toward an International Cultural Studies* (1996). His work has appeared in journals such as *Polygraph* and *American Literary History* and in collections such as *The Post-Colonial Critic: Interviews, Strategies, Dialogues: Gayatri Chakravorty Spivak* (1990) and *Reading the Shape of the World: Toward an International Cultural Studies* (1996).

MARY ANN DOANE is a Professor of Modern Culture and Media at Brown University. She is the author of *The Desire to Desire: The Woman's Film of the 1940s* (1987) and *Femmes Fatales: Feminism, Film Theory, Psychoanalysis* (1991). She is the co-editor of *Re-Vision: Essays in Feminist Film Criticism* (1984). Her work has appeared in journals such as *Differences, Critical Inquiry, Frauen und Film, Cinefocus, Kultur og Klass, Camera Obscura, East West Film Journal, Quarterly Review of Film and Video, Discourse, Poetics Today,* and *Wide Angle* and has been included in collections such as *Cinema and Language* (1983), *Feminism and Psychoanalysis* (1989), *The Films of G. W. Pabst: An Extraterritorial Cinema* (1990), *Psychoanalysis and Cinema* (1990), and *Writing on the Body: Female Embodiment and Feminist Theory* (1997).

TAYLOR DOWNING is Managing Director of Flashback Television, London. He is the author of *Olympia.* He is co-producer of *Cold War,* a 24-part series made in London for Turner Broadcasting and the BBC, and co-author of a book of the series (with Sir Jeremy Issacs).

GARY EDGERTON is Professor and Chairperson of the Department of Communication and Theatre Arts at Old Dominion University. He is the author of *American Film Exhibition and an Analysis of the Motion Picture Industry's Market Structure* (1983). He is the editor of *Film and the Arts in Symbiosis: A Resource Guide* (1988) and *In the Eye of the Beholder: Critical Perspectives in Popular Film and Television* (1997). His work has appeared in journals such as *Quarterly Review of Film Studies, Film and History, Journal of Film and Video, Journal of Popular Film and Television, The Journal of American Culture,* and *Literature and Film Quarterly.* His essays have appeared in *Technohistory: Using the History of American Technology in Interdisciplinary Research* (1996), *Reflections in a Male Eye: John Huston and the American Experience* (1993), and *Symbiosis: Popular Culture and Other Fields* (1988).

NAOMI GREENE is Professor of French at the University of California, Santa Barbara. She is the author of *Antonin Artaud: Poet Without Words* (1971), *René Clair: A Guide to References and Resources* (1985), *Pier Paolo Pasolini: Cinema as Heresy* (1990), and *Landscapes of Loss: The National Past in Postwar French Cinema* (1999). Her work has appeared in journals such as *Bucknell Review, Italian Quarterly, The French Review, Journal of the American Association of Teachers of French, Hors Cadre: Le Cinema a Travers Champs Disciplinaires,* and *Cinema Journal.* Her work has been included in collections such as *Auschwitz and After: Race, Culture, and "the Jewish Question" in France* (1994) and *Cinema, Colonialism, Postcolonialism: Perspectives from the French and Francophone World* (1996).

MIRIAM BRATU HANSEN is Andrew W. Mellon and Ferdinand Schevill Distinguished Service Professor in the Humanities and Chair of the Committee on Cinema and Media Studies at the University of Chicago. She is the author of *Babel and Babylon: Spectatorship in American Silent Film* (1991). Her work has appeared in journals such as *Qui Parle, Critical Inquiry, Frauen und Film, Amerikastudien, New German Critique, October, Raritan: A Quarterly Review, Screen, Persistence of Vision, South Atlantic Quarterly, Cinefocus, Public Culture, Camera Obscura, Discourse,* and *Cinema Journal* and in collections such as *Film und Literatur: Literarische Texte und der Neue Deutsche Film* (1984), *Myth and Enlightenment in American Literature* (1985), *German Film and Literature: Adaptations and Transformations* (1986), *Zur Verteidigung der Vernunft gegen ihre Liebhaber und Verachter* (1993), *Public Sphere and Experience: Toward an Analysis of the Bourgeois and Proletarian Public Sphere* (1993), *Gender and Cinema: Feminist Interventions, Part II* (1993), *Holocaust Remembrance: The Shapes of Memory* (1994), *Cinema and the Invention of Modern Life* (1995), and *Spielberg's Holocaust: Critical Perspectives on Schindler's List* (1997).

SUE HARPER teaches film and cultural history at the University of Portsmouth. She is the author of *Picturing the Past: The Rise and Fall of the British Costume Film* (1994). Her work has appeared in journals such as *Screen* and *Red Letters.* Her work has also been included in collections such as *The Politics of Theory* (1983).

SUMIKO HIGASHI is Professor of History at SUNY College at Brockport. She is the author of *Virgins, Vamps, and Flappers: The American Silent Movie Heroine* (1978), *Cecil B. DeMille: A Guide to References and Resources* (1985), and *Cecil B. DeMille and American Culture: The Silent Era* (1994). Higashi's work has appeared in journals such as *Cinema Journal* and has been included in collections such as *From Hanoi to Hollywood: The Vietnam War in American Film* (1990), *Unspeakable Images: Ethnicity and the American Cinema* (1991), *Revisioning History: Film and the Construction of a New Past* (1995), and *The Persistence of History: Cinema, Television, and the Modern Event* (1996).

ANTON KAES is Professor of German at the University of California, Berkeley. He is the author of *Expressionismus in Amerika* (1975), *Deutschlandbilder: die Wiederkehr der Geschichte als Film* (1987), and *From Hitler to Heimat: The Return of History as Film* (1989). He is the editor of *Kino-Debatte* (1975) and *Weimarer Republik: Manifeste und Dokumente zur deutschen Literatur 1918–1933* (1983). He is the co-editor of *Literatur für viele: Studien zur Trivialliteratur und Massenkommunikation im 19. Und 20. Jahrhundert* (1975), *Probleme der Moderne: Studien zur deutschen literatur von Nietzsche bis Brecht: Festschrift für Walter Sokel* (1983), *Geschichte des deutschen Films* (1993), and *Weimar Republic Sourcebook* (1994). His work has been published in journals such as *Monatshefte fur Deutschen Unterricht, Deutsche Sprache und Literatur, New German Critque, Qui Parle,* and *The German Quarterly.* His work has also been included in collections such as *Sinn aus Unsinn: Dada International* (1982), *Erkennen und Deuten: Essays zur Literatur und Literaturtheorie, Edgar Lohner in Memoriam* (1983), *America and the Germans* (1985), *Medium film—das Ende der Literatur* (1986), *German Film and Literature: Adaptations and Transformations* (1986), *High and Low Cultures: German Attempts at Mediation* (1994), and *Yale Companion to Jewish Writing and Thought in German Culture, 1096–1996* (1997).

MARCIA LANDY is Distinguished Service Professor of English and Film Studies with a secondary appointment in the French and Italian Department at the University of Pittsburgh. She is the author of *Fascism in Film: The Italian Commercial Cinema, 1930–1943* (1986), *British Genres: Cinema and Society, 1930–1960* (1991), *Film, Politics, and Gramsci* (1994), *Cinematic Uses of the Past* (1996), *The Folklore of Consensus: Theatricality in the Italian Cinema, 1930–1943* (1998), and *Italian Film* (2000). She is the co-author of *Queen Christina* (1995) and the editor of *Imitations of Life: A Reader on Film and Television Melodrama* (1991). Her work has appeared in such journals as *Film Criticism, Boundary 2, Cinema Journal, Post Script, Annali d'Italianistica, Jump Cut, Journal of Film and Video, Screen, Screening the Past, Critical Quarterly, Rethinking Marxism, New German Critique, Critical Studies, University of Massachusetts Review,* and *The French Review* and in collections such as *Postcolonial Discourse and Changing Cultural Contexts, Theory and Criticism, The British Cinema Book, Humanity at the Limit: The Impact of the Holocaust on Christians and Jews, The Western Reader, Soft Beds and Hard Battles: The Boulting Brothers and Post War British Culture,* and *American Horrors.*

SHAWN ROSENHEIM is Professor of English at Williams College. He is the author of *Cryptographic Imagination: Secret Writing from Edgar Poe to the Internet* (1997). He is the co-editor of *American Face of Edgar Allan Poe* (1995). His work has appeared in journals such as *Film Quarterly* and *ELH* and in collections such as *The Persistence of History: Cinema, Television, and the Modern Event* (1966) and *Edgar Allan Poe: A Critical Biography* (1998).

ROBERT ROSENSTONE is Professor of History at the California Institute of Technology. He is the author of *Protest from the Right* (1968), *Crusade of the Left: The Lincoln Battalion in the Spanish Civil War* (1980), *Mirror in the Shrine: American Encounters with Meiji Japan* (1988), *Romantic Revolutionary: A Biography of John Reed* (1990), and *Visions of the Past: The Challenge of Film to Our Idea of History* (1995). He is the editor of *Seasons of Rebellion: Protest and Radicalism in Recent America* (1980) and *Revisioning History: Film and the Construction of a New Past* (1995). His work has appeared in journals such as the *American Historical Review, Comparative Studies in Society and History,* and *Cineaste* and in collections such as *The Persistence of History: Cinema, Television, and the Modern Event* (1996).

PIERRE SORLIN is a professor of sociology at the University of Paris III and works in the Audiovisual Department at the Instituto Parri in Bologna. He is the author of *Sociologie du Cinéma: ouverture pour l'histoire de demain* (1977), *Film in History: Restaging the Past* (1980), *European Cinema, European Societies, 1939–1990* (1991), *Mass Media* (1994), *L'Art sans règles, ou, Manet contre Flaubert* (1995), *Italian National Cinema 1896–1996* (1996), and *Fils de Nadar: le "siècle" de l'image analogique* (1997). He is the co-author of *Lire les textes, écrire l'histoire* (1982). His work has appeared in journals such as *Cinefocus, Franco-Italica, Serie d'histoire litteraire, Paragraph: A Journal of Modern Critical Theory,* and *Hors-Cadre: Le Cinema a Travers Champs Disciplinaires.* His work has also been included in collections such as *Esthetique plurielle* (1996) and *Art et fiction* (1997).

MARIA WYKE is Senior Lecturer in Classics at the University of Reading (UK). She is the author of *Projecting the Past: Ancient Rome, Cinema, and History* (1997), the editor of *Gender and the Body in the Ancient Mediterranean* (1998), and co-editor of *Women in Ancient Societies: An Illusion of the Night* (1994) and *Uses and Abuses of Antiquity* (1999).

ISMAIL XAVIER is Professor of Cinema in the School of Communication at the University of São Paulo. He is the author of *Discurso cinematográfico: a opacidade e a transparência* (1977); *Sétima arte, um culto moderno: o idealismo estético e o cinema* (1978); *Sertão mar: Glauber Rocha e a estética da fome* (1983); *Alegorias do subdesenvolvimento: cinema novo, tropicalismo, cinema marginal* (1993); and *Allegories of Underdevelopment: Aesthetics and Politics in Modern Brazilian Cinema* (1997). He is co-author of *Desafio do cinema: a política do estado e a política dos autores* (1985) and the editor of *Experiência do cinema: antologia* (1983). Xavier's work has been included in such collections as *New Latin American Cinema, I: Theory, Practices, and Transcontinental Articulations; Studies of National Cinemas* (1997); *Mediating Two Worlds: Cinematic Encounters in the Americas* (1993); and *Resisting Images: Essays on Cinema and History.*

Index